Impressively, the case studies collected in this book come from West, Central, East, and Southern Africa. They insightfully and innovatively cover the pivotal issue of communications rights from diverse perspectives – from digital inclusion and communication rights of marginalised communities to ordinary citizens' battles with Internet shutdowns and the struggles to legislate intellectual property rights in contexts of digitalisation. In putting together this book, Tendai Chari and Ufuoma Akpojivi have given students, researchers, policymakers, media professionals, and rights activists a must-have and must-read piece of work.

Dr Teke Ngomba, *Associate Professor of Media Studies Aarhus University, Denmark*

In this edited collection, Tendai Chari and Ufuoma Akpojivi assemble an array of engaging and thought-provoking case studies related to communication rights in Africa. The book will be a valuable reference point for those concerned with understanding and furthering communication rights in the African context and beyond.

Dr Giles Moss, *Associate Professor in Media and Politics, School of Media and Communication, University of Leeds, United Kingdom*

Communication Rights in Africa

This ground-breaking volume examines enduring and emerging discourses around communication rights in Africa, arguing that they should be considered an integral component of the human rights discourse in Africa.

Drawing on a broad range of case studies across the continent, the volume considers what constitutes communication rights in Africa, who should protect them, against whom, and how communication rights relate to broader human rights. While the case studies highlight the variation in communicative rights experiences between countries, they also coalesce around common tropes and practices for the implementation and expression of communication rights. Deploying a variety of innovative theoretical and methodological approaches, the chapters scrutinise different facets of communication rights in the context of both offline and digital communication realities. The contributions provide illuminating accounts on language rights, digital exclusion, digital activism, citizen journalism, media regulation and censorship, protection of intellectual property rights, politics of mobile data, and politicisation of social media.

This is the first collection to consider communication in Africa using a rights-based lens. The book will appeal to researchers, academics, communication activists, and media practitioners at all levels in the fields of media studies, journalism, human rights, political science, public policy, as well as general readers who are keen to know about the status of communication rights in Africa.

Tendai Chari is an Associate Professor of Media Studies and a National Research Foundation (NRF) C3 Rated Researcher at the University of Venda, South Africa. He holds a PhD in media studies from the University of Witwatersrand, South Africa. Previously, he lectured at several universities in Africa, including the University of Zimbabwe (where he was head of the media programme in the English department), the National University of Science and Technology and Fort Hare University (South Africa). Chari is widely published in the field of media and communication studies, and his research focuses on political communication with a broadened horizon on the interface between digital media and politics, media and conflict, and media ethics and popular culture. His other publications have appeared in the *Journal of African Media Studies*, *African Identities*, *Communicatio: South African Journal on Media and Communications*, *African Journalism Studies*, and *the Journal of African Elections*. He is the co-editor of *Global Pandemics and Media Ethics: Issues and Perspectives* (Routledge, 2022, co-edited with Professor Martin N. Ndlela), *African Football, Identity Politics and Global Media Narratives: The Legacy of FIFA 2010 World Cup* (2014 Palgrave Macmillan; co-edited with Professor Nhamo A. Mhiripiri); *Media Law, Ethics, and Policy in the Digital Age* (IGI Global Publishing, 2017; also with Professor Nhamo A. Mhiripiri); and *Political Transition in Southern Africa: Democratic Consolidation or Change of Façade?* He is a recipient of several grants and fellowships, which include the African Peace Building Network Fellowship (2017), the African Peacebuilding Book Publishing Manuscript grant (2018), the African Humanities Program (AHP) of the American Council of Learned Societies (ACLS) Post-Doctoral Fellowship (2022). Chari is working on finalising his single-authored book titled *Diaspora Media and Homeland Conflict: Coloniality of Conflict Journalism in Zimbabwe* (Routledge 2023).

Ufuoma Akpojivi (PhD) is Policy, Research and Learning Lead at Advocates for International Development (A4ID), United Kingdom. Before this, he was an associate professor at the University of the Witwatersrand, South Africa and a visiting professor at the School of Media and Communication, Pan-Atlantic University, Nigeria. He holds a PhD and MA in communications studies from the University of Leeds, United Kingdom. His research interests cut across media policy, democracy, citizenship, new media technologies, and political communications, and he has widely published on these issues. He is a National Research Foundation (NRF) South Africa, C2 Rated Researcher and a recipient of numerous teaching and learning awards such as the Vice Chancellor Individual Teaching and Learning Award (2017), Faculty of Humanities Individual Teaching and Learning Award (2017), Vice Chancellor Team Teaching and Learning Award (2016), and Faculty of Humanities Team Teaching and Learning Award (2016). He is the author of *Media Reforms and Democratization in Emerging Democracies of Sub-Saharan Africa* (Palgrave 2018) and *Social Movements, and Digital Activism in Africa* (Palgrave, 2023).

Routledge African Media, Culture and Communication Studies

This series features innovative and original research on African media, culture and communication from scholars both within and outside of Africa. With Africa still under-represented in media and cultural studies literature, this series provides a much-needed platform for comparative and interdisciplinary research that highlights the perspectives and needs of Africans as consumers and producers.

Digital Dissidence and Social Media Censorship in Africa
Edited by Farooq A. Kperogi

African Language Media
Edited by Phillip Mpofu, Israel A. Fadipe and Thulani Tshabangu

Communication Rights in Africa
Emerging Discourses and Perspectives
Edited by Tendai Chari and Ufuoma Akpojivi

For more information about this series, please visit: www.routledge.com/Routledge-African-Media-Culture-and-Communication-Studies/book-series/RAM

Communication Rights in Africa

Emerging Discourses and Perspectives

Edited by Tendai Chari
and Ufuoma Akpojivi

LONDON AND NEW YORK

First published 2024
by Routledge
4 Park Square, Milton Park, Abingdon, Oxon OX14 4RN

and by Routledge
605 Third Avenue, New York, NY 10158

Routledge is an imprint of the Taylor & Francis Group, an informa business

© 2024 selection and editorial matter, Tendai Chari and Ufuoma Akpojivi; individual chapters, the contributors

The right of Tendai Chari and Ufuoma Akpojivi to be identified as the authors of the editorial material, and of the authors for their individual chapters, has been asserted in accordance with sections 77 and 78 of the Copyright, Designs and Patents Act 1988.

All rights reserved. No part of this book may be reprinted or reproduced or utilised in any form or by any electronic, mechanical, or other means, now known or hereafter invented, including photocopying and recording, or in any information storage or retrieval system, without permission in writing from the publishers.

Trademark notice: Product or corporate names may be trademarks or registered trademarks, and are used only for identification and explanation without intent to infringe.

British Library Cataloguing-in-Publication Data
A catalogue record for this book is available from the British Library

Library of Congress Cataloging-in-Publication Data
Names: Chari, Tendai, editor. | Akpojivi, Ufuoma, editor.
Title: Communication rights in Africa : emerging discourses and perspectives / edited by Tendai Chari and Ufuoma Akpojivi.
Other titles: Routledge African media, culture and communication studies.
Description: New York : Routledge, 2024. | Series: Routledge African media, culture and communication studies | Includes bibliographical references and index. | Summary: "This ground-breaking volume examines enduring and emerging discourses around communication rights in Africa, arguing that they should be considered an integral component of the human rights discourse in Africa. Drawing on a broad range of case studies across the continent, the volume considers what constitutes communication rights in Africa, who should protect them, against whom and how communication rights relate to broader human rights. While the case studies highlight the variation in communicative rights experiences between countries, they also coalesce around common tropes and practices for the implementation and expression of communication rights. Deploying a variety of innovative theoretical and methodological approaches, the chapters scrutinise different facets of communication rights in the context of both offline and digital communication realities. The contributions provide illuminating accounts on language rights, digital exclusion, digital activism, citizen journalism, media regulation and censorship, protection of intellectual property rights, politics of mobile data and politicisation of social media. This is the first collection to consider communication in Africa using a rights-based lens. The book will appeal to researchers, academics, communication activists, and media practitioners at all levels in the fields of media studies, journalism, human rights, political science, public policy, as well as general readers who are keen to know about the status of communication rights in Africa"— Provided by publisher.
Identifiers: LCCN 2023015148 (print) | LCCN 2023015149 (ebook) | ISBN 9781032482835 (hardback) | ISBN 9781032482842 (paperback) | ISBN 9781003388289 (ebook)
Subjects: LCSH: Freedom of expression—Africa. | Communication—Social aspects—Africa. | Human rights—Africa.
Classification: LCC JC599.A35 C656 2024 (print) | LCC JC599.A35 (ebook) | DDC 323.44096—dcundefined
LC record available at https://lccn.loc.gov/2023015148
LC ebook record available at https://lccn.loc.gov/2023015149

ISBN: 978-1-032-48283-5
ISBN: 978-1-032-48284-2
ISBN: 978-1-003-38828-9

DOI: 10.4324/9781003388289

Typeset in Sabon
by Apex CoVantage, LLC

This book is dedicated to our families for providing all the support, love, comfort, and encouragement during the editing of this book.

Contents

List of figures xiv
List of tables xv
Acknowledgements xvi
List of contributors xvii
List of abbreviations xx

Introduction: Communication Rights in Africa – Theoretical
and Practical Considerations 1
TENDAI CHARI AND UFUOMA AKPOJIVI

PART I
Cultural and Minority Rights 19

1 Language-Cultural Barrier in Ubang Community: A Critical
  Assessment of the Communication Rights of Women
  and The Girl-Child 21
  CHIKE MGBEADICHIE

2 Silicon Savannah or Digitising Marginalisation? A Reflection
  of Kenya's Government Digitisation Policies, Strategies,
  and Projects 38
  JOB MWAURA

3 Please Do Not Call It Human Right: A Southern
  Epistemological Perspective on the Digital Inclusion
  of People With Disabilities in South Africa 55
  LORENZO DALVIT

4 The Interdependence of Communication, Political, and Socio-Economic Rights: Examining the Lived Experiences of Digitally Marginalised Netizens Before and During the COVID-19 Lockdown in Lagos State, Nigeria 70
OLUTOBI AKINGBADE

PART II
Digital Citizenship 89

5 *Cabo Delgado Também é Moçambique*: The Paths of Youth Digital Activism in a Restrictive Context 91
DÉRCIO TSANDZANA

6 Citizen Journalism and the Entrenchment of Communication Rights in Zimbabwe 110
EARNEST MUDZENGI AND WELLINGTON GADZIKWA

PART III
Freedom, Censorship, and Intellectual Property Rights 127

7 "The Right to Tell My Story as I Please": Regulation and Self-Censorship in the Nigerian Film Industry 129
IKECHUKWU OBIAYA

8 A Critical Review of Intellectual Property Rights: The Case of Nigeria 146
AIFUWA EDOSOMWAN

9 Internet Shutdowns in Semi-Authoritarian Regimes: The Case of Cameroon 165
PETER TIAKO NGANGUM

10 Fake News Versus Freedom of Expression: Legislating Media Trademarks Infringements on Social Media Platforms in Kenya and South Africa 183
BRIAN HUNGWE

PART IV
Politics of Digital Infrastructures 201

11 Politics of Digital Infrastructures in the Global South:
The Case of #DataMustFall Campaign in South Africa 203
TENDAI CHARI

12 Silence and Silent the SóróSoké Generation:
The Politicisation of Social Media in Nigeria 223
UFUOMA AKPOJIVI

Index 243

Figures

5.1	Access to the Internet in Mozambique	98
5.2	Facebook advertising audience overview	99
5.3	Illustration of the campaign "Cabo Delgado is also Mozambique"	101
5.4	We don't want support; we just want the war to end	103
5.5	Explanation of the steps for sending campaign support and strategies for virtual action	104

Tables

1.1 Examples of separate sounds of Ofre and Arasere 26
2.1 The number of Ajira centres in the 15 pastoralist counties in Kenya 51
8.1 Summary of copyright milestones in Nigeria 158

Acknowledgements

Editing this volume was a rewarding experience we could have never imagined. There are many people without whose efforts this book could not have seen the light of day. We would like to sincerely express our sincere gratitude to all the contributors for their dedication, commitment, and sacrifice. Without them this book would not have materialised. A very special thanks to the anonymous reviewers of our book proposal. Their rigorous and insightful reviews made this book possible. Our since gratitude goes to the production team at Routledge, Taylor and Francis for the instrumental role they played in steering the book project. Rosie Anderson, Editorial Assistant (Global Development/African Studies) deserves special mention. She provided guidance and advice throughout the entire process of compiling and editing this volume. Helena Hurd, Editor (Global Development/African Studies) was receptive to the idea of a book on communication rights in Africa. We thank her for superintending the book project in its initial phase. Also, we are grateful to the University of Witwatersrand, South Africa NRF Vitamin C Programme, whose funds enabled us to have all the chapters proofread. Last, but not least, we are eternally grateful to our family members for all the support they gave us throughout the entire period of editing this book.

Contributors

Olutobi Akingbade is currently a vice-chancellor's postdoctoral research fellow at the Centre for the Advancement of Non-Racialism and Democracy, Nelson Mandela University, South Africa. His research focus examines the intersections of various forms of journalism and media with frames of public health communication and questions of social justice, democracy, and citizenship in sub-Saharan Africa. He completed his master's and doctorate degrees at the School of Journalism and Media Studies, Rhodes University, South Africa.

Lorenzo Dalvit is Associate Professor of Digital Media and Cultural Studies at Rhodes University in Makhanda (South Africa). His areas of academic interest include digital media theory and education and digital inequalities and disability. He recently published a chapter in *The Routledge Companion to Disability and Media* and another in *Vulnerable People and Digital Inclusion: Theoretical and Applied Perspectives*, published by Palgrave Macmillan.

Aifuwa Edosomwan holds a master's in media and communication from the School of Media and Communication, Pan-Atlantic University in Lagos, Nigeria. He is a lecturer at the Pan-Atlantic University, and his areas of interest are the creative industries and media studies. He is currently working on research in the area of representations in films.

Wellington Gadzikwa (PhD) is Senior Lecturer in Journalism and Media Studies at Africa University in Zimbabwe. He previously held the same position at the University of Zimbabwe. He is a published scholar with several chapters in books and peer-reviewed journals. His research and publication interests are in journalism standards and practice, media framing, tabloids, and tabloidisation.

Brian Hungwe is a journalist with over two decades of experience. Formerly, he was a correspondent for the British Broadcasting Corporation (BBC), South African Broadcasting Corporation (SABC), Zimbabwe Independent, and freelanced for the British Daily Telegraph and Mail & Guardian. He holds a National Diploma in Mass Communications (Harare Polytechnic);

LLBS (UZ); LLM Constitutional & Human Rights Law (MSU); LLM Internet Defamation, by Research (UKZN); currently, he is a PhD candidate in intellectual property law (Wits), researching on the implications of the Internet on South Africa's copyright holders' remuneration, taking lessons from the European Union and Ghana. He has published several journal articles and book chapters on media law, constitutional and human rights law, intellectual property law, and defamation law. He practises law and is also a consultant, and his areas of interest, over and above the aforementioned published areas, are construction law, international commercial arbitration, contract law, administration law, and public international law. He is working on a book, *Defamation Law in the Digital Era*.

Chike Mgbeadichie teaches cultural analysis and critical thinking at the School of Media and Communication, Pan-Atlantic University, Lagos, Nigeria. He holds a PhD in English from the University of Exeter, UK, where he studied African literature with emphasis on African culture and critical theories. He was trained at the University of Leeds, UK, from where he obtained an MA in English literature. His research interests include African literature; media and cultural studies; African critical theory; media-in-African literature; and migration discourses. His articles have appeared in a couple of highly rated journals such as *Research in African Literatures*, *African Research Reviews*, and *Journal of African Languages and Literary Studies*. He has contributed chapters in some book projects. His book on Afrocentrism is awaiting publication in press.

Earnest Mudzengi is a researcher and communication rights activist. His study interests are in media policy, communication and citizenship, citizen journalism, political communication, community media, constitutionalism, and civil society. He has previously authored and reviewed academic material in subjects that include investigative journalism, media management, global media structures, and constitutionalism.

Job Mwaura is Postdoctoral Research Fellow at Wits Centre for Journalism at the University of the Witwatersrand. He was previously a research fellow at the South African Research Chair in Science Communication at the Centre for Science Communication at Stellenbosch University in South Africa. He completed a postdoctoral research fellowship at the University of Cape Town, at the Institute for Humanities in Africa (HUMA). Dr Job Mwaura completed his doctoral studies in the Department of Media Studies at the University of the Witwatersrand (Wits), South Africa. He holds an MSc in communication and journalism from Moi University, Kenya. He researches and publishes on digital media in Africa, African studies, digital culture activism, and social justice.

Peter Tiako Ngangum is a member of the Centre de Recherche en Information et Communication (ReSIC) of the Université Libre de Bruxelles (ULB). He holds a PhD in information and communication sciences from the ULB, an MA in mass communication from the University of Leicester, an MSc in environmental sciences from the University of Greenwich, London, and a BA in English from the University of Yaoundé, Cameroon. His research in the fields of journalists' safety, media law and regulation, media ethics, media and counterterrorism laws, journalism, and new media has been published as book chapters and in several international peer-reviewed journals. He was a panellist and academic assessor of UNESCO's report on World Trends in Freedom of Expression and Media Development and has participated in a large number of media-based international conferences, where he presented papers on a wide range of topics around media studies and journalism. His latest participation was in November 2022 at the 8th Annual International Conference on the Safety of Journalists, Oslo Metropolitan University, Norway. He teaches courses in media law and regulation, media ethics, and media systems. Also, he is a media consultant and trainer.

Ikechukwu Obiaya is Senior Lecturer, School of Media and Communication at the Pan-Atlantic University. He obtained a BA degree, with combined honours in English and literature, from the University of Benin. This was followed by a master's degree from the University of Ibadan, also in English literature. He obtained his PhD from the University of Navarra, Spain, and his thesis was a study of the impact of state intervention, through the NFVCB, on the Nigerian film industry.

Obiaya has also carried out some studies on the audience of the Nigerian video film as well as on technical workers in the industry. He has a varied practical experience of the media having worked at various moments in both a broadcast house and a publishing company.

Dércio Tsandzana is a Mozambican PhD in political science at Sciences Po (France), and he holds an MA in political science from the same university. Since 2013, Tsandzana has been working on youth, Internet, social media, and political participation in Mozambique, including online activism for Global Voices International. Alongside his PhD, Tsandzana undertook research work focusing on digital rights and data privacy with the Electoral Institute for Sustainable Democracy in Africa (EISA), the Collaboration on International ICT Policy for East and Southern Africa (CIPESA), Paradigm Initiative (PIN), Meta (Facebook), Association for Progressive Communications (APC), and the African Declaration on Internet Rights and Freedoms. His latest article is titled "The Political Participation of Youth in Mozambique's 2019 General Elections" (*Journal of African Elections*, 2022).

Abbreviations

Chapter 1: Chike Mgbeadichie

UN – United Nations

Chapter 2: Job Mwaura

GDP – Gross Domestic Product
ICTs – Information and Communication Technologies
UNDHR – Universal Declaration of Human Rights
SSA – Sub-Saharan Africa
KNBS – Kenya Population Housing Census
ASALs – Arid and Semi-Arid Lands
NEMIS – National Education Management and Information Systems
UPI – Unique Personal Number
KUCCPS – Kenya Universities and Colleges Central Placement Service
PPIP – Public Procurement Information Portal

Chapter 3: Lorenzo Dalvit

DPS – Disabled People of South Africa
WTO – World Trade Organisation
USA – United States of America
GDPR – General Data Protection Regulation
NPC – National Paralympic Committee
LGBTQ – Lesbian, Gay, Bisexual, Transgender and Queer
UNCRDP – United Nations Convention on the Rights of People with Disabilities
REPUDA – The Promotion of Equality and Prevention of Unfair Discrimination Act
SHRC – South African Human Rights Commission
NCPD – National Council for People with Disabilities
DWSA – Disability Women of South Africa
ITU – International Telecommunication Union

Chapter 4: Olutobi Akingbade

SARS – Special Anti-Robbery Squad
ICTs – Information and Communication Technologies
IPA – Interpretive Phenomenological Analysis

Chapter 5: Dércio Tsandzana

UNDHR – United Nations Universal Declaration of Human Rights
EU – European Union
ITU – International Telecommunication Union
IPS – Intrusion Prevention Systems
APT – Advanced Persistent Threat
INTIC – National Institute of Information and Communication Technologies

Chapter 6: Earnest Mudzengi and Wellington Gadzikwa

UNESCO – United Nations Scientific and Cultural Organisation
ZBC – Zimbabwe Broadcasting Corporation
ZANU-PF – Zimbabwe African National Union Patriotic Front
ZACRAS – Zimbabwe Association of Community Radio Stations
DSTV – Digital Satellite Television
ZEC – Zimbabwe Electoral Commission
SMS – Short Message Service
CNN – Cable News Network
MISA – Zimbabwe-Media Institute of Southern Africa Zimbabwe
CITE – Centre for Innovation and Technology

Chapter 7: Ikechukwu Obiaya

AMCOP – Association of Movie Content Owners and Producers/Distributors of Nigeria
DSTV – Digital Satellite Television
DVD – Digital Video Disc
KSCB – Kano State Censorship Board
LSFCB – Lagos State Film and Censor Board
MOPPAN – Motion Picture Practitioners Association of Nigeria
NFVCB – National Film and Video Censors Board
UNESCO – United Nations Educational Scientific and Cultural Organization
VOD – Video on Demand

Chapter 8: Aifuwa Edosomwan

AVRS – Audio Visual Rights Society of Nigeria
CD – Compact Disc
CMO – Collective Management Organisation

COSON – Copyright Society of Nigeria
DVD – Digital Video Disc
EFCC – Economic and Financial Crime Commission
ICPC – Independent Corrupt Practice Commission
ICT – Information and Communications Technology
IP – Intellectual Property
MCSN – Musical Copyright Society of Nigeria
NCC – Nigerian Copyright Commission
NFVCB – National Film and Video Censors Board
PwC – Price Waterhouse Coopers
STRAP – Strategic Anti-Privacy Operations
VCD – Video Compact Disk
WHO – World Health Organisation
WIPO – World Intellectual Property Organisation

Chapter 9: Peter Tiako Ngangum

ICT – Information and Communication Technology
ISP – Internet Service Providers

Chapter 10: Brian Hungwe

ACHPR – African Charter on Human and People's Rights
AP – Associated Press
BAKE – Bloggers Association of Kenya
BBC – British Broadcasting Corporation
CNN – Cable News Network
COVID-19 – Coronavirus disease
ICCPR – International Covenant on Civil and Political Rights
ICESCR – International Covenant on Economic, Social and Cultural Rights
INS – International News Service
IP – Intellectual Property
IPRs – Intellectual Property Rights
SMPs – Social Media Platforms
TRIPS – Trade-Related Aspects of Intellectual Property Rights
UNESCO – United Nations Educational Scientific and Cultural Organization

Chapter 11: Tendai Chari

ANC – African National Congress
COVID-19 – Coronavirus Disease
CWU – Communication Workers Union
DJ – Disc Jockey
FM – Frequency Modulation
ICASA – Independent Communications Authority of South Africa

ICT – Information Communication Technology
MTN – Mobile Telephone Network
NWICO – New World Information and Communication Order
SMs – Social Media
SONA – State of the Nation Address

Chapter 12: Ufuoma Akpojivi

API – Application Programming Interface
AU – African Union
CAC – Cyberspace Administration of China
CEO – Chief Executive Officer
ICT – Information Communication Technology
NCC – Nigerian Communications Commission
NITDA – National Information Technology Development Agency
NOI – Ngozi Okonjo Iweala
OTT – Over The Top
POPIA – Protection of Personal Information Act
PRIDA – Policy and Regulation Initiative for Digital Africa
VPN – Virtual Private Network

Introduction
Communication Rights in Africa – Theoretical and Practical Considerations

Tendai Chari and Ufuoma Akpojivi

> *The discourse of communication rights (CR) is currently going through a renewal and resurrection of some sorts. Of sorts, because it is not going through a thorough, root and branch renewal, but is undergoing a patch-work by concerned academics and communication activists who are committed to clarifying its meaning, mapping its conceptual framework and activists who are committed to clarifying its meaning, mapping its conceptual framework and elucidating the links between its theory and practice.*
>
> (Thomas, 2011: 217)

This quotation illuminates on the evolutionary perspective on communication rights canvassed in this book, where communication rights are viewed as a dynamic discourse transcending temporal and spatial boundaries (Hamelink, 1994, 2004a, 2004b, 2008; Alegre & O'Siochru, 2005; Alegre & O'Siochru, 2005). The point of departure in this book is that there is no common understanding of "communication rights", as its understanding and interpretation is shaped by local, regional, and national contexts, and it is these local and regional nuances which must be taken into account for conceptual clarity. Thus, communication rights is inseparable from the African continent's political, economic, and social struggles as much as the struggle for human rights cannot be divorced from the continent's anti-colonial and anti-imperial struggles.

Despite this long history, the concept is marred with controversy due to lack of conceptual clarity (Musiani et al., 2009). On the African continent, these controversies are intertwined with and amplified by legacies of colonialism, globalization, and the entrenchment of neoliberalism, wherein the new communication environment reinforces cleavages of the old political order, meaning that citizens remain "subjects" (Mamndani, 1996). Against this backdrop, the concept of the right to communicate should be regarded as a "concept in progress" (Ruuhonen, 2004: 1). Approaches to the role of communications differ significantly across cultures since communication rights encompass a multiplicity of rights. There is a persistent impasse with regard to the meaning and substance of communication rights, particularly in postcolonial contexts such as Africa. The coterie of unsettled questions includes, who should protect communication rights, how, against whom, and how communication rights should be realized in a digital context. French media expert and the then-Director of Radio and Visual Services in the United Nations (UN) Office of Public Information, Jean d' Arcy is credited for being the first to directly make reference to "the right to communicate" in 1969 when he wrote:

> The time will come when the Universal Declaration of Human Rights will have to encompass a more extensive right than man's right to information, first laid 21 years ago in Article 19. This is the right to communicate. It is the angle from which the future development of communications will have to be considered if it is to be fully understood.
> (D'Arcy, 1969: 1)

Within a few years, the issue was elevated to the front burner of geopolitics after which the right to communicate became an integral component of the New World Information and Communication Order (NWICO). Although its scope and specifics were not clear, particularly with regard to whether it would be an individual or a collective right as well as "its relationship to existing rights, the precise wording, and the legal form in which it would be incorporated" also remains unclear to date (CRIS, 2005: 19). NWICO coincided with a number of developments in the political sphere, the most notable being the attainment of political independence by states in what was generally known as the "Third World". This led to some kind of rebalancing of power within the United Nations framework, which provided a platform for former colonial states to assert their anti-colonial philosophies as well as resist the hegemony of Western nations. This gave birth to the New International Economic Order (NIEO), the precursor to NWICO, and it was within the context of NIEO that opposition to the "free flow" of information supported by the West, led by the United States, was vehemently resisted by the newly independent states in the Global South. Thus, NIEO gave way to NWICO, and the right to communicate discourse found formal acknowledgement within NWICO. Underpinned by what were known as "the 4Ds" (Development, Democratization, Decolonization, and Demonopolization) (Hamelink, 1994), NWICO was informed by the essential role of media and communication in the context of decolonization and nation-building, existential threats of foreign media on "national identity, cultural integrity and political and economic sovereignty" (CRIS, 2005: 16). Thus, concerns about cultural imperialism and its long-term implications on nation-building, state sovereignty, and cultural identity were voiced mainly by "Third World" countries but were supported by some developing countries such as France, Canada, and Finland (CRIS, 2005: 16). Between 1973 and 1976, several meetings convened under the auspices of the Non-Aligned Movement (NAM) tackled concerns with regard to the unequal flow of information from the Global North to the Global South, homogenization of cultures, misrepresentation of minority cultures, the growing trend of concentration of media industries and conglomerates in the Global North, increasing control of new communication technologies, and media production by the West, which enabled Western countries to "trespass" into the newly independent states in the Global South (CRIS, 2005). However, there were huge disagreements between NAM and Western countries, led by the United States and the United Kingdom. A showdown was avoided only after the appointment of the Sean MacBride Commission, which was tasked with the responsibility to investigate the contentious issues around "the right to communicate" as ventilated by various parties within the NWICO framework. In a submission on the right to communicate, d' Arcy opined that:

> From the very first, this fundamental right was implicit in, and underlay all the freedoms that have successfully been won: Freedom of opinion, freedom of expression, freedom of the press, freedom of information.
> (CRIS, 2005: 16)

Although the NWICO debate eventually collapsed after the withdrawal of the United States (1984) and the United Kingdom (1985), the MacBride report (1980), although far from perfect, came up with a number of important recommendations, one of which affirmed the fact that "communication is a basic individual right, as well as a collective one required by all communities and nations" (McBride, 1980: 253). The report also noted that:

> Freedom of information – and, more specifically the right to seek, receive and impart information – is a fundamental human right: indeed, a prerequisite for many others. The inherent nature of communication means that its fullest possible exercise and potential depend on the surrounding political, social and economic conditions, the most vital of these being democracy within countries and equal, democratic relations between them. It is in this context that the democratization of communication at national and international levels, as well as the larger role of communication in democratizing society acquires utmost importance.
> (McBride, 1980: 253)

Notwithstanding some of its flaws, the McBride report was momentous and gave the concept "the right to communicate" its formal recognition and endorsement and opened the way for further exploration when it stated:

> Communication needs in a democratic society should be met by the extension of specific rights such as the right to privacy, the right to participate in publication – all elements of a new concept, the right to communicate. In developing what might be called a new era of social rights, we suggest, all the implications of the right to communicate be further explored.
> (McBride, 1980: 265)

From the Right to Communicate to Communication Rights

While the "right to communicate" and "communication rights" are closely linked, and are sometimes used interchangeably, they have distinct histories and tactics; hence they are not the same (CRIS, 2005). On the one hand, the right to communicate is linked to the NWICO debate and relates to the need to put in place a formal legal framework that acknowledges communication as a right and "makes intuitive sense as a basic human right" (CRIS, 2015: 19). On the other hand, "communication rights" emphasize the fact that there exist already a number of international rights that underpin communication "but are too often ignored and require active mobilization and assertion" (CRIS, 2005: 19). The "right to communicate" could be viewed by opponents of NWICO as a veiled attempt to smuggle the NWICO debate onto the agenda of the World Summit on the Information Society (WSIS) through the back door. For opponents of NWICO, the right to communicate invokes attempts to curtail the free flow of information and legitimation of governmental control. Proponents of the right to communicate recognize that most of its components already exist, albeit in different forms, in existing human rights charters, but insist that the right to communicate should be provided for explicitly and in its own right rather than as an appendage of existing rights.

The term communication rights was the more preferred term during the discourse of the World Summit on the Information Society and relates to existing human rights that relate to communication (CRIS, 2005). Communication rights signal a shift from the establishment of an autonomous right to communicate towards assertion, amplification, or rejuvenation of already existing communication rights. Communication Rights in the Information Society (CRIS), a movement that was at the forefront of campaigning for communication rights during WSIS identified five pillars of communication rights, namely

- Communicating in the public sphere – focuses on the role of media and communication in fostering democratic participation.
- Communicating knowledge for equity and creativity – relates to the terms and means through which knowledge generated by society is either communicated or suppressed by different groups.
- Civil rights in communication – focuses on the way in which civil rights relate to the communication process in society.
- Cultural rights in communication – is about the communication of diverse cultures, cultural forms, and identities at the individual and collective levels (CRIS, 2005).

Although the right to communicate received considerable endorsements, it was excluded within the WSIS due to fear of stirring controversy. Hoffmann (2009: 25) notes how the term "the right to communicate" became "a victim of ferocious ideological disputes, mutual distrust and incidental uprisings of paranoia, which eventually made it impossible to consider the merits of all arguments in a rational manner". Hamelink (cited in Hoffmann, 2009) notes that the term right to communicate became taboo and "politically incorrect", and by the 1990s, it had disappeared from public discourse as UNESCO abandoned its earlier efforts to formulate the right to communicate as an international legal framework as it tried to endear itself with the West. As a result, the right to communicate discourse was quietly replaced by the term "communication rights", which was considered more palatable by the Western nations. Unlike in NWICO, where the right to communicate discourse was championed by governments, the communication rights debate within the context of WSIS was advocated for by smaller grassroots movements as part of their social justice campaigns to ensure that local communities had control of the media, thereby increasing access to marginalized communities. It should be noted that the communication rights movement grew exponentially; unlike during NWICO, it faced resistance not from states and governments but from global media and telecommunication monopoly companies averse to regulation and control.

Digital Rights

The term "digital rights" is somewhat slippery as it is understood differently in different contexts. However, most scholars use it interchangeably with "Internet rights" (Karppinen & Puukko, 2020; Kaye & Reventlow, 2017). Digital rights could be viewed as a component of the communication rights discourse, which dates back to the NWICO debate. In the context of the new digital communication environment, demands that digital rights should be recognized as human rights have been mounting, and a number of civil society organizations were advocating for digital rights using the motto "digital rights are human rights" (Schejter, 2022: 1833). Schejter asserts that "in recent years, the right to communicate has become synonymous with the rise of 'new media', in particular, the Internet and other broadband, Internet-Protocol -based services" (2022: 1832). Mathiesen (2014: 3) equates digital rights or the right to access information online to a moral right. Cerf (2012) disagrees, arguing that digital rights are derivative rights and cannot be equated to fundamental human rights. Karppinen and Puukko (2020: 304) argue that despite failing to gain traction in earlier times, the discourse of communication rights has been resurrected by various political actors under the guise of Internet or digital rights. They identify four main discourses around digital rights, namely:

- Digital Rights as Protection of Negative Liberties – These rights are associated with opposition to attempts to impose laws and restrictions on free speech and privacy on the Internet Karppinen and Puukko (2020: 313).
- Private Rights and State Obligations – This is a more positive conception of rights whereby regulation is not necessarily viewed as an obstacle to the

realization of individual rights. Rather, the realization of human rights is seen as creating obligations for national and supranational bodies (Karppinen & Puukko, 2020: 314).
- Rights as a Vehicle of "Informational Justice" – These rights focus on equal access and the individual's capabilities, whereby rights are conceived as vehicles of information justice. Thus, rights do not just end with individual capabilities or entitlements but also have to do with broader issues like "concentration of power in the hands of the few and means to protect vulnerable groups online" (Karppinen & Puukko, 2020: 317).
- Rights and Business: Affordances Provided by Platforms – In this case, digital rights are viewed as affordances or entitlements provided by platform companies or digital intermediaries such as Facebook, Google, Twitter, and so on. A digital affordance is defined as "a type of action or a characteristic of actions that a technology enables through its design instead of something imposed by states, either by inaction or by means of regulation" (Karppinen & Puukko, 2020: 319).

While the "death" of NWICO ensured that the right to communicate discourse fizzled out from both academic and activist discourses on communication, the new communication landscape spawned by the digital revolution reignited and reactivated most of the issues and concerns which had dominated the NWICO debate. Although there were emerging concerns peculiar to the digital environment, most of the controversies associated with NWICO reincarnated. Among the range of residual issues and emerging concerns that justify a relook at communication rights include the persistence of media monopolies and oligopolies; media concentration, which results in media content tilting towards profit-maximization and reduced diversity of voices; and weakening of cultural identities and increased homogenization of cultural identities linked with the proliferation of "unsuitable" individualist and consumerist content (CRIS, 2005: 29). The new digital environment and the concomitant mushrooming of the so-called alternative media have not led to diversity of voices in the media. CRIS states:

> The trouble is that increased freedom of expression is not generating a corresponding flowering in media diversity, including diversity of content and plurality of sources. While sheer volume of media outlets and channels has increased, evidence suggests that following an initial opening in hitherto repressed countries – the diversity of views represented, and of the sources and formats of those views, is very narrow. This is largely the result of commercialization of media and a focus on generating profits, and of the concentration of ownership into fewer and fewer global corporations . . . The net effect of a corporate, consumerist and northern bias in global mass media, inadequate local media in most poor countries, and little or no media directly focusing on and arising from people's needs and interests.
>
> (CRIS, 2005: 29–30)

Hope that the Internet, described by Larry Diamond (2010: 70) as a "liberation technology" would address some of the deficits of mainstream media outlined in the previous quotation appear to be fading, if not turning into a utopian vision because it has, in some instances, engendered exclusion rather than inclusion owing to the digital divide (see Mwaura, and Dalvit, in this volume). Studies have pointed out how very little has changed with regard to the impact of the Internet on democratic participation because of obstacles such as inequalities in access, skills, and relevant content language representation (Hoffmann, 2009: 27). Access to the Internet and other digital infrastructures, particularly access to mobile data in Africa, is an everyday struggle. On the one hand, the open architecture of digital media has facilitated the subaltern to partake in national conversations and assert their cultural identities. On the other hand, challenges of Internet connectivity and exclusionary business practices, such as astronomical prices of data and gadgets, threaten prospects for inclusivity in the digital sphere, the focus of Chari's chapter, in this volume.

Concerns have also been raised about the spread of fake news, misinformation, disinformation and hate speech, and copyright and intellectual property infringements on social media networks and how these in turn subvert the rights of others and what legitimate regulatory measures can be implemented by the state without undercutting the rights of citizens. Balancing communication rights and other human rights within a digital environment is a delicate exercise, as some African governments, in their attempt to curtail the spread of fake news, hate speech, and critical voices, have either shutdown Internet services (Mare, 2020; Chari, 2022) or formulated restrictive regulatory mechanisms as witnessed in Uganda, Ethiopia, and Nigeria amongst others (see Olaniyan & Akpojivi, 2021), an issue addressed by Ngangum, in this volume. Also, the focus of Hungwe and Edosomwan's chapters in this volume.

Concerns about the intensification of commodification of information propelled by the dominance of neoliberalism market have heightened demands for the right to self-expression and equal access to digital technologies and infrastructures, in a context of an ever-increasing digital divide. The extent to which communication should be geared towards the preservation of national identity and national development in Africa resonates with earlier concerns during the NWICO debate but also connects with contemporary demands for decolonization of communication through the protection of cultural diversity in a context where indigenous African cultures are increasingly marginalized while dissenting voices are jettisoned from public discourses (Article 19, 2003; Anawalt, 2020).

Communication Rights and Digital Citizenship

The emergence of information communication technology (ICT) necessitates rethinking the meaning of citizenship to broaden our understanding of the potential of digital media (Hoffman, 2004). While the notion of digital citizenship is new, the Internet and its affordances have redefined the way in which citizens perform their citizenship. Before the emergence and proliferation of new media technologies and their affordances, citizenship and its inclusionary aspect were limited to physical or offline sphere communities wherein any citizens could demand their rights (political, economic, and communication) (see Lister, 2007). Lister (1996) argues that exclusion and inclusion reflect both sides of citizenship, as citizenship in contemporary society has witnessed the contestation between the exclusionary and inclusionary rights of people. For instance, outside the exclusion of people and their rights from specific communities within a nation state, there has been an increasing demand for communication rights in most postcolonial African states due to the shrinking communicative space (see Mudzengi and Gadzikwa's chapter in this volume). The 2021 Freedom House report noted that there was a growing trend of moving towards authoritarianism as the basic tenet of democracy (freedom of expression and media), which sums communicative rights, is in decline, as governments are circumventing "the norms and institutions meant to support basic liberties" associated with citizenship. Such circumvention in governments' strict control of mainstream media (print and broadcast) has restricted the communicative rights of their citizens which are essential in strengthening democracy. Mare (2014) argues that the flawed nature of democracy in most postcolonial African states has seen the rise of protests across the continent and the use of new media technologies in these protests (see also Tsandzana in this volume).

On the flip side of the coin, the Internet is credited for creating opportunities to participate in the governance process by enabling citizens to form communities (online) with which they identify, engage, and participate in societal discourses (Mossberger et al., 2008). Despite the different societal cleavages, citizens are able to form an online space for public deliberations, therefore enabling them to express their communicative rights. Thus, the Internet plays a central role in the formation and realization of digital citizenship, as it enables the creation of what Habermas termed the "public sphere", where these citizens meet visually to deliberately mobilize and press for social changes (see Tsandzana's chapter in this volume). Consequently, Diamond (2010) posits that the ability of citizens to express themselves by "facilitating independent communication" and form and strengthen emergent civil society has made the Internet and its affordances liberating technologies. According to Diamond, these technologies "enable citizens to report news, expose wrongdoing, express opinions, mobilise protest, monitor elections, scrutinise government, deepen participation, and expand the horizons of freedom" (2010: 70). However, the realization of digital citizenship and the potential to strengthen democracy, as alluded to by Diamond, are linked to communication and its recognition by nation states. Article 19 of the universal declaration of human rights states that everyone has the right to freedom of opinion, receive and impact on information. This right is salient to digital citizens and in their protection and promotion of their activities, as the digital space facilitated by the Internet and ICT has interpenetrated every aspect of our lives (Isin & Ruppert, 2020).

The active participation of the private sector in investing in communication and information infrastructure and the deployment of modern technologies such as the Global System for Mobile communication (GSM) (see Chakravartty & Sarikakis, 2006) led to the connectivity of citizens and enhanced democracy and civil rights. Ndukwe (2005), drawing from the Nigerian experience, held that the liberalization of the telecommunication sector saw the proliferation of mobile services across the country and enabled citizens to participate in national discourse. This juxtaposes Aker and Mbiti's (2010) argument that the last two decades have enabled access to communicative space on the African continent, as the widespread use of mobile phones has created new possibilities and shifted the focus from simple communication tools to service delivery. According to them, while buttressing this idea, there is no African country where there is no mobile phone signal or ICT usage, and this has empowered citizens to contribute to the sociopolitical, economic, and cultural discourse of their respective nation states. Citizens could easily use these technologies to express themselves and demand accountability and good governance, which is a bane in most postcolonial African states. These technologies have enabled and changed the dynamics of citizens and state relationship, as the gap between the state and citizens has been bridged and citizens can obtain information, create spaces for deliberation and maintain social relationships (Bosch, 2018). This change in the relationship between the citizens and the states has led to the perceived notion of inclusionary citizenship, as citizens could easily mobilize, engage, and demand service delivery, as witnessed in the social movement protests that have characterized the continent from Arab Spring, Occupy movements, and #MustFall. Consequently, Nyamnjoh (2016) argued that we live in an era where everything must fall due to the potential of social media in aiding and enabling citizens in their demand for good governance.

However, the extent to which digital technologies have enhanced citizens' capacity to receive and impart information, which is the backbone of digital citizenship, has been tampered with, particularly given the numerous obstacles in accessing digital technologies in Africa. Mallen (2021) argues that there can be no right without freedom, and freedom of communication is one right that every human should have as it is the foundation and determines the relationship with politics, culture, and ethics. According to Mallen (2021: 9), "since the beginning of their existence, humans have felt the need to express themselves and to communicate with other humans", and the exclusion or restriction of this is evil and hinders the attainment of truth (Mill, 1859). Theoretically, this position makes communication rights to seek, receive, and impart information a universal principle, and they are germane to digital citizenship (Corredoira, 2021). Thus, normative (offline) citizenship communicative rights encompass both old and new media usage. However, in practice, some nation states are reluctant to extend communicative rights to the digital sphere, arguing that it is difficult to implement it due to the absence of legislation (Corredoira 2021). A review of the African continent shows that there is no African country that has formulated or passed digital rights legislation and inclusion despite the rapid proliferation of the Internet and ICTs (Egbunike, 2020). Instead, African states have passed laws that allow for excessive taxation, digital shutdown (digital blackout), surveillance, and imprisonment to impede digital citizenship, exclude people, and discourage digital activism and mobilization that have been enabled by the Internet. Furthermore, while it can be argued that some people within the continent can be regarded as digital citizens due to their access to the Internet and ability to bypass government restrictions, others are excluded, as digital citizenship requires "educational competencies, technology access and skills and problems such as poverty, illiteracy, and unequal educational opportunities prevent more people from full participation online and society more generally" (Mossberger et al., 2008: x).

The ability of citizens to exercise full digital rights and be included in the digital sphere depends on access, educational skills, infrastructural cost, and language. Most often, in the discourse of communication rights, the focus is on access while other vital aspects that can hinder or exclude some groups in society are neglected. In Africa, the digital divide remains a major factor which excludes citizens from enjoying their rights in the digital sphere, as there are vast infrastructural inequalities and disparities between societies. Most often, these infrastructures are situated within urban areas due to economic reasons, as the service providers seek to recoup their investment quickly. According to Adeleke (2020), the digital divide in most postcolonial African states stems from economic and social inequalities, and there is a split between urban and rural and north and south. This implies that in a continent where a vast majority of its populace reside in rural areas, they are excluded from the communicative space. Even when these infrastructures are present, the high cost of voice and data services discourages and excludes people from this digital citizenship, and their ability to communicate and participate in societal activities (Moyo & Munoriyarwa, 2021, Akpojivi, 2018), as they are more interested in their survival. According to Statista (2022), the average cost of one gigabyte of mobile Internet in sub-Saharan Africa is $4.47, making it one of the highest worldwide. Consequently, resistance in some African states demanding affordable and better mobile services (see Moyo & Munoriyarwa, 2021, and Obadare, 2006). In addition, poor network service and digital divides, exuberant costs of communication (data and voice calls), and lack of electricity and regulatory instincts of the state (see Moyo & Munoriyarwa, 2021, Obadare, 2006) exacerbate the digital divide in Africa (an issue explored by Ngangum in this volume). According to the Accessnow 2021 report, 12 African countries shut down the Internet 19 times in Africa in 2021 (Accessnow, 2021); likewise, states such as Uganda, Lesotho, Burkina Faso, Tanzania, and Nigeria, among others have introduced and sought to introduce a regulatory framework that will make social media users pay social media taxes, register with regulatory authorities, and criminalized communication about the state (Karombo, 2020, Olaniyan & Akpojivi, 2021). All these are strategies used by the state to restrict the communicative rights of citizens and exercise the banality of the state (Mbembe, 1992). To Mbembe (1992), this banality of power is not about just the "implicit or explicit" forms in which these states used restrictive forms to curtail communicative rights or established their arbitrary rule but the routines "repeated daily actions and gestures" in which this banality exists. The daily and repeated actions of most postcolonial African states tend to exclude communications rights, and this is evident in the increasing attempts of the state to move to the online and digital spheres, which have enabled citizens in democratic culture. This exclusionary act thus raises questions about the status of communication rights in Africa and the level of commitment of national governments in promoting and protecting these rights. It speaks to not only the fluidity and unpredictability of communication rights in Africa but also their dynamism in the changing digital communication landscape.

Apart from regulatory restrictions, language barriers have played a significant role in hindering access to digital rights in Africa. Colonial languages such as English, France, Spanish, Portuguese, and Afrikaans are the main official languages, and the Internet content is predominantly in these languages while indigenous African languages are marginalized, thereby perpetuating exclusion. Africa is home to hundreds of indigenous languages and dialects, and the inability of people to access the Internet or communicate using their indigenous languages or dialect means they are being excluded. According to (Mossberger et al., 2008), language acts as a barrier to digital citizenship as it influences access and participation, and this goes against the fundamental principles of the right to communication grounded in the ability of people to "fellowship, participation, empowerment and mutual understanding" (Hamelink and Hoffmann 2008 cited in Moyo (2010: 429). Consequently, the notion that digital citizenship and its associated communicative rights are far from being fully realized on the continent, as institutional and non-institutional factors impede people from entering the digital sphere and participating in political, economic, and cultural discourses.

International Perspectives on Communication Rights

The right to communication is a fundamental human right that is encapsulated in international conventions such as United Nations Article 19 of the Universal Declaration of Human Rights. Article 19 states that "everyone has the right to freedom of opinion and expression, the right includes freedom to hold opinions without interference and to seek, receive and impart information and ideas through any media regardless of frontiers". This provision is holistic and distinct, meaning that communicative rights are applicable to all, irrespective of race, gender, colour, religion, class, and language. Also, it means that there is no geographic restriction, as it is universal "regardless of frontiers" and includes the rights of everyone to seek, receive, and impart any information on any platform, whether mainstream media or new media (Corredoira, 2021).

Therefore, the universal declaration of human rights has become the framework upon which nation states' democratic principles are evaluated (Akpojivi, 2018), and this has likewise influenced the supranational approach to communication rights within the African continent. For instance, Article 9 of the African Charter on Human and People's Rights states that "Every individual shall have the right to receive information. Every individual shall have the right to express and disseminate his opinions within the law". This provision has been criticized for its skewed approach to communication rights, which is not encompassing and not enforceable due to the non-interference policy of the African Union (Akpojivi, 2018). According to Moyo (2010), the lack of political will of African leaders to recognize the communication rights of their citizens has been one of the downsides of the African charter on human rights. This political will can be seen in two ways, namely recognizing the rights of their citizens to seek, receive, and impart information irrespective of the platform (mainstream or new media) and the universality of these rights and principles. Thus, this has influenced most bills of rights that are formulated in a "give and take nature" to maintain the desire to control and restrict the communicative rights of citizens (see Akpojivi, 2018, Ronning & Kupe, 2000).

Such an approach has further influenced subsequent policies and regulations concerning communication rights in the digital age. Since the Internet allows citizens so much potential to hold their leaders accountable via activism, the desire to control and limit communicative rights online has grown, and this is evidenced in legislation that promotes excessive taxation, digital shutdown (digital blackout), surveillance, and imprisonment to impede digital citizenship. Therefore, there are no policies that guarantee digital citizenship and its communicative rights within the African continent. However, available policies such as "digital transformation strategy for Africa (2020–2030)" and the Policy and Regulation Initiative for Digital Africa (PRIDA) are tailored to foster the digital economy, as both policies recognize technology as a central tool in the empowerment of the growing youths and in fostering the digital economy (see Akpojivi's chapter in this volume). Likewise, the AU Data Policy Framework (African Union, 2022) is concerned with an effective data governance system in a global economy that will ensure safeguarding of human rights. Additionally, the Africa Union (AU) policy guidelines on digitizing teaching and learning in Africa is about how technology can be appropriated effectively in teaching and learning to overcome the challenges COVID-19 poses to teaching and learning on the continent (Africa Union, 2022). In all of these, there is a policy gap within the continent, and such a gap raises questions about how the communicative rights of Africans can be guaranteed in a continent that is faced with political, economic, and cultural imbalances. Can the desired digital economy and free trade in Africa, which existing policy attests to, be attained without clear policy guidelines to guarantee communication rights both online and offline? Nevertheless, despite these policy gaps, the digital transformation strategy for Africa and policy guidelines on digitalizing teaching and learning in Africa touch on one aspect of digital citizenship, that is, technological/digital literacy. Digital education and literacy are key to the attainment of digital citizenship, as they address technical knowledge and expose citizens to the collective benefit (economic and political) of digital citizenship. Therefore, giving a ray of hope that in the near future, if these policies are effectively implemented, there will be digitally savvy citizens who are educated and have the skills to use of technology to advance democratic citizenship.

This volume comprises 12 chapters and an introduction, organized into four parts. Part 1 focuses on cultural and minority rights. Part II examines digital citizenship. Part III is on freedom, censorship, and intellectual property rights issues, and Part IV addresses the issue of the politics of digital infrastructures. In the introductory chapter, Tendai Chari and Ufuoma Akpojivi provide a theoretical and historical overview of the concept of communication rights and its variant, "the right to communicate", demonstrating their origins, the social, economic, and political circumstances in which they evolved and the controversies associated with these concepts. Part I of the edited volume, which focuses on cultural and minority rights, opens with Chapter 1 by Chike Mgbeadichie, who examines the "unique" language and cultural phenomenon of the Ubang community of the Cross River state in Nigeria, where men and the boy-child speak two languages (the language of men and the language of women) while women and the girl-child speak the language of women. Mgbeadichie considers the possible impact of this language differentiation and peculiarity on the communication rights of women and the girl-child, arguing that due to this language differentiation, women and the girl-child become second-class citizens in the community despite their metalinguistic knowledge. In Chapter 2, Job Mwaura focuses on the "unintended" consequences of the government of Kenya's digitization initiatives on the pastoral communities of that country. Drawing on interviews and document analysis, Mwaura highlights how, despite their noble intentions, the government's digitalization projects are exacerbating rather than enhancing digital exclusion among the pastoralist communities in Kenya. He proffers suggestions on possible ways through which digitization projects can foster inclusivity among these communities. The theme of digital inclusivity is picked by Lorenzo Dalvit in Chapter 3. Deploying a decolonial perspective, Dalvit critiques existing narratives around digital inclusion of people living with disabilities in South Africa. He argues that the rights-based approach pertaining to the digital rights of people living with disabilities is rooted in Western epistemologies which makes it difficult to define and quantify both disability and inclusion. For Dalvit, this has far-reaching implications, as the gap between policy and practice might increase digital inequalities. To address the challenge of coloniality of language, Dalvit advocates overcoming the pathologization of disability and a shift from the current neoliberal paradigm to which South Africa and many other African countries subscribe. In Chapter 4,

Olutobi Akingbade's contribution connects with Mwaura and Dalvit's focus on digital marginalization of vulnerable groups. While Mwaura focuses on the pastoralist communities in Kenya, and Dalvit on people with disabilities in South Africa, Akingbade focuses on digitally marginalized netizens during the COVID-19 pandemic in Nigeria. Drawing on semi-structured interviews, Akingbade explores how young Nigerians utilized social media before and during the COVID-19 pandemic. He reveals how young Nigerians regularly used the Internet and social media not just for entertainment, but also to exercise their democratic right to expression. The chapter illuminates the interface between communication and political and socio-economic rights in the context of a developing African country marked by digital inequalities. In Chapter 5, Dércio Tsandzana examines the digital activism of *Cabo Delgado Também é Moçambique*, a Mozambican social movement which mobilized through social media to attract the government's attention about the political conflict in the Cabo Delgado region. Tsandzana highlights how digital platforms enabled youthful activists of the movement to mobilize for a national cause regarding terrorism in the conflict-affected region, as well as how these platforms promoted political participation and civic engagement among the activists. Tsandzana argues that despite low levels of Internet connectivity, Moçambique is witnessing significant youth digital activism, even in a context where freedom of expression and civic activities are restricted. In Chapter 6, Ernest Mudzengi and Wellington Gadzikwa tackle the issue of citizen journalism and communication rights in Zimbabwe. Grounded on Jürgen Habermas's public sphere concept and Antonio Gramsci's theory of Hegemony, Mudzengi and Gadzikwa posit that current citizen journalism practices have been corrupted by corporate monopolies. According to Mudzengi and Gadzikwa, the transformative and democratic potential of citizen journalism has been corrupted by corporate and state capture. They argue that for citizen journalism to redeem itself, it must embrace an inclusive social movement building ethos which is free from vested interests. They see citizen journalism as a possible vehicle for promoting the communication rights of subaltern groups, only if freed from political and corporate capture.

Part III of the volume, which focuses on freedom, censorship, and intellectual property rights, opens with Chapter 7 by Ikechukwu Obiaya, who explores the way in which Nigerian film-makers negotiate regulatory obstacles and censorship imposed by the state. Obiaya found out that to evade censorship of their works, Nigerian film-makers either engage in self-censorship or find creative ways of telling their stories to sidestep these obstacles. Obiaya contends that despite the fact that the right to communicate is enshrined in the Nigerian constitution and international human rights conventions and protocols ratified by Nigeria, the right of Nigerian film-makers to tell their stories was often abused by state actors. Chapter 8 by Aifuwa Edosomwan focuses on the thorny issue of intellectual property rights protection and law enforcement. Edosomwan critically evaluates recent developments with regard to the protection of intellectual property rights and enforcement of laws

Introduction 15

in Nigeria. The chapter shines the spotlight on the Nigerian Copyright Commission's efforts towards improving the policy framework for the protection of intellectual property rights, surveying various pieces of legislation that have been reviewed to align with the current digital technology environment. He exposes how weak enforcement of copyright laws in Nigeria has negatively impacted on critical sectors of the Nigerian economy, and how workers in the creative industry have been prejudiced of their dues. Edosomwan argues that loopholes in existing copyright laws have contributed to loss of revenue due to the national fiscus. In Chapter 9, Peter Tiako Ngangum focuses on yet another contentious issue on the African continent – Internet shutdowns. Drawing on document analysis and interviews, Ngangum examines Internet shutdowns in the Anglophone regions of Cameroon. Ngangum reveals how Internet shutdowns in Cameroon are linked to a host of other kinds of censorship and information suppression tactics such as taxation, licensing of media houses, surveillance regulations, website-takedown, social media bans, closing down of media houses, and suspension and/or banning of journalists. Ngangum concludes that despite the existence of human rights laws and principles, there is very little or no transparency and accountability with regard to Internet shutdowns. Thus, in the absence of a fair balance between protecting media freedom, access to information, exercising communication rights, and upholding principles of public policy, Internet shutdowns should be viewed as a disproportionate way of regulating the media. In Chapter 10, Brian Hungwe turns to an equally vexatious question of fake news, freedom of expression, and trademark infringements. Adopting a doctrinal research approach, Hungwe compares the digital misappropriation of media trademarks to spread fake news as harmful infringements on intellectual property rights in South Africa and Kenya. He dissects the impact of fake news on media trademarks, bringing to the fore contending legal arguments for balancing the right to freedom of expression and the Misappropriation Doctrine, which makes a case against the misappropriation of valuable assets such as media trademarks. Hungwe argues that media trademarks are pillars of trust and national discourse references which must be protected in the public interest.

Part IV of the volume is devoted to the politics of digital infrastructures in the African context. Chapter 11 by Tendai Chari explores the controversial issue of the politics of mobile data. Deploying the concept of digital rights and social movement theories, Chari explores the struggle over the price of mobile data in South Africa, using #DataMustFall as a case study. The chapter highlights how economic "deprivation" motivated the formation of the campaign, the hybrid modes of activism which it employed, its milestones, as well as setbacks. Chari illuminates on the way in which the notion of digital rights intersects with the politics of digital infrastructures in an unequal society, revealing the ambiguity and complexity of the notion of digital rights in a neoliberal context whereby citizens' digital rights are at variance with corporate interests. Chapter 12, which is the final chapter in the volume, by Ufuoma Akpojivi examines the politicization of social media in Nigeria. Employing

Jürgen Habermas's concept of the public sphere and Mill's On Liberty theory, and using the 2021 Twitter ban in Nigeria as a case study, involving a critical discourses of over 500,000 tweets, Akpojivi dissects the contestation between tech giants, the state, and citizens over the regulation of free speech in Nigeria and its implications for communication rights. Akpojivi demonstrates how communicative platforms such as Twitter were being politicized through Internet shutdowns and how such politicization reflected the contours of a complicated postcolonial state–citizen relationship whereby the state justified such control on the grounds of "state security" while citizens resisted government efforts to control digital infrastructures by using Virtual Private Networks (VPN) to speak back to power. Akpojivi calls for a rethink of how communication rights can be realized in a country such as Nigeria, which seeks to promote a digital economy and digital citizenship, yet the state maintains its authoritarian enclave by splinternet and curtailing the communication rights of citizens.

References

Accessnow (2021). *2021 Report*. Online: www.accessnow.org/internet-shutdowns-africa-keepiton-2021/, accessed 12/01/2023

Adeleke. R. (2020). Digital Divide in Nigeria: The Role of Regional Differentials. *African Journal of Science, Technology, Innovation and Development*, 13, 3: 333–346.

African Union (2022). *AU Data Policy Framework*. Addis Ababa: AU.

Africa Union (n.d.). *Policy Guidelines on Digitalising Teaching and learning in Africa*. Addis Ababa: AU.

Aker, J., and Mbiti, I. (2010). Mobile Phones and Economic Development in Africa. *Journal of Economic Perspectives*, 24, 3: 207–232.

Akpojivi, U. (2018). Euphoria and Delusion of Digital Activism: Case Study of ZumaMustFall. In F. Endong (Ed.), *Exploring The Role of Social Media in Transnational Advocacy*. Pennsylvania: IGI Global.

Akpojivi, U. (2018). *Media Reforms and Democratisation in Emerging Democracies of Sub-Saharan Africa*. New York: Palgrave.

Alegre, A., and O'Siochru, S. (2005). Communication Rights. In A. Ambros, V. Peugeot and D. Pimienta (Eds.), *World Matters: Multicultural Perspectives on Information Societies*, pp. 475–502. Caen: C&F Publishers.

Anawalt, H.C. (2020). The Right to Communicate. *Denver Journal of International Law & Policy*, 13, 2–3: 219–236.

Bosch, T. (2018). Digital Media and Political Citizenship: Facebook and Politics in South Africa. In B. Mutsvairo and B. Karam (Eds.), *Political Communications in Africa: From Mandela to Magufuli*, pp. 145–158. London: Routledge.

Cerf, G.V. (2012, 4 January). "Internet Access is Not a Human Right. *New York Times*. Online: https://www.nytimes.com/2012/01/05/opinion/internet-access-is-not-a-human-right.html, accessed 30 January, 2021.

Chakravartty, P., and Sarikakis, K. (2006). *Media Policy and Globalisation*. Edinburg: Edinburg University Press.

Chari, T. (2022). Between State Interests and Citizen Digital Rights: Making Sense of Internet Shutdowns in Zimbabwe. In F.A. Kperogi (Ed.), *Digital Dissidence and Social Media Censorship in Africa*, p. 76. London: Routledge.

Corredoira, L. (2021). Communication Rights in an Internet-Based Society Why is the Principle of Universality So Important? In L. Corredoria, I. Mallen and R. Presuel (Eds.), *The Handbook of Communication Rights, Law, and Ethics*, pp. 30–46. Hoboken, NJ: Wiley Blackwell.

CRIS. (2005). Assessing Communication Rights: A Handbook. *CRIS Campaign*. Online: https://archive.ccrvoices.org/cdn.agilitycms.com/centre-for-communication-rights/Images/Articles/pdf/cris-manual-en.pdf, accessed 6/01/2023.

D' Arcy, J. (1969) Direct Broadcast Satellites and the Right to Communicate. *EBU Review*, 118, 14–18.

Diamond, L. (2010). Liberation Technology. *Journal of Democracy*, 21, 3: 69–83.

Egbunike, N. (2020). *Digital Rights in Africa is Still Far from the Internet Freedom We Desire: What's the Future of Digital Rights in Africa?* Online: https://globalvoices.org/2020/10/01/digital-rights-in-africa-is-still-far-from-the-internet-freedom-we-desire/, accessed 15/01/2023

Freedom House (2021). *The Global Expansion of Authoritarian Rule*. Online: https://freedomhouse.org/report/freedom-world/2022/global-expansion-authoritarian-rule, accessed 10/01/2023

Hamelink, C.J. (1994). *The Politics of World Information: A Human Rights Perspective*. London: Sage.

Hamelink, C.J. (2004a). Did WSIS Achieve Anything at All? *Gazette: The International Journal for Communication Studies*, 66, 3–4: 281–290.

Hamelink, C.J. (2004b). Towards a Human Right to Communicate. *Canadian Journal of Communication*, 29: 205–212.

Hamelink, C., and Hoffman, J. (2008). The State of the Right to Communicate. *Global Media Journal*, 7, 13: 1–16.

Hoffman, J. (2004). *Citizenship beyond the State*. London: Sage.

Hoffmann, J. (2009). *Communication Rights, Democracy & Legitimacy: The European Union*. Amsterdam: Academic Publishing AG & Co.

Isin, E., and Ruppert, E. (2020). *Being Digital Citizens*. London: Rowman & Littlefield International.

Karombo, T. (2020). *More African Governments are Quietly Tightening Rules and Laws on Social Media*. Online: https://qz.com/africa/1915941/lesotho-uganda-tanzania-introduce-social-media-rules, accessed 07/01/2023

Karppinen, K., and Puukko, O. (2020) Four Discourses of Digital Rights: Promises and Problems of Rights-Based Politics. *Journal of Information Policy*, 10: 304–328.

Kaye, D., and Reventlow, N. (2017). *Digital Rights are Human Rights*. Online: https://slate.com/technology/2017/12/digital-rights-are-human-rights.html, accessed 06/07/2023

Lister, R. (1996). Citizenship, Welfare Rights and Local Government. In J. Demaine and H. Entwistle (Eds.), *Beyond Communitarianism*. London: Palgrave.

Lister, R. (2007). Inclusive Citizenship: Realising the Potential. *Citizenship Studies*, 11, 1: 49–61.

Mallen, I. (2021). Freedom as the Essential Basis for Communication Rights. In L. Corredoria, I. Mallen and R. Presuel (Eds.), *The Handbook of Communication Rights, Law and Ethics: Seeking Universality Equality, Freedom and Dignity*. Hoboken, NJ: Blackwell.

Mamndani, M. (1996). *Citizen and Subject: Contemporary Africa and the Legacy of Late Colonialism*. Princetown, NJ: Princetown University Press.

Mare, A. (2014). Social Media: The New Protest Drums in Southern Africa? In B. Pătruț and M. Pătruț (Eds.), *Social Media in Politics. Public Administration and Information Technology* (vol. 13). Cham: Springer. https://doi.org/10.1007/978-3-319-04666-2_17

Mare, A. (2020). Internet Shutdowns in Africa State-Ordered Internet Shutdowns and Digital Authoritarianism in Zimbabwe. *International Journal of Communication*, 14, 4244–4263.

Mathiesen, K. (2014). Human Rights for the Digital Age. *Journal of Mass Media Ethics*, 29, 1: 2–18.

Mbembe, A. (1992). The Banality of Power and the Aesthetics of Vulgarity in the Postcolony. *Public Culture*, 4, 2: 1–30.

McBride, S. (1980). *One Voices One World*. Paris: UNESCO.

Mill, S. (1859). *On Liberty* (4th ed.). London: Longman.

Mossberger, K., Tolbert, C., and McNeal, R. (2008). *Digital Citizenship The Internet, Society, and Participation*. Cambridge: The MIT Press.

Moyo, D., and Munoriyarwa, A. (2021). Data Must Fall: Mobile Data Pricing, Regulatory Paralysis and Citizen Action in South Africa. *Information, Communication & Society*, 24, 3: 365–389.

Moyo, L. (2010). Language, Culture and Communication Rights of Ethnic Minorities in South Africa: A Human Rights Approach. *The International Communication Gazette*, 72, 4–5: 425–440.

Musiani, F., Pava, E., and Padovani, C. (2009). Investigating Discourses on Human Rights in the Digital Age: Emerging Norms and Policy Challenges. In *International Association for Media and Communication Research* (IAMCR, Annual Congress on "Human Rights and Communication", July 2009), pp. 359–378. Mexico: Mexico. Online: https://hal-mines-paristech.archives-ouvertes.fr/hal-00448231

Ndukwe, E. (2005, 31 May). *Telecommunications in Nigeria: The Next Frontier*. A Paper Presented at the New Age/NCC Seminar.

Nyamnjoh, F. (2016). *RhodesMustFall: Nibbling at Resilient Colonialism in South Africa*. Bamenda: Langaa RPCIG.

Obadare, E. (2006). Playing Politics with the Mobile Phone in Nigeria: Civil Society, Big Business and the State. *Review of African Political Economy*, 107, 73–111.

Olaniyan, A., and Akpojivi, U. (2021). Transforming Communication, Social Media, Counter-Hegemony and the Struggle for the Soul of Nigeria. *Information, Communication & Society*, 24, 3: 422–437.

Ruuhonen, M. (2004). *A Review of the Right to Communicate: Possibilities of Communication Rights in an Information Society*. Unpublished MA Dissertation. Department of Journalism and Mass Communication, University of Tempere. Online: https://trepo.tuni.fi/handle/10024/92003, accessed 12/01/2023

Ronning, H., and Kupe, T. (1999) "The Dual Legacy of Democracy and Authoritarianism". In J. Curran and M. Park (Eds.), *De-Westernizing Media Studies*, pp. 157–177. London: Routledge.

Schejter, A. (2022). 'It Is Not Good for the Person to Be Alone': The Capabilities Approach and the Right to Communicate. Convergence. *The International Journal of Research into New Media Technologies*, 28, 6: 1826–1840.

Statista (2022). *Average Price for 1GB of Mobile Data in Africa as of 2022, by Country*. Online: www.statista.com/statistics/1180939/average-price-for-mobile-data-in-africa/, accessed 20/01/2023

Thomas, P.N. (2011). *Negotiating Communication Rights: Case Studies from India*. New Delhi: Sage.

Part I
Cultural and Minority Rights

1 Language-Cultural Barrier in Ubang Community
A Critical Assessment of the Communication Rights of Women and the Girl-Child

Chike Mgbeadichie

Introduction

Language is a critical part of human existence and a fundamental right of all human beings necessary for fostering interactivity and connectivity among different peoples of the world (Brady et al., 2016). Everyone sends and receives communicative messages through different modes: speaking, listening, reading, writing, and other non-verbal means. Any attempt to limit the communication capacity of any human being amounts to reducing the full potential and essence of the human existence (Bloomfield, 1933; McLeod, 2018). To ensure this human right, the United Nation's 1948 declaration argues that freedom of opinion and expression and freedom without distinction of language are sacrosanct communication right of all human beings (Article 19, United Nations, 1948).

However, in Ubang community in Cross River state of Nigeria, men and the boy-child are culturally empowered to speak two languages (Ofre, the language of men and Arasere, the language of women), but women and the girl-child speak only Arasere, even though they understand Ofre. By culture stipulating women/girl-child to Arasere, and men/boy-child to speak two languages, the Ubang culture has introduced a unique language-cultural issue that needs analysing. This language-cultural phenomenon is likely problematic because it goes against the United Nations (UN) declaration of freedom of expression without distinction of language. Because the acquisition of language in itself is an act of "becoming a person" and a member of a particular society (Nelson, 2003; Shatz, 1994), the language-cultural situation in Ubang portends for women and the girl-child the status of a lesser-human with reduced and limited self-worth. This chapter examines the language use among the Ubang people to assess how the language-cultural phenomenon, a specific cultural pattern, affects the communication rights of women and the girl-child in the community and to underscore the impact it might have on them.

The chapter begins with a brief background on the Ubang people to shed light on cultural patterns and ethos of the Ubang with a view to unravel the position ascribed to women in the said ethnic group. It then analyses the dual-language phenomenon in Ubang, providing several important dimensions of this unique linguistic pattern in the community. This is followed by an overview and a summary of the theoretical framework and methodology that underpin the research and next, a comprehensive section with a discussion on the impact of the Ubang dual-language practice on the rights of women and the girl-child.

The Ubang Community

Little has been written by historians, sociologists, anthropologists, or cultural experts about the Ubang. The Ubang is a unique community in Obudu local government area of Cross River State in Nigeria. It is situated on latitude 9 degree east of the state and longitude 6.3 degree north. There are three villages in Ubang: Okwersing, Ofambe, and Okiro. According to Abue et al. (2018: 75), Ubang is a gender-sensitive linguistic clan where men speak Ofre, a completely different language from the women who speak Arasere. The linguistic situation of this community becomes even more fascinating in the sense that whilst men and women have separate languages, men and the boy-child are culturally empowered to speak both languages. Women and the girl-child, according to cultural norms, are supposed to speak Arasere only. This language-cultural phenomenon creates a structure of superiority and inferiority of the genders. In this case, men who are culturally empowered to speak two languages assume an even more superior stance compared to women who are restricted to a single language.

Like every other cultural group in Nigeria, Ubang is known for its unique cultural world view, which shapes the people of the community. Some of such cultural principles are respect for the elderly; belief in the supernatural; perseverance and fortitude; the diverse roles and responsibilities of male and female in the formation of the family; the language phenomenon (Ingwe, 2014: 6); and the ownership rights of the Ubang woman where her body is supposed to be the property of her in-laws whilst her head is owned by her birth family (Chrisler, 2013: 4). Ubang is known to wrap its traditions on the people in such a way that even when a person leaves the community, such a person remains deeply connected to the customs of the land. From the knowledge of the Ubang people, it could be argued that the culture of this community impedes on the fundamental rights of women in different ways. In this chapter, however, the focus is not on other cultural practices that discriminate against women, for instance, the contravention of Ubang women's sexual and reproductive rights as argued by Undie and Izugbara (2011), but to assess how the language-cultural phenomenon affects the communication rights of women and the girl-child in the community.

The Dual-Language Phenomenon in Ubang Community

To understand the dual-language phenomenon in Ubang, I refer to a documentary video available on YouTube where an Ubang Chief, Oliver Ibang, describes the phenomenon. This video henceforth shall be coded as YouTube video (1). In YouTube video (1), Ibang argues that boys grow up speaking the female language and at the same time are taught the men's language by their fathers. This language-cultural situation is put more clearly by Abue et al. (2018: 80) "mothers are instructed by the Ubang culture to teach their daughters and sons the Arasere language at an early age, but fathers are supposed to teach only their sons the Ofre language". This cultural practice gives the boy-child/men two languages but leaves the girl-child/women with one. Thus, the boy-child assumes a superior position compared to his sisters and even his mother in the community.

Even though women speak Arasere and might understand a bit of Ofre by observing the men speak in the community, it is obvious that the boy-child/men are at an advantage over the women. Having learnt both languages as taught by their mothers and fathers, the boy-child grows with competence in both languages while the girl-child has one. At age 10, Ibang says the boy-child is expected to switch communication using the men's language. He says:

> There is a stage where the male discovers he is not using his rightful language. Nobody will tell him; he would change to the male language. When he starts speaking the men's language, you know maturity is coming into him.[1]

When a child fails to make such language switch between 10 years and 12 years, such a child is considered abnormal. However, such abnormality could be as a result of a couple of factors which a further study might reveal. By being cultural bilinguals, Ubang males possess more social nuances and competence in the community. They understand their world, the world of the females, and the entire community. As for the females, they could be handicapped to some extent in exploring their world compared to their male counterparts.

The origin of this dual-language phenomenon is fascinating. In video (1), Oliver Ibang and other residents in the community say that this unique language situation was given to them by God. In this video that privileges textuality over sound, these people argue that God's plan was to give each ethnic group two languages. But after creating the two languages for Ubang, God realized there were not enough languages to go round all ethnic groups, so God stopped. This suggests why Ubang has the benefit of two languages which makes them different from other ethnic groups. From this media text, it is clear that the linguistic binary of the Ubang has been sustained over the years by the people's creation of myths through their strong reliance and reverence to God. The Ubang believe in the supernatural and God at the centre of their world. They believe that God does not make mistakes and cannot be challenged, hence the Ubang have come to accept this language system as both a supernatural and cultural gift.

Not only has culture and the belief in the supernatural helped in the preservation of the linguistic binary in Ubang, but myths also contribute critically to the perpetration of gender inequality through the nurturing and sustenance of a discriminatory communicative culture between the genders. Myths, whether cultural or supernatural, lend some form of credibility to the explanations of actions of a people. It offers justification and validation of beliefs—healing, renewal, and some form of inspiration to others (Rollo, 1983: 3). The renewal and inspiration that myth offers can be counter-productive to the marginalized in a society. Whilst uplifting to those at an advantage in a social system, it creates a docile mindset for the marginalized to accept any status ascribed to them. Because myths are many times ingrained in the world view of a people, it becomes difficult to find critics of practices that are sustained by mythic nuances. Thus, to critique the discriminatory communicative culture in Ubang, it is essential that linguists and scholars interrogate deeply the creation and cultural myths that have sustained this practice.

The question about the complication of the Ubang creation myth and linguistic gifting could be an adaptation of, or borrowing from, the Judeo-Christian creation mythology. This form of borrowing resonates with what Edward Said refers to as "traveling theory" to interrogate the foundational logic of their linguistic practice. Travel theory is a critical ideology where "people and schools of criticism, ideas and theories travel – from person to person, from situation to situation, from one period to another" (Said, 1983: 226). The Ubang had borrowed from the Judeo-Christian biblical creation narrative to establish the beginning of their language peculiarity and by that the Judeo-Christian creation mythology has travelled. In adapting the Judeo-Christian creation mythology to give credence to their linguistic gifting, the Ubang manipulate the original myth by some modifications to fit their peculiarity; they presented a distorted Judeo-Christian creation myth by ascribing a separate language to men and women which is absolutely not the case in the original theory. This is expected because Said makes it clear that in travel theory, "translation, simplifications and contradictions of the original may be transgressed" (Said, 1994: 439). Whether as some critics argue that the period referenced in the biblical creation myth is most likely to be later than the creation of the Ubang stock considering that archaeological and paleontological findings indicate that the earliest forms of human evolution occurred in Africa before humans spread to other continents, one may still rely on the Judeo-Christian creation mythology as a foundation to explain the Ubang language dynamics, since the biblical stories command absolute believability amongst a good number of peoples, especially Christians, across the world.

What easily comes to mind when one thinks of the dual-language situation in Ubang is the idea of bilingualism. Although bilingualism does not clearly describe the phenomenon in this community, one might use the knowledge thereof to attempt an understanding of the language situation in Ubang. Bilingualism is simply a situation where two languages are used alternatively by persons in daily conversations and social interactions. Hamers and Blanc (2000: 6) put it clearly:

> Bilinguality is the psychological state of an individual who has access to more than one linguistic code as a means of social communication; the degree of access will vary along a number of dimensions which are psychological, cognitive, psycholinguistic, social psychological, sociological, sociolinguistic, sociocultural and linguistic.

Bilingualism is not an occasional use of two languages by a bilingual person. It is much more than that. For Haugen (1956: 94), bilingualism suggests that the bilingual person constantly expresses a "whole range" mastery of the skills and understanding of the two languages. The criterion of being bilingual, therefore, demands that a speaker of a language produces meaningful expressions in another language (Diellza, 2019). Ubang males fit this bubble.

In Ubang, men and the boy-child are culturally empowered to be bilinguals. They display mastery of Ofre and at the same time have competence in Arasere. They exhibit dynamism in the interplay of the conceptual and linguistic levels of both languages which is based on bidirectional movements. How men and the boy-child are able to sustain conversations in different situations using either of the languages is fascinating and perhaps might be the focus for another study. Kecskes (2006) in a study on dual-language phenomenon suggests that preverbal thought for bilinguals is linguistically formulated and appears on the surface in the form of expressions which may contain elements from either or both languages and unique structural mixes produced by the bilingual individual. Such ability to mix elements from both languages creates a superior persona for the Ubang males in comparison to their female counterparts. Another way the bilingual Ubang males display language dynamism is through their ability to code-switch. Code-switching, as Kecskes (2006: 260) argues, involves a cooperative rather than a competitive relationship between language channels. Ubang men have the competence to keep both languages separately and ensure they cooperate when expressing preverbal thoughts. The role of participating languages in bilingual production of sentences/utterances keeps changing in the course of language production and depends on conceptual–pragmatic factors such as the speaker's intention or topic. With bilingualism, Ubang males have an advantage over the females in conversations because they have the space – using a language which the females have no mastery of – to possibly manipulate their intentions or twist topics in conversations.

Ubang males are cultural bilinguals not bi-dialectals. This means that they are culturally empowered to speak two distinct languages and not a variation of one language. This is worth stressing because there are doubts as to the veracity of the clear distinctions between Ofre and Arasere. However, social linguists such as Undie and her well-known father, Victor Uchendu, have produced studies to support this claim. According to Undie (2007), who has

Table 1.1 Examples of separate sounds of Ofre and Arasere

Ofre	English	Arasere
abu	dog	*okwakwe*
kitchi	tree	*okweng*
bamuie	water	*amu*
nko	cup	*ogbala*
nki	clothing	*ariga*
bibiang	bush	*deyire*
ibue	goat	*obi*

done extensive work on the Ubang culture but nothing on the impact of the language-cultural phenomenon on women, the languages of Ubang, Ofre and Arasere, have no robust orthography (Undie, 2007: 297). Several attempts by the community to invite national and foreign linguistic experts to the community to help with this challenge have not been successful. This does not take away the important role the languages play in the lives of the Ubang. Ofre and Arasere are spoken extensively in Ubang. According to Abue et al. (2018), these two languages have all the elements of every language. He disagrees with Undie that Ubang languages have a weak orthography. For him, these languages can be written and read. There are letters of the languages. He argues further that Ofre and Arasere have separate phonology, morphology, syntax, semantic, and pragmatic features. A few examples of the separate sounds of the two languages are shown in Table 1.1.

I am not from Ubang community; neither am I from Cross River. I am Igbo from the south-eastern part of Nigeria and an academic with interest in cultural studies to examine how culture impacts human development. This informs my interest in studying the culture and perceived language inequalities of the Ubang and its implications thereof. I do not therefore claim to have native knowledge of the Ubang community; what I know is that ideas from this study could serve as springboard for scholars of cultural studies in their interrogations of language rights in a postcolonial state like Nigeria.

Theoretical Framework

This chapter adopts Hymes's (1962) theory of ethnographic cultural communication. The theory, made popular by Geertz (1973) and Philipsen (1975), describes the communicative particularities of a cultural community in expounding the communicative uniqueness of the people. The theory argues that certain cultural communication paradigms such as of the cultural concept of *community* (the interactions within the community), *conversation* (aspects of Arasere/Ofre languages), and *codes* (system of meaning and ideals women and girl-child generate in the community) should be critically examined.

Just as Edward Hall (1959: 217) wrote, "Culture is communication and communication is culture", the ethnographic cultural communication theory requires that, to underscore the communicative particularities of any cultural community like Ubang, one needs to rethink the idea of culture strictly from the perspective of the communication paradigm of that given community. To understand the language-cultural dimension in Ubang in accordance with this theory, we should thus view culture as a code or system of meanings and ideals. After all, Philipsen (1989: 260), defining culture as communication, argues that culture is "a historically transmitted system of symbols, meanings, premises, routines, and rules". By this, we place communication in the forefront of cultural discourses and thus, to understand the culture of a community, one must first understand the communication paradigm of the people within the community to evaluate what Hall (1959: 54) calls "the intersubjective resources available for the people in generating a given meaning or meanings from an observed act". Based on this theory, this chapter will critically analyse and interpret the embedded resources, patterns, and skills employed by Ubang women and the girl-child in generating meanings and codes to make sense of their world.

Given that the ethnographic cultural communication theory takes culture through communication to be both integrative and transformative (Bradford, 1992; Carbaugh, 1990), it will be fascinating to understand how females in Ubang feel integrated under this unique language-cultural pattern. For this theory, the culture of a community lacks integration and transformation if the communication structures are problematic.

Methodology

This chapter adopts a descriptive research design approach. Data for analysis were derived from two YouTube videos available online on the dual-language phenomenon in Ubang as well as semi-structured interviews with five purposely selected natives of Ubang community across well-notable demographic representations in the community: two school teachers, 45 and 40 years, who are also wives and mothers with male and female children; two fathers, 55 and 58 years, who also have male and female children; and another woman, 50 years, with university education, who is a wife and mother with male and female children. To protect the identity of the respondents, I will refer to the five of them henceforth as R1 (man, 55 years), R2 (man, 58 years) R3 (woman, 45 years), R4 (woman, 40 years), and R5 (woman, 50 years). The three women were useful in providing critical views and opinions on Ubang women on the impact of this language-cultural patterns on females. They equally helped the researcher articulate the possible impact of this language system on the development and formation of male and female children in the community. This is important because, for ethical reasons, it would be inappropriate to speak directly to a child, male or female, whose knowledge of this system might not be completely formed. The men interviewed provided views representative of the male folk in Ubang. The interviews were juxtaposed against the textual and visual contents available on the two YouTube videos for critical analysis. Because this is a unique study with little written on it so far, interviews with critical stakeholders in the community are important to understand and unpack "the experiences of people, the facts and meanings they ascribe based on their experiences" Kvale (1996: 35). With the data from these interviews and contents from the videos, one is able to critically analyse and assess the impact of this breach of communication rights of women and the girl-child in Ubang as well as suggest ways to reassert the language rights of women without eroding the cultural ethos of the Ubang people.

It is worth stating that the researcher had initially designed a part of the data gathering to be focused group discussions with a sizeable number of persons, but that did not happen because, at the last minute, the host who was supposed to arrange this meeting with the community suggested we cancel the meeting for security reasons in the region. However, the researcher was able to have robust recorded telephone conversations with representatives of the selected demography for the study. When the researcher contacted people from Ubang, almost everyone refused granting any interviews; leaving the researcher with the option of snowballing. In fact, when I got the consent of the three female interviewees, they constantly reminded me that they would like to remain anonymous as the views they would be expressing are not going to be popular amongst women and men in the community.

The analyses were at two levels. The first aspect is a thematic analyses of responses from interviews to deepen understanding of the impact of such language-cultural practice in the community. Through visual and textual readings, the second unpacks the significant contents from the two YouTube videos. Taken together, these two levels of information (media texts and interviews) were juxtaposed against each other to show the convergence and divergence in their readings of the language situation in Ubang.

Thematic Analysis

Drawn from the interviews conducted, I placed the discussions on the impact of the language-cultural phenomenon on Ubang females into themes.

Cognitive Advantage, Confidence, and Inhibitory Control

Studies have shown clearly that bilingual people, especially children, demonstrate a number of cognitive advantages that are related to their need to understand social and contextual cues (Cheung et al., 2010; Goetz, 2003; Damon & Eisenberg, 1998; Halle & Daneri, 2014; Saarni, 1997). This is not different in the Ubang situation. R4 suggests that, although people in the community live as though all is well with them and are happy with the language patterns in Ubang, a few women have reservations about the situation and the advantage it offers the male over the female in the community. She says that, as a mother of five with three sons and two daughters, she has seen her sons grow in conscious intellectual activities such as thinking, reasoning, or remembering, beyond their sisters:

> Out of all my five children, I can say that the three boys are smarter and intelligent than their sisters. I don't know why this is the case, but I think it may be a "man's thing".

R4 was unable to say whether this cognitive advantage is directly connected to males being cultural bilinguals.

R3 on this point thinks that the situation breaks females but is uplifting for males. She argues that her daughters, aged 6 and 9, have enquired why they are not taught Ofre by their father, but their brother who is 4 years joins them to learn Arasere:

> [M]y girls have complained many times to me that they want to learn Ofre because their brother joins them to learn Arasere. This is beginning to trouble me because they ask plenty questions at their age about this situation and I don't have answers to give them. The older one even said, sometime, that we love the boy more than them.

Although they still grow to have fair knowledge of Ofre by way of observing and listening to male discussions, there is no doubt that the males in the community who were taught both languages at childhood have a greater advantage over the females. She thinks that this language-cultural phenomenon is affecting the socialization of her daughters and their confidence. Because the male in the homes are culturally empowered to speak two languages, one can deduce that "as bilinguals, they have the ability to communicate feelings in different appropriate ways" (Cervantes, 2002: 151). In fact, Bialystok and Martin (2004) and Kovács and Mehler (2009) argue that bilingual persons when compared to their monolingual counterparts, demonstrate greater inhibitory control. By this, we mean the ability to suppress irrelevant stimuli and behavioural responses, motor impulse control which is sometimes referred to as stopping impulsivity. Both R4 and R3 alluded to this point. They think that their male children show more inhibitory control compared to their sisters. Even though behavioural experts have extensively concluded that females in an ideal situation possess superior cognitive advantage, inhibitory control, and confidence over their male counterparts (see Ide, 2011; Mansouri et al., 2016), the Ubang community through its language-cultural dynamics have reversed this trend. Thus, because the peculiarity of the language practice is unnatural, it is important to rethink critically this language-cultural tradition, which affects the psycho-social development of females in Ubang.

Bilinguals, in this case cultural bilinguals, perform better in perspective-taking tasks (Greenberg et al., 2013). Perspective-taking task refers to tasks that inform a person to attend to or switch personalities. In other words, the ability to conceal mood, feeling, or disposition. R3, R4, and R5 think that their boys display this extensively both at home and in the community. In fact, when asked to describe the behaviour of their sons as different from their daughters, they provided similar responses that it is near impossible to know what their sons have in mind because they tend to switch between "selves' to take-on other personas. This, in my opinion, helps the male adapt to situations around him to his advantage. However, Ubang females who lack this skill as a result of their monolingual nature are at a disadvantage. When asked to describe the females in the community, R1 and R2 said they noticed females of all age brackets are not as smart and enterprising as males in Ubang. For these male respondents, this is how God made Ubang female; noting that they have their fantastic qualities which the males lack and that the males are bearing a double burden of protecting the females from persons who might want to manipulate their weaknesses.

Beyond the perspective-taking tasks, an extensive body of literature has shown that bilingual persons surpass their monolingual counterparts on a number of executive function tasks (see Bialystok & Martin, 2004; Bialystok et al., 2010; Carlson & Meltzoff, 2008; Yang et al., 2011). Responses from the interviews with R1, R2, R3, R4, and R5 prove this as well. For R1, males, whether boys or men, pay attention more than females: "our men and boys understand and pay attention to things very well. I don't tell my boys things more than once and they do it better". Attention to details is a function task that is expected of an executive. What this suggests is that males, giving the Ubang situation, are better executives than the females. This portends a great problem for the females if they would ever achieve their full potentials in the community and beyond. Also, the power of bilingualism provides the Ubang males the ability and executive function to understand different viewpoints of an issue as well as remaining focused to complete a task. In the views of R3, R4, and R5, when asked to describe their husbands, they see their husbands as persons who are much more focused than them and diverse in opinions. Although the female respondents think these qualities are as a result of the natural make-up of the Ubang men, studies suggest that these qualities which place male above female can be traced and linked to the bilingual nature of men in the community. This bilingual culture offers males the ability to horn these skills, making them better and superior human to the female. If one argues that monolingualism (Ellis, 2008) in the case of Ubang makes a person more introverted and somewhat timid, one will not be entirely wrong. R5 who chronicles females in her own understanding thinks that Ubang females, although hardworking, can be introverts which sometimes makes her appear timid. She is of the opinion that women will need to be more self-expressive instead of being over reliant on the men to lead the way in all things in the community. This is one of the many ways this language situation affects women in the community.

Ubang females, as a result of their monolingual language phenomenon, show less control in cognitive behaviours such as mental flexibility, self-monitoring and power, initiation of activity, and planning. This can be deduced because Bialystok and Barac (2012: 12) argue that bilingual persons demonstrate an executive control system associated with such behaviours as planning, initiation of activity, mental flexibility, self-monitoring, and power. Ubang males are known to always take charge in all matters. R3 says it is by tradition that the male takes charge and plans for the household and community. Females, she says, are responsible for other things, but not planning and initiating activities:

> We cannot plan for our houses when our husbands or our mature sons are around; our tradition forbids it. We are not in control; they are the ones to take charge every time, but we still have our work in the house (sic).

If she demonstrates executive control even in his absence, she must seek and get the approval of her husband. By this token, it becomes evident that females have handed over their lives to the males who have acquired these planning, initiation of activity, mental flexibility, self-monitoring, and power skills as a result of their bilingual heritage in the community. It is worth stressing that the cultural superiority of males over females is not new in the different cultures in Nigeria. What is new in the Ubang case is the mechanism through which males have acquired this position, and that mechanism is what I call "cultural bilingualism".

Advanced Metalinguistic Knowledge

Critics have shown that bilingual persons possess better metalinguistic understanding compared to their monolingual counterparts (Bialystok & Barac, 2012; Ricciardelli, 1992; Galambos & Goldin-Meadow, 1990). R3 and R4 who are teachers in the community say that they noticed that males display greater skills in examining, discussing, and thinking about language and that they show better understanding and outperform the females in grammar and reading comprehension. Whilst this has become normalized and accepted in the community, one can easily trace this to the language-cultural phenomenon in the community. It is thus evident that Ubang females are negatively impacted as a result of the language culture in the community. Therefore, it is important to begin to critique such a cultural system that places a group at an advantage over the other in so many social aspects.

Despite the downsides of this language-cultural phenomenon in Ubang on females, R1 sees nothing wrong with the language pattern in the community. He questions the view of what he calls the "imported tiny minority into Ubang to destroy the unique language situation we have". He is of the view that anyone who sees anything wrong with the language pattern in Ubang, which has been in existence for thousands of years, is truly not an Ubang person. In fact, he says he is not surprised if anyone holds a contrary opinion on the Ubang language culture, because of late, he has noticed an increase in interests from different persons on the Ubang phenomenon, and he thinks their interest is not to represent the Ubang people but the interest of the researcher's organization or personal goal.

Second-Class Personas

Although nearly all Ubang women seem comfortable with this language-cultural structure, which they say is a unique gift from God, the female interviewees for this study seem to disagree with this generalized opinion. On a general question about the culture of Ubang in empowering both male and female fairly and equally, R3, R4, and R5 are of the opinion that some aspects of the Ubang culture make girls and women feel inferior and second class to men. R5 describes a situation where many women try to speak Ofre but laugh it off after making lots of mistake: "I have seen occasions where some women in hidden places mimic Ofre but finds it funny due to the mistakes they make and then return to speaking Arasere". She says she feels sorry for such women who do not know the implication of not being able to speak Ofre whilst their sons could speak Ofre and Arasere. In fact, she even says that some mothers approach their sons for knowledge on Ofre, wondering how condescending such is to the full potential and realization of the dreams and aspirations of women as equal members of the Ubang community. When asked how this language system affects women, R3 thinks the impact of this on women is felt at marriage. She claims that young ladies in the community think of marriage very quickly to fill up the void of their inability to speak Ofre instead of pursuing a career. One can deduce that, because the woman is constructed to need the man who is structured by the community as having a cognitive advantage, confidence, and inhibitory control over women as well as possessing a higher metalinguistic knowledge, young women tend to go into marriages with men to partake of the higher qualities the culture has subtly given to men. This situation, no doubt, project women as second to men in the community.

Textual and Visual Analysis of the YouTube Videos

The two documentary videos (YouTube Video 1 "African Language Not Heard Nor Documented" www.youtube.com/watch?v=LbNMifxpyfI&t=36s & YouTube Video 2 "Ubang: The Nigerian village where men, women speak different languages" www.youtube.com/watch?v=iDcZMwmB-EQ) that I have chosen to analyse in this study capture the unique language-culture of the Ubang community.

Although not much can be deduced from video (1)[2] other than the few significant aspects which have already been used to contextualize the dual-language situation in Ubang, one striking textual note that is worth mentioning is a quoted statement from Undie CC, whom I have earlier referred to in this study. The video on 4:32 minutes displayed the following: "This is a dual-sex culture, men and women operate in almost two separate spheres.

It's like they're in separate worlds, but sometimes those worlds come together and you see that pattern in the language as well". Conspicuously, the language-cultural pattern of Ubang has placed men and women in separate worlds. They operate as unequal beings and exhibit sensibilities as sometimes two binary opposites. On occasions when these two worlds come together, it is certain, as argued previously, that the world of the woman gives in to the superiority of the men's world.

If video (1) used textual notes and focus music to paint the Ubang dual-language phenomenon, video (2) is a typical documentary-style video where interviews and voice of God narration were used. Hence, a visual reading will be useful to unpack the nuances contained therein. In the documentary, there was a conspicuous smug performance of power by the chief in the community as he gesticulates about the privilege of the males to speak their own language and that of the women at the same time, which is not the case with the women. To deepen this argument of male power in Ubang, I take a critical look at the camera angle in the interview of the chief in the video. Experts of cinematography will suggest that the angle of camera deployed in the said interview is of the low-angle dimension. Low angle occurs "when the camera is fixed anywhere below the eye line and points upwards. These can symbolically delegate a status of power or authority to the character in the frame by making the character appear more dominant" (Cinematography Fundamentals, 2022). The video in this way, whether consciously or not, captures the supremacy status of men in Ubang. However, the camera angle used during conversations with a few women as observed in the video is high angle, the opposite of low angle. "High angle shots occur when the camera is placed at a high point so that it looks down at the characters. This makes the characters look small and inconsequential" (Cinematography Fundamentals, 2022). It thus projects a low confidence status on the monolingual Ubang women. Not only is the camera angle of interest at this time, lighting, which is another fascinating data from the visual, contributes to the framing of the status of Ubang male. In the interview of the chief, there is a careful use of lighting to add colour and create focus on the character. Whether chronicled from the visual analysis or the interviews, the bilingual Ubang men have assumed the leadership status whilst the monolingual females are the followers.

Whilst significant aspects of the two videos corroborate the views expressed by the respondents that were interviewed for this study, there are other clear points of departure between the videos and the interviews in the analysis of the language situation. For instance, in the interview, it is obvious that the women were angry with the language situation in their community, but in the two videos the case differs. We notice in the videos that the women who spoke were smiling, cheerful, proud, and extremely accepting of the language dynamics in their community. Despite these videos communicating some sense of happiness on the faces of the women, the cutaways of women and young children replete in video (1) depict sadness and forlornness as the textual notes on the language phenomenon appeared and disappeared.

This perhaps suggests the need to rethink such a cultural practice that affects the condition of women in the community. It is therefore necessary to stress this convergence and divergence between the interview and videos to show the level of enlightenment that is needed to expose the effect this language-cultural pattern has on women and the girl-child.

Conclusion and Recommendations

This chapter has articulated clearly that the language-cultural phenomenon in Ubang impacts females negatively, even though this view is hushed and not easily and freely shared by females in the community. It has shown that, to empower women in developing economies and across the globe, cultural patterns like language are a crucial pointer to unpack. Culture plays an important role in forming, reforming, and, in the case of Ubang, breaking a people. As argued by the ethnographic cultural communication theory postulated by Hymes (1962), the culture of a community lacks integration and transformation if the communication structures are problematic. Having analysed the communication paradigm and its impact on females in Ubang, one can safely conclude that the cultural communication structures in Ubang is insipid and non-integrative for the people of Ubang and should be given a second look by the people tasked with the responsibility to protect the Ubang community and her people.

Whilst this chapter is in no way advocating a radicalization of the cultural peculiarity of the Ubang, which is one of Africa's legacies and linguistic/communicative uniqueness, it advocates a nuanced revision of the dual-language practice to become integrative by allowing both males and females to freely use the two languages, instead of restricting women to only one. The chapter thus encourages the Ubang chiefs to revisit this subtle, yet obvious, language dichotomy amongst the genders to see ways it can better support and uplift women and the girl-child to be full persons of equal rights as males in the community. To achieve this, Ubang women need to speak up more and not dismiss the possibility of the impact this language phenomenon might be having on the girl-child and females in general. There is need to educate Ubang females on the importance and gains of men being cultural bilinguals in the community and in the same vein, the losses of women as cultural monolinguals. From the encounter with the chief and others in the analysed videos, it is essential that linguists and other scholars take on the challenge to revisit the conceptualization of "mother tongue" in Ubang at a time when mothers, the primary caregivers, through whom a person acquires and learns a language from birth, are already disempowered by language in the community. In this vein, can one argue that Ubang still has a mother tongue? By steering the discussion away from gendered bilingualism to address the questions of communicative rights and power associated with it, this chapter has initiated new ways of understanding cultural dynamics among the Ubang people.

Notes

1 www.youtube.com/watch?v=LbNMifxpyfI&t=36s
2 YouTube Video (1) is a 6:32-minutes video that privileges textual notes over sound. There are a few occasions where voiced statements were used to convey meanings and messages in the documentary whilst a large part of the video is filled with textual notes on the Ubang dynamics. Along the textual notes are cutaway images of the Ubang people and landscape. The documentary employs a suitable focus music, which played as the written texts appeared and disappeared. The focus music, I argue, is a deliberate choice to critically prepare the minds of viewers to appreciate, think deep, and concentrate on the written texts about the uniqueness of the Ubang language phenomenon.

References

Abue, A., Christopher, R., & Sunday, A. (2018). 'The Qualitative Dermatoglyphics Patterns in Both Hands for Males and Females in Ubang Clan, Cross River State, Nigeria'. *Advances in Anthropology*, 8(2), 73–81. http://dx.doi.org/10.4236/aa.2018.82004

Bialystok, E., & Barac, R. (2012). 'Emerging Bilingualism: Dissociating Advantages for Metalinguistic Awareness and Executive Control'. *Cognition*, 122, 67–73. http://dx.doi.org/10.1016/j.cognition.2011.08.003

Bialystok, E., Barac, R., Blaye, A., & Poulin-Dubois, D. (2010). 'Wordmapping and Executive Functioning in Young Monolingual and Bilingual Children'. *Journal of Cognition and Development*, 11(4), 485–508. http://dx.doi.org/10.1080/15248372.2010.516420

Bialystok, E., & Martin, M. (2004). 'Attention and Inhibition in Bilingual Children: Evidence from the Dimensional Change Card Sort Task'. *Developmental Science*, 7(3), 325–339. https://doi.org/10.1111/j.1467-7687.2004.00351.x

Bloomfield, L. (1933). *Language*. New York: Henry Holt.

Bradford, H. (1992) 'Theories of Culture and Communication'. *Communication Theory*, 1, 50–70.

Brady, N., Bruce, S., Goldman, A., Erickson, K., Mineo, B., Ogletree, B., Paul, D., Romski, M., Sevcik, R., Siegel, E., Schoonover, J., Snell, M., Sylvester, L., & Wilkinson, K. (2016). 'Communication Services and Support for Individuals with Severe Disabilities: Guidance for Assessment and Intervention'. *American Journal on Intellectual and Development Disabilities*, 121(2), 121–138. http://dx.doi.org/10.1352/1944-7558-121.2.121

Carbaugh, D. (1990). 'Toward a Perspective on Cultural Communication and Intercultural Contact'. *Semiotica*, 80(2), 15–35.

Carlson, S. M., & Meltzoff, A. N. (2008). 'Bilingual Experience and Executive Functioning in Young Children'. *Developmental Science*, 11(2), 282–298. http://dx.doi.org/10.1111/j.1467-7687.2008.00675.x

Cervantes, C. A. (2002). 'Explanatory Emotion Talk in Mexican Immigrant and Mexican American Families'. *Hispanic Journal of Behavioral Sciences*, 24(2), 138–163. https://doi.org/10.1177/0739986302024002003

Cheung, H., et al. (2010). Sociolinguistic Awareness and False Belief in Young Cantonese Learners of English. *Journal of Experimental Child Psychology*, 107(2), 188–194. https://doi.org/10.1016/j.jecp.2010.05.001

Chrisler, J. C. (2013). 'A Global Approach to Reproductive Justice-Psychological and Legal Aspects and Implications'. *William. & Mary Journal of Women & the Law*, 20(1), 1–25.

'Cinematography Fundamentals with WWI Virtual Academy: 5 Types of Camera Angles'. *WWI Virtual Academy: Online Media Education*. https://wwivirtualacademy.com/cinematography-fundamentals-with-wwi-virtual-academy-5-types-of-camera-angles/, Accessed 27 September, 2022.

Damon, W., & Eisenberg, N. (Eds.) (1998). *Handbook of Child Psychology: Social, Emotional, and Personality Development*. New York: Wiley.

Diellza, H. (2019). 'The Phenomenon of Bilingualism in Rahovec's Spoken Language'. *Advances in Language and Literary Studies*, 10(3), 122–127.

Ellis, E. (2008). 'Defining and Investigating Monolingualism'. *Sociolinguistic Studies*, 2(3), 311–330. http://dx.doi.org/10.1558/sols.v2i3.311

Galambos, S. J., & Goldin-Meadow, S. (1990). 'The Effects of Learning Two Languages on Levels of Metalinguistic Awareness'. *Cognition*, 34, 1–56. http://dx.doi.org/10.1016/0010-0277(90)90030-N

Geertz, C. (1973). *The Interpretation of Cultures: Selected Essays*. New York: Basic Books.

Goetz, P.J. (2003). 'The Effects of Bilingualism on Theory of Mind Development'. *Bilingualism: Language and Cognition*, 6(1), 1–15. https://doi.org/10.1017/S1366728903001007

Greenberg, A., Bellana, B., & Bialystok, E. (2013). 'Perspective-Taking Ability in Bilingual Children: Extending Advantages in Executive Control to Spatial Reasoning'. *Cognitive Development*, 28(1), 41–50. https://doi:10.1016/j.cogdev.2012.10.002

Hall, E. (1959). *The Silent Language*. New York: Doubleday.

Halle, T., & Daneri, P. (2014). 'The Social – Emotional Development of Dual Language Learners: Looking Back at Existing Research and Moving Forward with Purpose'. *Early Childhood Research Quarterly*, 29(4), 734–749.

Hamers, J. F. & Blanc, M. H. A. (2000). *Biliguality and Bilingualism* (Second edition). Cambridge: Cambridge University Press.

Haugen, E. (1956). *Bilingualism in the Americas: A Bibliography and Research Guide*. New York: Einar.

Hymes, D. (1962). 'The Ethnography of Speaking'. In T. Gladwin & W. Strurtevant (Eds.), *Anthropology and Human Behavior* (pp. 15–53). Washington, DC: Anthropological Society of Washington.

Ide, J. (2011). 'A Cerebellar Thalamic Cortical Circuit for Error-Related Cognitive Control'. *Neuroimage*, 54(1), 455–464.

Ingwe, R. (2014). 'Between Cultural and Natural Heritage: Pluralism in Planning Tourism Products for Rescuing the Lost (Ogoja) Province, North-Central, Cross River State, Nigeria'. *Journal for Geography/Revija za Geografijo*, 9(2), 12–25.

Kecskes, I. (2006). 'The dual language model to explain code-switching: A cognitive-pragmatic approach'. *Intercultural Pragmatics*, 3(3), 257–284. *Bilingualism: Language and Cognition*, 14(3), 412–422. http://dx.doi.org/10.1515/IP.2006.017

Kovács, M., & Mehler, J. (2009). 'Cognitive Gains in 7-month-old Bilingual Infants'. *Psychological and Cognitive Sciences*, 106(16), 6556–6560. https://doi.org/10.1073/pnas.0811323106

Kvale, S. (1996). *Interviews: An Introduction to Qualitative Research Interviewing*. London: Sage Publications.

Mansouri, F., Fehring, D., Gaillard, A., Jaberzadeh, S., & Parkington, H. (2016). 'Sex Dependency of Inhibitory Control Functions'. *Biology of Sex Differences*, 7(11), 1–13.
McLeod, S. (2018). 'Communication Rights: Fundamental Human Rights for All'. *International Journal of Speech Language Pathology*, 20(1), 3–11. http://dx.doi.org/10.1080/17549507.2018.1428687
Nelson, K. (2003). 'Narrative and Self, Myth and Memory'. In R. Fivush & C. Haden (Eds.), *Connecting Culture and Memory: The Social Construction of an Autobiographical Self* (pp. 486–511). Mahwah: Erlbaum.
Philipsen, G. (1975). 'Speaking 'Like a Man' in Teamsterville: Culture Patterns of Role Enactment in an Urban Neighborhood'. *Quarterly Journal of Speech*, 61(1), 13–22.
Philipsen, G. (1989). 'An Ethnographic Approach to Communication Studies'. In B. Dervin, I. Grossberg, B.J. O'keefe, & F. Wartella (Eds.), *Rethinking Communication* (pp. 258–268). Newbury Park: Sage.
Ricciardelli, L. A. (1992). 'Bilingualism and Cognitive Development in Relation to Threshold Theory'. *Journal of Psycholinguistic Research*, 21(4), 301–316. http://dx.doi.org/10.1007/BF01067515.
Rollo, M. (1983). 'Myth and Culture: Their Death and Transformation'. *Cross Currents*, 33(1), 1–7.
Saarni, C. (1997). 'Emotional Competence and Self-Regulation in Childhood'. In P. Salovey & D. Sluyter (Eds.), *Emotional Development and Emotional Intelligence* (pp. 35–66). New York: Basic Books.
Said, E. (1983). *Traveling Theory, the World, the Text, and the Critic*. Cambridge: Harvard University Press.
Said, E. (1994). "Traveling Theory Reconsidered." In R. Polhemus & R. Henkle (Eds.), *Critical Reconsiderations: The Relationship of Fiction and Life* (pp. 251–268). Redwood City: Stanford University Press.
Shatz, M. (1994). *A Toddler's Life: Becoming a Person*. New York: Oxford University Press.
Undie, C. C. (2007). 'My Father's Daughter: Becoming a "Real" Anthropologist among the Ubang of Southeast Nigeria'. *Dialectical Anthropology*, 31(1–3), 293–305. http://dx.doi.org/10.1007/s10624-007-9013-x
Undie, C. C., & Izugbara, C. O. (2011). 'Unpacking Rights in Indigenous African Societies: Indigenous Culture and the Question of Sexual and Reproductive Rights in Africa'. *BMC International Health and Human Rights*, 11 (Suppl. 3), S2. http://dx.doi.org/10.1186/1472-698x-11-s3-s2
United Nations. (1948). *Universal Declaration of Human Rights*. www.un.org/en/universal-declarationhuman-rights/, Accessed 10 April, 2022.
Yang, S., Yang, H., & Lust, B. (2011). 'Early Childhood Bilingualism Leads to Advances in Executive Attention: Dissociating Culture and Language'. *Bilingualism: Language and Cognition*, 14(3), 412–422. http://dx.doi.org/10.1017/S1366728910000611
YouTube Documentary Video on Ubang – 'African Language Not Heard Nor Documented (Ubang Community in Southern Nigeria)'. www.youtube.com/watch?v=LbNMifxpyfI&t=36s, Accessed 20 June, 2022.
YouTube Documentary Video on Ubang – 'Ubang: The Nigerian Village Where Men, Women Speak Different Languages'. www.youtube.com/watch?v=iDcZMwmB-EQ, Accessed 19 June, 2022.

2 Silicon Savannah or Digitising Marginalisation?

A Reflection of Kenya's Government Digitisation Policies, Strategies, and Projects

Job Mwaura

Introduction

It is widely believed that adopting information and communication technologies (ICTs) by governments and other actors can expand African economies, financial inclusion, and citizens' services and necessitate free trade between countries. However, the adoption of ICTs by governments, especially in Africa in the last few years, has faced considerable challenges, which range from poor governance, corruption, inequalities, insufficient infrastructure that supports the adoption and expansion of ICTs, and the lack of technical know-how. Although various African governments have made progress towards adopting ICTs in their economies, the digital divide continues to widen.

The ability to receive, process, store, and produce messages are at the heart of human interactions and is recognised as a fundamental human right. In 1948, United Nations enunciated communication as a fundamental human right. Article 19 of the Universal Declaration of Human Rights states that "Everyone has the right to freedom of opinion and expression; this right includes freedom to hold opinions without interference and to seek, receive and impart information and ideas through any media and regardless of frontiers" (UN General Assembly, 1948). Nevertheless, communication involves complex practices and processes depending on various sociopolitical and cultural issues. Uppal et al. (2019) acknowledged that communication occurs within the frameworks of society, politics, and culture, anchored in national and local symbolic universes and imaginaries. Increased use of computer technologies within information and communication has necessitated increased digital communication and rethinking of digital rights. Communication and digital rights have been recognised as human rights in many global contexts. Both digital and communication rights include the right to access, privacy, freedom of expression, and so on. Therefore, I conceptualise digital rights in this chapter as interrelated to communication rights.

As of December 2021, internet penetration in Africa stood at 43.1% against a global average of 66.2%, according to Statista Research Department (2022). According to a survey result by Pew Research, a median of 41% across the six sub-Saharan African countries surveyed said they regularly use

DOI: 10.4324/9781003388289-4

the internet or possess an internet-capable smartphone (Silver and Johnson (2018). Other statistics also indicate that sub-Saharan Africa has a lower internet-use level than any other regional area. It was estimated by GSMA that by the end of 2020, 28% of the sub-Saharan African population were connected to the mobile internet and this number is now expected to rise to 40% of the population by 2025 (Delaporte et al., 2021, 2022).

Despite these low figures and the number of existing challenges in adopting ICTs in African economies, some countries have emerged as technological hubs in the global technosphere. For instance, Kenya is popularly known as a "silicon savannah" due to its many technological innovations providing local solutions to its populations (Omanga & Mainye, 2019). For instance, the mobile money transfer M-Pesa has provided financial solutions for many individuals, particularly the unbanked population. In addition, the crisis mapping application *Ushahidi*, which was first used in Kenya, has provided solutions during a crisis. Many countries have adopted these applications and services beyond the African continent. According to a report by Forbes in July 2019, Nigeria and South Africa continue to be the most advanced tech ecosystems, with 85 and 80 active tech hubs, respectively (Friederici et al., 2020). The report further states that Lagos is now the top creative city by the number of hubs (40+) while Western Cape, Gauteng, and Durban are the centres of the tech hubs scene in South Africa.

Mobile phone penetration in Africa has made remarkable progress over the last two decades, and most of the internet is accessed on mobile phones (Delaporte et al., 2021). Further, internet usage trends are similar to those seen for mobile and smartphone use, with more skilled, younger, and higher-income individuals more likely to go online. Anderson (2019) noted a disparity in that in many African countries, men are much more likely to use the internet than women.

This context paints a complex scenario in the African technosphere, most of which are brought about by sociopolitical and economic issues. Furthermore, policies created by some African governments have exacerbated the disparities in the state of ICTs in Africa. For African countries to make strides in digital economies, efforts must be made to make policies more inclusive to avoid marginalising specific populations. This chapter aims to analyse some government policies, strategies, and projects in Kenya, specifically focusing on how they have marginalised pastoralist communities. The chapter aims to answer two questions: How have the government digitisation projects marginalised pastoralist communities in Kenya? How can the government hasten inclusion in digitisation projects among pastoralist communities in Kenya?

Kenya's Pastoralist Communities

The term pastoralism has been defined variously in mobility, agriculture, and economics studies. Scholars in this area of study conceptualise pastoralism as an economic practice and a cultural identity. However, they are cautious to note that the latter does not necessarily mean the former (Krätli et al., 2013). Pastoralism is generally defined by a focus on an economic practice based on animal production to take advantage of the characteristic instability of most rangeland environments, where primary resources such as nutrients and water for livestock can be depended on in the form of volatile and short-lived concentrations rather than in standardised and stable distributions (Krätli et al., 2013). Elsewhere, pastoralism is seen as a production structure in which 50% of the gross household income (i.e., the overall amount of commercialised production plus the approximate value of household subsistence production) comes from livestock or agricultural operations (Swift, 1988). For some time, "nomadism" was used to refer to "pastoralism", which concentrated on a single technique – migration, not the production and distribution mechanism through which it is employed and held negative connotations of people travelling for unknown psycho-cultural purposes, which needed to be resolved in the interest of quality and society (Baxter, 1994). Lately, scholars have argued that the term pastoralism must be applied to individuals or households within communities holding such values that have been compelled by hardship to rely on non-livestock livelihoods and also to affluent households within such groups that have effectively diversified into commerce, transport, agriculture, or government jobs (Morton & Meadows, 2000).

Researchers like Rass (2006) estimate that there are about 120 million pastoralists/agro-pastoralists worldwide, of which 50 million live in sub-Saharan Africa (SSA), by integrating data from different sources. Within sub-Saharan Africa, Sudan and Somalia, Ethiopia and Kenya are said to have the highest pastoral/agro-pastoral populations. In Kenya, it is estimated that 20% of the national population are pastoralists (Nyariki et al., 2009). Going by the 2019 Kenya Population and Housing Census, the total population in Kenya is 47.5 million (KNBS, 2019), which makes the number of pastoralist communities to be 9.5 million, according to Rass's estimates.

Various studies have been conducted in the last few years regarding Information Communication Technologies (ICTs) adoption among pastoralist communities. In an article examining the usage of mobile phones among livestock traders among Borana pastoralists of Southern Ethiopia, Debsu et al. (2016) noted that there was increased adoption of ICTs among people in these communities. Their research noted that the pastoralists used mobile phones to access information on grazing, weather, and market conditions. However, they also noticed that various factors, including the inadequate reach of mobile phone networks, regular power and network outages, and inaccessibility of battery-recharging services, limited the reach and usage of mobile phones in pastoral areas. Inefficient electricity distribution, weak networks, and low wages affect cell phone ownership and usage in the Borana region.

In another study by Waters-Bayer and Bayer (2016), the authors examine how hi-tech influenced pastoralism and how pastoralists have adopted hi-tech with a focus on Africa, Australia, and Central Asia. They noted that advances in ICT and transport link pastoralists to the rest of the world even more directly and efficiently than in the past, whether in Africa, Mongolia, Australia, or the Americas. Better connectivity would undoubtedly lead to more improvements in how they coordinate their life and work. Moreover, they conclude by noting that while pastoralists in many countries are challenged by hi-tech ventures that consume finite resources, hi-tech solutions that complement a mobile development system and are implemented in a socially responsible manner may also modernise pastoral life and help ensure its future (Waters-Bayer and Bayer (2016).

Khalai (2016) researched how mobile technologies can be leveraged for crowdsourcing and disseminating information on livestock and livestock products. They noted that while ICT has become an essential means of information distribution in developing countries, the available cutting-edge research strategies have not yet been taken advantage of by both pastoralists and organisations employed in Kenya's Arid and Semi-Arid Lands (ASALs). Findings from this study indicated that most initiatives to use ICTs in gathering and distributing information have failed in situations with no other support structures for pastoralists. However, they noted that an agent in the form of drought monitors, food monitors, Community Animal Health Workers, and government administrators are vital support to phone-based approaches in collecting and disseminating information (Khalai, 2016).

The Maasai people living in some parts of Kenya and Tanzania are well-known pastoralist communities. In a paper interrogating the continued marginalisation of the Maasai people against the myth of rising Africa, Otenyo noted that the Africa growing myth and infiltration of ICTs in rural areas hide the dispossession of Maasai's means of livelihood, thus worsening the groups' conditions of living (2017). There has always been a growing attitude that pastoralism is not a valuable economic activity. However, research has revealed that in a place like Kenya, the pastoralism sector has an economic worth of US$1.13 billion, with the livestock sector and non-livestock sector accounting for 92% (US$1.04 billion) and 8% (US$0.0903 billion), respectively (Nyariki & Amwata, 2019). Nyariki and Amwata (2019) further note that pastoralism contributes 10–44% of African countries' gross domestic product (GDP), with more than 1.3 billion people benefitting from the livestock value chain.

This chapter reveals that there is continued marginalisation of pastoralist communities in many ways, including the marginalisation of access to ICTs; yet the pastoralism sector is a valuable economic activity in many parts of the world, particularly Africa. While a change in such trends would essentially begin at the government policy level in the Kenyan context, there has been a failure by the Kenyan government to commit to making ICTs accessible to all and sundry. On the other hand, studies on holistic digital inclusion in ICTs have tended to focus on women, the youth, and individuals living in marginalised communities such as slums (Alaoui, 2022). There has been less focus on digital inequalities among the pastoralist communities. This chapter aims at contributing to these existing discussions since it remains crucial that all stakeholders consider digital and communication rights as a present imperative as well as an emerging future concern. In the next section, I theorise the complex nature of inequalities in the context of digital technologies.

Complexities of Digital Inequalities

Sociopolitical and economic inequalities have existed for thousands of years. Kohler et al. (2017) note that inequality began to spread widely in European and Asian communities as far back as 11,000 years ago. Scholars also trace the spread of "inequality" as having begun during the agrarian revolution – the cultivation of plants and domestication of large animals such as cows and horses, as well as the growing social stratifications (Ragnedda, 2020). The irony is that while inequality gaps existed between those who owned animals and those who did not in ancient communities in Europe and Asia, the current situation of digital inequality primarily exists between pastoralists (communities which rely on animal rearing as a means of production) and with those who are not pastoralists. As noted by Ragnedda (2020), these animals owned by ancient communities were used to plough land and transport goods, which led to the creation of landless peasants on the one side and elite individuals who accumulated wealth on the other side.

Inequalities have always been at the heart of cultural and social theorists, and there is a consensus among them that inequalities do not occur naturally but are caused by sociopolitical choices (Lahsen & Ribot, 2022; Oualy, 2021; Savage et al., 2022). Inequalities result from multiple factors in society at the micro and macro levels. Ragnedda (2020) notes that sometimes, there is a tendency in society to equate inequality solely to an economic problem. This results in neglecting other forms of inequality like sociopolitical, cultural, economic, and digital inequalities and how they manifest themselves in society. While it is true that people are usually concerned about economic issues, others are increasingly concerned with inequality of government participation and access to resources, inequality of educational opportunities, access to climate change risk management, and, eventually, adequate access to and use of technology. From this, we can deduce that inequality is a complex and multifaceted phenomenon deeply rooted in socio-economic, political, and cultural processes.

The emergence of modern digital technologies has strengthened existing inequalities, not only in the lack of fair access and usage requirements for ICTs but also in the way that skewed algorithms and AI perpetuate socially organised disparities for specific communities. In the recent past, most jobs have moved online. Ragnedda (2020) further noted that digital inequalities are complex and can be based on gender, age, and ethnic or social group features that have been entrenched in sociocultural hierarchies over the years. Since most jobs have been digitised, certain social classes, particularly those who lack affordance and have no access to digital technologies like the pastoralists in this context, are more likely to be excluded. The economic gap between such disadvantaged groups would therefore continue to grow, which would also mean that due to the fast pace of digitisation, they are unlikely to access justice and other welfare state resources (Dressel & Farid, 2018).

The areas where most pastoralists in Kenya live include the following counties: Isiolo, Mandera, Wajir, Garissa, Marsabit, Turkana, West Pokot, Baringo, Laikipia, Samburu, Tana River, Lamu, Kajiado, and Narok, most of which fall within arid and semi-arid climatic conditions. The counties are also characterised by complex issues ranging from poverty, insecurity from cattle rustlers and invasion of terrorist groups, poor leadership, neglect from the government, poor infrastructure that makes some counties inaccessible, and many other issues. These issues do not, therefore, allow for the thriving of a digital economy, leading to a complex vicious circle of inequalities.

Methodology

This study adopted a qualitative research design to collect and analyse data. The study adopted two data generation techniques – document analysis and interviews. The study analysed documents on the digital economy published by the Government of Kenya through its Ministry of Information Communication and Technology and the Huduma Namba Bill 2021. These documents set out critical digital strategies, policies, and plans for Kenya and were therefore considered necessary for analysis. In addition, six in-depth interviews were conducted with individuals from pastoralist communities in Kenya's Marsabit, Garissa, Mandera, and Isiolo counties. Purposive sampling was used to recruit participants who included four men and two women.

Digital Marginalisation of Pastoralist Communities

In the interviews held for this chapter, the respondents narrated the difficulties pastoralists were experiencing in realising digital development. When they were asked to state why digital infrastructures were slow in the pastoralist communities generally as compared to other counties, this is what they mentioned:

Respondent A: Our location has never had a tarmacked road. There are only four sub-counties in Marsabit, and places like Kiambu county[1] has twelve sub-counties. Electricity is rare and solar power is unrealisable. When government establishes projects, such as digital projects, they are allocated to administrative units inaccessible to many rural communities. There is minimal effort by the government to uplift the livelihoods of the pastoralist communities.
Respondent B: One of the biggest problems is illiteracy and lack of information. This has been because of neglect by the government. When the government rolls out free education, very few pastoralist communities

are aware of it. When they see those who have gone to school with no jobs, they quickly choose cattle rearing. When government opportunities are advertised on government websites or in newspapers, pastoralists and nomadic communities have a limited way of receiving such information. Newspapers do not reach those areas, and available radio stations tend to focus more on politics.

Respondent E: We have a leadership problem in the pastoralist counties. Every election year, we elect them, but they do very little to push for development agenda. We feel very neglected when it comes to development. The poor infrastructure cannot support digitalisation in these counties. People have no access to good roads or electricity, and most of those communities do not even know what fibre optics is, just to give an example. Many cannot afford a smartphone or even a computer.

The respondents' arguments mainly focus on lousy governance and agenda-related neglect. The growth of digital infrastructure is seldom ever realised in those countries due to the weak infrastructure. A regrettable political trend in Kenya is that areas with a high population are given more priority for government initiatives since they influence votes. In contrast, areas with a low population are shunned. Since administrative units are based on population size, the main effects of this are that there are few administrative districts in pastoralist-populated areas, poor infrastructure, neglected schools, few or no markets for selling their livestock, and a lack of interest from private companies like telecoms to invest in such areas due to the low returns on their investments. It is undoubtedly a significant desire for the government to digitise activities like procurement procedures, information access, and other government services. However, they suffer when specific populations are excluded from such an agenda.

Chapter 33 of the Kenyan constitution addresses the freedom of expression, and section 1(a) states, "Every person has the right to freedom of expression, which includes freedom to seek, receive or impart information or ideas". The respondents from the pastoralists communities were asked to state the extent to which poor digital infrastructures hindered their constitutional right to freedom of expression, and this was their response:

Respondent A: Our geographic disadvantages are significant, as I already indicated. Exercising one's right to freedom of expression includes accessing and receiving information. Our constitutional rights as pastoralists would be violated if the government moved all its operations and information online because we would have trouble obtaining it.

Respondent B: These initiatives to digitise all government functions may impede our freedom of expression. Although it might be advantageous for many who have access to digital infrastructures, it disadvantages others, such as pastoralists, who do not. How can I get it, for instance, if all government contracts are only published online and Marsabit, where I am

from, has a poor internet connection? How many pastoralists can apply for a passport if they are informed they can only do it online? It will be challenging if the government disregards our need for digital access.
Respondent F: The police inspector general has been hosting Q&A sessions on Twitter, as I have seen on social media. Those who participate are undoubtedly those who live in metropolitan areas, have access to the internet, and can afford it. Pastoralists have enormous security concerns in Isiolo, like where I am from. How can people with limited access to digital infrastructure, like pastoralists, engage in online forums? They would be unable to express themselves.

The pastoralist communities' constitutional rights and privileges, such as freedom of expression, are curtailed when the Government of Kenya fails to develop digital infrastructure in counties where pastoralist communities live. It is the government's responsibility to provide a conducive environment where investments in digital infrastructure can take place or spearhead the development of the same without discriminating against them based on ethnicity or geographical location.

Kenya's Digital Identity Systems and Their Exclusionary Nature

The Kenyan government has been intending to change the legal framework governing Kenya's identification system since independence through the introduction of Huduma Namba. If enacted, the Huduma Bill 2021 states that Huduma Namba would become compulsory to access at least 17 essential government services. These services include the issuance of a passport, registration or renewal of a driving licence, financial market transactions, registration of a cell phone, payment of taxes, lawful marriage, voting, opening a bank account, accessing health services and several other aspects. The government termed it (Huduma Card) as a "single source of truth"[2] about people's identity in Kenya.

The roll-out of the digital identity card (Huduma Namba Card) received a mixed reaction from Kenyans due to its unprocedural nature. In November 2020, despite the backlash and court orders to stop Huduma Namba registration, the government rolled out the exercise. Even when no legislation supported the exercise, the government made it mandatory for all Kenyans to register for Huduma Namba. #ResistHudumaNamba movement quickly erupted, creating a massive discussion in Kenya's online and offline spaces for several months in 2019, including court processes and protests (Mwaura, 2019). The Huduma Bill 2020 proposed to collect the following contentious data from citizens: fingerprints, hand geometry, earlobe geometry, retina and iris patterns, toe impression, voice waves, signatures, blood typing (DNA), and photographs, and the same have been retained in the Huduma Bill 2021.

In the context of this chapter, the introduction of a digital identity system has the potential to be exclusionary if introduced in Kenya. In what ways does the digitisation of the identity system become retrogressive or marginalise communities and, in this context, the pastoralist communities? Since independence, the issuance of identity cards in Kenya has been unequal and exclusionary. In interviews conducted for this study with individuals from pastoralist communities, they lamented that issuing ID cards in counties inhabited by pastoralist communities sometimes took up to two years. Their applications for identity cards are subjected to double check, unlike those of Kenyans living in other counties. Some of the respondents for this study had this to say when asked about the situation with identity cards in pastoralist areas:

Respondent B: We have an issue when applying for digital identity cards. There is always a suspicion on whether we deserve the document or not since we are viewed as less of Kenyans. There is this suspicion that we come from Somalia, and we need to produce extra documents to prove our identity, including being asked to produce the identity card of our grandparents. To get an ID faster, one would need to travel to other counties away from the pastoralists' counties to apply.

Respondent C: You must have a birth certificate to have an ID. To have a birth certificate, you must have a birth notification. A birth notification is a registration of birth document that happens in a government hospital and is used to process birth certificates. Most of the births in these pastoralist counties occur in homes because access to hospitals is challenging. When one clocks 18 years, the legal age to have an ID, individuals sometimes travel long distances to access government offices to apply for them. On applying, they sometimes wait less than a year to have an ID. Sometimes, the ID does not come, and after two years of waiting, they are forced to apply again. Others give up the application, mainly because the government issues citizens with IDs until the age of 24.

Respondent D: For a person to travel out of the pastoralist areas, they are met with several police roadblocks where everyone is asked to show their identity cards. Failure to produce the ID means the journey is cut short. We must show our IDs because we are not considered "Kenyan" enough. We belong to the Cushitic ethnic group primarily found in the horn of Africa, and our looks are different from the Bantu and Nilotic communities in Kenya. So, our looks bring about suspicion because they think we come from Somalia or Ethiopia.

Currently, the difficulties of acquiring identity documents (IDs and birth certificates) among pastoralist communities disadvantage them in many ways. For instance, you must show your identification document to apply for government tenders and to access many government services, like healthcare insurance.

Nevertheless, would a consolidated digital identity programme offer any recourse to the problems that pastoralist communities face? This is unlikely and would lead to further marginalisation of such communities. To begin with, the digital identity programme fails to acknowledge that some of these counties would fail to support the digital registration of persons. With the few government offices in pastoralist communities, poor communication networks, unreliable power, insecurity issues, their nomadic lifestyle, and a host of other challenges, it becomes impracticable to collect digital data in those areas. Second, consolidation of government-related documents issued to citizens into a single digital identity card is a good plan, especially for those who have quicker turnaround application periods. However, individuals from pastoralist communities who get many bottlenecks, especially in the application of identity cards, may not benefit much from it. The inability to acquire digital identity cards means citizens from these geographical areas would miss out on accessing 17 government services because of the consolidation.

Related to the digital identity programme, when the Government of Kenya changed the school curriculum (kindergarten, primary, secondary, and tertiary levels), it also introduced the National Education Management Information System (NEMIS) portal. Students are required to register in the portal and are issued a Unique Personal Identifier (UPI) after producing a birth certificate, or an ID number, or an Alien number. The introduction of such systems is meant to trace students' progress through the education system in Kenya, but this has been contentious, as expected. Communities from marginalised areas, like the pastoralist communities, are, in the first instance, confronted with inadequate access to such digital infrastructures. Because of the requirements to be registered in the digital systems, some parents withdraw their children from the education system, thus becoming a double jeopardy and aggravating the cycle of poverty within the pastoralist communities. When asked to comment on the National Education Management Information System, respondents in this study had this to say:

Respondent B: Although I have little experience with NEMIS, the requirements to have students from pastoralist areas use an online system to register for exams is discriminatory. First, the system requires students to show birth certificates which are challenging to obtain. In addition, the few schools in pastoralist areas are located in remote areas with hardly any digital infrastructure. Some of the schools have students learning under trees. How is such a school able to afford a computer to register students?

Respondent C: When I registered for my national examination in 2015, schools where pastoralist communities live had problems registering students because of the mandatory birth certificates. Some of those who did not produce birth certificates gave up and went home to graze cattle, and they dropped out of school.

Respondent F: There was a time when the ministry of education required pupils sitting for national examinations to produce birth certificates, and pupils from North Eastern had problems producing the certificate. Thank

God that was scrapped, and pupils can now register without it. However, generally speaking, that requirement would have continued to lock out many pupils who either did not have birth certificates or had delays in the application for birth certificates.

For such crucial digital information management systems to be equitably adopted, proper support systems should first be set up. In January 2020, The Ministry of Education in Kenya issued a directive to schools across the country that stated that schools which did not register their students on NEMIS on time risked losing government funding for the year (The Star Newspaper, January 07, 2020). Although there are no available details on whether any school lost funding due to not registering pupils on NEMIS, this could be viewed as double punishment to communities living in pastoralist areas. In the first place, they have difficulties getting the required documents and second, there is poor infrastructure to support digital systems.

Further, the institution charged with the placement of students in post-secondary institutions – Kenya Universities and Colleges Central Placement Service (KUCCPS) – in May of 2022 admitted that there was a low uptake of college slots from the north-eastern region of Kenya (occupied mainly by pastoralist communities) because of "low access to the information on placement or lack internet services in their localities, making it hard for them to apply" (*The Star Newspaper*, May 30, 2022). Essentially, potential students are meant to apply for post-secondary school placement in the KUCCPS digital portal, and the allocation of scholarships is also done there. The institution admitted that most students had low access to information on placement or lacked internet services in their localities, making it hard for them to apply.

Unequitable Government Policies and Projects

The Kenyan government has, on several occasions, tried to lay out other strategies, policies, and projects that would help mitigate digital marginalisation in Kenya. In May 2019, Kenya launched the first Digital Economy Blueprint, which was meant to be Kenya's "contribution to Smart Africa Alliance initiative, which was working towards digitising the economies and trade of 24 countries across the African continent" (*Aptantech News* June 2019). The second draft of the document named "Digital Economy Strategy" was released in October 2020 by the Ministry of Information, Communication, Technology, Innovation and Youth Affairs in Kenya. The document defined Digital Economy as "the entirety of sectors that operate using digitally enabled communications and networks leveraging the internet, mobile and other technologies" (Republic of Kenya, 2019). The first draft of the document identified five pillars of the digital economy: digital government, digital business, infrastructure, innovation-driven entrepreneurship, and digital skills and values. The second draft of the Digital Economy Strategy maintained the five pillars but also included the digital inclusion of marginalised people/communities as a critical area of focus in realising a Kenyan digital economy.

While the first draft (Digital Economy Blueprint) mentioned sociopolitical, cultural, and economic issues globally, it failed to mention or appreciate the uniqueness of such issues in the Kenyan context. The second draft (Digital Economy Strategy), on the other hand, recognised these contextual issues but also focused on how to work towards the digital exclusion of women, youth, persons living with disabilities, and "others". Even though this is a commendable endeavour, it is unfair to label pastoralists and communities residing in the 13 pastoralist and nomadic counties as "others", and efforts to ensure their inclusion in the digital economy are likely to go unappreciated.

While the two documents mention challenges to uptake of digital technologies, the acknowledgement ends there and does not attempt to offer how these challenges would be overcome. As noted earlier, most pastoralist communities live in locations that do not have or have inadequate road networks, poor ICT networks, for example, mobile phone coverage, fibre optic cables, and even poor electricity network. These infrastructural issues would hinder the digitisation of the Kenyan economy, especially in pastoralist areas. Complete digitisation of the economy would therefore mean that specific communities get excluded from participating in governance issues.

Various levels of government are already implementing some aspects of Kenya's Digital Economy Blueprint/Strategy. Business between the government and citizens has already been up and running for several years now with the assistance of digital technologies (e.g. tendering and payments). The third chapter of the Digital Economy Strategy begins by stating that:

> The backbone of a digital economy is a robust marketplace that leverages technology to ensure that every citizen and business can trade goods, information, and services. As the economy continues to digitise, the lines between "digital trade" and "non-digital" trade [have] continued to blur. The digital trade sub-sector of this pillar, therefore, prioritises the initiatives that can drive the uptake of e-commerce in Kenya.

The Government of Kenya has established a Public Procurement Information Portal (PPIP) where many government tenders are advertised, but they are also advertised in the daily newspapers. Some tender documents viewed in the portal for this study showed that while others require a physical application, some government institutions require documents to be submitted online. In one particular instance, where one of the counties in the pastoralist region (Turkana County) advertised for a tender invitation in the daily newspapers (Daily Nation Newspaper, May 12, 2022), which was also advertised in the PPIP, it indicated that bidders needed to access tender documents from a website and send documents through an email address.

To participate in such bids, applicants needed to have a certain level of digital literacy. They would be required to have access to digital networks and digital gadgets like laptops, printers, and scanners. While this business process makes work easier, faster, and transparent, it is also exclusionary. Pastoralist communities that would not have access to power, digital networks, and other communication infrastructure and have high levels of illiteracy (including digital illiteracy) cannot participate in such business bids.

The Uncertainties of Digital Centres

In 2009, through a public–private partnership, the Government of Kenya established telecentres across the country named "pasha", a Swahili word for "inform". The centres were established to ensure digital inclusion of all citizens, especially those from marginalised communities. The establishment of pash centres was done through the Ministry of Information, Communication, and Technology (ICT), with funding from other private organisations. After this project was piloted and several pasha centres were established and funded, there is no information available on their current existence from the Ministry of ICT, and the Pasha website (www.pasha.co.ke) was closed in May 2021.

With increasing unemployment in Kenya, the Government of Kenya, through the Ministry of ICT, Innovation and Youth Affairs, established the *Ajira Digital Program* (*Ajira* is a Swahili word meaning "labour") to offer digital training to the youth through upskilling to provide them with skills necessary to take up digital/online freelancing jobs and also "position Kenya as a choice labour destination for multinational companies as well as encourage local companies and public sector to create digital work" (Ajira Digital Program's linked page). In partnership with private companies like Mastercard, Ajira centres have been established nationwide to train one million youth.

While these digital projects are essential to bridge existing digital gaps by increasing access and skills, their inconsistency and inequitable nature make them inefficient for a country that has vast gaps of inequalities. First, Pasha digital centres were a good idea in taking digital access to pastoralist areas and other rural areas in Kenya. Proper funding and upscaling to ensure they continued to exist were necessary. Second, Ajira digital centres are a noble idea for the youth's digital upskilling and preparing them for digital labour. However, they are unevenly rolled out in the country. For instance, of the 142 Ajira digital centres across the country, only nine exist in counties inhabited by pastoralists. Table 2.1 shows the distribution of Ajira digital centres in pastoralist counties.

These trends in establishing digital government projects ought to be equitable in their roll-out to ensure specific communities are not marginalised. Ajira digital centres are concentrated in urban centres such as the four Kenyan cities of Nairobi, Kisumu, Mombasa, and Nakuru while urban centres in pastoralist counties hardly get any. This deepens the level of marginalisation in these counties.

Table 2.1 The number of Ajira centres in the 15 pastoralist counties in Kenya

Counties	Ajira centres
Garissa	0
Wajir	0
Lamu	0
Turkana	0
Tana River	0
Mandera	0
Marsabit	0
Isiolo	0
Samburu	0
West Pokot	3
Kilifi	2
Elgeyo Marakwet	0
Baringo	4
Narok	0
Laikipia	0

Source: (Data obtained from Ajira Digital Website – https://ajiradigital.go.ke/#/centres, on November 17 2022)

Conclusion

This chapter examined how government digitisation projects have marginalised pastoralist communities through their digital policies and projects. It began by giving a broader context of digitisation in Kenya and the pastoralist context in Kenya. It also reflected in detail on the broader issues of the digital marginalisation of pastoralist communities and presented empirical data from interviews and other documents. Since Kenya is on the verge of rolling out a digital identity system, the chapter discussed how proposed Kenya's Digital Identity Management Systems (Huduma Namba Bill) and the existing information management systems like NEMIS have the potential to marginalise communities living in pastoralist counties. To find out the efforts the government has been putting in place to bridge digital gaps, the chapter examined two proposed digital strategy documents – The Kenya Digital Economy Blue Print and the Digital Economy Strategy – and briefly two government-led digital projects – Pasha centres and Ajira digital centres.

As noted, digital strategy documents have the potential to marginalise pastoralist communities in a significant way. The document does not explicitly mention or recognise marginalised pastoralist communities who are grouped as "others", and the document fails to offer recourse for such communities. As noted in the analysis of the proposed Huduma Namba and the existing (NEMIS), the digitisation of registrations of persons marginalises the already vulnerable pastoralist population. While a well-functioning and inclusive population management programme are essential, individuals from pastoralist communities are likely to be left out. First, they are not adequately digitised in terms of skills and infrastructures; second, they do not have the affordance of digital devices even to access government services. In addition, for a long time, the Kenyan government has made it difficult for members of some ethnic groups, including Nubians, Somalis, Maasais, Boranas, Indians, and Arabs, to apply for national ID cards. Digitising the issuance of digital IDs does not take away the earlier problems but exacerbates them.

The digitisation of government operations and government services is a welcome move, and time and again, scholars have stated that such moves can lead to accelerated economic growth. However, such projects should ensure that all stakeholders, especially taxpayers, benefit equally. As Waters-Bayer and Bayer (2016) state, hi-tech systems should be implemented socially responsibly to ensure the modernisation of pastoral life and help ensure its future. Further, for inclusive digitisation of government projects to take place, the government needs to be sensitive to the needs of all the people they serve. In places with high levels of inequalities, such radical digitisation projects must be rolled out in phases.

Further, to mitigate this, the government should first deal with the underlying and historical injustices that have characterised geographical locations where pastoralists live before rolling out countrywide digitisation projects. When specific locations continue to benefit from such services while others only dream of them, that becomes a recipe for a vicious circle of marginalisation. The government is therefore obliged to create policies that would accelerate the development of essential aspects of the economy in pastoralist areas, such as infrastructure, security, and other essentials, before the digitisation of government services and operations.

Notes

1 Kiambu county is located in central Kenya near the capital, Nairobi.
2 This is as cited in the second draft (October 2020) of the Digital Economy Strategy.

References

Alaoui, A. M. (2022). ICT and social media: How to avoid social exclusion. In López Peláez, A., Suh, S. M. and Zelenev, S. (eds.), *Digital Transformation and Social Well-Being: Promoting an Inclusive Society* (1st ed, pp. 169–180). London: Routledge.
Anderson M. (2019, June 13). Mobile technology and home broadband 2019. *Pew Research Center*. Retrieved from www.pewresearch.org/internet/2019/06/13/mobile-technology-and-home-broadband-2019/. Accessed on 24th June 2022.
Baxter, P. (1994). Pastoralists are people: Why development for pastoralists, not the development of pastoralism. *Rural Extension Bulletin (United Kingdom)*. Retrieved from https://agris.fao.org/agris-search/search.do?recordID=GB9415305. Accessed on 22nd July 2022.
Debsu, D. N., Little, P. D., Tiki, W., Guagliardo, S. A. J., and Kitron, U. (2016). Mobile phones for mobile people: The role of information and communication technology (ICT) among livestock traders and Borana pastoralists of southern Ethiopia. *Nomadic Peoples*, 20(1), pp. 35–61. https://doi.org/10.3197/np.2016.200104.

Delaporte, A., and Bahia, K., (2022, October). The state of mobile internet connectivity 2022. *GSM Association*. Retrieved from https://www.gsma.com/r/wp-content/uploads/2022/12/The-State-of-Mobile-Internet-Connectivity-Report-2022.pdf?utm_source=website&utm_medium=download-button&utm_campaign=somic22. Accessed on 24th January 2023

Delaporte, A., Bahia, K., Carboni, I., Cruz, G., Jeffrie, N., Sibthorpe, C., . . . and Groenestege, M. T. (2021, September). The state of mobile internet connectivity 2021. *GSM Association*. Retrieved from https://www.gsma.com/r/wp-content/uploads/2021/09/The-State-of-Mobile-Internet-Connectivity-Report-2021.pdf. Accessed on 24th January 2023.

Dressel, J., and Farid, H. (2018). The accuracy, fairness, and limits of predicting recidivism. *Science Advances*, 4(1). https://doi.org/10.1126/sciadv.aao5580.

Friederici, N., Wahome, M., and Graham, M. (2020). *Digital Entrepreneurship in Africa: How a Continent is Escaping Silicon Valley's Long Shadow*. Cambridge: The MIT Press.

Kenya National Bureau of Statistics. (2019). *Kenya Population and Housing Census*. Nairobi: Kenya National Bureau of Statistics.

Khalai, D., Banerjee, R. R., and Mude, A. G. (2016). Analysing the use of ICT in demand and access to information and services for pastoralists. *Paper presented at the Tropentag 2016 Conference on Solidarity in a Competing World – Fair Use of Resources*, Vienna, Austria, 19–21 September. Nairobi: ILRI. Retrieved from https://cgspace.cgiar.org/handle/10568/77006. Accessed on 4th February 2022.

Kohler, T. A., Smith, M. E., Bogaard, A., Feinman, G. M., Peterson, C. E., Betzenhauser, A., Pailes, M., Stone, E. C., Marie Prentiss, A., Dennehy, T. J., and Ellyson, L. J. (2017). Greater post-Neolithic wealth disparities in Eurasia than in North America and Mesoamerica. *Nature*, 551(7682), pp. 619–622. https://doi.org/10.1038/nature24646.

Krätli, S., Huelsebusch, C., Brooks, S., and Kaufmann, B., (2013). Pastoralism: A critical asset for food security under global climate change. *Animal Frontiers*, 3(1), pp. 42–50. https://doi.org/10.2527/af.2013-0007.

Lahsen, M., and Ribot, J. (2022). Politics of attributing extreme events and disasters to climate change. *Wiley Interdisciplinary Reviews: Climate Change*, 13(1), e750.

Morton, J., and Meadows, N. (2000). Pastoralism and sustainable livelihoods: An emerging agenda. *Natural Resources Institute Policy Series*, 11. Retrieved from https://gala.gre.ac.uk/id/eprint/11124/. Accessed on 8th July 2022.

Mwaura, J. (2019). #Resisthudumanamba: Kenyan government at a crossroad. *AoIR Selected Papers of Internet Research*. Brisbane. http://spir.aoir.org.

Nyariki, D. M., and Amwata, D. A. (2019). The value of pastoralism in Kenya: Application of total economic value approach. *Pastoralism*, 9(1), pp. 1–13. https://doi.org/10.1186/s13570-019-0144-x.

Nyariki, D. M., Wakesho Mwang'Ombe, A., and Thompson, D. M. (2009). Land-use change and livestock production challenges in an integrated system: The Masai-Mara ecosystem, Kenya. *Journal of Human Ecology*, 26(3), pp. 163–173. https://doi.org/10.1080/09709274.2009.11906178.

Omanga, D., and Mainye, P. C. (2019). North-South collaborations as a way of 'not knowing Africa': Researching digital technologies in Kenya. *Journal of African Cultural Studies*, 31(3), pp. 273–275.

Otenyo, E. E. (2017). Being left behind amidst Africa's rising imagery: The Maasai in the world of information and communication technologies (ICTs). *Australasian*

Journal of Information Systems, 21, pp. 1–15. https://doi.org/10.3127/ajis. v21i0.1526.

Oualy, J. M. R. (2021). Income inequality and socio-political instability in Sub-Saharan Africa. *Managing Global Transitions*, 19(1), pp. 49–72.

Ragnedda, M. (2020). *Enhancing Digital Equity: Connecting the Digital Underclass.* Cham; Berlin: Springer Nature. https://doi.org/10.1007/978-3-030-49079-9.

Rass, N. (2006). *Policies and Strategies to Address the Vulnerability of Pastoralists in Sub-Saharan Africa. Food and Agriculture Organization.* Rome: FAO (Pro-poor Livestock Policy Initiative (PPLPI) Working Paper Series, 37). Retrieved from https://citeseerx.ist.psu.edu/document?repid=rep1&type=pdf&doi=886cfe0228c8 404dfdcc83a39a582e7d25027e3b. Accessed on 8th July 2022.

Republic of Kenya. (2019). Digital economy blueprint. Powering Kenya's transformation. Ministry of Information, Communications and Technology, pp. 1–96. Retrieved from http://www.ict.go.ke/wp-content/uploads/2019/05/Kenya-Digital-Economy-2019.pdf. Accessed on 18th September 2022.

Savage, T., Akroyd, J., Mosbach, S., Hillman, M., Sielker, F., and Kraft, M. (2022). Universal digital twin – The impact of heat pumps on social inequality. *Advances in Applied Energy*, 5(22), p. 100079. Retrieved from www.sciencedirect.com/science/article/pii/S2666792421000718. Accessed on 22nd July 2022.

Silver, L., and Johnson, C. (2018). Internet seen as having positive impact in Sub-Saharan Africa. *Pew Research Center's Global Attitudes Project.* Retrieved from www.pewresearch.org/global/2018/10/09/internet-connectivity-seen-as-having-positive-impact-on-life-in-sub-saharan-africa/. Accessed on 8th July 2022.

Statista Research Department. (2022, March 8). Most used social media 2021. *Statista.* Retrieved from www.statista.com/statistics/272014/global-social-networks-ranked-by-number-of-users/. Accessed on 21st April 2022.

Swift, J. (1988). Major issues in pastoral development with special emphasis on selected African countries. *FAO.* Retrieved from https://agris.fao.org/agris-search/search.do?recordID=XF9103143. Accessed on 8th July 2022.

United Nations General Assembly. (1948). *Universal Declaration of Human Rights.* Retrieved from http://www.un.org/en/universal-declaration-human-rights. Accessed on 8th July 2022.

Uppal, C., Sartoretto, P., and Cheruiyot, D. (2019). The case for communication rights: A rights-based approach to media development. *Global Media and Communication*, 15(3), pp. 323–343.

Waters-Bayer, A., and Bayer, W. (2016). Pastoralists in the 21st century: "lo-tech" meets "hi-tech". In *Proceedings of the 10th International Rangeland Congress. Saskatoon, SK: Canada* (pp. 24–31). Saskatoon: The International Rangeland Congress.

3 Please Do Not Call It Human Right

A Southern Epistemological Perspective on the Digital Inclusion of People With Disabilities in South Africa

Lorenzo Dalvit

Introduction

South Africa's recent past is infamously emblematic of egregious human rights abuses. The system, known as apartheid and dismantled in 1994, attracted extensive international condemnation because of its violence and brutality (West, 1987). As an integral part of this "colonialism of a special kind", institutionalised segregation and discrimination run along primarily racial and spatial lines. Non-Whites were severely restricted in terms of where they could live and travel; which work they could do; which health, educational, recreation, and other facilities they could access; and so on (Nightingale et al., 1990). Besides classifying individuals as Africans, Coloured or Asians, institutionalised discrimination was extended to other dimensions such as gender and disability. People with disabilities were considered second-class citizens across different domains, and organisations such as Disabled People of South Africa (DPS) played a role in the anti-apartheid struggle (Howell et al., 2006). To different extents, South Africans with disabilities of all colours suffered at the hands of the racist, sexist, and ableist state. More than a quarter of a century from the democratic transition of 1994, the legacy of human rights abuses persists in diverse domains such as healthcare (Baldwin-Ragaven et al., 2000; Sirkin et al., 2018), education (Gallo, 2020; Badat, 2012), and the administration of justice (Van Hout & Wessels, 2021).

Today's South Africa is one of the world's most unequal countries, scoring 0.709 on the Human Development Index (2020). South Africa boasts one of the largest economies on the African continent. Internet penetration, primarily via mobile phones, is estimated at approximately 60% (DataReportal, 2020). As noted by Donner and Gitau (2009), such mobile-centric Internet is far from the fast, broadband, uncapped, and relatively cheap experience in most of the West, which informs academic literature. Stark offline inequalities extend to the digital domain, and those along the lines of (dis)ability are no exception. For people with disabilities, the ubiquity of digital technology makes digital inclusion more and more a necessity rather than a choice or a right. A critical reflection on the limitations and pitfalls

DOI: 10.4324/9781003388289-5

of current approaches to digital inclusion in a Global South milieu is timeous, given growing concerns about the influence and reach of poorly regulated informational superpowers based in the West. This conceptual chapter seeks to problematise an understanding of the digital inclusion of people with disabilities as a human right. A decolonial approach based on the work of scholars such as Maldonado-Torres (2007) and de Sousa Santos (2009) is explored to problematise a dominant approach informed by medical, social, and experiential models.

Digital Inequalities

Inequalities in the digital domain have been a key area of scholarly concern for over two decades. The notion of a digital "divide", in circulation since the 1990s and whose original proponent remains somewhat uncertain (see Ragnedda, 2019), appears somewhat obsolete today and has largely been replaced by the reference to inequalities. Such inequalities are present between and within countries and can be articulated along multiple levels and dimensions. The so-called developing countries (mainly located in the Southern Hemisphere) are often defined in deficit terms in contrast with a technologically advanced North. Terms such as "development", "leapfrog", bridging the gap", and the like in reports, policy documents, and some scholarly research often reflect a technologically deterministic conception of digital innovation supposedly driving linear and uncritically positive social change (Gomez & Pather, 2011). However, far from being a neutral tool, digital technology is imbued with the ideological tenets of the culture which produced it and controls it. Hwang (2007) argues that discursive constructions of access and inclusion serve as Western (and particularly US) hegemonic tools. The author cites the World Trade Organisation (WTO) Agreement on Basic Telecommunications Services as an example of a measure by the United States to counter its decline in economic and political supremacy. Information superpowers such as Amazon, Apple, Facebook, Google, and Microsoft, whose headquarters are located in the United States dominate the digital domain and can exert considerable influence on the flow of information in countries around the world (see Moore & Tambini, 2018). It is therefore no surprise that, as noted by Chari (2022) with reference to Internet.org in India, countries with a colonial past view with suspicion initiatives by large corporations underpinned by the rhetoric of connectivity.

Neo-Marxist scholars (see Dean, 2005; Zuboff, 2015; Fuchs, 2016) highlight the exploitative nature of these platforms as quintessential incarnations of a new form of capitalism based on data extraction and surveillance. Couldry and Mejias (2019) look beyond contemporary forms of profit generations through profit-oriented social media capitalist actors for whom data is "the new oil" and identify in historical colonialism the only comparable process to the emergence of a new social order, such as is currently the case. The authors recognise that it would be unrealistic to expect either individual resistance to have an impact or corporations to start behaving ethically. Citing the European General Data Protection Regulation (GDPR) as a seminal example of regulation protecting humans' right to privacy, an evolution is noted from a concern with protection of individuals from state power to a concern with the combination of data from multiple sources to inform decision-making. In the geographical Global South, however, the protection of activists and journalists from monitoring by repressive governments still seems to be the main (if not the only) issue worthy of scholarly concern (see Duncan, 2018), and digital rights appear as an extravagant luxury one can hardly afford. Within decolonial scholarship, the term Global South refers not so much to a geographical entity but to a shared condition of suffering and resistance (De Sousa Santos, 2012). Such a nuanced understanding accounts for the existence of Global South realities also within Europe and North America. At the same time, the term is best understood as capturing the complex multiverse of experiences one finds in former colonies (often located in the Southern Hemisphere). In these contexts, the legacy of colonialism includes a bifurcated public resulting in profound social inequalities, reflected in the digital domain.

Digital inequalities can be conceptualised at multiple levels and from different theoretical viewpoints. With specific reference to the African context, Ragnedda (2019) summarises three levels. The first level, associated with early stages of ICT penetration, concerns the distinction between those who have physical access to digital devices, infrastructure, and connectivity and those who do not. Most people with disabilities in South Africa are digitally excluded by virtue of their material conditions, the cost of data, and poor network coverage in areas where they live. The second level refers to the uses and skills necessary to take advantage of digital technology. Innovations such as touchscreen mobile phones require a steep learning curve for some people with disabilities (e.g. the visually impaired). The third level of digital inequality pertains to the benefits one may accrue from digital inclusion. At the same time, Ragnedda et al. (2022) note the mutually reinforcing effect of digital and social exclusion. Mutsvairo and Ragnedda (2019a) emphasise the complementarity of digital, economic, and sociocultural elements as a quintessential characteristic of sub-Saharan Africa. One of the major consequences is the emergence of a democratic digital divide resulting from digital exclusion and marginalisation (Mutsvairo & Ragnedda, 2019b; Moyo, 2020).

Rights and Disability in South Africa

South Africa's legal system is sophisticated and independent from political power. The Constitution (1996) is regarded as one of the most progressive in the world. It is one of a handful which explicitly mentions disability (see Heap et al., 2009). Its provisions are given effect in various pieces of legislation, for example, the South African Schools Act 84 of 1996, the Employment Equity Act 55 of 1998, the Promotion of Equality and Prevention of Unfair

Discrimination Act 4 of 2000, the Mental Health Care Act 17 of 2002, the Social Assistance Act 13 of 2004, and the Children's Act 38 of 2005. Holness (2021) notes the limitations of tackling disability issues through generic legislation. The 2015 White Paper on the Rights of Persons with Disabilities provides a comprehensive framework focusing specifically on disability. Kamga (2016) recognises that while this represents a positive development, Chapter 9 institutions such as the Human Rights Commission or the Public Protector as well as Civil Society Organisations need to be capacitated to monitor its implementation.

The South African Human Rights Commission (SHRC) recognises disability as one of its strategic focus areas. Besides convening workshops involving Civil Society Organisations and compiling periodic reports, the Commission initiates investigations into the abuse of the rights of people with disabilities and conducts site visits to schools and care facilities. While cases involving disability fall within the purview of the Public Protector, its relatively scarce resources tend to be employed to focus on more topical areas of concern, such as gender discrimination (The Conversation, 2016). South Africa boasts a vibrant civil society forged during the struggle against apartheid, during which organisations like Disabled Persons of South Africa (DPSA) played an active role in terms of legal protection and challenging perceptions. At present, organisations focusing specifically on disability range from generic ones like the National Council for People with Disabilities (NCPD) to population and domain-specific ones like the Disabled Women of South Africa (DWSA) and the National Paralympic Committee (NPC). At the government level, the bodies primarily tasked with protecting and advancing the rights of people with disabilities are the Department of Women, Youth and Persons with Disabilities and the Department of Social Development, with other departments being tasked with policymaking and implementation in the respective domains.

The rights-based approach on which policy documents rely and on which much of the formal civil society sector draws is recognised as a hard-fought victory against the apartheid past and against the obsolete understandings of disability it relied on (Heap et al., 2009). Consistent with either medical or charitable approaches, people with disabilities were considered helpless victims of circumstances who could not speak out for themselves. The current framework is inspired by the social model (Shakespeare, 2006; see also Howell et al., 2006), which foregrounds the social construction of disability over an outdated focus on impairment and its associated deficits. Such a progressive approach, however, is not beyond criticism. While the liberal human rights model served an important purpose in legitimising the post-apartheid state (see Wilson, 2001), two decades of scholarly research suggest that this approach failed the most vulnerable groups, such as immigrants, the poor, LGBTQ, and people with disabilities (see Crush, 2001; Mubangizi & Mubangizi, 2005; Brown, 2012; Pascoe et al., 2018; Hart et al., 2022). The ability to enforce rights depends on awareness as well as material conditions such as proximity and access to the courts, funds to pay for a lawyer, and, most importantly, a sense of empowerment as citizens in relation to the state and others. For South Africans with disabilities, these depend to a large extent on their socio-economic background, where they live, the language they speak, and so on. Bornman et al. (2016) highlight the challenges faced by people with disabilities in court proceedings. For example, people with deafness, speech, or intellectual impairment face specific challenges during court proceedings and their preparation. Given the centrality of appropriate language use, reliance on testimony based on memory and uncovering an objective "truth", police officers and legal counsellors may even discourage prosecution if they feel chances of success are limited.

Decolonial Critique

Decolonial scholarship provides an extensive critique of the concept of human rights. Maldonado-Torres (2017) captures the historical roots of the human rights discourse as a response to the tragic events of the Second World War in Europe and its aftermath. He coined the phrase "coloniality of human rights" to capture the role of the concept as both a product and a tool of colonial and neocolonial global power relationships. Its supposed universality reflects the persistent centrality of Western understandings enforced in the Global South through institutional arrangements inherited from the colonial period. De Sousa Santos and Martins (2021) emphasise the multiple experiences and different conceptualisations of rights depending on Southern epistemological understandings of personhood and dignity. Understandings of concepts such as "dignity", "ability", "inclusion", and even "disability" itself are heavily influenced by one's cultural, social, and linguistic background. As an example, the official figure of 7.5% of the South African population living with disabilities (Statistics South Africa, 2011) is almost certainly an underestimate or misrepresentation as it relies on the Western medical model of subjective evaluation of one's ability to perform certain tasks. By contrast, in isiXhosa (one of the most widely spoken official South African languages), the terms for disability (*isidalwa*) and people with disabilities (*abantu abakubazekileyo*) are not semantically related to ability. As a further example of the limits of a Eurocentric epistemological perspective, in policy documents (see Department of Communication South Africa, 2017), the concept of informed consent to (self)representation appears to be oblivious of a context of relatively low English proficiency and unequal power relationships between, for example, people with disabilities and institutional representatives.

In relation to the Global South, digital media is (often uncritically) credited with promoting democracy and social justice (see Morozov, 2011). Digital inclusion for all is inscribed as a desirable goal in policy documents and is generally accepted as an unconditionally positive pursuit by public opinion. The Disability and ICT Strategy of the South African Department of Communication (2012: 1) explicitly refers to the need to "build a people-centred information society that takes into account the needs of all, including people with disabilities". Such statements are underpinned by the principle of universal access, which has been problematised in scholarly literature (see Winter, 2013). Lievrouw and Livingstone (2006) argue that one of the quintessential characteristics of digital media is its ubiquity. This refers not only to its pervasiveness in every domain of daily life but also to its impact on every person, whether they are users or not. As an example, Arora (2016), notes that e-government services are becoming the norm even in the Global South, and access to digital technology is a prerequisite for enjoying benefits and support systems. In particular, the need to share biometric data as a requirement to access government services uncovers the imperative to connect as a form of control which may engender new forms of exclusion. For example, retinal scans or fingerprints may be difficult or impossible to collect and verify for people with degenerative conditions affecting their eyesight or for those who lost their limbs. While advanced infrastructure, proactive civil society organisations, and sophisticated legislation may enable people with disabilities living in the West to get around such issues, the most vulnerable and marginalised have little recourse.

The Eurocentric construction of the "human" as a Western, modern human is paramount in the notion of human rights as highlighted by de Sousa Santos (2007; 2009) and Maldonado-Torres (2016). People with disabilities in South Africa are required to approximate a Western modern ideal by embracing digital inclusion and by performing their condition according to expectations. Furthermore, the pathologisation of disability and ensuing bureaucratisation enforce discrete categories arranged in a hierarchical relationship. As noted by De Sousa Santos (2012), such a process is a quintessential epistemological tool to enforce colonialism and patriarchy, and a similar consideration can be made with respect to disability.

Digital Inclusion Policy and Practice

A recognised gap between policy and practice (United Nations, 2017; eNCA, 2016; CIPESA, 2021) risks entrenching, exacerbating, and extending existing inequalities to the digital domain. An emerging body of research documents challenges and new forms of exclusion/invisibility of people with disabilities online, such as lack of access to or inaccessible software/hardware, a steep learning curve, or the practice of hiding one's disability to avoid pity or stigma. Statements such as the one that follows attest to the persistence of a saviour mentality in the online space and reflect a tendency to conceptualise issues within the terms of reference dictated by Western modernity:

> We have an abundance of disability service organisations and a deficit in human rights advocates for disabled people and that's one of the reasons why some disability organisations are not providing the most needed services, and also failing at fighting for rights.
>
> (@ekverstania, 2020)

South Africa's National Development Plan (NDP) acknowledges Information and Communication Technology (ICT) as a key instrument for the inclusion of people with disabilities. It gives effect to Chapters 9 and 21 of the United Nations Convention on the Rights of People with Disabilities (United Nations, 2006). The former deals with accessibility. Examples from the implementation of assistive technologies in education highlight challenges such as chronic lack of resources and a piecemeal approach (Lyner-Cleophas, 2019; van Niekerk et al., 2019). Tax rebates on personal income are available for assistive devices, which include generic ones like mobile phones and tablets where specific impairments warrant it. This approach poses two sets of problems. First, the focus on impairment is based on a medical model of disability which has been extensively criticised in the literature (Shakespeare, 2006; Howell et al., 2006). To access these benefits, taxpayers with disabilities need their condition to be confirmed by a registered health professional. The regulation has not been amended to accept a declaration by a traditional healer (van Zyl, 2011). Despite traditional medicine enjoying some formal recognition, the taxpayer would have to assume the burden of proof.

The second issue with the rebate on income tax approach is that only a relatively small portion of the population is employed in the formal sector. If one considers the intersectional nature of disability, this measure stands to benefit a relatively small percentage of people with disabilities. Many people with disabilities who live below the poverty line rely on family support and government grants. South Africa is one of the few countries in Africa to make provisions for a disability grant. Such provision is often the main source of income for entire families (Macgregor, 2006). While the price of entry-level smartphones makes them accessible to people from the lowest socio-economic backgrounds, the cost of data in South Africa remains one of the highest in the world (Moyo & Munoriyarwa, 2021). It should also be noted that accessibility features, though available by default on almost any device, can be resource-intensive. As an example, using the default screen reader on an entry-level Android phone can slow it down to the point of being unusable. Furthermore, human language technology such as screen readers is often unavailable or at the initial stages of development in African languages (Schlünz et al., 2017). These languages are spoken by the majority of the South African population and especially by a large portion of the most marginalised. Far from ensuring social inclusion, access to digital technology may reproduce inequalities and exclusion.

Article 21 of the UNCRPD focuses on freedom of expression or opinion and access to information. Annable et al. (2007) note that accessing health or impairment-specific information is an important contribution of Internet access for people with disabilities. The Promotion of Equality and Prevention of Unfair Discrimination Act (PEPUDA), Act 4 of 2000, gives effect to Section 9(3) of the Constitution by protecting against discrimination on the basis of, *inter alia*, disability. However, open discrimination and derogatory language find expression online, for example, blogs, comments, social media pages, and so on (Mudavanhu, 2017, Tiger, 2021). Such incidents are difficult to police and those affected have little legal recourse (Holness, 2021). A decolonial perspective of the coverage of violence against people with disabilities in South African news (see Dalvit, 2022a, 2022b) suggests that the difficulties of obtaining reparation through legal means can be understood as part of the legacy of past oppression. Furthermore, McDougall (2006) highlights how media narratives around (dis)ability as a pitiable condition result in accommodation being considered as a merciful concession rather than a right for people with disabilities. This is exemplified by online comments such as

> Wonderful news! We are constantly fighting for the empowerment of persons with disabilities and we are delighted to see the involvement of our government in an attempt to create awareness around disabilities and the persons who live with them! Thank you, sir @CyrilRamaphosa.
> (@The_NCPD, 2019)

The enthusiastic tone of the message, the use of the word "attempt", and the focus on awareness imply that dignity and respect are not legal entitlements for people with disabilities but rather a best effort, a concession to be celebrated and to be thankful for.

Privacy and Autonomy

As noted by Willems (2012), civil society organisations are expected to compensate for the shortcomings of dysfunctional postcolonial governments. As noted by Grech (2015), with specific reference to disability, such dysfunctionality is measured against an ideal invariably defined according to Western standards. Drawing on Mamdani (2018) reflections on the tensions and paradoxes inherent to postcolonial societies, Eurocentric solutions can be conceptualised only in terms of turning "subjects" into "citizens", that is, promoting awareness of one's rights through the support of formal organisations which conform to Western standards. Willems (2012) recognises the fallacies of such an approach in an African context, where the relationship with the state can be understood in different ways, for example, as ritual, convivial, and so on. By simply advocating "more of the same", the aforementioned tweet risks contributing to strengthening a system which has little (if any) liberating potential. Ndlovu-Gatsheni (2013) proposes a radical critique by arguing that democratic and human rights discourses constrain the horizons of the possible and calls for liberatory struggles in Africa to be qualitatively different from their counterparts in the West.

Within decolonial literature (see Mignolo, 2007; 2011), liberation is considered the result of a radical delinking and reconstructing process, in contrast with emancipation, which is understood as "narrowing the gap" without ever actually bridging it. A story titled "Bridging the Digital Divide for People with Disabilities" (South African Government, 2013) and documenting the donation of ICT equipment to a school for learners with disabilities provide some opportunities for reflection. First of all, the fact that this is a donation implies an act of generosity by the sponsor (in this case a Mobile Telecommunicator), in contrast with the claim that "Disability people have a right to access to ICT equipment such as mobile devices and computers". Second, the fact that the minister presiding over the donation event *hoped* "that this is the beginning of many more centres like this one" may seem to suggest an attempt to shift the responsibility for the deployment of ICT in schools (inscribed in the White Paper on E-Education of 2004) to private funders. Finally, the remark that for learners, access to ICT tools "will make it easier for them to carry on with their studies and equip them with skills needed in the workplace" reveals a Eurocentric understanding of success as an individual accomplishment and economic independence. This may well be at odds with an emphasis on contributing to one's family or community, for instance, which informs the values of many in the Global South (Grech, 2015). As a more general consideration, the supposed "success stories" (either focusing on digital inclusion or propagated through digital media) about people with disabilities tend to foreground exceptional cases or circumstances, for example, high-achievers or once-off events while relegating the lived experiences of oppression and marginalisation by the vast majority of people with disabilities to the background (see Dalvit, 2022).

Human rights have sometimes been critiqued by state actors as part of a neocolonial project to yield unchecked power and escape accountability (Ndlovu-Gatsheni, 2009). Such argument.(see Oyowe, 2013) highlights the incompatibility between the primacy of communal harmony (which characterises the moral philosophy of Ubuntu) and of individual liberty (underpinning human rights). Other authors prefer to foreground the shared emphasis on dignity understood as the capacity to identify with and extend solidarity to others (see Metz, 2011). Autonomy and independence from public control within the private domain are fundamental underpinnings of the normative concept of the public sphere (Susen, 2011). Over a decade and a half ago, Goldstuck (2008) noted that Internet access for members of marginalised groups is often at the community or household rather than the individual level. Phone sharing, which has been extensively researched in Africa (Dalvit, 2014), appears to engender new forms of dependency for people with disabilities (McDougall, 2006; see also Dalvit, 2019). The progressive shift of digital technology use from public to private spaces does not necessarily mean people with disabilities are any more included but might very well render their dependency on friends and family members less visible. Power relationships in the home are particularly difficult to regulate. At the same time, intrusions into the private space by private corporations in the absence of (and sometimes in opposition to or despite of) state regulation are increasingly common (see Zuboff, 2015).

Conclusions and Recommendations

This chapter problematised understanding of the digital inclusion of people with disabilities as a human right. The gap between progressive legislation and implementation challenges is often attributed to a dysfunctional government, weak civil society, and lack of awareness or resources. While these remain challenges to be addressed as a matter of urgency, a decolonial perspective highlights how the legacy of past oppression against people with disabilities persists in the digital domain. Besides the challenges associated with ensuring physical and epistemological access and regulating the online space, an emancipatory orientation limits the horizon of possible avenues of transformation. A quarter of a century of experience suggests that, for South Africans with disabilities, human rights in the digital and other domains are to a large extent, unenforceable. Furthermore, advancements in the form of individual success or piecemeal interventions serve to mask the persistence of old and the emergence of new ableist practices in the digital domain. At the same time, there is little assurance that further investment in the current approach would yield positive social change.

As ICT plays an increasingly important role in every aspect of daily life, people with disabilities risk being increasingly marginalised. Heeding the call by decolonial scholars such as Ndlovu-Gatsheni, a radically different approach taking a truly African perspective as its starting point needs to be explored. In terms of challenging coloniality of power, that is, the persistence of institutional arrangements inherited from the colonial period, transnational action should follow a double approach. On the one hand, a strengthening of institutions such as the African Union would provide greater leverage in countering the hegemony of undemocratic and Western-centric bodies such as the International Telecommunication Union (ITU), The World Trade Organisation, and the World Bank. Second, people with disabilities in different countries should leverage digital technology to lobby for equal rights independent of one's geographical location. In terms of challenging coloniality of knowledge, that is, beliefs and world views that justify and reinforce colonial power relationships, it is important to overcome the pathologisation of disability and consequent reliance on accommodations and redress based on people with disabilities motivating, advocating, demonstrating, and so on. Adopting the principle of accessibility by design, for instance, would shift the responsibility to software developers and service providers to ensure that nobody is excluded, regardless of their (dis)ability. Finally, disability should be recognised as an integral component of human experience. This may entail an explicit recognition of users with disabilities as drivers of technological innovation (e.g. in the case of autocompletion while typing or of voice recognition) and not as afterthoughts to be catered for "if practically possible". I realise these recommendations rely on a shift away from the current neoliberal paradigm to which many African states, including South Africa appear to subscribe.

References

Annable, G., Goggin, G., and Stienstra, D. (2007). Accessibility, disability, and inclusion in information technologies: Introduction. *The Information Society*, 23(3), 145–147.

Arora, P. (2016). Bottom of the data pyramid: Big data and the global south. *International Journal of Communication*, 10(2016), 1681–1699.

Badat, S. (2012). Redressing the colonial/apartheid legacy: Social equity, redress, and higher education admissions in democratic South Africa. In Z., Hasan and M., Nussbaum (eds), *Equalizing Access: Affirmative Action in Higher Education in India, United States, and South Africa* (pp. 121–150). New Delhi: Oxford University Press.

Baldwin-Ragaven, L., London, L., and De Gruchy, J. (2000). Learning from our apartheid past: Human rights challenges for health professionals in contemporary South Africa. *Ethnicity & Health*, 5(3–4), 227–241.

Bornman, J., White, R., Johnson, E., and Bryen, D. N. (2016). Identifying barriers in the South African criminal justice system: Implications for individuals with severe communication disability. *Acta Criminologica: African Journal of Criminology & Victimology*, 29(1), 1–17.

Brown, R. (2012). Corrective rape in South Africa: A continuing plight despite an international human rights response. *Annual Survey of International & Comparative Law*, 18(1), 45–66.

Chari, V. (2022). Internet. org and the rhetoric of connectivity. *Communication and Critical/Cultural Studies*, 19(1), 54–73.

CIPESA (2021, December 3). *CIPESA Working on Advancing Digital Inclusion for Persons with Disabilities in Africa*. Retrieved from: https://cipesa.org/2021/12/cipesa-working-on-advancing-digital-inclusion-for-persons-with-disabilities-in-africa/. Accessed on 23 July 2022.

Couldry, N., and Mejias, U. A. (2019). Data colonialism: Rethinking big data's relation to the contemporary subject. *Television & New Media*, 20(4), 336–349.

Crush, J. (2001). The dark side of democracy: Migration, xenophobia and human rights in South Africa. *International Migration*, 38(6), 103–133.

Dalvit, L. (2014). Why care about sharing? Shared phones and shared networks in rural areas: African trends. *Rhodes Journalism Review*, 2014(34), 81–84.

Dalvit, L. (2019). Mobile phones and visual impairment in South Africa: Experiences from a small town. In G., Goggin, K., Ellis, B., Haller and R., Curtis (eds), *The Routledge Companion to Disability and Media* (pp. 285–294). New York: Routledge.

Dalvit, L. (2022). A Decolonial perspective on online media discourses in the context of violence against people with disabilities in South Africa. *Comunicação e Sociedade*, 41, 169–187.

Dalvit, L. (2022). Differently included: A decolonial perspective on disability and digital media in South Africa. In P., Tsatsou (ed), *Vulnerable People and Digital Inclusion: Theoretical and Applied Perspectives*. Geneva: Palgrave Macmillan.

DataReportal. (2020, February 18). Digital 2020: South Africa (S. Kemp, Ed.). *DataReportal – Global Digital Insights*. Retrieved from: https://datareportal.com/reports/digital-2020-south-africa. Accessed on 23 July 2022.

De Sousa Santos, B. (2012). Public sphere and epistemologies of the South. *Africa Development*, 37(1), 43–67.

De Sousa Santos, B., and Martins, B. S. (Eds.). (2021). *The Pluriverse of Human Rights: The Diversity of Struggles for Dignity: The Diversity of Struggles for Dignity*. London: Routledge.

Dean, J. (2005). Communicative capitalism: Circulation and the foreclosure of politics. *Cultural Politics*, 1(1), 51–74.

Department of Communication South Africa. (2017, January 1). *Disability and ICT Strategy*. Retrieved from: www.gov.za/sites/default/files/gcis_document/201409/disability-and-ict-strategya.pdf. Accessed on 23 July 2022.

Donner, J., and Gitau, S. (2009). *New Paths: Exploring Mobile-centric Internet Use in South Africa*. Paper presented at the Africa Perspective on the Role of Mobile Technologies in Fostering Social Development, Maputo (pp. 1–11). Retrieved from: http://www.w3.org/2008/10/MW4D_WS/papers/donner.pdf. Accessed on 23 July 2022.

Duncan, J. (2018). Taking the spy machine south: Communications surveillance in Sub-Saharan Africa. In B., Mutsvairo (ed), *The Palgrave Handbook of Media and Communication Research in Africa* (pp. 153–176). Cham: Palgrave Macmillan.

eNCA. (2016, March 21). Disabled South Africans still fighting to be recognised on human rights day. *YouTube*. Retrieved from: www.youtube.com/watch?v=LcS2iMFxqps. Accessed on 23 July 2022.

Fuchs, C. (2016). Digital labor and imperialism. *Monthly Review*, 67(8), 14.

Gallo, M. A. (2020). *Bantu Education, and Its Living Educational and Socioeconomic Legacy in Apartheid and Post-Apartheid South Africa*. Bachelor of Arts Thesis. New York: Fordham University.

Goldstuck, A. (2008). *Internet Access in South Africa 2008, A Comprehensive Study of the Internet Access Market in South Africa*. Johannesburg: World Wide Worx.

Gomez, R., and Pather, S. (2011). ICT evaluation: Are we asking the right questions? *The Electronic Journal of Information Systems in Developing Countries*, 50(5), 1–14.

Grech, S. (2015). Decolonising eurocentric disability studies: Why colonialism matters in the disability and global South debate. *Social Identities*, 21(1), 6–21.

Hart, T., Wickenden, J. M., Thompson, S., Pienaar, G., Rubaba, T., and Bohler-Muller, N. (2022). *Literature Review to Support a Survey to Understand the Socio-economic, Wellbeing and Human Rights Related Experiences of People with Disabilities during Covid-19 Lockdown in South Africa*. Brighton: Institute of Development Studies.

Heap, M., Lorenzo, T., and Thomas, J. (2009). 'We've moved away from disability as a health issue, it's a human rights issue': Reflecting on 10 years of the right to equality in South Africa. *Disability & Society*, 24(7), 857–868.

Holness, W. (2021). Hate crime based on disability in South Africa. Lessons for law reform. *SA Crime Quarterly*, 70, 2–11.

Howell, C., Chalklen, S., and Alberts, T. (2006). A history of the disability rights movement in South Africa. In B., Watermeyer, L., Swartz, T., Lorenzo, M., Schneider and M., Priestley (eds), *Disability and Social Change: A South African Agenda* (pp. 46–84). Cape Town: HSRC Press.

Hwang, J. (2007). *Deconstructing the Discourse of the Global Digital Divide in the Age of Neo-Liberal Global Economy*. PhD Dissertation. Retrieved from: https://etda.libraries.psu.edu/catalog/7363. Accessed on 23 July 2022.

Kamga, S. D. (2016). Disability rights in South Africa: Prospects for their realisation under the white paper on the rights of persons with disabilities. *South African Journal on Human Rights*, 32(3), 569–580.

Lievrouw, L. A., and Livingstone, S. (2006). Introduction to the updated student edition. In L. A., Liewrouw and S., Livingstone (eds), *Handbook of New Media: Social Shaping and Social Consequences of ICTs* (pp. 1–14). London: SAGE Publications.

Lyner-Cleophas, M. (2019). Assistive technology enables inclusion in higher education: The role of Higher and Further Education Disability Services Association. *African Journal of Disability*, 8, 1–6.

Macgregor, H. (2006). 'The grant is what I eat': The politics of social security and disability in the post-apartheid South African State. *Journal of Biosocial Science*, 38(1), 43–55.

Maldonado-Torres, N. (2007). On the coloniality of being: Contributions to the development of a concept. *Cultural Studies*, 21(2–3), 240–270.

Maldonado-Torres, N. (2016). Outline of ten theses on coloniality and decoloniality. *Foundation Frantz Fanon*. Retrieved from https://fondation-frantzfanon.com/wp-content/uploads/2018/10/maldonado-torres_outline_of_ten_theses-10.23.16.pdf. Accessed on 23 July 2022.

Maldonado-Torres, N. (2017). On the coloniality of human rights. *Revista critica de ciências sociais*, (114), 117–136.

Mamdani, M. (2018). Citizen and subject. In *Citizen and Subject*. Princeton: Princeton University Press.

McDougall, K. (2006). Ag shame' and superheroes: Stereotype and the signification of disability. In B., Watermeyer, L., Swartz, T., Lorenzo, M., Schneider and M., Priestley (eds), *Disability and Social Change: A South African Agenda* (pp. 387–400). Cape Town: HSRC Press.

Metz, T. (2011). Ubuntu as a moral theory and human rights in South Africa. *African Human Rights Law Journal*, 11(2), 532–559.

Mignolo, W. D. (2007). Introduction: Coloniality of power and de-colonial thinking. *Cultural Studies*, 21(2–3), 155–167.

Mignolo, W. D. (2011). Epistemic disobedience and the decolonial option: A manifesto. *Transmodernity*, 1(2), 3–23.

Moore, M., and Tambini, D. (Eds.). (2018). *Digital Dominance: The power of Google, Amazon, Facebook, and Apple*. Oxford: Oxford University Press.

Morozov, E. (2011). *The Net Delusion: How Not to Liberate the World*. London: Penguin.

Moyo, D., and Munoriyarwa, A. (2021). 'Data must fall': Mobile data pricing, regulatory paralysis and citizen action in South Africa. *Information, Communication & Society*, 24(3), 365–380.

Moyo, L. (2020). The end of the public sphere: Social media, civic virtue, and the democratic divide. In M., Ragnedda and A., Gladkova (eds), *Digital Inequalities in the Global South* (pp. 269–285). Cham: Palgrave Macmillan.

Mubangizi, J. C., and Mubangizi, B. C. (2005). Poverty, human rights law and socio-economic realities in South Africa. *Development Southern Africa*, 22(2), 277–290.

Mudavanhu, S. L. (2017). Comrades, students, baboons and criminals: An analysis of "othering" on Facebook in relation to the# rhodesmustfall/# feesmustfall movement at the University of Cape Town. *African Journalism Studies*, 38(2), 21–48.

Mutsvairo, B., and Ragnedda, M. (2019a). Comprehending the digital disparities in Africa. In B., Mutsvairo and M., Ragnedda (eds), *Mapping the Digital Divide in Africa: A Mediated Analysis* (pp. 13–26). Amsterdam: Amsterdam University Press.

Mutsvairo, B., and Ragnedda, M. (2019b). Does digital exclusion undermine social media's democratizing capacity? *New Global Studies*, 13(3), 357–364.

NCPD [@The_NCPD]. (2019, February 27). Wonderful news! We are constantly fighting for the empowerment of persons with disabilities and we are delighted to see the involvement of our government in an attempt to create awareness around disabilities and the persons who live with them! Thank you, sir @CyrilRamaphosa [Tweet]. Retrieved from: https://twitter.com/The_NCPD/status/1100764540587991040?s=20. Accessed on 23 July 2022.

Ndlovu-Gatsheni, S. J. (2009). Making sense of Mugabeism in local and global politics: 'So Blair, keep your England and let me keep my Zimbabwe'. *Third World Quarterly*, 30(6), 1139–1158.

Ndlovu-Gatsheni, S. J. (2013). *Empire, Global Coloniality and African Subjectivity*. New York: Berghahn Books.

Nightingale, E. O., Hannibal, K., Geiger, H. J., Hartmann, L., Lawrence, R., and Spurlock, J. (1990). Apartheid medicine: Health and human rights in South Africa. *JAMA*, 264(16), 2097–2102.

Oyowe, A. O. (2013). Strange bedfellows: Rethinking ubuntu and human rights in South Africa. *African Human Rights Law Journal*, 13(1), 103–124.

Pascoe, M., Klop, D., Mdlalo, T., and Ndhambi, M. (2018). Beyond lip service: Towards human rights-driven guidelines for South African speech-language pathologists. *International Journal of Speech-Language Pathology*, 20(1), 67–74.

Ragnedda, M. (2019). Conceptualising the digital divide. In B., Mutsvairo and M., Ragnedda (eds), *Mapping Digital Divide in Africa: A Mediated Analysis* (pp. 27–44). Amsterdam: Amsterdam University Press.

Ragnedda, M., Ruiu, M. L., and Addeo, F. (2022). The self-reinforcing effect of digital and social exclusion: The inequality loop. *Telematics and Informatics*, 72(2022), 1–13.

Santos, D. B. (2007). Human rights as an emancipatory script? Cultural and political conditions. *Another Knowledge is Possible: Beyond Northern Epistemologies*, 3(1), 1–40.

Santos, D. B. (2009). If God were a human rights activist: Human rights and the challenge of political theologies. *Law, Social Justice & Global Development*, 2009(1), 1–42.

Schlünz, G. I., Wilken, I., Moors, C., Gumede, T., van der Walt, W., Calteaux, K., . . . and van Niekerk, K. (2017). Applications in accessibility of text-to-speech synthesis for South African languages: Initial system integration and user engagement. In *Proceedings of the South African Institute of Computer Scientists and Information Technologists* (pp. 1–10). New York: Association for Computing Machinery.

Shakespeare, T. (2006). The social model of disability. *The Disability Studies Reader*, 2, 197–204.

Sirkin, S., Iacopino, V., Grodin, M., and Danieli, Y. (2018). The role of health professionals in protecting and promoting human rights: A paradigm for professional responsibility. In Y., Danieli, E., Stamatopoulou and C., Dias (eds), *The Universal Declaration of Human Rights: Fifty Years and beyond* (pp. 357–369). New York: Routledge.

South African Government. (2013). *Bridging the Digital Divide for People with Disability*. Retrieved from: https://www.gov.za/bridging-digital-divide-people-disability. Accessed on 23 July 2022.

Statistics South Africa (StatsSA). (2011, January 1). *Stats SA Profiles Persons With Disabilities | Statistics South Africa*. Retrieved from: www.statssa.gov.za/?p=3180. Accessed on 23 July 2022.

Susen, S. (2011). Critical notes on Habermas's theory of the public sphere. *Sociological Analysis*, 5(1), 37–62.
Tania Melnyczuk [@ekverstania]. (2020, July 16). We have an abundance of disability service organisations and a deficit in human rights advocates for disabled people and that's one of the reasons why some disability organisations are not providing the most needed services, and also failing at fighting for rights. *Tweet*. Retrieved from: https://twitter.com/ekverstania/status/1283697597518159873?s=20. Accessed on 23 July 2022.
The Conversation. (2016, December 30). *Lesser-Known Stories of How Ordinary South Africans Felt the Effect of an Active Public Protector*. Retrieved from: https://theconversation.com/lesser-known-stories-of-how-ordinary-south-africans-felt-the-effect-of-an-active-public-protector-70300. Accessed on 23 July 2022.
Tiger [@idyan92]. (2021, June 4). Until they start shouting sharkFace with tears of joyFace with tears of joyFace with tears of joy but it was a good idea though. *Tweet*. Retrieved from https://twitter.com/idyan92/status/1400626024447102977. Accessed on 23 July 2022.
United Nations. (2006). *Convention on the Rights of Persons With Disabilities*. Retrieved from: https://www.un.org/disabilities/documents/convention/convoptprot-e.pdf. Accessed on 23 July 2022.
United Nations. (2017, January 26). My dreams are huge: Disability in South Africa. *YouTube*. Retrieved from: www.youtube.com/watch?v=1nMrux7GbyY. Accessed on 23 July 2022.
Van Hout, M. C., and Wessels, J. (2021). Human rights and the invisible nature of incarcerated women in post-apartheid South Africa: Prison system progress in adopting the Bangkok rules. *International Journal of Prisoner Health*, 18(3), 300–315.
van Niekerk, K., Dada, S., and Tönsing, K. (2019). Influences on selection of assistive technology for young children in South Africa: Perspectives from rehabilitation professionals. *Disability and Rehabilitation*, 41(8), 912–925.
van Zyl, F. (2011). Deductible medical expenses for income tax purposes: Traditional healers, pharmacists and cosmetic procedures. *Obiter*, 32(1), 171–188.
West, S. (1987). "War against kids" in Southern Africa. *The Black Scholar*, 18(6), 26–33.
Willems, W. (2012). Interrogating public sphere and popular culture as theoretical concepts on their value in African studies. *Africa Development*, 37(1), 11–26.
Wilson, R. A. (2001). *The Politics of Truth and Reconciliation in South Africa: Legitimizing the Post-Apartheid State*. Cambridge: Cambridge University Press.
Winter, J. S. (2013). Is Internet access a human right? Linking information and communication technology (ICT) development with global human rights efforts. *Global Studies Journal*, 5(3), 35–48.
Zuboff, S. (2015). Big other: Surveillance capitalism and the prospects of an information civilization. *Journal of Information Technology*, 30(1), 75–89.

4 The Interdependence of Communication, Political, and Socio-Economic Rights

Examining the Lived Experiences of Digitally Marginalised Netizens Before and During the COVID-19 Lockdown in Lagos State, Nigeria

Olutobi Akingbade

Introduction

An overview of relevant literature suggests that there is a dearth of studies that examine how youths from economically marginalised communities in the developing world use the internet and social media platforms in particular. This chapter contributes towards filling this gap in the literature. This is against the backdrop of a global discursive debate about internet access as a fundamental right for every citizen and its importance in fostering communication capabilities (Hamelink & Hoffman, 2008; Musiani et al., 2009; Melanson, 2010; Kravets, 2011). This chapter was motivated by assertions in the relevant literature that highlight the relevance of internet access and connectivity as a requirement for informed political participation and active democratic citizenship in today's contemporary world (Oyedemi, 2015; Mutsvairo, 2016; Olaniyan & Akpojivi, 2021).

Also serving as useful motivation for the analysis and discussion in this chapter is the way in which the emergence of information and communications technologies (ICTs) has over the years transformed communication and civic participation on the African continent and in Nigeria in particular (Mare, 2016; Uwalaka & Watkins, 2018; Olaniyan & Akpojivi, 2021). Within this context, this chapter also attempts to add to the discourse and debate on citizens' communication rights available in the literature (see, for instance, Hamelink & Hoffman, 2008; Kravets, 2011) by providing insights into its practical dimension and nuances before and during a pandemic episode in two low-income communities in Nigeria. Embedded in a qualitative research design, the chapter analyses transcripts from semi-structured interviews with 19 young adults resident in the low-income communities of Ajegunle and Amukoko in Lagos state, Nigeria.

The purposive sampling of youths is motivated by relevant studies (Järvinen et al., 2012; Kannan & Hongshuang, 2017), which indicate that

DOI: 10.4324/9781003388289-6

the youth are more active in their everyday use of ICTs and participation and consumption of information on the internet. More specifically, the motivation is a desire to understand whether – and how – this demographic group uses ICTs, especially social media, for democratic participation and expression. This stems from the seeming indifference and low participation rates in democratisation efforts that have been recorded over the years among many young adult Nigerians. Young adults from low-income communities were selected for this study because they exemplify the digital divide and constraints in continuous internet access being experienced on the African continent. Even though mobile internet availability has increased in Africa, digital divides are evident in Africa's poor and low-income communities where internet uptake and usage gaps remain high. The divide is growing between richer, urban, and better educated households with electricity supply and poorer households with erratic supply of electricity (Frankfurter et al., 2020).

ICTs and Communication Rights in Nigeria

Globally, the enhanced responsiveness, social presence of interaction, and new discursive opportunities that ICTs offer continue to serve as a qualitative and substantively different experience compared with traditional understandings and systems of communication form and practice. Nigeria is no exception, as advancements in ICTs continue to transform communicative ecologies in the country. This has facilitated the participation of subaltern groups and individuals in national, regional, and local conversations in Nigeria (Olaniran, 2014; Mutsvairo, 2016). Studies highlight how various groups of previously passive audiences have at different times become engaged, being able to benefit from the affordances of digital, social, and mobile media to access alternative news stories and share and publicise their perspectives on national, regional, and local issues (Akinfemisoye, 2013; Kperogi, 2018; Akingbade, 2021). Gauging the impact of digital media in facilitating social and political change might be difficult and unpredictable. Yet, several studies (e.g. Kperogi, 2020; Olaniyan & Akpojivi, 2021) have acknowledged the possibility of a new political culture of public accountability, owing to citizens' use of social media platforms to champion issues that mainstream media ordinarily would ignore or fail to prioritise. This is against the background of citizens' growing distrust of Nigeria's mainstream media and criticism that it has neglected its crucial role of producing in-depth investigative, advocacy, and adversarial journalism, which was common during military rule (Dare, 2007, 2011). While mainstream media was well known and regarded – prior to military regimes and during the agitations against colonial rule – as a major source of political education, it is now accused of being complicit in the corrupt practices of the political class (Kperogi, 2012).

The goal of equality and social justice underpinning the philosophical and theoretical debates emphasising the right of every citizen to self-expression and equal access to ICTs is well captured in the relevant literature. However, there are practical inhibitors in Nigeria. Just like most developing and postcolonial states, these inhibitors in Nigeria include expensive networks, data and devices, the absence of reliable internet connectivity, and other challenges that constitute the digital divide across the country. The current rate of internet penetration in Nigeria is below 56 per cent (DataReportal, 2023), which suggests that almost half of the total population is excluded from participation in the digital sphere. With unemployment on the increase – a condition made worse by the COVID-19 lockdown – millions of Nigerians within the internet penetration range find it difficult to consistently maintain paid access to the internet. Even when they do, active engagements with conventional politics and state governance via the digital sphere become unsustainable.

While government officials and non-governmental and not-for-profit organisations make their stance clear at different fora that every Nigerian has a right to access ICTs, and the affordances they provide such as self-expression and access to relevant information, the reality for millions of Nigerian citizens contradicts this position. Another contradictory reality is the attempt by Nigeria's government to enforce stringent regulatory measures regarding citizens' use of social media platforms widely adopted as a mobile communicative tool due to transformation in ICTs. An example is a proposed bill, sponsored in 2013 by one of the senators in Nigeria's upper legislative chamber, which sought to criminalise political messaging through social media that was deemed abusive and critical of the state and government officials (Akpojivi, 2018). Although the bill was not passed into law, similar bills have been considered by the Nigerian senate; the "National Commission for the Prohibition of Hate Speech" seeks to control social media communication and proposes death penalty for anyone found guilty of propagating hate speech (Olaniyan & Akpojivi, 2021). Academics, activists, civil society, and other stakeholders have emphasised that this and other similar bills are deliberately sponsored by the political class to gag citizens from expressing their rights to freedom of speech while also controlling those media organisations that are beginning to draw on citizens' voices as expressed through social media for their programming (Ewang, 2019; Olaniyan & Akpojivi, 2021). Although the threat of a death sentence proposed as a penalty for those found guilty has been dropped following an outcry of public displeasure and criticism, sponsors and supporters of the bill insist it is in Nigeria's best interest.

While there are legitimate concerns about how advances in ICTs have amplified the avalanche of clickbait, hoaxes, fake news, conspiracy theories, misinformation, and disinformation, this must be delicately balanced with citizens' human and communication rights. Absence of balance is evident in the government's continued attempts to curtail citizens' use of the digital public sphere, despite this being inconsistent with democratic values and international standards regarding freedom of expression and communication rights. A disregard for citizens' rights was exemplified in the seven-month ban on Twitter by the Nigerian government. This action led to citizens' inability to legally access one of the key platforms where they receive alternative news, freely express their views on news stories and pertinent issues, and hold conversations. Twitter's place as a sphere where citizens dialogue and agitate for social change is evidenced in how the 2020 #EndSARS campaign morphed from the platform into street protests. Using the social media platform, Nigerian youths, including those abroad, mobilised themselves and convened on the streets in protest against police brutality and the excesses of the state's Special Anti-Robbery Squad (SARS) – a now disbanded tactical unit of the Nigerian police notorious for its extortion and cruelty against youths suspected of crime.

Even though power is multidimensional, and there are different types and levels of powerplay in the ICT industry (Castells, 2011), the role of the state in facilitating the provision of affordable access to ICTs for all citizens cannot be overemphasised. While the government is expected to remain committed to combating fake news, hate speech and the like, this must not be used as a fig leaf to systematically curtail citizens' freedom of speech and communication rights.

Theoretical Framework

This chapter draws on the concept of the public sphere which is central to understanding media and communication processes in the political arena. Key contributions are credited to German philosopher and Frankfurt School sociologist Jurgen Habermas, who conceived the public sphere as a realm of social life in which private individuals come together to form public opinion on matters of public concern (Habermas, 1974). The theorising brings to the fore the philosophical concept and consciousness of "publics" and their importance in mediating between society and state authority by holding the latter accountable to the former via "publicity" (Habermas, 1974; Crossley & Roberts, 2004). The theorising also foregrounded the public use of rational, informed discussion and reason as a form of political confrontation, whereby participants set aside their differences in birth or fortune to communicate with one another as peers (Habermas, 1989; Fraser, 1990). The public sphere was thus theorised as a democratic mode of societal coordination, communication, and unfettered debate, unlike state power and market economies that are prone to domination and reification (Fraser, 1990; Calhoun, 1996).

However, the popularity of non-print forms of mass media led to individualised media consumption whereby the type and quality of media had implications for individuals' sense of self and their role and public participation as citizens (Habermas, 1989; Mare, 2016). Unequal access to and control over the public sphere, which operated by appearance only as mediated political communication was carried out by an elite, specifically journalists and public actors – whose appearance in journalism constructed them as opinion leaders (Habermas, 1974; Garnham, 2007; Bruns & Highfield, 2016). With ordinary citizens viewed as audience members who merely observe events as they unfold on "the virtual stage of mediated communication", this vertical, top-down model has over the years continued to inhibit citizens' civic participation (Bruns & Highfield, 2016: 99). This has led to complexities that continue to inhibit an ideal communicative environment where plurality of opinions and communication rights would be accommodated and upheld. This explains the usefulness of recent scholarship on counterpublics that has paid significant attention to the potential of ICTs in supporting and sustaining multiple public spheres (Shirky, 2011; Jackson & Welles, 2015; Choi & Cho, 2017). A great degree of this attention is directed specifically to social media and social networking sites. This attention, to some extent, can be attributed to the capacity of social media platforms to reconfigure communicative power relations such that citizens are able to challenge the monopoly on media production and dissemination by state and commercial institutions (Shirky, 2011; Fenton, 2012). Alongside the theorising on the public sphere, this chapter draws on this recent scholarship and relevant conceptualisations. Included is the assertion that social media platforms aid democracy, as they increase the number of spaces available for deliberation and dissent and legitimise collective experiences of unrecognition, expropriation, and marginalisation (Fenton, 2012; Choi & Cho, 2017). This is made possible because social media platforms do not require a unified message to challenge mainstream discourses and have fast become one of the notable mediated spaces where marginalised voices can deliberate collectively with the potential to impact wider publics (Wasserman, 2011; Shirky, 2011; Jackson & Welles, 2015).

In relation to citizens' rights to freely communicate and deliberate in the public sphere, this theoretical framework provides a useful way of unpacking the dynamics and complexities of study participants' communication experiences and civic engagements before and during the COVID-19 pandemic. This line of enquiry and analysis is in consonance with relevant studies, which highlight how different categories of a previously passive audience in Nigeria have in recent times drawn on ICTs to ensure their opinions and voices are not excluded from the public sphere.

While social media platforms have been duly acknowledged for broadening political participation and communication, more critical studies that examine social media as a public sphere in the developing world are needed. This is considering the challenges posed by access, affordability, and connectivity that have left citizens either partially or permanently disconnected. Also, the seven-month Twitter ban in Nigeria exemplifies how citizens can be locked out or banned from social media platforms. This, among other key issues, demonstrates that the public sphere of social media is not as "public" as it might seem.

Methodology

As previously mentioned, this chapter follows the qualitative methodological approach. This is grounded in interpretative phenomenological analysis (IPA) – an approach that uses critical and in-depth analysis of research participants' lived experiences to examine and underscore the essence of a specific phenomenon (Patton, 1990). To provide an in-depth analysis of any predefined phenomenon, the IPA approach emphasises a deliberate focus on "small, purposively-selected and carefully situated samples" within a specific socio-historical context (Smith et al., 2009: 29). This informs the purposeful selection of 19 young adult Nigerians from densely populated low-income communities characterised by inequalities, marginalisation, and a low standard of living that make consistent internet access difficult and challenging. Born and resident in the low-income communities of Ajegunle and Amukoko in Lagos state, Nigeria, the young adults' levels of education range from high school certificate to college diploma. Eleven of the young adults (five males, six females) are from Ajegunle while eight (four males, four females) are from Amukoko. Both Ajegunle and Amukoko are multi-ethnic communities with many households at the lower end of the economic scale. Most services and infrastructures in these two low-income communities are either absent or lack adequate maintenance (Agbola & Agunbiade, 2009). These include water supply, sewage, sanitation and waste disposal, electricity, roads and drainage, health centres, and so on. Although great talents in sports and entertainment have emerged from Ajegunle and Amukoko among other law-abiding people who diligently go about their day-to-day activities, these communities are, however, also notable for social vices like thuggery, banditry, and other criminal tendencies and unwholesome activities (Olajide, 2010; Onyegbula, 2015).

The data discussed in this chapter was collected through semi-structured interviews conducted in the month of April 2020 with each of the 19 participants. Semi-structured interview, a notable method of data collection in qualitative research, was used because of its flexibility, conversational approach, and allowance for a blend of closed and open-ended questions, accompanied by follow-up questions, probes, and comments (Adams, 2015). As a result of constraints in physical mobility due to the COVID-19 lockdown, the interviews were conducted online using social media. Specifically, the interviews were conducted through video calls on Facebook and WhatsApp. This approach was based on assertions in the literature (e.g. Drabble et al., 2016; Janghorban et al., 2014) which establish the usefulness of online interviews as a means of gathering research data due to constraints in physical mobility. Also, the inhibition that comes with online interviews was mitigated because the researcher had established familiarity, rapport, and trust with the young adults during participant recruitment and the first phase of the study, conducted physically in early March 2020 before lockdown. The researcher provided each of the 19 participants with data bundles, which covered costs of internet connectivity. Research and ethics approval processes were completed, which included obtaining written and verbal consent from each respondent after providing detailed information about the research project.

The analysis and discussion presented here are based on thematic coding of the transcripts of the recordings from the interviews. Pseudonyms are used in the presentation of the data, because participants were guaranteed anonymity to create an avenue where they would be able to speak as freely as possible and provide detailed narratives.

Online Communication and Engagements via Social Media Before the COVID-19 Outbreak

During participants' selection process and each of the interview sessions, the young adults enlisted for the study were asked if and how they participated in political processes and general communication about the Nigerian polity. These and other similar follow-up questions were asked with the aim of bringing to the fore the extent of their civic engagement and communication and their understandings about these processes prior to the outbreak of COVID-19 and the subsequent lockdown. The detailed narratives provided by participants suggest that social media has been an integral part of their everyday actions and activities prior to the outbreak of COVID-19. Social media platforms, particularly Facebook, Twitter, and WhatsApp were referred to as key sources for receiving, sharing, and discussing news and other key information.

> Even before this COVID lockdown I've always found social media very useful because I am able to follow latest news and analysis through the apps. Facebook, for me, is a way to not just check what is trending in fashion and entertainment but also to see what is going on in the political space and in the country generally . . . on my FB and twitter I am able to chat about news with friends and put my views out there . . . For several months now, at least for over a year, I have been following *Tribune's* FB and twitter pages on my phone and I am able to easily share my perspective about different stuff and also interact with others.
> (Vic from Ajegunle; interview 6)

This excerpt illustrates that participants do not use social media to only socialise and get updates about entertainment and fashion. They also find the platforms useful for gathering news and relevant information about the Nigerian state and the political process in the country and for sharing their views and opinions. A useful lens for understanding this is provided by the theorising about social media as a sphere and realm of social life where citizens deliberate and make known their opinions and views about topical issues in the state.

Narratives provided by participants during the interview sessions also suggest that in their bid to conveniently participate in online conversations and debates about the Nigerian state and follow entertainment trends and stories, they prioritised owning smartphones over cheaper models that could not access social media. As is demonstrated by the previous excerpt – which references the *Nigerian Tribune*, a notable daily newspaper in the country –

these young adults make reference to social media channels of traditional (print and broadcast) media they follow on their smartphones as sources of some of the information they continuously access through their social media accounts. This highlights the unique and central position held by social media as a conduit for content from traditional media outlets. Also, this aligns with relevant studies (for instance, Larson, 2018; Willems, 2020) that have highlighted how the affordances of social media on smartphones continue to create a confluence of interactivity, immediacy, and intimacy which have aided the self-expression of people who were previously passive and transformed them into active audiences. This helps to understand the desire of this set of young Nigerians to always own a smartphone and stay active on social media, a sentiment strongly expressed during the interviews despite several complaints about financial challenges. Considering the cost implications of continuous and reliable internet connectivity, further questions were asked in an attempt to bring to the fore their thought processes and understandings about their communication and civic engagement online.

> Way before COVID, the only safe way that I've always known and used as a reasonable attempt to exchange ideas and discuss with those I don't stand a chance of meeting physically about nation building and about what is going on in Nigeria is through online conversations which I am able to do on my social media account. That, plus the entertainment aspect of social media, are major reasons why I always try to get internet access and stay online, even though it's super expensive to stay connected with my low-paying hustles. . . . At least being able to join major conversations on social media is something, since the popular media houses are not even accessible and are not ready to pay serious attention to our views and concerns . . . I'm open to ideas on how else to take up one's right to communicate and speak up without getting injured, kidnapped or even killed.
> (Anslem from Ajegunle; interview 3)

> Staying connected is certainly not cheap but you see those Twitter chats are not to be missed, especially those about Nigerian politics and sports. . . . That I even get to relate with others, share my concerns and views and just chat generally without getting waylaid and harmed is a big deal. The whole area is already unsafe so those chats are just like good and safe outlets where I can get heard.
> (Nne from Amukoko; interview 12)

These excerpts, among several other narratives from the interview transcripts, bring to the fore participants' understanding that online conversations through social media offer them a "safe way" to exchange ideas and discuss nation building[1] and the Nigerian state, thereby exercising their rights as citizens. This and other forms of interactivity and socialising – like uploading videos, posting photos and comments, and other forms of social media engagement or behaviour – were provided as key reasons why they prioritise maintaining paid access to the internet and being able to reach out, and to receive communication, at all times through their social media accounts.

The reference in the previous quotes to self-expression via social media as a "safe way" to exchange ideas and communicate views and opinions about nation building and the Nigerian state was also alluded to by other participants.

> Maybe I'm being too fearful, but I surely do not agree that it is safe to participate in peaceful protests or political meetings. . . . I would rather express myself on Twitter or Facebook. That's a safe zone for me. Physical chats about Nigerian politics must be behind closed doors and with only close friends and family. . . . Politicians only support stuff they can use for their selfish propaganda and even the big media houses would rather support these politicians rather than support our cause.
> (Ola from Amukoko; interview 13)

> I personally know of four persons around here that were recently harassed and seriously beaten up just because of their political views. The case was reported but it was not attended to. Speaking up at public meetings about the current state of the country is just not safe and to me it is a big risk. It is better to keep it on social media, at least that is what I do.
> (Seth from Ajegunle; interview 5)

While citizens from other demographic groupings might have divergent opinions depending on their vantage points, these young adults – based on their lived experiences – express dissatisfaction with the political office-holders in the country and say they only feel comfortable expressing their views online through social media engagements. They cited several instances of human rights violation, corruption, and the continued abuse of other democratic principles and values that they have witnessed over the years in their impoverished communities as reasons for their dissatisfaction with the political office holders. It is against this background of mistrust of political office-holders that they insist they prefer to communicate and engage online via social media with government officials than in-person through meetings and other fora. Peaceful protests and other similar engagements, they argue, never yield desired results and most times lead to chaos and threat to life. This is what the young adult (Anslem) earlier quoted is referring to, when he mentions that he is "open to ideas on how else to take up one's right to communicate and speak up without getting injured, kidnapped or even killed".

The position of these young adults can be further understood by looking at several citizens who have either lost their lives or ended up wounded during in-person civic engagements in Nigeria. Examples include meetings and rallies organised by civil society in 2012 in protest against the soaring increase in fuel prices and those organised by Nigerian youths in 2020 against police brutality. These events led to loss of lives and many injuries due to the government's intolerance and use of force to silence citizens' voices and agitations (Loomis, 2012; Obiezu, 2021). Kidnappings for political and economic ends that have become commonplace in Nigeria also provide useful insights into the stance of these youths. Now known as one of the kidnapping hotspots in the world, over 2,500 citizens were reported kidnapped in Nigeria in 2020 (Okoli, 2022; Gbadamosi, 2022).

Also evident in the transcripts from the interview sessions is the stance of study participants that many journalists in the traditional media rarely produce news bulletins and in-depth reports that bring their voices of dissatisfaction and mistrust for Nigeria's political class to the fore. They maintained this stance affirming that they see the news reports from the mainstream media via their social media platforms. This is the understanding of the participant who, as earlier quoted, says that "being able to join major conversations on social media is something, since the popular media houses are not even accessible and are not ready to pay serious attention to our views and concerns". The word "our" in this context refers to subalterns from low-income communities like Ajegunle and Amukoko who, save for their access to the digital public sphere, feel marginalised, unrepresented, and excluded from the critical communications going on at all levels in Nigeria's democratic state. In line with the theoretical framings outlined earlier, these young Nigerians' use of social media helps them to exercise the right to communicate – despite their lived experiences of unrecognition and marginalisation, alongside the monopoly on media reportage, production, and dissemination by state and traditional print and broadcast institutions.

Online Communication and Engagements via Social Media During the COVID-19 Lockdown

It is within the context of the earlier analysis and discussion that participants complain about their inability to maintain paid access to the internet during COVID-19 lockdown, due to their low-paying jobs and – for the participants who had lost their jobs – unemployment. As a result of lockdown regulations enforced by the government, eight of the 19 young adults complained that their salaries and allowances which even ordinarily were inadequate to meet their daily needs had been either stopped or reduced by almost half while the other 11 complained of job loss.

> Can you imagine being under this boring lockdown and not able to even know what's going on around the country, since there's no money to subscribe and connect to the internet, and as per the usual thing there's no electricity so the boredom is just something crazy . . . The

lockdown was supposed to be two weeks and now they've extended it again. The small job I'm surviving on only pays based on the number of hours I work and now because of the lockdown there's no way to go out to hustle, and with no savings there's no hope of internet connection . . . In this case, how can I even chat online and discuss with people when the simple way I do that is no longer possible . . . so those from rich and wealthy backgrounds can maintain regular access to the internet and use their Twitter, Facebook and other social media to connect, communicate and generally socialise, but we the poor people do not have a right to that even though we are also citizens, or maybe we are no longer citizens during this lockdown.

(Aduks from Amukoko; interview 17)

This quotation exemplifies participants' feelings of exclusion from the digital public sphere during the lockdown, having been accustomed to using social media as a "safe way" to express the right to communicate and deliberate with other netizens. This again brings to the fore the challenge of access to internet connectivity and unequal communicative power relations, despite the evolving expressions of citizens' rights to communicate in the context of digitality – which is not just evidenced in the literature but has also been demonstrated in the case of this study's participants. The inability of study participants to access the internet and express themselves during the lockdown reinforced their socio-economic realities. This led to these youths comparing their experiences with those of other Nigerians with better living conditions and finances that could sustain unlimited internet access irrespective of COVID-19 lockdown. This is evident in the aforementioned excerpt, where the participant – in comparing herself with other citizens on the upper end of the social scale – refers to herself and others in her socio-economic strata as poor people who do not have rights to regular internet access. This excerpt and several other narratives in the transcripts from the interviews suggest that citizens' inability to maintain their continued participation in the digital public sphere during severe situations like the COVID-19 lockdown does not just reinforce their socio-economic realities but leads them to question their status as citizens.

Despite the reconfiguration of communicative power that social media offers, participants' lack of financial means during the lockdown made it impossible for them to benefit from this reconfiguration. This explains the palpable frustration observed during the interview sessions. The frustration was underpinned by their inability to communicate and participate in conversations via social media, as they have always done previously. For the interview participants, social media remains a "safe way" to exercise the right to communicate as citizens and speak truth to power while also being entertained by other forms of social media engagement and behaviour. This can also be understood by drawing on relevant studies which indicate that social media served as a means through which people reduced boredom and frustration during COVID-19 lockdown (Depoux et al., 2020; Akingbade, 2021).

Blaming the government for their exclusion from the digital public sphere, this study's participants expressed their anger at the political office-holders who according to them have always been insensitive to their plight; never having cared about putting palliative measures in place to help them cope with the lockdown. Also complaining that they have been exposed to severe hunger as a result of the lockdown, these youths – who are not oblivious to the marginalisation and low standard of living in their impoverished communities – interpreted their exclusion from the digital public sphere within the context of their lived experiences.

> It's not surprising that we're forced to go on an unnecessary lockdown without any meaningful attempt to make plans for our welfare. . . . Our politicians have never been concerned about our welfare in this part of the state. . . . What sense does it make if we die of hunger while trying not to die of covid. Hunger is the issue here not covid and that is what people must know. . . . But then there is no hope of getting on social media to chat as usual and discuss since the lockdown has led to me losing the job where I get money to subscribe and communicate with others.
> (Ife from Amukoko; interview 15)

Through different but similar narratives, study participants insisted that hunger is deadlier than the COVID-19 outbreak, which they say should not have warranted a total lockdown. This set of youths also affirmed that if the government had created a good environment for businesses to thrive and made it a policy to ensure the support of unemployed and underemployed youths, they could have been able to sustain their internet subscription plans during the pandemic. Further emphasising the government's failure to provide basic needs, seven of the youths specifically cited the epileptic power supply in Nigeria and asserted that a government that has failed to fix this challenge should not be expected to understand citizens' need for constant access to the internet.

> That we cannot boast of at least a steady eight-hour supply of electricity and other things that are very basic stuff in some parts of the world already say something about our political rulers. If we are lacking basic stuff how then can we even expect our selfish leaders to understand the urgent need for steady internet access and how that will help us in many ways as young Nigerians. . . . To many of these politicians, not having internet access is even a good thing to them since we won't be able to actively talk back using social media as some of us are already beginning to do quite well.
> (Fav from Ajegunle; interview 8)

> This lockdown has really brought hunger and pain to the extent that I can no longer pay for my internet subscription. . . . I really did not know how much I've been addicted to following political news and other gist on social media until this lockdown. . . . I've missed chatting about news with others on Twitter and Facebook. It's become a major part of me and now it's beginning to look like I lost a body part because that's really one of the very few things I am able to do as a naija youth and citizen living in a hood many don't really care about.
>
> (Jay from Ajegunle; interview 10)

A key highlight from participants' narratives is that their use of social media represents a core of their agency as citizens in Nigeria's democratic state. Their inability to access the digital public sphere during the COVID-19 lockdown paved the way for an overwhelming sense of unrecognition and marginalisation, which their access to the internet and social media use helped to manage and to some extent keep at bay prior to the lockdown. Even though they have always felt less of a citizen in Nigeria, their inability to exercise their agency via the digital public sphere provoked several thoughts about their rights as citizens who do not have a say in how they are governed. Querying the lockdown regulations in their impoverished communities, where physical distancing and other COVID-19 control measures remain unrealistic due to several households sharing the same communal space and bathroom facilities, they stated they would have at least shared this and other similar perspectives online if only they had been able to maintain their access to what they have come to see as a "safe space". The argument that social media serves as useful spaces to express dissent and legitimise collective lived experiences (Fenton, 2012; Choi & Cho, 2017) offers a useful lens with which this can be contextualised.

Conclusion

This chapter has demonstrated how an enlisted set of young adult Nigerians who prioritise their regular access to the internet use social media not just for entertainment but as a safe space to exercise the right to democratic self-expression and communication with other netizens. This chapter also demonstrated how this has over time become a core of their agency as citizens who do not trust their political office-holders to protect their freedom of expression and communication rights during in-person engagements. This, among several other actions targeted towards curtailing citizens' democratic rights, comes from routine violation of Nigerians' freedom to express themselves and question their elected officials about how they are governed.

Also underscored in this chapter is how study participants' continued determination to prioritise internet access, despite several constraints and challenges, became unsustainable during COVID-19 lockdown. The frustration that came with this might become more relatable looking at studies (Synovitz, 2020; Thomson & Ip, 2020) that have highlighted how different levels of lockdown regulations and severe restrictions that characterised the pandemic outbreak have been referred to as authoritarian and an evasion of democratic processes and citizens' rights. This is also understandable considering that ICTs are essential to youths' daily social and cultural engagements. However, citizens – like the participants in this study who are able to use their social media to avoid being limited to the vertical, top-down communication model that has turned many into passive and docile onlookers – have a tendency to become uneasy when they feel marginalised and excluded from the public sphere during a state-ordered lockdown.

While the findings presented in this chapter are consistent with studies which suggest that the internet, social media, and the ubiquity of smartphones – underpinned by new technologies – remain a key factor in increasing political activism, communication, and democratic citizenship in Africa, a more significant point inherent in these findings is the nexus between communication and political and socio-economic rights. Exercising communication rights via social media comes with a severe cost implication for the young Nigerians who are the focus of this study and many other citizens from similar backgrounds. Even though political communication, debates, and other agitations have been channelled through social media platforms by this study's participants due to reasons already outlined, these engagements become halted when they are under dire socio-economic pressure, such as that caused by the pandemic. This demonstrates the interdependence of communication and political and socio-economic rights and how it plays a key role in democratic expression and in the democratisation process of a developing country. It is important for civil society, activists, and other stakeholders who work to advance democratic tenets in the developing world to recognise and appreciate this reality. This also points to the need for further critical research engagements that would examine the public sphere of social media and how it is not as "public" as it might seem.

The Nigerian state holds a strategic and powerful role in ensuring citizens are not excluded from the digital public sphere. However, it is pertinent to state that the expectation for political office-holders to go beyond verbal commitment in ensuring the protection of citizens' rights to communicate via the internet does not necessarily mean free access for all citizens. As this study's participants affirmed, a government that creates a good and sustainable environment for businesses to thrive – especially those that primarily focus on ICT innovations and solutions in the developing world – goes a long way in making internet access available and affordable. Established businesses directly or indirectly contribute to making internet access affordable and available to more citizens. In line with the assertion of Oyedemi (2015), apart from the state coming up with suitable legislation that affirms citizens' rights to the internet and ICTs, the industry must be monitored through regulatory oversight that ensures citizens have cheaper and quicker internet access. The oversight should include actionable plans that ensure households at the lower end of the economic scale are provided with subsidies.

However, all these technocratic interventions remain impossible if core principles that underlie citizens' rights to free and democratic participation are not respected by political office holders. Democracy in developing states like Nigeria cannot be effectively nurtured to maturation if these political office-holders and others at the helm of affairs at all levels of governance fail to understand that communication rights are not being advocated for just because they are good in and of themselves. Rather, they are being advocated for because they serve a major purpose in advancing democracy. The banning of Twitter by the Nigerian government alongside other clampdowns through vague hate speech bills indicates a loss of perspective on how communication rights serve democracy. This comes off as an excuse by political office-holders to tip the delicate balance between combatting fake news and upholding citizens' communication rights in favour of unaccountable governance.

Note

1 Nation building, from the understanding of the participant cited and also as alluded to by others during the interview sessions, refers to sincere communications, debates, and engagements that contribute to the betterment of Nigeria and her citizenry and not just the betterment of a group of people in the country.

References

Adams, W. (2015). Conducting semi-structured interviews. In K. E. Newcomer, H. P. Hatry and J. S. Wholey (Eds.), *Handbook of Practical Program Evaluation* (pp. 492–505). San Francisco: Jossey-Bass.

Agbola, T., and Agunbiade, E. (2009). Urbanization, slum development and security of tenure: The challenges of meeting millennium development goal 7 in Metropolitan Lagos, Nigeria. In A. de Sherbiniin, A. Rahman, A. Barbieri, J. Fotso and Y. Zhu (Eds.), *Urban Population-Environment Dynamics in the Developing World: Case Studies and Lessons Learned* (pp. 77–106). Paris: Workshop Report by the Committee for International Cooperation in National Research in Demography.

Akinfemisoye, M. (2013). Challenging hegemonic media practices: Of 'alternative' media and Nigeria's democracy. *African Journalism Studies*, 34(1), 7–20.

Akingbade, O. (2021). Social media use, disbelief and (mis)information during a pandemic: An examination of young adult Nigerians' interactions with COVID-19 public health messaging. *African Journal of Information and Communication (AJIC)*, 28, 1–18.

Akpojivi, U. (2018). *Media Reforms and Democratization in Emerging Democracies of Sub-Saharan Africa*. London: Palgrave Macmillan.

Bruns, A., and Highfield, T. (2016). Is habermas on Twitter? Social media and the public sphere. In G. Enli, A. Bruns, A. O. Larsson, E. Skogerbo and C. Christensen (Eds.), *The Routledge Companion to Social Media and Politics* (pp. 56–73). London: Routledge.

Calhoun, C. (1996). Introduction: Habermas and the public sphere. In C. Calhoun (Ed.), *Habermas and the Public Sphere. Studies in Contemporary German Social thought* (pp. 1–50). Cambridge, MA: The MIT Press.

Castells, M. (2011). A network theory of power. *International Journal of Communication*, 5, 773–787.

Choi, S. Y., and Cho, Y. (2017). Generating counter-public spheres through social media: Two social movements in neoliberalised South Korea. *Javnost-The Public*, 24(1), 15–33.

Crossley, N., and Roberts, J. M. (2004). *After Habermas: New Perspectives on the Public Sphere* (Sociological Review Monograph). Oxford and Malden, MA: Blackwell Pub.

Dare, S. (2007). *Guerilla Journalism: Dispatches from the Underground*. Ibadan: Kraft Books Limited.

Dare, S. (2011). The rise of citizen journalism in Nigeria – A case study of sahara reporters. *Reuters Institute*. Accessed on September 26, 2021. https://reutersinstitute.politics.ox.ac.uk/our-research/rise-citizen-journalism-nigeria-case-study-sahara-reporters.

DataReportal. (2023, February 13). Digital 2023: Nigeria. Accessed on April 30, 2023. https://datareportal.com/reports/digital-2023-nigeria.

Depoux, A., Martin, S., Karafillakis, E., Preet, R., Wilder-Smith, A., and Larson, H. (2020). The pandemic of social media panic travels faster than the COVID-19 outbreak. *Journal of Travel Medicine*, 27(3), 1–2. https://doi.org/10.1093/jtm/taaa031.

Drabble, L., Trocki, K. F., Salcedo, B., Walker, P. C., and Korcha, R. A. (2016). Conducting qualitative interviews by telephone: Lessons learned from a study of alcohol use among sexual minority and heterosexual women. *Qualitative Social Work*, 15(1), 118–133. https://doi.org/10.1177/1473325015585613.

Ewang, A. (2019, June 28). Nigeria's wavering commitment to freedom of expression. *Human Rights Watch*. Accessed on May 22, 2022. www.hrw.org/news/2019/06/28/nigerias-wavering-commitment-freedom-expression.

Fenton, N. (2012). The internet and social networking. In J. Curran, N. Fenton and D. Freedman (Eds.), *Misunderstanding the Internet*. New York: Routledge.

Frankfurter, Z. J., Kokoszka, K., Newhouse, D. L., Silwal, A. R., and Tian, S. (2020). Measuring internet in access in Sub-Saharan Africa (SSA). *World Bank Group Report*. Accessed on May 26, 2022. https://openknowledge.worldbank.org/bitstream/handle/10986/34302/Measuring-Internet-in-Access-in-Sub-Saharan-Africa-SSA.pdf?sequence=1/.

Fraser, N. (1990). Rethinking the public sphere: A contribution to the critique of actually existing democracy. *Social Text*, 25/26, 56–80. https://doi.org/10.2307/466240.

Garnham, N. (2007). Habermas and the public sphere. *Global Media and Communication*, 3(2), 201–214.

Gbadamosi, N. (2022, May 4). Can nigeria ever end its kidnap-for-ransom industry? *Foreign Policy*. Accessed on May 29, 2022. https://foreignpolicy.com/2022/05/04/nigeria-kidnapping-abduction-law-security/.

Habermas, J. (1974). The public sphere: An encyclopedia article (1964). *New German Critique*, 3, 49–55.

Habermas, J. (1989). *The Structural Transformation of the Public Sphere*, trans. Thomas Burger. Cambridge, MA: MIT Press.

Hamelink, C., and Hoffman, J. (2008). The state of the right to communicate. *Global Media Journal*, 7(13), 1–16.

Jackson, S. J., and Foucault Welles, B. (2015). Hijacking #myNYPD: Social media dissent and networked counterpublics. *Journal of Communication*, 65(6), 932–952.

Janghorban, R., Roudsari, R. L., and Taghipour, A. (2014). Skype interviewing: The new generation of online synchronous interview in qualitative research. *International Journal of Qualitative Studies on Health and Well-being*, 9(1), 1–3. https://doi.org/10.3402/qhw.v9.24152.

Järvinen, J., Tollinen, A., Karjaluoto, H., and Jayawardhena, C. (2012). Digital and social media marketing usage in B2B industrial section. *Marketing Management Journal*, 22(2), 102–117.

Kannan, K., and Hongshuang, A. (2017). Digital marketing: A framework, review and research agenda. *International Journal of Research in Marketing*, 34(1), 22–45. https://doi.org/10.1016/j.ijresmar.2016.11.006.

Kperogi, F. A. (2012). The evolution and challenges of online journalism in nigeria. In E. Siapera and A. Veglis (Eds.), *The Handbook of Global Online Journalism* (pp. 445–461). Oxford: Wiley-Blackwell.

Kperogi, F. A. (2018). Networked social journalism: Media, citizen participation and democracy in Nigeria. In B. Mutsvairo (Ed.), *Participatory Politics and Citizen Journalism in a Networked Africa* (pp. 19–33). Houndmills: Palgrave Macmillan.

Kperogi, F. A. (2020). *Nigeria's Digital Diaspora: Citizen Media, Democracy, and Participation*. Rochester: University of Rochester Press.

Kravets, D. (2011, June 3). U.N. Report declares internet access a human right. *WIRED*. Accessed on March 11, 2022. www.wired.com/2011/06/internet-a-human-right/.

Larson, H. J. (2018). The biggest pandemic risk? Viral misinformation. *Nature*, 562(7726), 309–310. https://doi.org/10.1038/d41586-018-07034-4

Loomis, N. (2012, January 08). 3 killed as nigerians strike against end of fuel subsidy. *VOA News*. Accessed on March 14, 2022. www.voanews.com/a/nigerians-strike-against-end-of-fuel-subsidy-136941073/150481.html.

Mare, A. (2016). Baba Jukwa and the digital repertoires of connective action in a 'Competitive Authoritarian Regime': The case of Zimbabwe. In B. Mutsvairo (Ed.), *Digital Activism in Social Media Era: Critical Reflections on Emerging Trends in Sub-Saharan Africa* (pp. 45–68). Houndmills: Palgrave MacMillan.

Melanson, M. (2010, July 1). Life, liberty & broadband access: Finland makes internet a right. *New York Times*. Accessed on March 16, 2022. https://archive.nytimes.com/www.nytimes.com/external/readwriteweb/2010/07/01/01readwriteweb-life-liberty – broadband-access-finland-make-80005.html.

Musiani, F., Pava, E., and Padovani, C. (2009) Investigating evolving discourses on human rights in the digital age: Emerging norms and policy challenges. *International Association for Media and Communication Research (IAMCR); Annual Congress on Human Rights and Communication*, July, Mexico, pp. 359–378. Accessed on March 19, 2022. https://hal-mines-paristech.archives-ouvertes.fr/hal-00448231/document.

Mutsvairo, B. (2016). Dovetailing desires for democracy with new ICTs' potentiality as platform for activism. In B. Mutsvairo (Ed.), *Digital Activism in the Social Media Era: Critical Reflections on Emerging Trends in Sub-Saharan Africa* (pp. 3–25). Houndmills: Palgrave Macmillan.

Obiezu, T. (2021, October 21). Nigerian protesters against police brutality demand justice a year later. *VOA News*. Accessed on January 19, 2022. www.voanews.com/a/nigerian-protesters-against-police-brutality-demand-justice-a-year-later/6279700.html.

Okoli, A. C. (2022, June 17). Who's at risk of being kidnapped in Nigeria? *The Conversation*. Accessed on July 19, 2022. https://theconversation.com/whos-at-risk-of-being-kidnapped-in-nigeria-184217#:~:text=Nigeria%20ranks%20among%20the%20kidnapping,has%20been%20reported%20as%20571.

Olajide, O. (2010). Urban poverty and environmental conditions in informal settlements of Ajegunle, Lagos Nigeria. In M. Schrenk, V. Popovich and P. Zeile (Eds.), *Cities for Everyone. Liveable, Healthy, Prosperous* (pp. 827–836). REAL CORP 2010 Proceedings/Tagungsband Vienna.

Olaniran, S. (2014). Social media and changing communication patterns among students: An analysis of Twitter use by University of Jos students. *Covenant Journal of Communication (CJOC)*, 2(1), 40–60.

Olaniyan, A., and Akpojivi, U. (2021). Transforming communication, social media, counter-hegemony and the struggle for the soul of Nigeria. *Information, Communication & Society*, 24(3), 422–437.

Onyegbula, E. (2015). Amukoko residents cry for help over activities of hoodlums. *Vanguard News Report*. Accessed on July 21, 2022. www.vanguardngr.com/2015/12/amukoko-residents-cry-for-help-over-activities-of-hoodlums/.

Oyedemi, T. (2015). Internet access as citizen's right? Citizenship in the digital age. *Citizenship Studies*, 19(3–4), 450–464.

Patton, M. Q. (1990). *Qualitative Evaluation and Research Methods* (2nd ed.). Newbury Park, CA: Sage.

Shirky, C. (2011). The political power of social media: Technology, the public sphere, and political change. *Foreign Affairs*, 90(1), 28–41.

Smith, J. A., Flower, P., Tindall, L., and Larkin, M. (2009). Interpretative phenomenological analysis: Theory, method and research. *Qualitative Research in Psychology*, 6(4), 346–347.

Synovitz, R. (2020, December 30). COVID-19 crackdowns, expanded authoritarianism, and the post-pandemic world. *Radio Free Europe/Radio Liberty*. Accessed on March 2, 2022. www.rferl.org/a/authoritarianism-crackdowns-covid-human-rights-coronavirus/31026181.html.

Thomson, S., and Ip, E. C. (2020). COVID-19 emergency measures and the impending authoritarian pandemic. *Journal of Law and the Biosciences*, 7(1), 1–33.

Uwalaka, T., and Watkins, J. (2018). "Social media as the fifth estate in Nigeria: An analysis of the 2012 occupy nigeria protest." *African Journalism Studies*, 39(4), 22–41.

Wasserman, H. (2011). Mobile phones, popular media, and everyday African democracy: Transmissions and transgressions. *Popular Communication*, 9(2), 146–158. https://doi.org/10.1080/15405702.2011.562097.

Willems, W. (2020). Beyond platform-centrism and digital universalism: The relational affordances of mobile social media publics. *Information, Communication & Society*, 24(12), 1–17. https://doi.org/10.1080/1369118X.2020.1718177.

Part II
Digital Citizenship

5 *Cabo Delgado Também é Moçambique*
The Paths of Youth Digital Activism in a Restrictive Context

Dércio Tsandzana

Introduction

Mozambique has low levels of Internet access (21%; Hootsuite, 2023) – which increases social inequalities in the use of virtual spaces and amplifies the "digital divide" (Vassilakopoulou, 2021) in the country. This situation has also an impact on how digital rights are enforced in the country. This chapter examines the activities of a civic movement called *Cabo Delgado Também é Moçambique* (Cabo Delgado is also Mozambique) that, through digital and communication platforms, managed to mobilise young people for a national cause regarding terrorism in Mozambique. It is important to note that over the past few years, different youth initiatives have flourished in Mozambique which tend to use the digital space as tools for political discussion, especially in urban spaces (Tsandzana, 2018). However, replicating and expanding these initiatives throughout digital media remain a challenge.

The choice of studying this movement is motivated by the need to understand how digital platforms are used to promote different rights such as political participation and civic engagement in Mozambique. In fact, as United Nations Human Rights Council report noted in 2011, because of "the transformative nature of the digital technologies" access to these technologies and the ability to use them effectively should be seen as "an indispensable tool for realizing a range of human rights". The debate has centred on trying to understand to what extent the Internet can become a human right and what is its weight in the face of other fundamental rights without which human beings cannot live. It is a controversial debate, if we consider that many people on the continent still lack Internet access and infrastructures. Considering that perspective, we can conclude that Mozambique is very far from making Internet access as a human right.

The subject we address in this chapter is not at all new, as some scholars have demonstrated that the "flourishing of social media and digital technologies over the past decade and a half has had considerable impacts on all aspects of society, including in the area of activism" (O'Brien, 2021: 1). To demonstrate this reality, digital spaces have been transforming not only how information is transmitted but also what impact that communication

DOI: 10.4324/9781003388289-8

has on youth engagement, including in contexts like Mozambique. At the same time, there has also been resistance and criticism that the technologies can also be used to police and prevent certain voices, reinforcing existing hierarchies, digital surveillance, and strengthening power structures (Morozov, 2011). In the case of Mozambique, there is evidence that the digital rights of citizens are not respected by the political authorities (Tsandzana, 2020). For example, almost every mobilisation organised through social networks has been threatened and suppressed by the police, as was the case of the failed demonstration in July 2022 against the price of transport and fuel in Maputo.

Some researchers point out the impact of digital and online activism, to emphasise that although there is some relationship between virtual and offline activism, it cannot be assumed that digital platforms are synonymous with political engagement (Brimacombe et al., 2018). In general, there is a wide-ranging debate on the role of young people in the political arena around the world (Cammaerts et al., 2014). There is the idea that young people have evolved to an informal dimension where politics has come to be seen as synonymous with activism or the use of digital platforms as a primary solution. Some scholars argue that there is a "youth deficit" implying that adults need to socialise and politicise young people (Earl et al., 2017).

The main argument is that virtual digital platforms have not only transformed the way young people get involved in politics but have also brought "new arenas" of political engagement that no longer pass uniquely through the formal dimension such as political parties but also through informal mechanisms such as boycotts, occupations, or public demonstrations in social movement (Terren & Soler-i-Martí, 2021). In countries where young people are considered the demographic majority like Mozambique, there is the general belief that this population is the driving force behind many initiatives that seek to use the power of the digital space as an important tool (Honwana, 2014). However, this reality is often not easy, as the exercise of digital rights is often inhibited by violations on the part of political authorities or lack of conditions to have digital access in contexts where Internet affordability is still a challenge. Considering this atmosphere, I interpret as restrictive context an environment where the enjoyment of fundamental rights, such as the right to information and association, is prevented by the country's political actors and security forces.

This chapter is divided into seven sections. The first section, which is the introduction, addresses the general discussion around digital rights, youth, and social movements. The second section introduces the literature on digital rights. The third section discusses the emergence of digital rights in the global space. The fourth section addresses the context of digital rights in Mozambique. The fifth and sixth sections discuss the case study on Mozambique, and the last section gives an overall conclusion and proposals for future research.

The State of Art About Digital Rights: Definition and Controversies

Digital rights are a set of universal human rights that ensures everybody – regardless of their gender, age, race, sexuality, and more – has equal access to an open Internet that is governed in an inclusive, accountable, and transparent manner to ensure peoples' fundamental freedoms and rights.
(APC – Association for Progressive Communications, 2020)

What are digital rights? How do they work? Who protects them and how to use them? These are questions that the literature for years has tried to answer but without success (Pangrazio & Sefton-Green, 2021). The term digital has been linked with virtual or everything that is not in physical space. Equally, it is understood as having to do with our actions as users of digital platforms, containing questions about privacy, open data, or protection and security. For this chapter, the intention is not necessarily to answer what human rights are but to understand how they are operationalised in a context like Mozambique. As noted by Özkula (2021), following the Arab Spring, many publications and reports have discussed and advanced knowledge on digital activism in Africa. However, it is understood that there no consensus on its conceptual scope.

Civil society's use of social media has been a major highlight for promoting social movements and digital activism. It has been observed that civil society actors adopt digital tools to address concerns and present claims that are important to them in their context. We have observed that digital technology can enable the easy spread of information through established networks while also reaching new users and adherents on social movements. Related to this, there is an emergence of "digital rights", a notion that has recently generated several declarations, policies, and civic initiatives across the world (Karppinen et al., 2020). In general, it is known that digital rights have a long history as a mechanism to facilitate activism at the global level.

In the case of Mozambique, the low levels of connectivity and activity in the digital space seem to indicate that digital and communication rights are less present in the country. As shown by Karppinen (2020: 306), from a critical perspective,

> current debates on digital rights often fail to acknowledge that rights are not simply rules and defences against power: rights claim often emerge from civil society but can also be used as vehicles of power that encode and institutionalize specific normative ideals, relations of power, and structures of governance.

Even without consensus on its definition, digital rights are seen as a mechanism that facilitates and enables the enjoyment of other fundamental rights found in physical space. Digital technologies allow people to connect through online platforms and therefore enjoy rights such as demonstration and public association. In this chapter, digital rights are understood as mechanisms to facilitate the exercise of rights such as political participation and the right to assembly, acts which have been constantly impeded by the political power in Mozambique. Different organisations have been engaged to report violations against digital rights on the Internet. For example, KeepItOn is a campaign coordinated by Access Now and its partners. It tracks many cases of Internet shutdowns across the world.

Some scholars (Oyedemi, 2015) argue that digital rights can be considered as human rights in the Internet era. To this end, the right to have privacy and freedom of expression is seen as an extension to the achievement of inalienable rights that are described in the United Nations Universal Declaration of Human Rights (UNDHR) – putting people offline is a form of violation of these rights (UN, 2011). But to what extent is this applicable to contexts like Mozambique where basic rights like access to information and association are lacking? There are several political and civic statements that address the issue of digital rights. For example, in January 2022, the European Union (EU) Commission proposed to the European Parliament the adoption of a declaration of principles and rights that can guide the EU towards a real digital transformation in the continent.

In Africa, the adoption of the "African Declaration on Internet Rights and Freedoms" is an important achievement. As stated on its website, "The Declaration" is a Pan-African initiative to promote human rights standards and principles of openness in Internet policy formulation and implementation on the continent. However, as demonstrated in this section, much of the literature (Karppinen, 2020; Pangrazio & Sefton-Green, 2021) on digital rights has been based on contexts that are not very real for countries like Mozambique. In other words, not all countries have the same conditions to provide digital rights to their citizens, given the difficulties and insufficiency of infrastructure or capacities. Hence, the need for a more localised approach as shown in the following section. Some authors refer to this problem as "digital coloniality" (Bon et al., 2022).

Digital Divide: Global South and Digital Rights

Scholars have argued that digital rights can be considered as human rights, which enable people to freely use, access, and publish their thoughts using platforms and tools, whether mobile or fixed, as well as the use of local community spaces (Munga, 2022). Currently, it can be stated that digital rights are not at all human rights in their fullness, but they can be mechanisms that facilitate the exercise of these rights (Hutt, 2015). Given these definitions, can we consider digital rights as synonymous of freedom for countries where inequalities persist?

Some authors noted, however, that

> despite the large impact of digital technology on the lives and future of all people on the planet, many people, especially from the Global South, are not included in the debates about the future of the digital society – this inequality is a systemic problem which has roots in the real world.
> (Bon et al., 2022: 61)

There is no single solution to change this reality, but it can be argued that technical investment, digital literacy, and the improvement of Internet infrastructure and access conditions can facilitate access in the Global South.

Heeks (2022) notes that there is a trend towards a significant reduction in digital rights abuse in the Global South. There is a tendency towards digital exclusion, which means that the digital transformations that are taking place around the globe are of little benefit to those who live outside the sphere of the most technologically developed countries (Heeks, 2022). In the case of Africa, it has been shown that digital inequalities are a continuation of other types of inequalities already existing on the continent (Heeks, 2022). Thus, there is huge scope to further increase the possibility of people to connect freely and democratically in Africa – this reality is still growing in countries like Mozambique.

The diversities and inequalities of connection in various countries of the South continue to grow. Data illustrate that the debate of digital inequality in the Global South started in the first years of the 21st century, as it allowed to situate the first trends of the use of digital tools in communication and interaction between people. However, we can observe that this approach remains relevant, as it enables an understanding of why many people do not have access to the Internet, mainly connecting on computers (ITU, 2021). Some scholars (Loh & Chib, 2019) have focused their analyses on evaluating inequalities in Internet access and the digital divide.

Heeks (2022) argues that inequality related to the digital space is not new and is part of how studies on this matter have been done over time and which represents a form of domination in development studies. In addition, there is a perception that the North has perpetuated domination against the Global South, as the export of technical capacities between the two geographic spheres is limited and the South serves only as a depository for obsolete technologies. In general, the literature on digital inequality in the Global South largely argues that inequalities in terms of access to the digital space only increase the already existing social problems, marked by a lack of digital literacy, as well as a lack of support for adults to use new technological tools and a lack of attention to vulnerable groups, such as youth and women (Karakara & Osabuohien, 2021; Pal et al., 2020).

Factors like limited infrastructures, lack of electricity, cost and quality of connectivity, and legislative frameworks are contributing towards digital inequalities in many sub-Saharan Africa countries. Compared to other regions, sub-Saharan Africa has the highest Internet usage costs per gigabyte of data. This accounts for the high rates of digital divide in part permanently explained by the limited economic conditions on the African continent (Munga, 2022). The International Telecommunication Union (ITU) indicates that globally 2.9 billion people remain offline, around 37% of the world's population. In 2021, only 33% of the population was using the Internet, meaning an estimated 871 million people are not realising digital dividends in Africa (GSMA, 2021).

In the international arena, Global Voices – multilingual community of writers, translators, academics, and digital rights activists – is one of the examples that have worked to reduce digital inequalities in the Global South. There are other local initiatives that have emerged to reduce the digital divide in the South, particularly in Africa. CIPESA – in collaboration on International ICT Policy for East and Southern Africa – works to promote effective and inclusive ICT policy and practice for improved governance, livelihoods, and human rights in Africa. Paradigm Initiative – PIN – is another leading organisation on digital rights for young people. PIN works to connect underserved young Africans with digital opportunities and ensures protection of their rights. However, their dependence on funding from organisations or countries in the North makes these initiatives highly dependent and unsustainable in their actions. The situation is similar to initiatives such as Free Basics, promoted by Facebook in several African countries. These initiatives are still anchored in a purely Northern domination dimension.

Background and Context

Mozambique has been plagued by conflict for more than half a century. The country's independence was won by military conquest against Portugal in June 1975. This was followed by a civil war that ended only with the signing of a peace agreement in October 1992. However, in 2013, the country went back to moments of political tension caused by a conflict in the centre of the country, which ended with the signing of a new peace agreement in 2015 and another in 2019. This means that the country is often in a scenario of permanent peace and conflict. The latest round of conflict began in October 2017 in the northern province of Cabo Delgado.

Since 2017, the attacks by extremist groups caused more than 900,000 internally displaced people and over 3,000 deaths. Several explanations have been offered about the causes of the conflict, but most remain unverified (Chichava, 2020). Since then, there is no accurate information on the phenomenon, although there are voices claiming that the Islamic State is behind the attacks and intends to occupy the gas production areas in Mozambique. Despite these claims, neither the perpetrators nor the origins of the violence have been clearly identified (Habibe et al., 2019).

The political identity, ideology, and demands of the extremists remain unknown. However, there are indications that the extremists have some known demographic characteristics (Matsinhe & Váloi, 2019). Morier-Genoud (2020) argues that the extremists probably switched to armed jihadism in consequence to the repression it suffered from mainstream Muslim organisations, and later the Mozambican state, even if the author also suggests alternative explanations for the origin and development of the insurgency, including the insurgents' connection to the Islamic State. However, this conflict was little discussed in Mozambique, and there was the impression that the government had forgotten what was really happening in Cabo Delgado, hence the emergence of voices and social movements.

Regarding digital rights, the political tension has resulted in the failure of the state to invest in communication infrastructure or regulate communicative infrastructure promoting censorship as a way of combatting the attacks and the implications on communicative rights in Mozambique. Even if there are no cases of Internet shutdown, the revision of the Press Law has caused much controversy. It has been developed without sufficient stakeholder input and includes provisions that many feel will be used against the media, offline and online. Some local voices also have noted that this is also not an appropriate moment to approve that law due to the risks of it being used to censor and intimidate the media while the country is facing insecurity in northern Mozambique (Tsandzana, 2022).

Methodology

This chapter aims to describe the actions that have been carried out by a youth movement called *Cabo Delgado Também é Moçambqiue*. We intend to understand how digital platforms were used to promote communication and mobilisation as part of the exercise of digital rights in Mozambique, describing actions that have been carried out by this movement in the country. Between October and November 2022, a total of 14 individuals participated in semi-structured interviews, which were structured around the following research questions: (a) For what purposes do activist practitioners use the digital space in Mozambique? (b) How were digital tools used to promote social mobilisation? (c) What are the challenges, limitations, and risks associated with digital activism in Mozambique?

Using WhatsApp calls, the discussions were audio-recorded, transcribed, and analysed for key themes that emerged. It includes "media and activism"; "social media and citizenship" and "social movements", and the Internet. The individuals are linked to the movement, mainly the managers (4) and activists (10). I have also collected data from digital platforms – nethnography (Kozinets, 2016) or "digital ethnography" (Dawson, 2019) used by the movement to promote the actions carried out between 2019 and 2021. Ethnography of the Internet is used as a practice in which the study of reality is done using digital tools (blogs, forums, vlogs, or chat spaces) to understand the dynamics of everyday life and its relationship between online and offline. The digital ethnography consisted of following a few publications made on the movement's Facebook page to capture the interactions throughout that period.

The selection of the interviewees followed a strategy based on the civic profile and history of the participants in the activist movement, based on their participation via the digital space in promoting the activities of the movement. The choice of the period was informed by the fact that it was during this interval that most of the activities of the activist movement had the greatest impact, coinciding at the same time with the greatest expansion of terrorism in Mozambique. The identity of the interviewees is not revealed, only pseudonyms and initials are used. The majority of the participants (14) are residents of the city of Maputo since the movement was born and became known from the capital city, but three of them are from other provinces (1 from Gaza in the South and 2 from Cabo Delgado in the North), aged between 18 and 35 years.

The Digital Landscape in Mozambique

Data indicate that there were 6.92 million Internet users (21%) in Mozambique in January 2023. Hootsuite's (2023) analysis indicates that Internet users in Mozambique increased by 848,000 (+14.0%) between 2022 and 2023. For perspective, these user figures reveal that 26.50 million people in Mozambique did not use the Internet at the start of 2023, meaning that 79% of the population remained offline at the beginning of the year. Sources from Hootsuite (2023) also noted that issues relating to COVID-19 continue to impact research into Internet adoption, so actual Internet user figures in Mozambique may be higher than these published numbers suggest (Figures 5.1 and 5.2).

In general, the use of the Internet in Mozambique is a challenge, as shown by data from Hootsuite (2023). It represents 21% (7 million) of a population

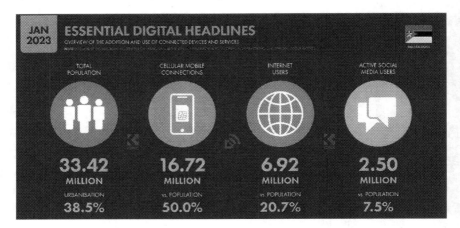

Figure 5.1 Access to the Internet in Mozambique

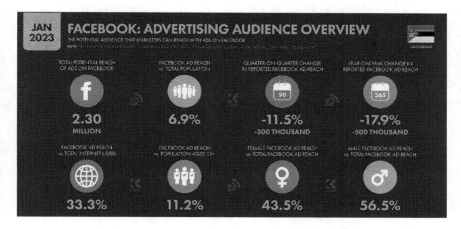

Figure 5.2 Facebook advertising audience overview

of 31 million, representing a penetration of 7.5%. Data published in Meta's advertising resources indicate that Facebook had 2.30 million users in Mozambique in early 2023. Numbers published in Twitter's advertising resources indicate that Twitter had 78,200 users in Mozambique in early 2023. This figure means that Twitter's ad reach in Mozambique was equivalent to 0.2% of the total population at the time. According to A4AI (2017), although local authorities have introduced several reforms in the technology sector, there is a need to move towards greater openness of the digital sector, allowing users easy and low-cost access, as well as improving signal provision by mobile communication and Internet providers. The same source has indicated that Mozambique has among the lowest mobile phone and Internet penetration rates, 30% and 10% respectively.

State of Digital Rights in Mozambique

The telecommunications market in Mozambique is structured in a vertical and integrated way, with three mobile communication companies and a state-owned fixed communication company (TDM) managed by the state. Of the mobile companies, Movitel and Vodacom are the best positioned, unlike the company TmCel, which is managed by the state in a loss-making way and with financial management problems. The debate about digital rights in Mozambique is new, as the country has no specific legislation on data protection or privacy, two important areas when we discuss about digital rights. However, there are other sources to understand privacy and digital obligations in Mozambique, including the Penal Code (2019); the Electronic Transactions Law (2017), and the National Cyber Security Policy and Strategy (2021).

In addition, the Constitution of the Republic of Mozambique (Government of the Republic of Mozambique, 2014 version) provides that all citizens are entitled to the protection of their private life and have the right to honour, good name, reputation, protection of their public image, and privacy. Furthermore, Article 71 of the Constitution identifies the need to legislate on access, generation, protection, and use of computerized personal data (either by public or by private entities); however, implementing legislation has not yet been approved. Article 252 of the Penal Code can be considered as fundamental to understanding digital rights in Mozambique, by mentioning the punishment of those who violate people's privacy, family intimacy using digital platforms.

Media freedom is of significant concern in Mozambique; the country was ranked 116 out of 180 countries in the Freedom of the Press and Expression Ranking published by Reporters Without Borders International in 2022. There is a big difference in connectivity between the different regions of the country – between rural and urban areas. For example, the capital Maputo has better connectivity compared to the other provinces. Problems of infrastructure and access to quality Internet services are the major challenges. As solution, the government created the Maluana Park, which is responsible for the management of e-government strategy and coordination in the technology sector in the country.

In 2021, Mozambique approved the National Cybersecurity Strategy. It aims to implement 25 projects by 2025 and establish a multi-sectoral council with a mandate to coordinate a governance framework. The government tends to include minimum cybersecurity requirements in public procurement contracts to meet minimum information and communication technology (ICT) requirements, but with the digital transition there is demand for outsourced solutions, such as encryption for network access, intrusion prevention systems (IPS), advanced persistent threat (APT), email phishing security, and cybersecurity training.

According to a report published in 2019 (RIA, 2019), Mozambique has a challenging path ahead if it is to realise the full potential of the ICT sector in developing its economy and to make progress on the ICT targets with regard to attainment of the United Nations' Sustainable Development Goals. Mozambique does not have a Data Protection Law. Equally, the country does not have a law on cybercrime, but it has a law on electronic transactions. In November 2022, the National Institute of Information and Communication Technologies (INTIC) published a proposal soliciting for comments around the new cybersecurity law, yet to be approved.

The Case Study

Started in 2017, *Cabo Delgado Também é Moçambique* (Cabo Delgado is also Mozambique) is a movement that was created by young people to defend the victims of terrorism in the northern part of Mozambique. It is composed of activists who were mobilised through social media networks to promote actions of support against the conflict taking place in Cabo Delgado. The name of the movement refers to the fact that the activists wanted to draw

Cabo Delgado Também é Moçambique 101

Figure 5.3 Illustration of the campaign "Cabo Delgado is also Mozambique"

attention to the need for the government authorities to pay more attention to what is happening in Cabo Delgado. By saying "it is also Mozambique" implies that the region was being neglected by the authorities by failing to resolve the conflict in that part of the country. The choice of black on the T-shirts also reflects a feeling of pain and distress about the situation.

> The attacks in Cabo Delgado started in 2017, but at the time the government was hiding information and they forgot that today we are in the digital space, and we can have more information. The reports only came through social media, so as a movement we decided to report what was happening in Cabo Delgado. The international community was our focus to call solidarity to the movement. It was not to challenge the Government, but to make our contribution to support victims of terrorism in Cabo Delgado.
> (Malaquias M., 9 November 2022)

The movement gained greater prominence when it began to be widely debated in the digital space, where an illustration (T-shirt, see Figure 5.3) with map of Cabo Delgado in red colours was created as a sign of the suffering the province was going through and with no response or action from the government. Given the closure of the offline civic space (Roberts, 2021a, 2021b) and lack of security for public demonstrations, the civic movement used the digital sphere as its main civic attraction – this was a form of youth activism through tools such as Facebook and WhatsApp.

Results and Discussion

Throughout the interviews, I asked three complementary questions related to the following: (1) the reasons for adopting the digital space as a tool for campaign action; (2) the profile of those who followed and participated in the campaign virtually; and (3) the obstacles faced in carrying out the virtual space campaign. Overall, there is a general idea that the virtual space has been transforming the civic actions in the country and that these platforms are indeed tools for political participation (Tsandzana, 2020). This feeling often has to do with a sense of security that the virtual space offers compared to what is experienced in the offline dimension.

> I think the virtual space is a tool for activism because the physical space is closed in Mozambique – equally the virtual space makes people more comfortable to give their opinions. People end up having more courage to speak out in the virtual arena and it's easy to get feedback. On Facebook there are more likes, and you feel that the cause can have followers.
> (Aly C., 9 November, 2022)

> Especially in contexts where civic space is under threat, such as Mozambique, digital is an alternative for human rights activists, although it is not 100% safe – virtual space reduces the risk and you can mobilise more people without many logistic difficult, especially because it requires few resources, except the cost of the Internet. It is also easy to have a support network, as well as to carry out actions without the actors being able to identify themselves.
> (Cídia C., 11 November 2022)

The idea that the virtual space is more open arises from the fact that cases of violation of civil rights such as demonstration and public mobilisation are constantly reported in Mozambique (Pereira & Forquilha, 2020). This scenario is created because there is a general idea that the political power is not open so that people can create protest movements, which is why the digital space is seen as an "escape route" or alternative tool to the physical space (Tsandzana, 2020a, 2020b). This reality reveals what is really happening if we take into account that since the movement "Cabo Delgado is also Mozambique" was in fact the only visible action and since its closure, no other similar campaign has been created in the country using the digital arena. However, this situation can be explained not only by the fact that there is a closure of the offline civic space in urban space as is the case in many countries in Africa (Mueller, 2018; Sanches, 2022) but also by the costs involved in running a virtual campaign (Internet costs) and the lack of organisational capacity.

Another aspect that was observed during the campaign was the fact that the objectives were not entirely to do with a national dimension but also to draw attention to the international stakeholders to look on Cabo Delgado (see Figure 5.4). In several interviews, it was revealed that the international community was the first to be considered, and that the best way to do this would be possible only through virtual tools such as Facebook and WhatsApp. This reveals in part the extent to which digital campaigns have a local source and perspective. In this case we are facing an example whose intention goes beyond national borders. Equally, this strategy may be similar with what the literature has revealed with regard to the way in which local campaigns

Figure 5.4 We don't want support; we just want the war to end

made on social media are a tool for international attention, especially during the Arab Spring (Wolfsfeld et al., 2013).

> It was a sensitive subject, and it was difficult to talk about terrorism on the street, so it was easy to use the digital space. We wanted to embrace young people as the main actors for our work. We also wanted to promote international attention and solidarity, because the local media was not open to helping us. We didn't plan to run a virtual campaign, it all started naturally.
> (Aly C., 9 November 2022)

Furthermore, the "Cabo Delgado is also Mozambique" campaign reveals how the movement not only raised awareness about the conflict but also served to collect financial support coming from users and donors. As shown in Figure 5.5, the movement's Facebook page shared all the steps that could be followed to send financial aid. In addition to that, the movement shared the strategies that should be used, as well as what to avoid for the success of the campaign.

> The first gain was that, since our campaign, people began to have an awareness of what was happening in Cabo Delgado. On Twitter there was a movement to understand what was happening in Cabo Delgado. We also gained financial support towards the movement, as well as more followers to our initiative.
> (Almina C., 10 November 2022)

> Our movement is really digital, our meetings were on WhatsApp because it was more dynamic. We did that campaign because we wanted

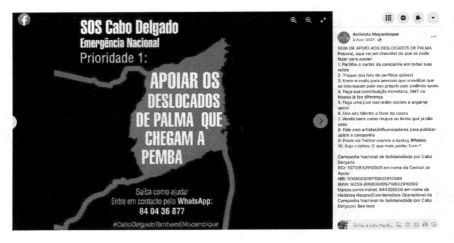

Figure 5.5 Explanation of the steps for sending campaign support and strategies for virtual action

to reach people who were outside Maputo, because it would be difficult to have logistics to implement our campaign – we would not have the same dynamics if we did our work in a physical. It is much more practical, even if our headquarters are in Maputo City – it helps us reach more people, and even outside of Mozambique we can reach people.

(Michella S., 12 November 2022)

I also wanted to understand the profile of people who supported the movement, as this element is important for capturing the sensitivity about the actors behind the campaign. Without much surprise, the result revealed that it was a movement made up mostly of urban young people who at least knew how to use a social network. This reality only reveals what the literature has explained about the predisposition of young people to use digital tools as a space for activism in urban spaces, whether in Africa (Matenda et al., 2020) or across the world (Keating & Melis, 2017). Equally, it was evident that this campaign went beyond Mozambique by including foreign actors, mostly students and non-governmental organisations.

They were activists who already had some interest in mobilising and supporting the movement, but then it extrapolated and captured more awareness over time. We also had civil society organisations, as well as representatives of other international entities.

(Hortência F., 9 November 2022)

Most of them were young people who had little access to information about Cabo Delgado – many people did not know, because the traditional media was more conservative in sharing information – people (the youth) were updated with us. We also had young people from political parties and members of civil society. We were a real channel of support and donation.

(Yuri F., 9 November 2022)

Finally, it was important to ask the activists involved what challenges they faced in carrying out their actions in the virtual space, given that as presented earlier, Mozambique has slightly limited Internet access, as well as conducting virtual campaigns is not an ongoing practice in the country. However, to our amazement, the issue of access costs was not necessarily raised as the first obstacle, as the following interviews illustrate.

There was a group of people who didn't understand our idea. We had people who criticised us because of our slogan. Some people didn't allow us to go ahead with the campaign. It was difficult to move from the virtual to the physical, some TV stations denied our approach.

(Aly C., 9 November 2022)

There was an attempt to block the campaign by people with links to the ruling party [Frelimo]. They [members of Frelimo] wanted to discredit the initiative through misinformation and publications that were not true.

(Mauro T., 10 November 2022)

The previous two quotes reveal that the public perception of the movement was not at all favourable to young people, insofar as there was a group that did not consider that action as necessary. Mentioning the resistance of the traditional media to diffuse the campaign is a synonym which reinforces the idea that the digital media is an alternative, as it may demonstrate the existence of hidden political interests in dominating the media space of television and radio. It is also interesting to understand to what extent the ruling party (Frelimo) had an impact on the campaign, by associating the promotion of misleading messages on social media networks to discredit the civic action of young people, which led to the campaign not being as successful in Cabo Delgado province.

The campaign worked through Maputo, most of the activists were in the capital – sometimes we asked for a volunteer locally (Cabo Delgado) to help us, but overall, we cannot speak of a campaign that was local, because local people did not join the cause. The slogan was seen in a negative way – people thought that it was against the Government – people were afraid to get together, it didn't have the same success that we can talk about in Maputo.

(Hadassa N., 15 November 2022)

The quote of an activist based in Cabo Delgado, the place where the campaign was intended to have an impact, reveals the minimal repercussion of virtual youth activism, which is one of the main criticisms of digital media as a mechanism of political participation. One interpretation would be that this reality is what the literature has designated as "echo chambers" (Cinelli et al., 2021), wherein Internet social networks give an impression of speaking to a wide audience while only serving to engage the same circle of actors and friends. However, we consider that Hadassa's speech may reveal that there was a "strange movement" speaking on behalf of the "host community". This fear of spreading local voices results from what is referred to in the title of this chapter as a "restrictive" or closing space for the exercise of civic and political participation by young people.

Conclusion

This chapter aimed to describe the action of a civic youth movement and its relationship with digital tools in Mozambique. With a view to understanding how the virtual space has been used as a space for activism, it was perceived that the youth digital activism has proved to be an escape from the closure that has been created at the level of physical space. It was also revealed that young people emerge as the demographic group that has the greatest interest in connecting with social causes through the Internet. In fact, the chapter suggests that even though Mozambique has registered low levels of Internet connection (23%), there is an emergence of youth digital activism that cannot be ignored, even if the civic space tends to be limited in the country.

The chapter revealed that despite the emergence of this movement "Cabo Delgado Também é Moçambique", there are still some gaps for such actions to be largely comprehensive, given the apparent lack of interest caused by the way the country is politically managed by the political forces, in particular the ruling party Frelimo. This may not only inhibit more young activists from joining the movements but may also give the impression that there is no civic action carried out by young people. I have observed the contrary reality, since not only what is political is formal and visible, but also what is informal and unconventional constitutes (new) forms of political and civic engagement.

As this chapter is practically one of the first attempts to analyse this movement or a virtual campaign, there were some limitations that can be addressed in future studies. The fact that there is little literature on Mozambique is still a barrier to be considered, as well as the fact that the Portuguese language is less highlighted in research on digital rights and activism. Equally, the little discursive culture of talking about activism on the part of young people proved to be another obstacle. From this perspective, as stated by Karppinen et al. (2020: 4), "a crucial challenge for research on digital rights is not only to help facilitate an emerging global consensus but to also clarify the concrete policy and practical implications of alternative visions and claims".

Finally, three future research options can be opened to understand the dynamics of digital rights in Mozambique: (1) from a legal point of view, there is an opportunity to discuss how Mozambique is prepared to respect citizens' digital rights in the country; (2) there is also a possibility to discuss about digital rights beyond simple Internet access, but above all its relation to human rights in contexts of conflict like Mozambique; and (3) there is a need to conduct studies that can involve other platforms like Twitter, even if the latter is not as widely used in the country as much as Facebook. All these areas should be seen in a complementary way to accurately shed deeper insights into the issue of digital rights in Mozambique.

References

A4AI. 2017, *Mozambique Affordability Report Highlights, Alliance for Affordable Internet*. https://a4ai.org/research/affordability-report-2017/. Accessed on 6 December 2022.

APC 2020, *Association for Progressive Communications, Coconet: What are Digital Rights?* https://www.apc.org/en/news/coconet-what-are-digital-rights. Accessed on 6 December 2022.

Assembly of the Republic. 2019, *Penal Code of Mozambique*. Maputo.

Bon, A., et al. 2022, 'Decolonizing technology and society: A perspective from the global south'. In Werthner, H., Prem, E., Lee, E. A., and Ghezzi, C. (eds), *Perspectives on Digital Humanism*, pp. 61–68. Berlin: Springer.

Brimacombe, T., Kant, R., Finau, G., Tarai, J., and Titifanue, J. 2018, 'A new frontier in digital activism: An exploration of digital feminism in Fiji'. *Asia & Pacific Policy Studies*, vol. 5, no. 3, pp. 508–521.

Cammaerts, B., and Anstead, N. 2014, 'The myth of youth apathy: Young europeans' critical attitudes toward democratic life'. *American Behavioral Scientist*, vol. 58, no. 5, pp. 645–664.

Chichava, S. 2020, *Os primeiros sinais do 'Al Shabaab' em Cabo Delgado: algumas histórias de Macomia e Ancuabe*. Maputo: IESE.

Cinelli, M., Morales, G., Galeazzi, A., and Starnini, M. 2021, 'The echo chamber effect on social media'. *Proceedings of the National Academy of Sciences – PNAS*, vol. 118, no. 9, pp. 1–8.

Dawson, C. 2019, *A-Z of Digital Research Methods*. London: Routledge.

Earl, J., Maher, T., and Elliott, T. 2017, 'Youth, activism, and social movements'. *Sociology Compass*, vol. 11, no. 4, pp. 1–14.

Government of the Republic of Mozambique. 2014, *Constitution of the Republic of Mozambique*. Maputo: Government Printer.

GSMA. 2021, *The State of Mobile Internet Connectivity 2021, Global System for Mobile Communications Association*. www.gsma.com/r/wp-content/uploads/2021/09/The-State-of-Mobile-Internet-Connectivity-Report-2021.pdf. Accessed on 6 December 2022.

Habibe, S., Forquilha, S., and Pereira, J. 2019, *Radicalização Islâmica no Norte de Moçambique: O Caso de Mocímboa da Praia*. Maputo: IESE.

Heeks, R., 2022, 'Digital inequality beyond the digital divide: Conceptualizing adverse digital incorporation in the Global South'. *Information Technology for Development*. vol. 28, no. 4, pp. 688704.

Honwana, A. 2014, *The Time of Youth: Work, Social Change and Politics in Africa*. Oxford: Kumarian Press.
Hootsuite. 2023, *Digital in Mozambique, Data Reportal*. https://datareportal.com/reports/digital-2023-mozambique. Accessed on 21 February 2023.
Hutt, R. 2015, What are your digital rights? *World Economic Forum*. https://www.weforum.org/agenda/2015/11/what-are-your-digital-rights-explainer/. Accessed on 6 December 2022.
ITU. 2021, *Measuring Digital Development, International Telecommunication Union*. Geneva: International Telecommunication Union.
Karakara, A., and Osabuohien, E. 2021, 'Threshold effects of ICT access and usage in Burkinabe and Ghanaian households'. *Information Technology for Development*, vol. 28, no. 3, pp. 511–531.
Karppinen, K., and Puukko, O. 2020, 'Four discourses of digital rights: Promises and problems of rights-based politics'. *Journal of Information Policy*, vol. 10, pp. 304–328.
Keating, A., and Melis, G. 2017, 'Social media and youth political engagement: Preaching to the converted or providing a new voice for youth?' *The British Journal of Politics and International Relations*, vol. 19, no. 4, pp. 877–894.
Kozinets, R. 2016, *Netnography: Redefined*. London: Sage publications.
Loh, Y. A. C., and Chib, A. 2019, 'Tackling social inequality in development: Beyond access to appropriation of ICTs for employability'. *Information Technology for Development*, vol. 25, no. 3, pp. 532–551.
Matenda, S., Naidoo, G., and Rugbeer, H. 2020, 'A study of young people's use of social media for social capital in Mthatha, Eastern Cape'. *Communitas*, vol. 25, no. 10, pp. 1–15.
Matsinhe, D., and Váloi, E. 2019, *The Genesis of Insurgency in Northern Mozambique*. Pretoria: Institute for Security Studies.
Morier-Genoud, E. 2020, 'The jihadi insurgency in Mozambique: Origins, nature and beginning'. *Journal of Eastern African Studies*, vol. 14, no. 3, pp. 396–412.
Morozov, E. 2011, *The Dark Side of Internet Freedom: The Net Delusion*. New York: Public Affairs.
Mueller, L. 2018, *Political Protest in Contemporary Africa*. Cambridge: Cambridge University Press.
Munga, J. 2022, *To Close Africa's Digital Divide, Policy Must Address the Usage Gap, Carnegie Endowment for International Peace*. https://carnegieendowment.org/2022/04/26/to-close-africa-s-digital-divide-policy-must-address-usage-gap-pub-86959. Accessed on 7 December 2022.
O'Brien, T. 2021, 'Digital activism, and the state, Tapuya: Latin American Science'. *Technology and Society*, vol. 4, no. 1, pp. 1–7.
Oyedemi, T. 2015, 'Internet access as citizen's right? Citizenship in the digital age'. *Citizenship Studies*, vol. 19, no. 3–4, pp. 450–464.
Özkula, S. 2021, 'What is digital activism anyway? Social constructions of the "digital" in contemporary activism'. *Journal of Digital Social Research*, vol. 3, no. 3, pp. 60–84.
Pal, A., et al. 2020, 'Contextual facilitators and barriers influencing the continued use of mobile payment services in a developing country: Insights from adopters in India'. *Information Technology for Development*, vol. 26, no. 2, pp. 394–420.
Pangrazio, L., and Sefton-Green, J. 2021, 'Digital rights, digital citizenship and digital literacy: What's the difference?' *Journal of New Approaches in Educational Research*, vol. 10, no. 1, pp. 15–27.

Pereira, C., and Forquilha, S. 2020, *Navigating Civic Spaces in Mozambique, Baseline Report*. Maputo: Institute for Social and Economic Studies.

RIA. 2019, *The State of ICT in Mozambique (Policy Paper 6)*. Cape Town: RIA.

Roberts, T. (ed.). 2021a, *Digital Rights in Closing Civic Space: Lessons from Ten African Countries*. Brighton: Institute of Development Studies.

Roberts, T. (ed.). 2021b, *Surveillance Law in Africa: A Review of Six Countries*. Brighton: Institute of Development Studies.

Sanches, E. (ed.). 2022, *Popular Protest, Political Opportunities, and Change in Africa*. London: Routledge.

Terren, L., and Soler-i-Martí, R. 2021, ' "Glocal" and transversal engagement in youth social movements: A twitter-based case study of Fridays for future-Barcelona'. *Frontiers in Political Science*, vol. 3, pp. 1–15.

Tsandzana, D. 2018, 'Juventude urbana e redes sociais em Moçambique: A participação política dos 'conectados desamparados". *Comunicação e Sociedade*, vol. 34, no. 2, pp. 252–265.

Tsandzana, D. 2020a, 'Country report: Mozambique'. In Singh, A., Majama, K., and Montinat, J. (eds), *The Struggle for the Realisation of the Right to Freedom of Expression in Southern Africa*, pp. 36–40. Nairobi: African Declaration on Internet Rights and Freedoms.

Tsandzana, D. 2020b, 'Redes sociais da Internet como "tubo de escape" juvenil no espaço político-urbano em Moçambique'. *Cadernos de Estudos Africanos*, vol. 40, no. 2, pp. 167–189.

Tsandzana, D. 2022, The need to strengthen a broad-based human rights movement in Mozambique. *Global Information Society Watch*, *Association for Progressive Communications*. www.giswatch.org/en/country-report/mozambique. Accessed on 6 December 2022.

United Nations Human Rights Council. 2011, *Report of the Special Rapporteur on the Promotion and Protection of the Right to Freedom of Opinion and Expression*. New York: United Nations.

Vassilakopoulou, P., and Hustad, E. 2021, 'Bridging digital divides: A literature review and research agenda for information systems research'. *Information Systems Frontiers*, pp. 1–15.

Wolfsfeld, G., Segev, E., and Sheafer, T. 2013, 'Social media and the arab spring: Politics comes first'. *The International Journal of Press/Politics*, vol. 18, no. 2, pp. 115–137.

6 Citizen Journalism and the Entrenchment of Communication Rights in Zimbabwe

Earnest Mudzengi and Wellington Gadzikwa

Introduction

Citizen journalism has been defined differently by different persuasions. From a technological determinist point of view, enmeshed in modernity and postmodernity, citizen journalism has been considered a process centred on technological tools and spaces such as the internet, the mobile phone, video cameras and other modern information and communication technologies and platforms. Benkler (2006), cited in Mutsvairo et al. (2012), conceives citizen journalism as a phenomenon of the emergency of a modern public sphere networked by digital tools such as the internet and mobile phones. Mutsvairo et al. (2012) characterise citizen journalism as that which happens when amateurs or untrained journalists engage in journalism. This definition and others that link citizen journalism to the rise of modern information and communication technologies tend to be ahistorical, considering citizen journalism's long history, predating new technologies and professional journalism itself (Hughes, 2011). Newspapers existed long before establishing the first professional journalism school at the University of Missouri in 1908, with citizen journalists at the centre of their production. The First Amendment of the American constitution was instituted long before the professionalisation of journalism, with the idea being to protect citizens who effectively practised journalism with no formal journalism training (Hughes, 2011). Journalism must not be confined to professionalism and technological determinism, which deprives it of being a public sphere platform through which citizens from across class divides are connected for communicative actions that promote and uphold the values of democracy, cultural diversity, and inclusive development. This chapter contends that citizen journalism must be open to all citizens who practise it as a function of human rights enjoyment, especially in restricted environments with limited self-expression platforms such as Zimbabwe.

The perspective for an open practice of citizen journalism is in line with the definition of citizen journalism as a citizen-centred form of journalism in which

> a citizen, or group of citizens play an active role in the process of collecting, reporting, analysing and disseminating news and information

DOI: 10.4324/9781003388289-9

with the intention of providing independent, reliable, accurate, wide-ranging and relevant information that is required for democracy and development.

(Bowman & Willis, 2003: 9)

This definition conceives citizens as active public sphere stakeholders whose participation in communication processes is key to democracy and development. This is echoed by Radsch (2013), who defines citizen journalism as an alternative and activist form of newsgathering and reporting that functions outside mainstream media institutions, often as a response to shortcomings in the professional journalistic field. What is clear from Bowman and Willis (2003) and Radsch (2013)'s definitions is that citizen journalism must be conceived from a broad, citizen-centred perspective that does not limit it to the use of new media, information and communication technologies and parochial professionalism practices driven by sectional interests, opposed to broad community needs. This resonates with Goode's (2009) conceptualisation of citizen journalism as a broad communicative practice that "is not an exclusively online phenomenon; is not confined to explicitly 'alternative' news sources, and includes 'meta journalism's well as the practices of journalism itself." The factoring of meta journalism is worth noting as it brings in a diversity of actors inside and outside "professional journalism" to contribute towards constructing, reiterating and even challenging the boundaries of acceptable journalistic practices (Carlsson, 2016). Bringing a diversity of actors into the journalistic space is necessary to ensure that journalism becomes a democratic public sphere in which citizens in different socioeconomic, cultural and political situations can enjoy socioeconomic, cultural and political rights as provided for in the Universal Declaration of Rights.

The "citizen" in citizen journalism connotes human beings who meaningfully belong to a particular polity and are entitled to enjoy the whole set of human rights. The subject–citizen debate is particularly relevant to the idea of citizen journalism practices that advance human rights in consideration of the Global South's context of coloniality, in which the configuration of citizenship has continued to be shaped in line with the socioeconomic and cultural order that was shaped by colonialism. In contrast to promoting democratic citizenship, the decentralisation of the colonial administrative system through indirect rule was a case of decentralised despotism in which traditional administrative structures were abused to submerge native Africans into subjects (Mamdani, 1996). This system has continued with African political and corporate elites being used as conduits for socio-economic, cultural and political systems that strip Global South citizens of their citizenship rights. Since the New World Information and Communication Order debates of the 1980s, the Global South has been protesting against asymmetrical global information flows that perpetuate dependency and coloniality (see, for instance, Carlsson, 2016; Obonyo, 2011; and Deloumeaux, 2022).

Information imbalances at the global level also extend to national levels, where media and communication platforms essentially serve the interest of a few at the expense of the majority. This, in Zimbabwe, is attributable to a number of factors that include mainstream media capture by the political–corporate complex (www.youtube.com/watch?v=aOVNI5cxWeE), a limiting digital divide (Mhiripiri & Mutsvairo, 2014; Mare, 2015), prohibitive data costs, unreliable communications infrastructure and economic constraints affecting both media houses and potential readers (www.techzim.co.zw/2013/10/newspaper-readership-in-zimbabwe-continues-to decline) among others. Broadcast media are largely confined to urban areas, with some border areas having to depend on neighbouring countries for broadcasting signals (Mano, 1997). These restrictions and limitations point to how mainstream media platforms are not democratic public spheres through which the broad spectra of the country's citizenry can enjoy communication rights in meaningful ways that edify democratic citizenship. With these limitations and restrictions in mainstream media, citizen journalism is seen as a communicative parallel market or alternative public sphere through which marginalised citizens can enjoy communication rights (Moyo, 2009).

As an alternative public sphere, citizen journalism should be oriented towards upholding and fostering holistic human rights enjoyment by all classes of people. Such enjoyment of human rights constitutes real democracy and inclusive development. Closely connected to this democratic imperative is the conceptualisation of citizen journalism as journalism "of the people, by the people and for the people" (Banda, 2010: 26). As Banda observes, equating citizen journalism with the people-centred definition of democracy signals the idea that this form of journalism is about democratic citizenship. Democratic citizenship, as posited by the Council of Europe (2021), pertains to greater participation, social cohesion, access, equity and solidarity. It is about inclusion rather than exclusion, participation rather than marginalisation and culture and values rather than simple procedures (such as voting). It is about actively shaping the understanding and practices of citizenship (Ibid.). These imperatives of democratic citizenship are being accorded token treatment by what is often referred to as mainstream or professional journalism, which is not living to the true meaning of a democratic public sphere characterised by diversity, inclusivity and equality.

As an alternative public sphere that embraces diverse socio-economic, cultural and political interests, citizen journalism is a vehicle through which subaltern or marginalised social groups within the Global South can engage in communicative actions that breed progressive community organising, solidarity and democratic and responsible citizenship. For this to be realised, citizen journalism must be oriented into an equalising communicative platform that effectively contributes towards transforming society from the obtaining state of elite capture to a more sustainable political and socio-economic trajectory punctuated by a cross-sectional enjoyment of socioeconomic and political rights, poverty eradication, pro-poor economic growth, environmental protection, gender justice, cross-generational sensitivity and climate justice.

These indicators of real democracy and inclusive development are outlined in the United Nations Scientific and Cultural Organization (UNESCO)'s Media Development Indicators (UNESCO, 2008). The dearth of these indicators defines the situation of coloniality in which Zimbabwe and other Global South communities are submerged. Whereas colonialism was a physical annexation in which colonising countries physically occupied the colonised countries, directly exploiting their resources and peoples, coloniality is a stealth form of domination, concealed in terms and forms of nicety that denote development, democracy and cooperation. It is a form of exploitation disguised in terms of "salvation, progress, modernisation and being good for everyone" (Mignolo, 2005: 6). Being part of the equation of coloniality, mainstream media that are compliant to the dictates of neoliberalism are portrayed in flowery liberal terms, which, instead of helping in addressing historical injustices, actually serve the purpose of sustaining systems that thrive on the continued marginalisation of subaltern social groups in the Global South. An equalising and democratising citizen journalism ought to be practised on a cross section of citizen and community media that are not only concerned with providing information, being a watchdog and paternalistically clarifying social values. They must also emphasise mobilisation and fostering enlightened and popular forms of communicative action underpinned by active and responsible citizenship (Baker & Chandler, 2004 with added emphasis).

Under category three of UNESCO's media development indicators is the imperative for media to exist as a platform for democratic discourse, with a critical role in sustaining and nurturing democracy, good governance and human rights. This obligates media to reflect and promote the socioeconomic, cultural and political positions, views, interests and concerns of all members of society, including marginalised social groups. The indicators also recognise media as a social actor endowed with orientations and qualities of addressing and redressing cases of socioeconomic inequalities, oppression and injustice. This can only be possible through citizen journalism platforms which marginalised groups can access, control and share.

To this end, and in attempting to transform Jürgen Habermas's (1962, 1989) initial public sphere conceptualisation, media must exist as a democratic public sphere through which a cross section of social groups are empowered to participate in socio-economic, cultural and political processes that promote, uphold and sustain a broad, inclusive enjoyment and exercise of human rights. Characterisation of media as a democratic public sphere marks a departure from ancient Germany and bourgeoisie public spheres that were caught up in the contextual realities of socioeconomic exploitation of enslaved people, dearth of gender parity, segregation of property rights, oligopoly capitalism, degrading working-class conditions and a racially motivated enlightenment project. Talking of a public sphere amid a perpetual prevalence of such conditions amounted to legitimising and normalising a state of permanent social exclusion in which the poor, women and other marginalised social groups are systematically relegated to the margins of political, economic, social and cultural processes. Neoliberal regimes of the contemporary era personify a scenario of institutionalised inequalities in which the state, media and other public institutions have been privatised for the selfish, monopolistic benefits of political and corporate elites.

Habermas (1989) was worried about the onset of oligopoly capitalism, more centralisation of the state, the emergence of mass media, continued class polarisation and such other factors, which he ascribed as causal factors in the disintegration of the bourgeoisie public sphere. He considered the ideal public sphere an exclusive affair typified by social exclusion. For instance, he considered competitive capitalism and free trade in the ideal public sphere not for the benefit of all but a few with mercantile and aristocratic privileges. His was a case of normalising a situation in which some lived as citizens while others were subjects within the same polity. Habermas's idea of communicative rationality, upon which communicative action must be based, has been considered illusory as it ignores unequal socioeconomic power relations in which Habermas's so-called public sphere existed. Without getting deeper into the realities of unequal power relations, such as that attendant to the bourgeoisie and the working class, Habermas's theory of communicative action based on rational argumentation tended to mask the reality of unequal social capital. Thus, Habermas's theoretical prescriptions were prone to promoting the existing socioeconomic order of inequalities as opposed to upsetting it. Where Michel Foucault perceived communication to be a reflection of pre-existing power relationships, Habermas theorised an unrealistic ideal of power-free communicative structures in which consensus could be achieved without due consideration of existing socioeconomic power inequalities. There was also an anomaly in which consensus was sought within a class binary in which a few belonging to the bourgeoisie class were the only ones who participated in the communicative space. This is reminiscent of a representative form of democracy in which a few people speak on behalf of others from a vantage point of being detached from the actual lived experiences of those being represented. This kind of representation has not ended with speaking for others but also extends to eating for others. Thus, the reality is that people get into politics for the sake of self-aggrandisement as opposed to representing the interests of the broad spectrum of citizens, including subaltern groups who live at the margins of a bourgeoisie-oriented society. This extends to mainstream media, which has been captured to become an instrument for fronting the hegemonic interests of self-centred elites. What has resulted from this is an elitist public sphere in which communicative actions are confined to the interests of a few political and corporate elites. In this configuration, subaltern social groups are stripped of citizenship to become mere consumers of information and media products that are produced and disseminated within the realm of elite interest. This has led to a situation in which there are publics that matter and those that do not matter. This calls for subaltern groups to have their public spheres rooted in their felt needs and interests. According to the framework underpinning this chapter, this can be made possible through citizen journalism.

Citizen journalism as a subaltern public sphere

Contemporary mainstream communication systems serve elite interests at the expense of marginalised groups who constitute the majority. As a subaltern public sphere, citizen journalism is conceptualised as a fallback platform through which people marginalised by elite-centred mainstream media and communication platforms can enjoy communication rights and other human rights in ways that lead to inclusive development and material satisfaction. Thus, citizen journalism must facilitate the enjoyment of communication rights by subalterns or people who are oppressed and systematically alienated from mainstream political, socioeconomic and communication activities (Mpofu, 2015). The debate (and communicative activity) within the subaltern public sphere must be robust and lead to true democratic emancipation (Papacharissi, 2004). Compared to the bourgeois public sphere that conforms to capital's exploitative dictates, citizen journalism is needed as a communicative system that disrupts and disentangles the exploitative and conformist mainstream. Citizen journalism, as seen from this perspective, liberates subaltern groups from media and communication structures that buttress and accommodate oppression. Stephansen (2016) observed that the imperative for an alternative and liberational public sphere calls for multi-pronged citizen journalism practices based on a cross section of citizen media. Such citizen media should be concerned about making public previously unreported issues and perspectives. They ought to cultivate social movement-building practices that create critical and assertive publics that assert their rights as citizens.

Citizen journalism can effectively contribute to the organisation of subaltern social groups into critical publics through community and citizen media approaches that advance active and critical participation of ordinary citizens in media production and media organisation (Bailey et al., 2008). This calls for empathetic media production and organisation systems shaped by the needs and interests of community members, especially those marginalised from mainstream socioeconomic and political processes. This is in line with a communicative pedagogical imperative in which audiences must play a central role in media and communication production processes. Citizen journalism provides citizens on the margins of mainstream media and communication systems with a platform to challenge ideological representations that perpetuate marginalisation. Through uncaptured citizen journalism, subaltern groups are empowered to showcase their everyday experiences, struggles and narratives that challenge oppression and repression. They are afforded platforms for communicative engagements that lead to community problem-solving through initiating actions and mobilisations towards the realisation of more sustainable communities (Mahamed et al., 2018). As such, citizen journalism cultivates awareness, consciousness and communicative actions that exert real democracy and development. Fuchs (2020) frames citizen journalism as a transformative form whose content and actions expose suppressed possibilities of existence, antagonisms of reality and potential for change. Insofar as it exposes antagonisms of reality, citizen journalism is rooted in the objective political. Objective politics is contrasted to subjective or partisan politics, which operates based on socioeconomic biases that disadvantage other members of society for the benefit of a privileged few. In line with imperatives about objective political and progressive pedagogy, citizen journalism must be practised in line with the ethical ethos of objectivity, fairness, independence and balance. It must not be a case of partisan activism and propaganda that derives from partisan political interests and emotions (Wall, 2019). Within this framework of ethics and independence, citizen journalism can be a transformative practice that rises above mainstream journalism's attempts to control and relegate it to the periphery (Ibid.).

Citizen journalism and social transformation of the subaltern

Being perpetually enmeshed in a multipronged crisis characterised by climate-induced disasters, resource plunder, coups, corruption, deepening poverty, gross social inequalities and other social ills, subaltern communities long for forms of journalism that contribute towards problem-solving and human rights promotion. Such forms of journalism resonate with social impact journalism, which, as pointed out by Wagemans et al. (2019); Gldensted (2015) and McIntyre (2015) is a form of journalism that is innovative, future-oriented and focused on finding solutions to problems afflicting society. It is an inclusive and active form of journalism that goes beyond mere reporting and in which journalists assume a more active role in developing and addressing events and issues being reported on. Gldensted (2015) draws parallels between social impact journalism and "constructive" journalism, which goes further than answering traditional journalism questions of "who, what, where, when, why, and what now?" In this respect, social impact journalism seeks to empower the generality of citizens, providing them with information tools and means that strengthen their belief in transformative change and facilitate their potential to bring about that change (Gldensted, 2015). Values of social impact journalism align with citizen journalism forms that accord audiences an active role in the conceptualisation and reporting of stories about their everyday experiences, fostering factors that enable individuals and societies to thrive for transformative change, characterised by a full enjoyment of human rights.

Citizen journalism is social impact journalism premised on the cause for transformative change where there are significant strides towards the full enjoyment of human rights. It is a problem-solving forum of journalism aimed at the attainment of the stage of development in which the generality of people have freedom from political, economic, ideological, epistemological and social domination installed by factors and systems such as colonialism, coloniality, authoritarianism, totalitarianism, exploitative neoliberalism and gender-based marginalisation. These are the key causal factors of problems affecting subaltern communities in the Global South. They can be resolved through an inclusive perspective of development, which entails overcoming significant obstacles to human happiness and attainment of material welfare, civil and political liberties, social peace and human security (Mkandawire, 2011; with emphasis added). As a result of media and communication systems submerged in marginalising systems of domination, most people have disengaged from the practice of active citizenship. With captured storytelling regimes that give marginalised people a sense of hopelessness, Gldensted (2015) advocates for a more active and involved form of journalism where journalists not only point out the wrongs but also show how to resolve these wrongs.

Stephansen (2016) adds that journalists must actively and objectively participate in processes wherein marginalised social groups are empowered to enjoy, exercise and assert their citizenship rights and obligations. This is achievable through relevant, appropriate and accessible media, which carry stories, conversations and communicative actions directly relevant to people's everyday experiences. As a form of social impact journalism, citizen journalism equips subaltern social groups with knowledge, skills and media advocacy scopes to deal with socioeconomic, cultural and political problems affecting their day-to-day survival. For instance, journalistic and communicative practices rooted in citizen journalism equip communities with knowledge, media advocacy tools and communicative platforms and networks that enable them to embrace climate-resilient agriculture to guarantee the enjoyment of their right to food. Citizen journalism can also yield social impact concerning poverty eradication, cultivating gender parity, sustainable environmental practices, good governance and other values of inclusive, democratic and sustainable development. Cultivating citizen agency towards resolving these and other community problems emanating from social exclusion, citizen journalism becomes a natural and democratic public sphere through which citizens in subalternism deliberate and engage in communicative actions towards their liberation.

All journalists must be citizen journalists

Contrary to the belief that citizen journalism is all about untrained amateurs who thrive on unethical practices, this chapter calls for research and practical attention to the practice of citizen journalism from the vantage point of passionate communication ethics and imperatives that include fairness, empathy, inclusivity, constructive engagement, diversity, independence and being community oriented. Due to the dearth of these values in the so-called professional journalism, there has been a clarion call for passionate communication ethics instead of emphasising professional media ethics that have become buzzwords in mainstream media (Wasserman, 2016). There should be an emphasis on passionate communication ethics that are attendant to aspired forms of citizen journalism practice. In that case, there will be a reduction in challenges such as brown envelope journalism, marginalising biases, capture, fake news and others that have resulted in trust gaps in traditional or mainstream journalism. With prospects for a more effective checking of the downsides of mainstream journalism, ethical and independent citizen journalism is the journalism for the future, and there are bright prospects in embracing it.

Journalists who, owing to poor working conditions, persistent victimisation and other restrictive conditions of service, have become part of the subaltern community embracing citizen journalism, thereby opening up possibilities for liberational communicative engagements between communities and journalists and among members of communities (Wagemans et al., 2019). Wagemans et al. (2019) further observed that subaltern communities would be empowered to engage in community-building actions that foster solidarity-based inclusiveness and diversity. Media spaces become spaces for organic community organising. They will be used to educate communities and raise their levels of consciousness concerning citizenship rights, citizenship responsibilities, and community problem-solving. From a developmental perspective, citizen journalism interventions will equip citizens with knowledge and platforms to effectively participate in policy processes at local, national and international levels. The international is included here in consideration of the globalisation of development goals and processes. Within globalisation, the benefits of rehashed citizen journalism practices will not only be felt at localised levels but also extend across the wider Global South community, ushering in potential for a global information and communication revolution in which the subaltern will be freed from the current state of repression emanating from partisan and commercialised journalistic processes. Digital and online communication tools and platforms are critical components towards the consummation of this revolutionary process as they facilitate the building of communicative networks and collaborations that push for transformative change. They must be viewed as a means to an end, not as an end in themselves, as conceived in earlier perspectives on citizen journalism.

Citizen journalism in the Zimbabwean context

The Zimbabwean landscape is characterised by a deepening capture of mainstream media (Melber et al., 2014). This applies to both government and privately controlled media. Concerning the former, the government continues to have a stranglehold over the broadcasting sector, with the Zimbabwe Broadcasting Corporation (ZBC) radio and television continuing to operate on a partisan basis in advancing the hegemonic interests of the ruling Zimbabwe African National Union-Patriotic Front (ZANU PF) party. The same is true of newspapers, radio stations and television stations under the

Zimbabwe Newspapers stable. Privately controlled media are captured by corporate interests. Being profit-oriented, privately controlled media are, to a more considerable extent, embracing an exploitative neoliberal status quo.

Zimbabwe has two privately owned national commercial radio stations, eight local commercial radio stations with provincial coverage and 20 community radio initiatives spread around the country and operating under the banner of the Zimbabwe Association of Community Radio Stations (ZACRAS). Three community radio initiatives affiliated with ZACRAS have since been licensed, and their prospects of going and remaining on air are at the mercy of donor funding. With widespread disaffection towards ZBC television programming, those who can afford it have turned to Digital Satellite Television (DSTV) provided by Multichoice Zimbabwe (https://zimfact.org/is_zimbabwe_media_serving_the_public/). This is over and above a sizeable number of licensed private newspapers, many of which are finding it difficult to operate due to economic constraints. While public anger and criticism over deteriorating socioeconomic and political conditions are often channelled, for example, through talk shows aired on private radio stations and through stories and opinion columns in newspapers, there has not been much in terms of turning words into transformative action. Existing private newspapers and radio stations do not operate as alternative communicative platforms through which actions that lead to social transformation are cultivated and organised.

This state of affairs highlights the need for a protracted and intensified practice of citizen journalism as an alternative and communicative platform through which social accountability, democracy and development can be exerted. As the Zimbabwean situation stands, citizen journalism is episodic, uncoordinated, personalised and fragmented.

The practice of citizen journalism by individuals

Considering the context in which the capture, privatisation and monopolisation of media and other public sphere institutions are submerging the majority of people into subjects without communicative liberties and other citizenship rights, effective practice of citizen journalism by individual citizens is an ideal that is aspired for in the interest of active, responsible and progressive citizenship in Zimbabwe. A vision for citizen journalism complemented by transformative citizen agency was conceptualised by Moyo (2009) in his analysis of the political communication situation surrounding Zimbabwe's 2008 harmonised elections. As the Zimbabwe Electoral Commission (ZEC) withheld the announcement of the presidential election results, and with mainstream media constrained to provide credible information as to what was going on, citizens resorted to their sources of information through the use of the mobile phone-based Short Message Service (SMS) and weblogs to exchange information on what was happening with respect to the inordinate delay in releasing the election results. Moyo (2009) argues that the exchange and circulation of information by citizens immensely contributed to national public opinion and actually influenced mainstream media content on the issue of delayed results. This citizen-driven exchange and circulation of information was, as Moyo (2009: 551) contends, a case of a "parallel market" of information that "contributed to the further exposure of the Mugabe regime's sinister machinations, thereby stopping the potential wholesale theft of the Zimbabwean people's victory in that election."

A critical and influential exchange of information between citizens has also been observed around the issue of *Gukurahundi*, a government-orchestrated military campaign of the mid-1980s in which thousands of Zimbabweans were killed in Midlands and Matebeleland provinces under the pretext of suppressing dissident activities. As noted by Mpofu (2015), citizen journalism through Web 2.0 platforms "revolutionised" political communication, enabling individual citizens from the minority Ndebele community to openly deliberate on this censored issue in ways aimed at agenda-setting towards closure and healing. Relatedly, the faceless Baba Jukwa's "news breaking" and reporting engagements on Facebook during the period surrounding the 2013 elections are believed to have impacted Zimbabwe's repressive media regulatory framework in ways that promote citizen agency scopes for citizens to interact freely, constructing their own desired realities in the face of stringent media laws (Sabao & Chingwaramusee, 2019; Mare, 2016).

These examples illustrate that there are scopes for individual citizens to engage in citizen journalism practices that cultivate democratic and developmental cultures. However, the practice of citizen journalism by citizens tends to be personalised and fragmented, lacking organic organising. Citizen media advocacy around the issue of the marginalisation of Matebeleland province, for instance, could be more effective if undertaken in collaboration with other marginalised communities in other provinces. The Baba Jukwa kind of engagement could gain more traction if executed from within the ethos of social movement building. The Baba Jukwa type of citizen journalism was more of man-based innuendo, rumour mongering and conjecture. Suppose they are to cultivate social movement building, citizen journalism initiatives need to be founded on a deep-rooted, ethical and widely encompassing civility and consciousness that cultivate protection and uphold citizenship rights. Sensational and rumouristic information spreading that speaks to partisan emotions has no place in this anticipated form of citizen journalism. The call for ethical, independent and organic citizen journalism calls for an end to narrow forms of Protestantism motivated by personality cults and opportunistic agendas.

Citizen journalism must be practised as a serious pursuit towards protecting citizenship rights. Those engaging in citizen journalism need to do so from a vantage point of active and responsible citizenship. This is not the case with the more significant number of individual citizens claiming to be engaging in citizen journalism in Zimbabwe, where a deepening state of political polarisation is being witnessed across the media realm, with engagements being characterised by name calling, sloganeering, self-aggrandisement, mimicry, conspicuous consumption, personality cult and outright lies. There is a growing trend in which individuals want to have as many followers on their social media pages as they can become influencers whom corporates can pay for marketing and advertising purposes. Thus, "social media" and "citizen media spaces" have, like mainstream media, been invaded by corporate tyranny and mimicry that are tempered by consumerism.

In China, celebrities' social media pages have been characterised as critical public sphere platforms, carrying debates on community problem-solving and critical ideological issues such as cultural and media imperialism orchestrated through global media outlets such as Cable News Network (CNN) (Reese & Dai, 2009). Images of a neoliberal-inspired showing off dominate Zimbabwe's so-called socialites. With mainstream media already submerged in corporate and authoritarian tyranny and influence, citizen and social media spaces are threatened by the same fate. This is proved by numerous studies that point to how online platforms are increasingly being manipulated for selfish corporate and authoritarian ends (see Mare, 2018; Mare, 2020; Stockmann & Gallagher, 2011; and Deibert, 2019). These studies point to the manipulation of the internet and social media spaces by vested political and corporate interests, resulting in citizens having limited scopes for utilising these platforms in ways that exert social accountability about pertinent issues such as service delivery, policy formulation, operations of extractive industries and others. To make matters worse, there are lower levels of consciousness and awareness to exercise citizenship rights and responsibilities, especially regarding socioeconomic and political rights. In most cases, citizens, especially those in rural areas, tend to get political information and direction from partisan platforms such as political party meetings and rallies[1] are beholden to politicians for political action, direction and discourse. In ideal terms, campaigns featured on Zimbabwean social media, such as *#Tajamuka* and *#ThisFlag*, must exist to foster a social movement-based consciousness tempered by active citizenship and ideological clarity. Deploying Mamdani's (1996) citizen and subject innovation and subaltern theories, Matsilele and Ruhanya (2021) have characterised *#Tajamuka* and *#This Flag* as social media dissidents and resistance movements. However, a critical look at these campaigns points to them as campaigns centred on a few individuals within civic organisations and political parties.

Civil society-supported citizen journalism

In an environment in which active citizenship through mainstream media spaces is curtailed, there is a need for a vibrant civic-based citizen journalism movement that can help protect citizens from vested political and corporate interests. Against this backdrop, civil society organisations, particularly those involved in promoting communication rights, have been embarking on citizen journalism capacity-building initiatives in Zimbabwe. In this context of capture, economic strain, political embeddedness and other factors affecting the reach and access of mainstream media, civil society has been trying to play a critical role in providing scopes for the existence of alternative public spheres that serve the informational and communication needs of marginalised and disadvantaged communities. Civic organisations that have engaged in citizen journalism capacity building include the Media Institute of Southern Africa-Zimbabwe Chapter (MISA-Zimbabwe), Radio Dialogue, Zimbabwe Association of Community Radio Stations (ZACRAS), Magamba, Centre for Innovation and Technology (CITE), Accountability Lab (Zimbabwe), Media Centre, Tell Zimbabwe Trust and Community Podium.

As stated by MISA-Zimbabwe's National Director,[2] and corroborated by the organisation's Advocacy Officer,[3] MISA-Zimbabwe's citizen journalism initiatives in communities were through the community newsletters project in which communities were capacitated to produce and publish newsletters that carried news by and about grassroots communities. The project was around after the 2008 elections, only to fold in 2010 owing to a lack of funding. It resumed before and shortly after the 2018 elections but has not been consistent due to a lack of sponsorship.

As gathered from Morris Zhowezha,[4] a citizen journalist who edited the MISA-Zimbabwe-sponsored Wedza newsletter, *Hwedza News*, the stories they published had a significant impact on such issues as the drilling of boreholes in some communities, helping in ensuring that the distribution of relief food and agricultural inputs was not done on a partisan basis and addressing of cases of corruption. Stories published by the newsletter also prompted better road maintenance, reduction and addressing of cases of human rights violations, including those of political intolerance, gender-based abuse and harmful cultural practices such as child marriages. Owing to the traction gained by the community newsletter, the Member of Parliament for the area ended up sponsoring a pro-ruling party newsletter to counter *Hwedza News* (Ibid.).

As stated by Kudzai Kwangwari,[5] former Radio Dialogue Programme Manager, Radio Dialogue attempted to have citizen journalists operating in line with the ethos of social movement building by fostering an environment in which citizen journalists were able to network and share their everyday problems and concerns, brainstorming on ways to address these problems and concerns through platforms such as discussion forums, WhatsApp and emails.

Another interesting citizen journalism initiative is by Magamba, a youth-based civic organisation that facilitates engagement between young people and decision-makers. The Magamba citizen journalism initiative, Open Parly, provides real-time access to parliamentary debates and processes through live tweeting, interviews and stories shared through online platforms. These activities are undertaken by trained journalists, mostly young journalism graduates. As indicated its[6] Project Officer, Nyasha Mukapiko, Open Parly is about opening parliament to the people so that they know what is happening in the August House. Provision of access to parliamentary proceedings is made through Facebook live streams and Twitter chat sessions on events such as Parliamentary Public hearings and Parliamentary Portfolio Committee hearings. Mukapiko describes Open Parly as both a citizen and a civil society initiative. He indicated that the project was mooted by citizens trained in citizen journalism through a civil society capacity-building initiative.

Conclusion

The practice of citizen journalism by individual citizens in Zimbabwe is limited by factors that include political polarisation, economic restrictions and manipulation by partisan and corporate interests. Emanating from this manipulation is the submerging of what should be citizen media spaces into platforms for shallow, partisan sloganeering and consumerist mimicry. Hashtag movements that have been touted as social movements have not existed as social movements but as extensions of partisan political agendas. Their prominence and traction have failed to go beyond their founders. They do not have much presence in communities and their organising scopes are not far-reaching, with their media presence and engagements being event-based and opportunistic. Notwithstanding sustainability challenges, limited grassroots community reach, elitism, limited collaboration and other challenges affecting civil society organisations, citizen journalism is better organised at the civil society or non-profit level, where there have been significant attempts to spread its tentacles to grassroots communities. Given the negative aspects of fragmentation emanating from individualised citizen journalism capacity-building projects being implemented by different civic organisations, coalitions and partnerships, there is a need for greater coordination and collaboration in supporting and implementing such projects. Citizen journalism capacitation must be carried from the vantage point of empowering citizens with a broad consciousness to protect and uphold citizenship rights.

Notes

1 See Boysen, Susan. 2012. "Change and 'New' Politics in Zimbabwe": Interim Report of a Nationwide Survey of Public Opinion in Zimbabwe: June–July 2012. Freedom House.
2 Interview with Tabani Moyo, MISA-Zimbabwe National Director, July 16, 2022.
3 Interview with Malvern Mukudu, MISA-Zimbabwe Advocacy Officer, July 5, 2022.
4 Interview with Morris Zhowezha, former editor of *Hwedza News*, July 18, 2022.
5 Interview with Kudzai Kwangwari, July 4, 2022.
6 Interview with Nyasha Mukapiko, July 6, 2022.

References

Bailey, O. G., Cammaert, B., and Carpentier N. 2008. *Understanding Alternative Media*. Maidenhead: McGraw Hill/Open University Press.
Baker, G., and Chandler, D. 2004. *Global civil society: contested futures*. Routledge.

Banda, F. 2010. *Citizen Journalism & Democracy in Africa*. Grahamstown: Highway Africa.
Benkler, Y. 2006. *The Wealth of Networks: How Social Production Transforms Markets and Freedom*. New Haven, Conn: Yale University Press.
Bowman, S., and Willis, C. 2003. *We Media: How Audiences are Shaping the Future of News & Information*. Retrieved September 19, 2003, from www.ndn.org/webdata/we_media/we_media.htm
Carlsson, M. 2016. Metajournalistic discourse and the meanings of journalism: Definitional control, boundary work, and legitimation. *Communication Theory*, 26(4): 349–368.
Deibert, R. J. 2019. The road to digital unfreedom: Three painful truths about social media. *Journal of Democracy*, 30: 25–39.
Fuchs, C. 2020. Towards a critical theory of communication as renewal and update of Marxist humanism in the age of digital capitalism. *Journal of Theory Social Behaviour*, 2020(50): 335–356. DOI: 10.1111/jtsb.12247
Gyldensted, C. (2015). *From Mirrors to Movers: Five Elements of Positive Psychology in Constructive Journalism*. Ggroup Publishing.
Goode, L. 2009. Social news, citizen journalism and democracy. *New Media & Society*, 11(8): 1287–1305.
Habermas, J. 1962 [1989]. *The Structural Transformation of the Public Sphere: An Inquiry Into a Category of Bourgeois Society*. Cambridge: MIT Press.
Hughes, W. 2011. "Citizen Journalism: Historical Roots and Contemporary Challenges" Honors College Capstone Experience/Thesis Projects (Paper 305). http://digitalcommons.wku.edu/stu_hon_theses/305
Mahamed, Mastura, Omar, Siti, Tamam, Ezhar, and Krauss, Steven. 2018. Citizen journalism in action: Empowering the rural community via citizen journalism. *International Journal of Academic Research in Business and Social Sciences*, 8. 10.6007/IJARBSS/v8-i11/4888.
Mamdani, M. 1996. *Citizen and Subject: Contemporary Africa and the Legacy of Late Colonialism*. Princeton, NJ: Princeton University Press.
Mano, W. 1997. Public service broadcasting in Zimbabwe: A brief on promise, performance and problems. In Andersen, E. W. (ed.), *Media, Democracy and Development*. IMK-Report 27 (pp. 5–40). Oslo: Department of Communication, University of Oslo.
Mare, A. 2015. *Facebook, youth and political action: A comparative study of Zimbabwe and South Africa*. Unpublished PhD thesis. Rhodes University, Grahamstown.
Mare, A. 2016. Baba Jukwa and the digital repertoires of connective action in a 'competitive authoritarian regime': The case of Zimbabwe. In Mutsvairo, B. (ed.), *Digital Activism in the Social Media Era* (pp. 45–68). London: Palgrave Macmillan.
Mare, A. 2018. Politics unusual? Facebook and political campaigning during the 2013 harmonised elections in Zimbabwe. *African Journalism Studies*, 39(1): 90–110. DOI: 10.1080/23743670.2018.1425150
Mare, A. 2020. "Sites of manufacturing consent or resistance? Post-2000 media and political contestation in Zimbabwe." In Tendi M., McGregor J. and Alexander J. (eds.), *The Oxford Handbook of Zimbabwean Politics*. Oxford: Oxford University Press.
Matsilele, T., and Ruhanya, P. 2021. Social media dissidence and activist resistance in Zimbabwe. *Media, Culture & Society*, 43(2): 381–394.

McIntyre, K. E. 2015. *Constructive Journalism: The Effects of Positive Emotions and solution Information in News Stories*. Doctoral Dissertation. Chapel Hill, NC: Chapel Hill Graduate School, University of North Carolina.

Melber, H., Moyo, D., and Chiumbu, S. H. (Eds.). (2004). *Media, Public Discourse and Political Contestation in Zimbabwe* (No. 27). Uppsala, Sweden: Nordic Africa Institute.

Mhiripiri, N. A., and Mutsvairo, B. 2014. Social media, new ICTs and the challenges facing the Zimbabwe democratic process. In Clarke, S., Jennex, M., Becker, E and Ari-Veikko A. (Eds.), *Crisis Management: Concepts, Methodologies, Tools, and Applications* (pp. 1281–1301). Hershey, PA: IGI Global.

Mignolo, W. D. 2005. *The Idea of Latin America*. Malden, MA: Blackwell Publishing.

Mkandawire, T. 2011. Running while others walk: Knowledge and the challenge of Africa's development. *Africa Development*, 36: 1–36.

Moyo, D. 2009. Citizen journalism and the parallel market of information in Zimbabwe's 2008 election. *Journalism Studies*, 10(4): 551–567. DOI: 10.1080/14616700902797291.

Mpofu, S. 2015. When the subaltern speaks: Citizen journalism and genocide 'victims" voices online. *African Journalism Studies*, 36(4): 82–101. DOI: 10.1080/23743670.2015.1119491

Mutsvairo, B., Columbus, S., and Leijendekker, I. 2012. African citizen journalists' ethics and the emerging networked public sphere. Retrieved August, 4, 2012. https://researchportal.northumbria.ac.uk/en/publications/african-citizen-journalists-ethics-and-the-emerging-networked-pub

Obonyo, L. 2011. Towards a theory of communication for Africa: The challenges for emerging democracies. *Communicatio: South African Journal for Communication Theory and Research*, 37(1): 1–20.

Papacharissi, Z. 2004. Democracy online: Civility, politeness, and the democratic potential of online political discussion groups. *New Media Society*, 6: 259–283.

Radsch, C. 2013. *The Revolutions will be Blogged: Cyberactivism and the 4th Estate in Egypt*. Doctoral Dissertation. Washington, DC: American University.

Reese, S. D., and Dai, J. 2009. The global news arena: China's new media critics. *Citizen Journalism: Global Perspectives*, 1: 221.

Sabao, C., and Chingwaramusee, V. R. 2019. Citizen journalism on Facebook and the challenges of media regulation in Zimbabwe: Baba Jukwa. In (names of editors) (eds.) *Journalism and Ethics: Breakthroughs in Research and Practice* (pp. 250–263). Hershey, PA: IGI Global.

Stephansen, H. 2016. Understanding citizen media as practice: Agents, processes, publics. In: Baker, M. and Blaagaard, B. (eds.), *Citizen Media and Public Spaces: Diverse Expressions of Citizenship and Dissent*. London: Routledge.

Stockmann, D., and Gallagher, M. E. 2011. Remote control: How the media sustain authoritarian rule in China. *Comparative Political Studies*, 44(4): 436–467.

UNESCO. 2008. UNESCO Media Development Indicators. UNESCO. New York.

Wagemans, A., Witschge, T., and Harbers, F. 2019. Impact as driving force of journalistic and social change. *Journalism*, 20(4): 552–567.

Wall, M. 2019. *Citizen Journalism: Practices, Propaganda, Pedagogy*. London: Routledge.

Wasserman, H. 2016. Listening past difference: Towards a compassionate ethics of communication. *STJ | Stellenbosch Theological Journal*, 1: 217. 10.17570/stj.2015.v1n2.a10.

Part III

Freedom, Censorship, and Intellectual Property Rights

7 "The Right to Tell My Story as I Please"

Regulation and Self-Censorship in the Nigerian Film Industry

Ikechukwu Obiaya

Introduction

The great achievement of the Nigerian film industry is its success in overcoming the barriers of African filmmaking to place its stories on a global stage (Okome, 2010; Obiaya, 2011). It has become "fundamental to Africa's self-representation" (Haynes, 2010) and is seen as "the most visible form of cultural machine on the African continent" (Krings & Okome, 2013b), "telling thousands of stories that speak to an audience of millions across the African continent" (Barrot, 2008). The films responded "to a craving for images to which a popular audience can relate" (Balogun, 2004), and this focus on local stories facilitated their wide reception across Africa in that the cross-border audiences were able to self-identify thanks to a "cultural proximity" (Krings & Okome, 2013b).

However, while the Nigerian filmmakers may have established their right to tell their stories on the global stage, that right is often challenged locally. The filmmakers are subject to the regulation of the National Film and Video Censors Board and, for those in the Hausa film sector, Kannywood, the additional, largely religion-guided regulation of the Kano State Censors Board. The filmmakers have always had to contend with the sociopolitical basis of censorship decisions (Obiaya, 2015). However, there is growing concern about an increased curbing of filmmakers' artistic freedom and their right to communication following regulatory decisions made in 2021 (Anon, 2021a, 2021b). Such regulation accompanies the constant accusations that the filmmakers have faced of promoting negative themes in their stories, perverting morals and giving the country a bad name.

The question that arises, therefore, is how do the filmmakers respond to such challenges? Do they engage in self-censorship by avoiding certain kinds of stories or do they find creative ways to sidestep these obstacles and still tell the stories they want? This chapter seeks to respond to these questions through a qualitative study consisting of interviews with filmmakers drawn from the different segments of the Nigerian film industry.

DOI: 10.4324/9781003388289-11

Some Background

Filmmaking in Nigeria began during the colonial times, but independent indigenous filmmaking dates back from 1970 (Ukadike, 1994). The early pioneers included persons like Francis Oladele, Ola Balogun, Hubert Ogunde, Moses Olaiya Adejumo, Sanya Dosunmu, Ladi Ladebo, Adamu Halilu and Eddie Ugbomah (Ukadike, 1994). This early phase of filmmaking in celluloid, with its attendant high costs, coincided with and was facilitated by Nigeria's economic boom. The subsequent crash of the economy, in the 1980s, brought an end to this first phase of Nigerian filmmaking (Obiaya, 2016). With the depreciation of the Naira, it became tremendously expensive to continue film production in celluloid given the high dependence on imported materials and the fact that postproduction was done outside the country. Thus, by the early 1990s, celluloid film production had virtually petered out.

The second phase of filmmaking began at the end of the 1980s as filmmakers began turning to video as a means of making their films. Although some video films had been released by 1989, the inaugural year for what would become a booming video film industry is considered to be 1992, the year in which Ken Nnebue's *Living in Bondage* was released (Haynes, 2007a). The following years saw an explosion in video film production, and video films were being churned out in the hundreds. Various factors accounted for this explosion in production: the production costs were low; the equipment was relatively easy to acquire and use; no entry barriers existed for filmmakers and, above all, there was a "large audience demand for entertainment" (Ukadike, 2002). The low cost of production – "absurdly low" according to Barrot (2008) – and the size of the audience also meant that the video films could be funded locally. All this led to the establishment of a vibrant video film industry.

The video filmmaking industry quickly acquired the moniker of "Nollywood," which has been widely applied to the Nigerian film industry. However, when applied in this way, the term fails to take into consideration the different strands of filmmaking in the country (Haynes, 2016). While it is true that Nollywood, referring to the films made largely in English, has been more prominent, there are equally vibrant strands of filmmaking in both Yoruba and Hausa (Johnson, 2000), with the latter known as Kannywood. The different strands are distinguished by their traditions and styles as well as, to a great extent, their audiences. Filmmaking is carried out in other ethnic languages in the country (McCain, 2013), but the level of production is much smaller than that of the three main production strands.

Stories, Popular Culture and Censors

One source of the popularity of the video films was the kind of stories that they told. The films took up a populist approach – they told the stories of the people for the people. Okoye (2007) describes the films as holding up a mirror to the people, a view echoed by Ofeimun (2004) and Okome (2007). Green-Simms (2012) indicates their closeness to everyday stories, and Haynes (2016) calls the industry a "chronicler of social history." This was true in a literal sense, particularly in the early days of the industry because it often happened that events in society became the subject of films. In the words of Adesokan (2004), "The current event, as news or observable phenomenon, is seen as a repository of ideas and themes from which to quarry a story." (A well-known example is Lancelot Imasuen's crime series, *Issabaka* (2001), which was based on the real-life events surrounding the Bakassi Boys, a community vigilante group in the east of the country.) Akpabio (2007: 91) points out that the success of the industry is perhaps due to this ability of the filmmakers "to emphasise contemporary realities which many Nigerians and Africans can relate to." The resulting cultural proximity (Krings & Okome, 2013a, 2013b; Obiaya, 2019) has facilitated the wide acceptance of the films across the African continent.

However, the filmmakers have faced a lot of criticism precisely for the themes and stories they have chosen to portray in their works. They have been attacked for the populist and commercial slant of their works (Obiaya, 2019), criticised for "over emphasising negative themes" (Akpabio, 2007), and accused of having a "thematic obsession with the occult world" (Ebewo, 2007). In response to all this, the filmmakers have continually stressed that they merely reflect what is going on in society and that they give the audience what it wants. They point out that, being rooted in their society, they draw their stories from what they observe around them. According to the filmmaker Tunde Kelani, "it is impossible for any responsible artiste to ignore all the problems socially, politically and economically" (NigeriaFilms.com, 2008). Ofeimun (2004), in defence of the filmmakers, criticises the self-deceitful "attempt to create a consensus around the need to make things look better in the films than they are in real life."

The "proximity of the films to popular imagination" (Haynes, 2007b) is explained by situating them within the paradigm of the African popular culture (Haynes, 2000). This paradigm makes it easier to understand the bond that exists between the films and the audience's response given that it posits popular culture as being, at the same time, both the source and the end of the product. "The fact that the audience and performers of popular art originate from the same masses introduces a certain dynamic into the relationship between producer and consumer" (Obiaya, 2019). Hence, Green-Simms (2012: 61) points out that the films possess the uniqueness of being "produced from below – which is to say that the class affiliations of the producers are often those of the mass consumers."

One could say that this *production from below* was reflected in the informal, all-comers nature of the industry. There were no gatekeepers, and the resultant flood of films eventually led to a public outcry for some form of regulation (Ugor, 2007). The response to this was the creation, in 1993, of the Nigeria Film and Video Censors Board (NFVCB). The law establishing the NFVCB empowers the Board to control the distribution, exhibition and marketing of films in the country. Filmmakers are expected to obtain approval for their films prior to releasing them into the market. According to its mandate, the Board can "deny approval not only to films considered indecent or likely to be injurious to morality but also to films that are undesirable in the public interest or that are likely to incite or encourage public disorder" (Obiaya, 2015).

However, in its years of operation, the Board has banned relatively few films (Ugor, 2007). Rather, emphasis is placed, when the need arises, on either requesting that certain scenes be modified or classifying the films as not fit for certain audiences. The Board, on its webpage, states that it looks "at issues such as drug use, horror, language, nudity, ritual, sex, sexual violence, theme, tribalism and racism, violence, or any content which could disrupt the peaceful state of the nation" (www.nfvcb.gov.ng/classification/). Thus, the Board has tended to come down hard on the overt depiction of scenes of sex and extreme violence. But, given the volatile nature of the multi-tribal and multi-religious mix in the country, the NFVCB has also paid particular attention to the sociopolitical considerations of its censorship decisions (Obiaya, 2015). This, for instance, was the fate of *The Milkmaid* (2020) for which the Board requested cuts of about 24 minutes due to sensitivities concerning references to Islam (Young, 2021). However, the Board has been accused of sometimes having exaggerated reactions. An example of this was the ban, in 2013, of *Fuelling Poverty*, a documentary that focused on corruption in the management of Nigeria's oil wealth. The Board's decision to ban the documentary based on concerns for national security was seen as inexplicable given that all the details covered in the documentary were already in the public domain (Edozien, 2013).

The National Film and Videos Censors Board was established by the federal government of Nigeria and therefore has jurisdiction over the entire country. However, given that Nigeria is a federation, its constitution provides for both shared and different powers that pertain to the central government and the state governments. The powers for establishing censorship bodies pertain to both the National Assembly and the state houses of assembly. In line with these powers, the governments of Kano and Lagos States set up their own state censorship boards in 2001 and 2004 respectively. The reasons for the establishment of the Lagos State Film and Censors Board (LSFCB) perhaps stem from the fact that Lagos is a key filmmaking hub. The LSFCB states on its website (https://lsfvcb.lagosstate.gov.ng/) that it has contributed to establishing standards and creating a conducive filmmaking environment. However, it does not maintain a very visible presence in the industry. This is quite a different case from that of the Kano State Censorship Board (KSCB).

The establishment of the KSCB came in the wake of the declaration of Shari'a law in Kano in 2000. Following the declaration, filmmaking was listed as one of the evils to be sanitised, and the production, exhibition and sales of films were subsequently banned in the state of Kano (McCain, 2013).

In the face of the loss of their livelihoods, the filmmakers of the thriving Hausa film industry agreed with the state government to create a censorship board that "would enable filmmakers to return to work, while also providing a political concession to the religious leaders who had urged a ban on the industry" (McCain, 2013: 229). The law establishing KSCB reproduces most of the criteria from the NFCVB Act, but it has additional regulations that reflect requirements of Shari'a law. Thus, to have access to the Kano markets, the filmmakers have to submit their films to both the NFVCB and the KSCB for approval (McCain, 2013). The KSCB has tended to come down hard on the filmmakers as the law has often been rigidly interpreted. In various moments, the activities of the industry have been suspended; filmmakers or films have been banned and the filmmakers have faced attacks, court trials, fines and incarceration (Ibrahim, 2013; McCain, 2013; Sylvester, 2021; Sahara Reporters, 2022). This exemplifies the view of Reitov (2021), who lists nationalism and religious orthodoxy as one of the challenges to artistic freedom. According to him, "Controlling the minds and expressions of people is based on fear, and the tool of control is spreading more fear, leading to self-censorship" (Reitov, 2021).

Self-Censorship: Public and Private

Censorship can be understood as a way to control the flow of information (Caso, 2008) largely through the suppression of this information in its different forms. Chia et al. (2004: 110) describe it as "an attempt to prevent media content from being circulated." Such control is usually attributed to the state or its agencies. For Shadmehr and Bernhardt (2015), the content of such censorship by the state is "bad news" that could lead to revolt while Bhowmik (2002) points out that "sex, violence and politics" are the three major areas in which film censorship operates worldwide. Censorship is, to a large extent, seen as negative, but Dwyer (2009) suggests that, when it is looked at more neutrally, censorship is not always something bad. Rather, "constraints of some kind may well be part of the very creative enterprise itself" (Dwyer, 2009: 29).

As has been pointed out, censorship is something usually attributed to governmental or other authorities. However, censorship is not something limited to agencies external to oneself. Hence, Cohen (2001: 9), in raising the question of whether censorship could also take the form of self-suppression, responds that "private censorship and self-censorship are not different in kind from governmental censorship." Cohen, thus, offers a more encompassing definition of censorship as "the exclusion of some discourse as the result of a judgment by an authoritative agent based on some ideological predisposition." While it is true that third parties are often the authoritative agents, the reality is that the artist also plays the role of the agent who makes judgements as regards what to supress. According to Dwyer (2009: 37), the expressive artist, in the bid to attain specific effects, "is always working with a set of self-imposed constraints. If anything goes, then there can be no meaning." Self-imposed constraints, or self-censorship, could therefore be considered as part of the creative process. But it could also arise from "respect for other people's religious beliefs or from a desire not to hurt people's feelings" (Klausen, 2010: 16).

However, such self-censorship that arises from the free choices of the individual must be distinguished from the self-censorship that is motivated by a sense of self-preservation. Cook and Heilmann (2013) offer the useful distinction between what they refer to as public self-censorship and private self-censorship. According to them, public self-censorship is the response of individuals to an existing public censorship regime. The individuals internalise the rules of the public censor and then censor themselves in respect of those rules. Private self-censorship, on the other hand, involves "the suppression by an agent of his or her own attitudes where a public censor is either absent or irrelevant" (Cook & Heilmann, 2013: 79). In this case, the decision on whether or not to publicly express something is based on the personal preferences of the individual and not on the impositions of an external body.

Research Methodology

As already indicated, the goal of this chapter is to identify how the Nigerian filmmakers cope with the limitations placed on them by censorship and whether it leads them to self-censorship. In line with the exploratory nature of the research, a qualitative approach was adopted. To this end, in-depth interviews were carried out with nine filmmakers drawn from the different segments of the industry. The filmmakers were purposively chosen to represent the three main sectors of the Nigerian film industry. The initial plan had been to interview five filmmakers from each of the three sectors, but this fell through due to the unavailability of some of the filmmakers and the limited timeframe. Three of the filmmakers – Ekene Mekwuenye, Chukwudi Chibuzor and Kemi Gbadamosi – were from Nollywood; four – Ahmad Sarari, Ishaq Sidi Ishaq, Khalid Musa and Sule Abubakar – were Kannywood filmmakers and two – Elder Adetunji Ojetola and Seun Olaiya – came from the Yoruba filmmaking sector. At the time of the interviews, Dr Ahmad Sarari was the president of the Motion Picture Practitioners Association of Nigeria (MOPPAN), an umbrella body for filmmakers in the north of the country while Elder Adetunji Ojetola was the national president of the Association of Movie Content Owners and Producers/Distributors of Nigeria (AMCOP), an umbrella body for Yoruba filmmakers. The choice of these particular filmmakers was based on convenience as they were the ones that readily agreed to be interviewed.

Given the geographical distance between the interviewer and the interviewees, all the interviews save one were carried out on the telephone at times convenient to the filmmakers. One of the interviewees preferred to respond in writing, and the questions were sent to him by email. His responses were returned in the same way. All the respondents agreed that interviews could be recorded and that their names could be used in the paper. However, due to the inability to obtain signed consent from two persons, their names were changed. They are referred to here as Chukwudi Chibuzor and Sule Abubakar. For the sake of convenience, all the respondents will be referred to subsequently by just their surnames.

All the filmmakers interviewed have had relatively extensive careers in the industry. The level of activity over the five years prior to the interview, in terms of the number of films produced, was quite varied, ranging from Musa, who indicated that he had not made any films in that time frame, to Olaiya who had directed over 50 films in the same period. Chibuzor said he had made over 30; Gbadamosi and Ojetola had made 12 and 11 respectively while Ishaq had made two. Mekwuenye said he had made eight but had released only two while Sarari distinguished between films he had directed himself (one) and films made under his company (10). Abubakar, who is also an actor, had produced three films but had acted in about 50 films.

Findings

It was established that the platforms on which the filmmakers released their films were relatively varied. According to Ojetola, speaking of the Yoruba filmmakers, "Up till now we still release them in DVDs, but that distribution is greatly challenged by these unscrupulous people pirating the films. So, the distribution steps have shifted to YouTube a lot now and very few VOD platforms" (A. Ojetola, personal communication, 19 May 2022). He also pointed to DSTV as being one of the platforms for distribution of their content. This was similar to the platforms indicated by the Kannywood filmmakers. According to Musa,

> YouTube seems to be the most patronised platform as our producers are yet to exploit the most profitable ones such as Netflix, Amazon and the rest for some obvious reasons – such as knowledge gap in online marketing and meeting the technical requirements of such platforms.
> (K. Musa, personal communication, 24 May 2022)

Ishaq also pointed out that "Most producers especially here over at the North, distribute their movies through TV channels . . . I think they only concentrate on doing movies for television stations. Even though there are other platforms like Northflix – *not Netflix*" (I. Ishaq, personal communication, 26 May 2022). Sarari mentioned distribution through film festivals and international film markets while Gbadamosi and Mekwuenye mentioned the cinemas. However, while Netflix was a target for most of the other filmmakers, only Mekwuenye indicated that he had distributed his films on that platform.

All the filmmakers indicated full awareness of the NFVCB and its censorship requirements. They said that their films were duly submitted to the NFVCB for classification prior to release, as specified by the law. According to Ojetola, fulfilment of this requirement was an essential condition for members of AMCOP, who "make up to 90% of executive producers of indigenous Yoruba films in Nigeria" (A. Ojetola, personal communication, 19 May 2022). This was confirmed by the other Yoruba filmmaker, Olaiya, who spoke of having a cordial relationship with the Censors Board. However, Mekwuenye indicates that he only submitted his film for classification if he intended to exhibit it in the cinemas.

> If I am going to cinema, yes. It's mandatory, so it's not even like I have a choice. But my last project, *One Lagos Night*, went straight to Netflix. So, . . . as I am talking now, I didn't go through them at all.
> (E. Mekwuenye, personal communication, 19 May 2022)

The four Kannywood filmmakers spoke about their awareness of the KSCB and its impact on their work. (It is notable that none of the four Lagos-based filmmakers mentioned any dealings with the Lagos State Film and Censors Board.) The Kano-based filmmakers indicated that they submit their films to both the NFVCB and the KSCB but acknowledge that there is a difference in the focus of both boards. According to Ishaq, the difference lies in that the KSCB

> controls contents that are within Kano State. And it's basically to protect culture and religion per se. They are not more or less particular about, like, technicalities of filmmaking. They are only concerned [with] the morality. . . . They have tried to intrude religion and culture into the censorship board.
> (I. Ishaq, personal communication, 26 May 2022)

Musa points out that

> However, the state agency usually becomes a stick in the hand of politicians used to [whip] the industry just for the purpose of appeasing public sentiment, to gain cheap political support. For this reason, the industry has been suppressed; its members incarcerated [often] for political reasons.
> (K. Musa, personal communication, 24 May 2022)

This view was supported by Sarari who stated that:

> In 2007, Kano State Censors Board arrested over 300 filmmakers. They harassed them, ransacked their houses, arrested them, took them to court and in hardly 15–20 minutes, sentenced them to prison. I was part of that saga. My junior brother was in prison for two months.
> (A. Sarari, personal communication, 24 May 2022)

The NFVCB, as part of its process, could ask a filmmaker to modify or delete scenes or, in extreme cases, ban the film outright. None of the filmmakers interviewed had ever had their films banned, but many of them did indicate that they had been asked to modify things in their films. "We were told to go and adjust and remove some things or reshoot," Olaiya said, and this was due to some nudity in a film. He however pointed out that this was a long time ago (S. Olaiya, personal communication, 22 May 2022). In Gbadamosi's case, she was not asked to modify the film,

> The only thing is that they gave me a [restricted classification]. I was hoping that they would give me for general viewing, and they did not. They said because of blood content and violence. And it was a documentary. I would have had to remove that for them to give me a general viewing, but it was restricted.
> (K. Gbadamosi, personal communication, 26 May 2022)

With reference to the KSCB, Abubakar had not had any personal experience of sanctions or requests for modifications but said that he had heard a lot of complaints from his colleagues. Ishaq also did not have personal experience but gave instances of the kind of issues that others have faced,

> Let me give you just an example: Like you have a wife; she's sick, you know, she's fainting, or she slumps; you cannot touch her. Do you understand? You cannot touch her, or you have a wife, you are married, a young couple getting married. And you don't show that romantic scenario. . . . Sometimes, if you expose that kind of scenario, or if mistakenly or deliberately somebody touches, like a guy touching a girl . . . they will tell you to remove that place. And that is, you know, limiting the creative aspect of it. And that is really killing the storytelling because it is not showing naturality; it is not showing that intimate relationship between couples.
> (I. Ishaq, personal communication, 26 May 2022)

With reference to the NFVCB, Ojetola stressed that the Board had taken the pains to carry them along by organising workshops to explain the rationale for the censorship requirements and decisions.

> For instance, if there is a gunshot somewhere or a murder, . . . first of all, they don't want to see blood. Some people will ask you, "how will you shoot somebody, and you say blood will not come out?" And it becomes an argument. And they say, if you have to show it, the mere act of that shooting is enough; [the message is transmitted without showing the blood].
> (A. Ojetola, personal communication, 19 May 2022)

According to him, the Board has explained

why they don't want smoking in our films, and . . . if you must show it, probably you want to depict a crime scene or whatever, you must explain why you must show such. . . . If you cross that line, definitely they will sanction you.
(A. Ojetola, personal communication, 19 May 2022)

Nevertheless, most of the filmmakers agreed that concerns about being censored placed limitations on their creative processes. Sarari pointed out that these limitations negatively affect the filmmaker's creativity and the market because it leads to a distortion of the stories. "Film is a mirror of the society, and for you to call attention of the people to any bad habit, you must portray how this is done" to draw out the corrective lessons (A. Sarari, personal communication, 24 May 2022). This was echoed by Chibuzor who indicated that people learn a lot from films. According to him,

Orientation is what is needed not stopping us from telling people about what is happening in our space. . . . If you don't show them these things, they will not know where to go and how to go there.
(C. Chibuzor, personal communication, 26 May 2022)

[The decisions of the Censors Board are] affecting us because it makes the film looks like a child's play; that is just the truth. I can't imagine how you will shoot somebody in the stomach, and you can't see blood. And you can't expect us to tell stories of the white men because what is happening in their country is not what is happening in our own. Every country tells the story about what is happening [to them] . . . India, Chinese . . . If you are shooting Chinese film here, you are joking because it is not part of us. So, when we talk of rituals, we all know that all these things naturally happen in our place. . . . And for you to say don't shoot this, don't shoot that, don't shoot that – what else do you want them to shoot? To shoot children going to school? Is going to school the only thing happening in the country?
(C. Chibuzor, personal communication, 26 May 2022)

Yes, it does affect a lot. I am actually on a film set right now, [and in the script of the film], there's a part that a soldier gets injured. So, we are worried that if there's blood, and we have to stop the blood, it would affect the censorship. And so we decided that instead we would cut to a shot that has the place already bandaged, so we would not get to see blood. So even though the blood would help for more emotional engagement, because of censorship, we had to strike that out and make it with no blood.
(K. Gbadamosi, personal communication, 26 May 2022)

> Violence is a reality in Nigeria everywhere. But when you shoot film and [present it to either of the censors' boards], they will tell you, "remove blood in it." Violence is a reality here in Nigeria; killing is everywhere, but they will tell you there is too much blood in your film; they will rate your film and so on and so on. . . . Everything is happening there. But if you are trying to tell a story about the reality of what is happening there, they will tell you no; you have to remove it.
> (S. Abubakar, personal communication, 26 May 2022)

However, Mekwuenye stated that concern about censorship is not a factor that he takes into consideration during his creative process.

> I am aware that there are no boundaries to where my film can go. There are over 200 countries in the world, so one country should not limit me to how I am going to tell my story. So, it only now means that I will have to do a separate cut for [Nigeria]. The people online are not restricted. Online is not a country; online is not a place; it's everywhere.
> (E. Mekwuenye, personal communication, 19 May 2022)

However, Mekwuenye did acknowledge that if he intends to show his films in the cinemas in Nigeria, then he will have no choice but to take censorship into consideration. But such a consideration will come up only after he has made the film and not before or during the creative process.

Most of the filmmakers admitted to carrying out a measure of self-censorship to avoid falling foul of the authorities but pointed out the adverse consequences. According to Ishaq, people tend to censor their own films knowing that "if it goes to Kano State Film and Video Censorship Board, they will ask them to remove it. So, they tend to censor it themselves before it reaches to that state" (I. Ishaq, personal communication, 26 May 2022). This, he pointed out, is a limitation of both creativity and storytelling. For Abubakar, it is largely an economic consideration. If a film were censored, and the director had to change something, it would mean going back to set and having to recall both the cast and the crew. This would have an impact on the budget for the film. Chibuzor also saw self-censorship as a business necessity but noted that "The only thing they have achieved is causing us to make bad films. They are making us not to be able to interpret the story well. That's the only thing they force us to do" (C. Chibuzor, personal communication, 26 May 2022).

Gbadamosi also recognised it as an economic consideration but saw it as "a give and take kind of situation." In some instances, she said, self-censorship is necessary to avoid being given a classification of restricted viewing, which would limit the number of persons that could see it, and thus affect the bottom line of the film. But in other instances, she said, "What we do is sometimes we accept and say we have to go all the way here and accept whatever form of restriction that we get" (K. Gbadamosi, personal communication, 26 May 2022).

Olaiya negated the notion of self-censorship through the deliberate avoidance of certain themes or images "because that is what will lead to affecting one's creativity while filming." Nevertheless, he admitted that "We try to make our film in such a way that we don't have problems with the audience and with Censors Board."

> For example, if my story tells me a character has to smoke or reveal this sort of things in film, at that particular point, if it is compulsory that I leave the smoke in the scene, I will just need to write on that scene, "smokers are liable to die young," which the Censors Board definitely will reason with.
> (S. Olaiya, personal communication, 22 May 2022)

In line with this, Ishaq, while recognising the challenges of censorship, expressed the belief that, regardless of such restrictions, the filmmaker can always tell whatever story he wants to tell. According to him, film has just one language, which is that of images and sound.

> If the stakeholders or if the filmmakers are educated, they can tell those stories without making the Kano State Film Censorship Board to raise an eyebrow on a scenario, on everything in your film. You can use semiotics to tell that story, convince people. That's to say, if you are really in this part of the country, you can use semiotics to tell your story. Where you don't need to touch something, you can use signs, or text or whatever you can use technically to tell that story.
> (I. Ishaq, personal communication, 26 May 2022)

Without calling it self-censorship, all the filmmakers recognised that personal considerations would always come into play in making judgements in their filmmaking. For instance, Gbadamosi indicated that there are things she would avoid in her films due to her personal values, but Abubakar said that the decision to do or not do something in a film would depend more on his mood in that moment and not because of his personal values. Olaiya indicated that his first audience was always himself while Ishaq recognised that the quality of one's film would be affected by the filmmaker's passion for the story. Mekwuenye, on his part, noted that stories are always told from the perspective of the storyteller. "So, I feel that every story that is being told [carries] a chunk of the personal beliefs and convictions of the storyteller" (E. Mekwuenye, personal communication, 19 May 2022).

These personal considerations, as the filmmakers were generally quick to point out, do not leave out a consideration of the audience. The judgements made in the creative process are also moderated by the concern for the audience. However, as Mekwuenye distinguished,

> The audience are the primary concern that I have when I am telling these stories. But I don't necessarily look at it as what would they like.

I make [my film] with the intention of telling a great story, and I know that if I told a great story that they would like it. I understand that the human mind wants to be entertained, and the human mind wants to be blown away with a great story. Sometimes we don't even know what kind of stories hit us until the stories hit us. So, where I concern myself is mainly in telling a great story.
(E. Mekwuenye, personal communication, 19 May 2022)

Discussion

The right to freedom of expression is enshrined in Section 39 of the 1999 Constitution of the Federal Republic of Nigeria. The constitution also indicates that this right includes the freedom to communicate one's ideas and information without interference. However, the Constitution makes clear that such a right is not limitless. In Article 3 of the same Section 39, it states that "Nothing in this section shall invalidate any law that is reasonably justifiable in a democratic society – (a) for the purpose of . . . regulating telephony, wireless broadcasting, television or the exhibition of cinematograph films" (Nigeria, 1999). Certainly, there may be valid reasons for censorship such as the need to preserve societal harmony and security; one's right to self-expression is, after all, always limited by the rights of others. However, what comes through from the findings is that when the power to censor is invested in an official body, it could very easily lead to an abuse of the right to self-expression. As one of the respondents noted, through such bodies, censorship could become a political tool used to unjustly suppress the views of others.

Such censorship is a violation of artistic freedom, which UNESCO (2019) defines as "the freedom to imagine, create and distribute diverse cultural expressions free of governmental censorship, political interference or the pressures of non-state actors." This freedom of expression as well as the freedom of individuals to choose their own cultural expressions are some of the principles emphasised in the Convention on the Protection and Promotion of the Diversity of Cultural Expressions (UNESCO, 2013), which Nigeria ratified in 2008 (UNESCO, 2021). Along with the constitution, therefore, sufficient protection has been provided for the filmmakers' rights to self-expression and to artistic freedom. It is however obvious that these rights are not respected in reality. As detailed by the respondents, the censorship that they have to undergo is to a large extent a violation of their rights, particularly since, as Reitov (2021) put it, such censorship is a bid to gain control of minds and expressions through fear.

The various experiences of the filmmakers make it clear that they face real challenges as regards censorship. But what also stands out is that there are differences of approach towards tackling the issue depending on the sector concerned. A clear difference between the sectors is obviously the fact that, whereas the Nollywood and Yoruba filmmakers have only the NFVCB to deal with, those of Kannywood have to contend with both the NFVCB and the KSCB. An important distinction exists in the mode of operation of both bodies. The NFVCB appears to tend more towards the role of classification and does not always outrightly censor films. Rather, while it has on relatively few occasions banned some films outright, its response to the inclusion in films of things it finds objectionable is to classify such films for more restricted viewing. For commercial reasons, this is not favourable to the filmmakers as it limits the number of viewers for their films. It thus creates a tension between the desire for profit and the filmmaker's self-expression. But this does not take away the right of the filmmakers to express themselves because they are still left with a choice. As Gbadamosi indicated, self-expression sometimes involves going all the way and accepting the more limited classification.

The KSCB, on the other hand, is more focused on censorship. Here, there is no such room for choice since it is not a question of classification. Certain things are outrightly forbidden because they are seen as not adequately reflecting the religious and moral requirements of society. The harsh consequences of violating the KSCB code threaten the freedom of self-expression. For the Nollywood and Yoruba filmmakers, the consequences of violating the guidelines of the Censors Board would be, in the worst-case scenario, the banning of the film concerned. But for the Kannywood filmmakers, such a violation could lead to arrest and imprisonment. This reality could, therefore, lead to an increased awareness in the filmmaker of the need to carry out a public self-censorship, thereby violating the freedom of artistic expression.

This, of course, is not to say that the filmmakers from the other sectors do not also carry out public self-censorship. As is obvious from the feedback from the respondents, a high level of public self-censorship exists among those filmmakers. However, while they do carry out such censorship, it can be seen that there appears to be more leeway to contravene the guidelines and settle for a restricted viewing classification or bypassing the Board's process completely by placing one's film on a platform that is beyond the moderation of the Board. This can be considered one of the creative ways in which filmmakers respond to censorship and still get to exercise their freedom of self- and artistic expression.

Although some of the filmmakers complained about the impact of censorship on the quality of their stories, they all agreed that it did not stop them from telling stories. Some of them also pointed out that there are creative ways of bypassing the limitations imposed by censorship. Constraints, as Dwyer states (cited earlier), are not always necessarily bad. They can, indeed, be considered a part of the creative process in that one is challenged to seek creative solutions to bypass those limitations. It is interesting that one of the filmmakers points to the lack of education as a limitation that stops people from identifying creative solutions. This reflects the low-barrier entry point of the industry in that one can enter the industry without formal training in filmmaking.

In addition to public self-censorship, there was also evidence of private self-censorship. The choices made by the filmmakers, as guided by personal preferences, can all be considered as belonging to the realm of private self-censorship. All the filmmakers agreed that personal considerations entered into their creative decisions in one way or another; this is a reality of the creative process in that no one creates in a vacuum. What an individual creates tends to be drawn from that person's nature and experiences, and it involves making choices of what to tell and what to suppress. This idea is further strengthened by the point made by the filmmakers that their stories are drawn from the reality of what is happening around them in society. In favour of the notion that the Nigerian films are a manifestation of popular culture, there is the notable concern of some of the filmmakers to use their films to correct societal ills. Being part of society, they are well positioned to recognise the ills and to draw attention to them. It therefore leaves one with the question of whether public censorship, in trying to protect audiences, does not end up contributing to a distorted on-screen image of society. Exercising the right to communication and self-expression could very well be seen as contributing to greater authenticity in societal representation.

Conclusion

The filmmakers' right to freedom of expression is enshrined in the Nigerian constitution. This right is at the basis of the right to artistic expression, which is promoted by a UNESCO convention ratified by Nigeria. The reality, however, is that these rights are often violated by the censorship of the filmmakers' work. To avoid possible adverse effects, they are often forced to resort to both private and public self-censorship. Nevertheless, they still find creative ways to sidestep the threat of censorship in their self-expression. But this does not change the fact that their right to freedom of expression is under attack. The threats of violence, imprisonment and economic loss are a great hindrance to this expression. It is also particularly challenging when such threats come from state actors because it leaves the filmmakers with little or no avenues for recourse.

References

Adesokan, A., 2004. Loud in Lagos: Nollywood videos. *Wasafiri*, 19(43), pp. 45–49.

Akpabio, E., 2007. Attitude of audience members to nollywood films. *Nordic Journal of African Studies*, 16(1), pp. 90–100.

Anon., 2021a. Censors board, stakeholders move to ban smoking in movies. *Punch*, 11 December. https://punchng.com/censors-board-stakeholders-move-to-ban-smoking-in-movies/

Anon., 2021b. NFVCB: Buhari regime bans movies glamourising villains. *Peoples Gazette*, 6 September. https://gazettengr.com/nfvcb-buhari-regime-bans-movies-glamourising-villains/ (Accessed: 15 December 2021).

Balogun, F., 2004. Booming videoeconomy: The case of Nigeria. In F. Pfaff, ed. *Focus on African Films*, pp. 172–181. Bloomington: Indiana University Press.

Barrot, P., ed., 2008. *Nollywood: The Video Phenomenon in Nigeria*. Oxford, Ibadan, Bloomington and Indianapolis: James Currey, HEBN Publishers and Indiana University Press.

Bhowmik, S., 2002. Politics of film censorship: Limits of tolerance. *Economic and Political Weekly*, 37(35), pp. 3574–3577.
Caso, F., 2008. *Global Issues: Censorship*. New York: Infobase Publishing.
Chia, S. C., Lu, K. H., and McLeod, D. M., 2004. Sex, lies, and video compact disc: A case study on tird-person perception and motivations for media censorship. *Communication Research*, 31, pp. 109–130.
Cohen, M., 2001. *Censorship in Canadian Literature*. Quebec City: Mcgill-Queen's University Press.
Cook, P., and Heilmann, C., 2013. Two types of self-censorship: Public and private. *Political Studies*, pp. 178–196.
Dwyer, S., 2009. Censorship. In P. Livingston and C. Plantinga, eds. *The Routledge Companion to Philosophy and Film*, pp. 29–38. Oxon and New York: Routledge.
Ebewo, P., 2007. The emerging video film industry in Nigeria: Challenges and prospects. *Journal of Film and Video*, 59(3), pp. 46–57.
Edozien, F., 2013. Nollywood: Censored at home, available on the internet. *The New York Times*, 22 April. https://archive.nytimes.com/rendezvous.blogs.nytimes.com/2013/04/22/nollywood-censored-at-home-available-on-the-internet/ (Accessed: 28 April 2023).
Green-Simms, L., 2012. Hustlers, home-wreckers and homoeroticism: Nollywood's beautiful faces. *Journal of African Cinemas*, 4(1), pp. 59–79.
Haynes, J., ed., 2000. *Nigerian Video Films*. Athens: Ohio University Centre for International Studies.
Haynes, J., 2007a. Nollywood in Lagos, lagos in nollywood films. *Africa Today*, 54(2), pp. 131–150.
Haynes, J., 2007b. Nnebue: The anatomy of power. *Film Internationa*, V(4), pp. 30–40.
Haynes, J., 2010. What is to be done? Film studies and nigerian and ghanaian videos. In M. Şaul and R. P. Austen, eds. *Viewing African Cinam*. Athens: Ohio University Press, pp. 11–25.
Haynes, J., 2016. *Nollywood: The Creation of Nigerian Film Genres*. Chicago and London: The University of Chicago Press.
Ibrahim, M. M., 2013. Hausa film: Compatible or incompatible with Islam? *Historical Journal of Film Radio and Television*, 2(2), pp. 65–179.
Johnson, D., 2000. Culture and art in Hausa video film. In J. Haynes, ed. *Nigerian Video Films*, pp. 200–208. Athens: Ohio University Center for International Studies.
Klausen, J., 2010. *The Cartoons that Shook the World*. New Haven, CT and London: Yale University Press.
Krings, M., and Okome, O., eds., 2013a. *Global Nollywood*. Bloomington: Indiana University Press.
Krings, M., and Okome, O., 2013b. Nollywood and its diaspora: An introduction. In M. Krings and O. Okome, eds. *Global Nollywood: The Transnational Dimensions of an African Video Film Industry*, pp. 1–22. Bloomington: Indiana University Press.
McCain, C., 2013. Nollywood, kannywood, and a decade of hausa film censorship. In D. Biltereyst and R. VandeWinkel, eds. *Silencing Cinema: Film Censorship around the World*, pp. 223–240. New York: Palgrave Macmillan.
Nigeria, 1999. *Constitution of the Federal Republic of Nigeria, 1999 [With the First, Second and Third Alterations]*. www.refworld.org/docid/44e344fa4.html (Accessed: 25 November 2022).

NigeriaFilms.com, 2008. *I Don't Believe In Nollywood – Tunde Kelani* [Online]. www.modernghana.com/movie/2205/3/I-DONT-BELIEVE-IN-NOLLYWOOD-TUNDE-KELANI (Accessed: 18 April 2008).
Obiaya, I., 2011. A break with the past: The nigerian video-film industry in the context of colonial filmmaking. *Film History*, 23(2), pp. 129–146.
Obiaya, I., 2015. Il nigerian film and video censors board: le basi socio-politiche della censura dei video nigeriani. In A. Jedlowski and G. Santanera, eds. *Lagos Calling: Nollywood e la reinvenzione del cinema in Africa*, pp. 93–114. Rome: Aracne.
Obiaya, I., 2016. *Sub-Saharan African Cinema: Influences and Prospects*. Pamplona: Servicio de Publicaciones de la Universidad de Navarra.
Obiaya, I., 2019. African cinema in the throes of commercialism and populism. In A. Ojebode, T. Adegbola, A. D. Mekonmen and E. C. Maractho, eds. *Camera, Commerce and Conscience: Afrowood and the Crisis of Purpose*, pp. 165–181. Ibadan: Greenminds Publishers.
Ofeimun, O., 2004. In defence of the films we have made. *West Africa Review*, 5.
Okome, O., 2007. *Nollywood: Spectatorship, Audience and the Sites of Consumption* [Online]. http://journals.sfu.ca/pocol/index.php/pct/article/view/763/425 (Accessed: November 2007).
Okome, O., 2010. Nollywood and its critics. In M. Saul and R. A. Austen, eds. *Viewing African Cinema in the Twenty-First Century*, pp. 26–41. Athens: Ohio University Press.
Okoye, C., 2007. Looking at ourselves in our mirror: Agency, counter-discourse, and the nigerian video film. *Film International*, 28, pp. 20–29.
Reitov, O. 2021. Five challenges to artistic freedom. *UNESCO*. https://en.unesco.org/Artistic-Expression (Accessed: 26 November 2022).
Sahara Reporters, 2022. Kano film director declared wanted By censors board attacked over movie considered immoral. *Sahara Reporters*, 9 May. https://saharareporters.com/2022/05/09/kano-film-director-declared-wanted-censors-board-attacked-over-movie-considered-immoral (Accessed: 5 October 2022).
Shadmehr, M., and Bernhardt, D., 2015. State censorship. *American Economie Journal: Microeconomics*, 7(2), pp. 280–507.
Sylvester, T., 2021. Kano government bans movies showing kidnapping, drug addiction and stealing. *KanyiDaily.com*, October. https://www.kanyidaily.com/2021/09/kano-government-bans-movies-showing-kidnapping-drug-addiction-and-stealing.html (Accessed: 14 April 2023).
Ugor, P., 2007. Censorship and the content of Nigerian home video films. *Postcolonial Text*. https://www.postcolonial.org/index.php/pct/article/viewFile/518/403 (Accessed: 14 April 2023).
Ukadike, F. N., 2002. *Questioning African Cinema: Conversations with Filmmakers*. Minneapolis, MN and London: University of Minnesota Press.
Ukadike, N. F., 1994. *Black African Cinema*. Berkeley: University of California Press.
UNESCO. 2013. *Convention on the Protection and Promotion of the Diversity of Cultural Expressions*. www.unesco.org/culture/en/2005convention/.
UNESCO. 2019. *Artistic Freedom*. https://en.unesco.org/creativity/sites/creativity/files/artistic_freedom_pdf_web.pdf (Accessed: 24 November 2022).
UNESCO. 2021. *Conventions – Nigeria | UNESCO*. https://en.unesco.org/countries/nigeria/conventions (Accessed: 25 November 2022).
Young, N., 2021. 'The milkmaid': Review. *Screen*, 22 January. https://www.screendaily.com/reviews/the-milkmaid-review/5156289.article (Accessed: 14 April 2023).

8 A Critical Review of Intellectual Property Rights

The Case of Nigeria

Aifuwa Edosomwan

Introduction

In recent years, the need to diversify the Nigerian economy from its monoproduct, oil dependent and import-driven structure to a vibrant economy driven by the service and manufacturing sectors has resurfaced in academic and sociopolitical parlances (Okosun & Aihie-ezomo, 2016). This is hinged on the years of neglect and lack of political will to articulate policies and initiatives that will enhance the nation's ability to exploit the abundance of its human capital spread across the different geopolitical regions in the country (Samuel, 2020).

Despite the non-supportive attitude of the Nigerian business environment and absence of a policy framework to harness and support the creative utilization of the human capital in the country, the creative industry has emerged as one of the bright lights of the Nigerian economy considering its contribution to the socio-economic development of the country. According to Governor of the Nigerian Central Bank, Godwin Emefiele, the creative industry is worth about $4.5 billion (Oyewole, 2021) and is projected to create about 2.7 million jobs across the entire value chain by 2025 (Babatunde, 2021).

However, the productive capacity of the industry is yet to fully materialize as perennial issues of property rights and protection continue to deprive players in the creative industry of their earnings. According to PricewaterhouseCoopers (PwC), intellectual theft, otherwise known as piracy, plagues the potential of the Nigerian creative industry (Akoyi et al., 2019). It was revealed that for every movie produced and sold in Nigeria, nine other copies are pirated and sold in different markets in the country (Moudio, 2013). Similarly, it was revealed that Nigeria is home to 80 percent of internationally pirated CDs as well as sale of about 40 percent of locally produced musical CDs (Akoyi et al., 2019).

The incidence of intellectual property theft in the Nigerian entertainment industry has been fuelled by the structure of film financing, production and distribution. It was reported that the film industry had relied on the capital, infrastructure and distribution network created to sponsor pirate media (Ridwan et al., 2013). Furthermore, it was argued that pirates play on the

DOI: 10.4324/9781003388289-12

ignorance of producers and marketers to infringe on their intellectual property. An analysis of the loophole in the distribution pattern shows that while producers prefer to master their production in VCDs and sell at a lower price, pirates use DVDs because they allow them to compress more films into a disc and sell at the same price as the original VCD (Essien, 2016). In the same vein, it has been argued that piracy gains traction in major distribution hot zones in the country. Lagos, Aba and Onitsha are major points for film distribution in Nigeria; however, these locations have been identified as hotspots for pirates from where they spread to other parts of Africa (Ridwan et al., 2013).

The spate of intellectual property theft in Nigeria has been accentuated by the rise of the internet and other online streaming platforms. The report showed that many music works online are uploaded without the knowledge of the creators, thereby depriving the creators of gains accrued from their creative ingenuity. To further confirm the severity of the situation, it was revealed that only 11 percent of musical works downloaded from streaming platforms are paid for by consumers and many others are downloaded for free, robbing the creators of their due revenue (Akoyi et al., 2019).

It must be emphasized that the effect of intellectual theft is observed in other sectors of the Nigerian economy. For instance, the Nigerian pharmaceutical industry has been suffering from the harmful sting of intellectual theft. A study conducted by the World Health Organization (WHO) reported that 64 percent of anti-malaria drugs in the country are falsified, and over 50% of food, drinks and drugs sold in Nigerian markets are substandard (Ojoye, 2016). Similarly, the potential of the ICT sector in Nigeria is maligned by the prevalence of unlawful use of software and other technological innovation. It was reported that 82 percent of software installed on personal computers of users is not licensed (Akoyi et al., 2019). Furthermore, it was revealed that due to the high cost of certified software, most Nigerians prefer to install pirated software on their personal computers. It was also disclosed that in 2016 Nigeria lost about $287 million to software theft (Akoyi et al., 2019).

To salvage the situation, the Nigerian government through the Nigerian Copyright Commission (NCC) moved to protect the intellectual property rights of creators within the industry. The establishment of the NCC was a response to the absence of a regulatory body to mainstream treaties governed by the World Intellectual Property Organization (WIPO). First, the government began to make amendments to the Nigerian Copyright Act to make it more relevant to modern realities. Following its enactment in 1988, the Copyright Act had gone through several amendments (1990, 1992, 1999, 2004, 2007 and 2012) to keep the regulations relevant in protecting the rights and interests of actors in the creative industry. These amendments have further equipped the NCC to sanitize the creative industry of intellectual theft. In addition, Nigeria became a member of WIPO in 1995 to ensure that its copyright regulations align with global best practices. WIPO was established to govern the existing and prospective international treaties regarding

IP protection and to promote coordination of national laws and cooperation in the administration of intellectual property (Edosomwan, 2019).

Despite government efforts to combat intellectual property infringements, incidence of intellectual property theft continues unabated in Nigeria. It has been argued that the enacted Nigerian Copyright Act and its subsequent amendments have been unable to curb intellectual property infringement because of overlapping regulations as well as poor funding of the NCC (Akoyi et al., 2019). In addition, it was argued that the regulations enacted to govern and protect intellectual property were inadequate, if not obsolete to meet the new technological realities. To this end, it became essential for the regulations protecting intellectual property to be updated to meet contemporary demands. Furthermore, it was observed that the enforcement abilities of the NCC has been questioned. It was reported that the commission handle 541 cases of people arrested for intellectual property theft but was able to convict only 54 between 2011 and 2015; representing about 10 percent of the offenders arrested (Edosomwan, 2019). In comparison with other African countries, Nigeria ranks 23 on the international property rights index with countries such as Mauritius, South Africa, Rwanda, Botswana and Ghana ranked leading the continent (Property Rights Alliance, 2022).

It is expected that Nigeria should be at the forefront of copyright protection on the African continent because of its strategic position as the giant of Africa as well as the expansive nature of its creative industry. The country's position among other African countries shows that there is a vacuum within the framework which must be addressed to protect the right of creatives in the country. Therefore, this chapter critically examines existing copyright laws in Nigeria to shed light on changes that have occurred over time, bearing in mind advancements in technology. The chapter further analyses provisions of the copyright laws concerning the enforcement powers of the NCC.

Critical Appraisal of the Copyright Laws in Nigeria

The history of copyright laws in Nigeria dates back to 1970 when the Copyright Act of 1970 was enacted as part of the Nigerian Criminal Code. The act was the first indigenous attempt at protecting intellectual property rights in Nigeria (Olatunji, 2013). Section 491 of the Criminal Code Act (1990) stated that:

> Any person who knowingly (a) makes for sale or hire any infringing copy of a work in which copyright subsists; (b) or sells or lets for hire, or by way of trade exposes or offers for sale or hire any infringing copy of any such work; (c) or distributes infringing copies of any such work either for the purposes of trade or to such an extent as to affect prejudicially the owner of the copyright; (d) or by way of trade exhibits in public any infringing copy of any such work, is guilty of a simple offence and is liable to a fine not exceeding four naira for every copy dealt with in contravention of this section of this Code, but not exceeding

one hundred naira in respect of the same transaction; or, on the case of a second or subsequent offence, either to such fine or to imprisonment for two months.

(Criminal Code Act, 1990)

The provisions in section 491 of the Act made an express definition of acts considered as copyright infringement and penalty for violators. However, the law did not make provision for the establishment of an independent regulatory body that oversees the enforcement of copyright infringements. In contrast, the Act empowered the Federal Commissioner for Trade to appoint authorities that would oversee the administration of prescriptive regulations (Asein, 2012). For instance, the Copyright Unit of the Department of Culture and the Minister of Finance were in charge of making and enforcing regulations regarding the issues in the creative industry and printing of copyrighted works (Asein, 2012). The absence of a government agency to perform regulatory functions under the 1970 Act paved way for uncontrolled infringements on intellectual property and the irrelevance of the Act after the civil war led to agitations for a repeal of the Act (Olatunji, 2013).

The military regime of general Ibrahim Babangida strove to stem the tide of copyright infringements in the country by amending the 1970 Copyright Act with the promulgation of Decree No 47 in 1988. A unique introduction under this decree was the establishment of a formal agency that would have the responsibility of administration and regulation of copyright issues in the country (Olatunji, 2013). This move birthed the Nigerian Copyright Council with the inauguration of its governing council in 1989. However, the scope of the council's responsibility was restricted to administrative purposes while it lacked real enforcement powers (Olatunji, 2013). Rather, the council's activities were visible in the conduct of workshops and seminars which were targeted at creating awareness and educating Nigerians on the need to exercise caution in the use of protected works of art. Despite this, the country's copyright infringement rate did not subside because the established council operated like a toothless bulldog (Asein, 2012). Between 1988, when the Copyright Council was established, and 1999, when the country transited into democratic governance, Decree No 47 had gone through two major amendments (1992 and 1999). A notable feature of the amendments was the renaming of the "Nigerian Copyright Council" as "Nigerian Copyright Commission" in 1996 and the expansion of the scope of its operation from mere administrative functions to entail a wider range of regulatory and enforcement roles. Section 34 (3) b-f of the Act detailed the responsibilities of the Commission as follows:

> b) monitor and supervise Nigeria's position in relation to international conventions and advise government thereon; c) advise and regulate conditions for the inclusion of bilateral and multilateral agreements between Nigeria and any other country; d) enlighten and inform the public on matters relating to copyright; e) maintain an effective

databank on authors and their works; f) be responsible for such other matters as relate to copyright in Nigeria as the Minister may from time to time direct.

(Federal Government of Nigeria, 1999)

The expansive capacity of NCC's role under the two amendments empowered the commission to pursue regulations that have come to define and shape the terrain of copyright regulations in the country. For instance, the Copyright (Video Rental) Regulations 1999, Copyright (Security Devices) Regulations 1993, Copyright (Optical Disc Plants) Regulations 2006, Copyright (Collective Management Organisation) Regulations 2007, Appointment of Copyright Inspectors Notice and Copyright (Levy on Materials) Order 2013 were outcomes of the enhanced capacities of the NCC to regulate and enforce laws in pursuit of a creative and conducive environment that rewards participants in the creative industry (Banwo-Ighodalo, 2016). The mode of enforcement of these regulations will form the crux of the discussion in the next section.

Copyright Regulations

Appointment of Copyright Inspectors

One of the major features of the 1999 amendments on the Copyright Act was the leverage given to the NCC in appointing copyright inspectors who act as the enforcement arm of the commission. According to Section 38 of the Copyright Act, the copyright inspector is saddled with the responsibility of enforcing compliance with the copyright provision. Section 38 of the Act vested the copyright investors with the powers

> a) to enter, inspect and examine any building or premises upon reasonable suspicion that such building/premises is being used for copyright infringement-related activities; b) to arrest upon reasonable belief that an offence has been committed under the Act; c) to examine or inquire for the purpose of ascertaining compliance with the Act; d) to require production of, inspect, examine or copy the register referred to under section 14; e) to enquire for necessary information from persons find in building/premises suspected as being used for infringement of copyright; f) to examine, test or analyse the premises suspected of being used for infringement of copyright including the power to take photographs of necessary evidence; and g) to exercise such other powers as the Commission may delegate to it to give effect to the provisions of the Act.

(Olatunji, 2013)

The effectiveness of the inspector officers was seen in the implementation of the anti-piracy raids across major music and movie touch points in the country. An example of the success of the copyright inspectors was seen in the implementation of the strategic anti-piracy (STRAP) operations carried out in 12 states across Nigeria between January and March 2016. The operation confiscated and destroyed products infringing on the copyright regulations valued at 2.4 billion Naira (Nigerian Copyright Commission, 2016). In spite of this, the 1999 amendment of the Copyright Act has been faulted on the loose definition of the qualification of persons appointed as copyright inspectors (Olatunji, 2013). For example, section 37 (3) of the regulation equates the authority of the copyright inspector with officers of the Nigerian police force. It states that:

> [A] copyright inspector shall have all the powers, rights and privileges of a police officer as defined under the Police Act and under any other relevant enactment pertaining to the investigation, prosecution or defence of a civil or criminal matter under this Act.
> (Federal Government of Nigeria, 1999)

Olatunji (2013) argued that equating copyright inspectors with officers of the Nigerian police force will require a further clarification on the criteria for selecting or appointing a copyright inspector. For example, will the appointment be considered if such a person has formal training in case investigation and security management which are core functions of the Nigerian police force? Should the copyright inspector be a serving member of the Nigerian police or other security agencies? The inability of the regulation to properly define the background of copyright inspector officers created a challenge around the recruitment process as well as the ability of the assigned persons to effectively function in that capacity. Furthermore, Akoyi et al. (2019) argued that the duplication and overlapping of roles between copyright inspectors and existing law enforcement agencies in Nigeria have been the challenge of intellectual property regulations in the country. The amendment saddled the copyright inspector officers with the same duty assigned to the Nigerian police force in investigating, arresting and prosecuting criminals. These complications are responsible for the lack of collaboration between the NCC and security operatives in prosecuting offenders.

Copyright (Video Rental) Regulations 1999

The copyright (video rental) regulation was enacted in 1999 in furtherance of the power given to the NCC to make laws that protect the earnings of creators in the Nigerian creative industry. Asein (2012) revealed that the regulation states that:

> The video rental regulation is designed to provide a mechanism through which legitimate cinematograph films in the video format can be made available for hiring without infringing the copyright provisions that prohibit the rental of works without the prior authorization of the owner of the copyright in the film.
> (Asein, 2012)

The regulation required anyone interested in engaging in the rental business to register with the NCC as contained in Section 37(4) which says that:

> All persons engaged in the business of rental, leasing, hiring, loaning or otherwise distributing cinematograph works, to the public for commercial purposes shall apply, in the prescribed forms, to the Nigerian Copyright Commission for accreditation to carry on such business.
> (Federal Government of Nigeria, 1999)

The regulation encouraged content creators (movie producers) to make available a rented copy of their work to rental outlets who are to pay royalty in return. Section 37(5) says:

> Each copyright owner shall make available to the accredited rental outlets specially packaged copies of his cinematograph film in library jackets or any other format as may be prescribed by the Commission to be designated as rental copies for the purpose of licensing the rental outlets to commercially distribute same to the public.
> (Federal Government of Nigeria, 1999)

The intention of the framework was to protect movie producers from exploitation since the country is yet to develop a sustainable way of mitigating the operations of film pirates. However, the framework has been criticized for its inability to establish a proper route through which producers are compensated for their work. More so, it was argued that the policy suffered a systemic failure as an investigation on the extent to which film rental outlets complied in registering with either the NCC or the NFVCB showed the rate of compliance was poor (Olatunji, 2013). For instance, Olatunji (2013) conducted an investigation on 20 video rental operators in Kwara State and found that none of the operators had registered with either the NCC or the NFVCB. One of the reasons observed for the poor compliance was the weak enforcement of the provision by the NCC as film rental operators disclosed that the commission had not performed its supervisory role to enforce compliance (Adewopo, 2011). More disturbing pieces of evidence emanated from Kwara State, where it was revealed that the majority of the films put out for rentals are pirated copies (Olatunji, 2013). This shows that poor enforcement of the video rental regulation was the clog impeding the efficient performance of the framework.

Copyright (Security Devices) Regulations 1999

The regulation was introduced to intensify the government's effort in the fight against piracy in the film and music industry in Nigeria. Section 21 (1) states that:

> The Commission, with the consent of the Minister may prescribe any design, label, mark, impression or any other anti-piracy device for use on, in, or in connection with any work in which copyright subsists.
> (Federal Government of Nigeria, 1999)

The regulation introduced the use of a hologram stamp as symbol of authenticity and originality on sound recordings and cinematograph films produced locally or imported with the intention of distributing for commercial purposes. The regulation requires local producers or importers to apply to the NCC for hologram accreditation, as the commission is the only authorized agency to issue it. As lofty as the idea was, it was not a foolproof arrangement as loopholes within the framework were exploited by perpetuators of intellectual property theft. For instance, it was revealed that the commission encountered difficulties in ascertaining the originality of works submitted for hologram accreditation (Nigerian Copyright Commission, 2012). It was argued that the framework also failed to reduce public exposure to counterfeit products because of the lack of awareness programmes to sensitize the public on ways of identifying original and counterfeit stamps since the commission envisaged the possibility of the hologram being counterfeited. Research conducted on movie consumers in Kwara State showed that the majority of respondents were unaware of the use of holograms as a mark of originality of CDs purchased. Rather, they rely on physical attributes such as the clarity of the pictures as well as the packaging (Olatunji, 2013).

Copyright (Optical Disc Plants) Regulations 2006

The Optical Disc Plant regulation aimed to tackle the issue of piracy from the source. The regulation was enacted in pursuant with Section 37(4) of the 1990 Copyright Act. The provisions under the Optical Disc Plant regulation stated that "no person shall manufacture optical discs or production parts in Nigeria unless such a person is duly registered by the Commission" (Nigerian Copyright Commission, 2016). In essence, the regulation targets monitoring the operations of local optical disc manufacturers and replicating plants in Nigeria as well as the importation of such products to curb the menace of illegal distribution, reproduction and marketing of counterfeited products (Olatunji, 2013). The commission identified the lack of regulation on the manufacturing and replicating plants as the source of piracy in Nigeria and as such moved to steer up initiatives that would ensure compliance among players in the line of business in fighting the rights infringement in the creative industry. The regulation ensured that operators of replicating plants must comply with stringent conditions such as registration of replicating plant, proper keeping of records and samples, inspections, sanctions and penalties for violation of regulations and prescribed fees. These efforts are geared at tightening the regulatory environment and ensuring that the commission can track elements within the market engaged in the shady practice. For instance, the regulation recommends that certificates are issued to replicating plants and they are assigned unique identification codes which help the commission track the source of CDs/DVDs in circulation.

Regarding the effectiveness of the regulation in stemming the rate of copyright infringement, the optical disc plant framework has been successful in other countries and Nigeria's implementation of the framework was applauded by the United States which had initially enlisted the country as one that allows the growth of piracy (Olatunji, 2013). However, three years after the introduction of the regulation, it was reported that many of the replicating plants were yet to be registered as required by the regulation (International Intellectual Property Alliance, 2009). Furthermore, it was disclosed that the rate at which the commission enforced the regulation is slow and limited to the big replicating plants in the country while other operators of CD duplication and burning are not prosecuted (Adedeji, 2011).

Copyright (Collective Management Organization) Regulations 2007

The Collective Management Organization (CMO) remains one of the most definitive regulations in the history of copyright regulation in Nigeria. The regulation introduced collecting societies named as CMOs who manage and collect royalties on behalf of right-holders. The CMOs enjoy the same right as the property holders and are entitled to 30 percent of right-holders' royalties (Olatunji, 2013). The regulation requires CMOs to register with the commission to obtain operating licences, which can be revoked and subject to renewal six months before the expiration of the current issue. The initiative to allow CMOs collect royalties on behalf of right-holders has been argued to present an effective mechanism that allows right-holders enjoy proceeds from their works with little or no effort.

The Nigerian music industry presents a clear example of application of the regulation as the enactment of the regulation paved the way for the establishment and consequent registration of Copyright Society of Nigeria (COSON) in 2010. COSON has been involved in the collection and management of royalties of its members, but the accusation of financial mismanagement by some of its members led to the withdrawal of its licence (Okeke & Ilesanmi, 2020). Before the withdrawal of its licence, COSON had partnered with MultiChoice Limited on the use of works of its members on their broadcast channels in Nigeria (Olatunji, 2013). Other collecting societies such as the Musical Copyright Society of Nigeria (MCSN) have emerged in the music industry to rival COSON in the quest to collect royalties on behalf of the artistes. However, the legal battle between the two societies has torn members apart on which society has the lawful right to perform this function. Until the recent proclamation by the Attorney General of the Federation, Abubakar Malami, approving the existence of MCSN as a CMO, COSON had operated as the single CMO in Nigeria (Okeke & Ilesanmi, 2020). Meanwhile, the suspension of COSON's licence has paved way for MSCN to operate as the accredited CMO in the country.

The success of the CMO in assisting artistes in securing their royalties has not been translated in the Nollywood movie industry as the absence of a CMO robs the industry's players of their hard-earned investment. It has been argued that the absence of a CMO in the Nollywood industry has contributed to the persistence of various illegal activities of copying, dubbing and burning of films into CDs and DVDs in the industry (Adelowo et al., 2010). In 2015, the Audio-Visual Rights Society of Nigeria (AVRS) became the sole CMO responsible for the collection of royalties on behalf of practitioners in the Nollywood industry. The extent to which AVRS has effectively curbed the unjust use of works created by practitioners in the Nollywood industry is scarce and would be a good point for future discourses.

Copyright (Levy on Materials) Order 2012

The levy on material order launched in 2012 is one of the proactive regulations in NCC's determination to revitalize the copyright environment in Nigeria. The order aimed at placing levies on materials that have the potential to be used in perpetuating infringement in intellectual property. Section 40 (1) states that "there shall be paid a levy on any material used or capable of being used to infringe copyright in a work" (Federal Government of Nigeria, 1999). The order empowered the minister to determine the levy payable and directed the NCC to oversee the disbursement of the levy among approved CMOs in the country. The sharing formula for the disbursements of the levy is as follows:

- 10 percent for promotion of creativity;
- 20 percent for anti-piracy programme of the Commission;
- 10 percent for administrative purpose to be shared equally among all government agencies involved in the implementation of this order;
- The remaining 60 percent shall be distributed equally among all approved collecting societies (Federal Government of Nigeria, 1999).

Analysis of the Levy on Materials order was aimed at reducing the rate at which materials that could be used to infringe copyright in a work were being imported into the country considering that local manufacturers for these items are inexistent. However, the order has been removed because of its inability to determine the purpose of its establishment either as a means of generating money for the NCC or to protect the royalties of authors (Olatunji, 2013). It was argued that the formula for sharing the proceeds from the levy collected showed the intent of the regulators in the formulation of the legislation as one that should cater for the daily operations of the NCC considering that the agency's activities have been impeded by poor funding. Given the sharing formula, it was further revealed that it was not clear how 60 percent of funds allocated to CMOs would be shared between the CMO and the right-holders. It should be noted that earlier regulation under the Collective Management Organization (CMO) regulation of 2007 had assigned 30 percent of right-holders' royalties to CMOs for administrative purposes. The levy on material order failed to specify how the funds generated would be shared and could be a source of conflict between CMOs and right-holders. In addition, it has been argued that the levy on material order, inasmuch as it seeks to discourage the importation of materials that could be used for copyright infringement; it shows the commission's inability to adequately combat copyright infringement in the country. The basis of the argument is predicated on the assumption that the commission tries to compensate the right-holder ahead of potential infringement on their works. From a business angle, the imposition of a levy will transfer the burden of pricing to the end users of the product; failing to dissuade manufacturers from engaging in copyright infringement since they are likely to transfer the additional cost incurred on the materials imported to the end users.

In a bid to make the nation's copyright laws relevant in the contemporary knowledge economy, the upper chamber of the Nigerian House of Assembly came up with a bill to outlaw the broadcast or reproduction of the online audiovisual work without the author's consent. The bill was passed by the House of Representatives on 27 July 2022, following its earlier passage by the Senate on 6 April 2022. *The Guardian* newspaper highlights the four cardinal objectives of the bill as:

> (a) strengthening the copyright regime in Nigeria to enhance the competitiveness of its creative industries in a digital and knowledge-based global economy; (b) effectively protecting the rights of authors to ensure just rewards and recognition for their intellectual efforts while also providing appropriate limitations and exceptions to guarantee access to creative works; encourage cultural interchange and advance public welfare; (c) facilitate Nigeria's compliance with obligations arising from relevant international copyright treaties, and (d) enhance the capacity of the Nigerian Copyright Commission for effective administration and enforcement of the provisions of the Copyright Act.
>
> (Ogwa, 2022)

The proposition tagged "A Bill for an Act to Repeal the Copyright Act CAP LFN 2004 and to Re-enact the Copyright Act 2021" was sponsored to protect the unauthorized use of creative audiovisual on social media platforms such as Facebook, Instagram, TikTok, Twitter among other platforms (Vanguard Newspaper, 2022). If passed, the bill further enhances the competitiveness of the Nigerian creative industry in the nascent digital economy as well as position authors on the right part of getting compensation and recognition for their works. A major fear with the enforcement of the regulation is not different from those that have plagued previous regulations and made them ineffective. For instance, the bill did not make provision for ways of investing financial resources in upscaling the capacities of the NCC in monitoring and effectively bringing to justice infringements perpetrated online.

Unlike previous laws, the 2021 Act empowers Copyright owners to take ownership of their work by monitoring the use of their works. Section 29(1) of the 2021 Copyright Act stated that:

> [T]he owner of copyright in a work, in respect of which copyright has been infringed, may issue notice of such infringement to the relevant service provider requesting the service provider to take down or disable access to any infringing content or link to such content, hosted on its systems or networks.
> (Federal Government of Nigeria, 2021)

Furthermore, the Act highlighted the responsibilities of service providers in protecting the unauthorized use of creative work online. Section 30(1–2) stated that:

> [A] service provider, upon receiving notice of infringement under Section 29 shall promptly notify the subscriber responsible for the content for which the notice relates informing him of the content of the notice; If within 48 hours of the receipt of the notice of takedown the subscriber fails to provide any information justifying the continued keeping of the content complained about, the service provider shall take down or disable access to the infringing content or links to such content hosted on its systems or networks, and thereafter, notify the owner of the copyright accordingly.
> (Federal Government of Nigeria, 2021)

The Act will be an effective measure in curbing indiscriminate use of creative content online and provides a good foundation for the regulation of social media in the country. In addition, the Act will enhance the competitiveness of the Nigerian creative industry in the nascent digital economy as well as position authors on the right part of getting compensation and recognition for their works. A major fear with the enforcement of the regulation is not different from those that have plagued previous regulations and made them ineffective. For instance, the Act did not make provision for ways of investing financial resources in upscaling the capacities of the NCC in monitoring and effectively bringing to justice infringements perpetrated online. A summary of the regulations and their provisions as well as weaknesses are summarized in Table 8.1.

Nigerian Copyright Commission and the Enforcement of Copyright Laws in Nigeria

The establishment of the Nigerian Copyright Commission has brought stability to the regulation of intellectual property rights in Nigeria. The agency has positioned Nigeria on the global map as a nation that frowns against the unlawful exploitation of authors and other players in the creative industry. Considering the enormous potential the creative industry possesses, the establishment of the NCC and consequent enactments and reviews of copyright

Table 8.1 Summary of copyright milestones in Nigeria

Copyright Milestones in Nigeria	Year	Provisions	Weaknesses
Copyright Act	1970	First indigenous attempt in protecting the intellectual property right in Nigeria. Federal Commissioner for Trade to appoint authorities that will oversee the administration of prescriptive regulations Copyright Unit of the Department of Culture and the Minister of Finance were in charge of making and enforcing regulations regarding the issues in the creative industry and printing of copyrighted	Failed to establish a definite body to enforce copyright laws
Promulgation of Decree No 47	1988	Establishment of the Nigerian Copyright Council The council was saddled with purely administrative roles Organized seminars and workshops in creating awareness on copyright infringements	The Nigerian Copyright Council lacked enforcement powers
Renaming of Nigerian Copyright Council as Nigerian Copyright Commission	1996	Expanded scope of NCC's operations Empowered to make laws, enforce and prosecute offenders	Poor funding Overlapping laws with other enforcement agencies Lack of collaborations with effective security agencies
Appointment of copyright inspectors	1999		Duplication and overlapping of roles with other security agencies in the country
Copyright (Video Rental) Regulations	1999	Licensing of rental association and encouraging authors to produce rental copies of their works	Poor supervisory role by NCC. Non-compliance by rental outlets to register with the NCC and NFVCB
Copyright (Security Devices) Regulations	1999	Introduction of hologram stamp	Poor public sensitization on the identification of authentic hologram stamp

Copyright (Optical Disc Plants) Regulations	2006	Registration of manufacturing and replicating plants	Slow enforcement of the regulation
Streamlined focus on big manufacturing and replicating plants
Many unregistered manufacturing and replicating plants even after three years of enactment
Copyright (Collective Management Organization) Regulations	2007	Introduction and registration of CMOs	Corruption allegations against CMOs
Copyright (Levy on Materials) Order	2012	Introduce levies on materials used for copyright infringements	Loose definition of sharing of levy generated
Transfer of pricing burden to end users
Exposed the weakness of NCC in fighting copy infringements in Nigeria Authors receiving compensation ahead of potential copy infringement on their work

laws in the country, Nigeria is yet to match the global best practices in the fight against intellectual property infringements. According to Statista (2022), Nigeria is ranked 120 on the global Intellectual Property (IP) ranking behind the United States, the United Kingdom and Germany, which occupied the first three spots, and South Africa, Kenya and Ghana, which are ranked forty-eighth, sixty-first and eighty-sixth in Africa respectively. Nigeria's inability to compete with nations on the global IP standard has been linked to the inefficiencies around the enforcement of property rights. Nwogu (2014) argued that poor enforcement strategy, inappropriate management of information, corruption and lack of skilled capacities at the NCC impedes the country's drive towards attaining global competitive height in IPR management.

More so, Olatunji (2013) argued that issues around IP enforcement in Nigeria can be adduced to the inefficiency of the NCC and its regulations. For instance, post-1996 reforms which gave the NCC powers to make regulations in the fight against copyright infringements saw the NCC appoint copyright inspectors who are saddled with the same responsibilities as officers of the Nigerian police force (Olatunji, 2013). A major question that crosses the mind is to explain the rationale for the appointment of a copyright inspector when collaboration could be struck with existing security agencies in the country to carry out such functions. This shows the extent of inter-agency cooperation that exists between the NCC and other security agencies in the country. For instance, it was argued that the working relationship between the NCC, the Nigerian Police Force and the Economic and Financial Crime Commission (EFCC) had not been the most convincing in the quest to combat copyright infringement in the country (Nigerian Copyright Commission, 2008). NCC (2008) report disclosed that lack of will among the officers of the Nigerian police force and the relegation of copyright matters as a minor case by the EFCC had put a strain on inter-agency collaboration in NCC's fight against copyright infringement in the country.

The digitization era has further exposed the weakness of the NCC in the fight against copyright infringement in the country. It was revealed that lack of sound knowledge among the officers of NCC and lack of access to modern technology and devices that aid detection of copy infringement impedes the commission's effectiveness in enforcing copyright laws (Adeyemi, 2020). Most of the officers of the NCC are ignorant of the issues involved in copyright protection (Adeyemi, 2020). This makes them incapable of properly enforcing the laws as expected. Furthermore, it was found that the incidence of corruption among officers of the NCC and their relationship with perpetrators of copyright infringements stalls the commission's efforts to execute justice. Similarly, the inefficiency in the Nigerian judicial system further contributes to the inefficient enforcement of copyright laws by the NCC. For instance, data revealed by Edosomwan (2019) showed how the slow judicial process hampers the ability of the NCC to enforce and prosecute copyright violators.

In furtherance of the debate on the enforcement capabilities of the NCC, it was argued that the existing copyright regulations in the country do not cover the rights of innovators of digital technology, which makes the enforcement capabilities of the agency obsolete and irrelevant to the demands of intellectual property theft in the digital economy (Adelabu & Oyeleye, 2022). The last revision to the copyright act in the country was in 2012, which shows that the government's commitment towards the protection of authorship in the creative industry does not match the verbal commitment given considering that the industry is contributing to reducing the unemployment rate in the country. Between 2012 and 2022, the nation experienced greater transformation in terms of innovative and disruptive capabilities in the internet technology space. The emergence of fintech and other software start-up companies springing up in different regions around the country is proof of the enormous transformation happening in the country's tech space. For instance, Flutterwave has grown from being just a Nigerian start-up to becoming the pride of Africa's start-up sector with a $3 billion valuation; the highest valuation for an African start-up (Kene-Okafor, 2022). Feats like this show the need to have relevant policies to protect the rights of authors in these spaces.

Conclusion

The chapter reviewed existing copyright laws and their amendments to show changes and milestones achieved by Nigeria in the protection of copyright and fights against intellectual theft in the country. The chapter established the relevance of intellectual right protection beyond the circuit of the creative industry to other areas of the nation's economy, such as the nascent software and technology and pharmaceutical sectors. Further, it has shown how weak the enforcement of copyright laws in the country has negatively impacted on critical sectors of the Nigerian economy and how authors are robbed of their credit and compensation for their creative works. The chapter attributed the continued loss of the nation's revenue to copyright infringements to the shortcomings associated with existing copyright laws in the country.

Historical and comparative analyses of the copyright regulations and amendments enforced in the country have shown that the country is yet to take a proactive approach to curb the spate of copyright infringement. The most appalling regulations were the levy on materials orders and the Copyright (Video Rental) Regulations of 2012 and 1999 respectively, which exposed the weakness of the NCC in curtailing the activities of copyright violators. Rather, the commission designed both frameworks to seek avenues to generate revenue for its administrative and promotional activities. Similarly, lack of conciseness in the designation of the role of copyright inspectors by the 1999 amendment with regard to the overlap in the discharge of their functions with that of the Nigerian police force showed that adequate consideration is needed in the formulation of future policies to protect against copyright

On the bright side of the regulations, the Copyright (Collective Management Organization) Regulations of 2007, which introduced CMO, is a major landmark that shaped the Nigerian music industry. The existence of collection societies such as COSON and MCSN has reduced the rate at which music artistes are exposed to incidences of copy infringement as these bodies work to collect royalties due to their members. These efforts, to a large extent, have increased the level of awareness among music artistes on copyright issues and royalties. The Nollywood industry is yet to attain the height experienced in the music industry because the industry had operated without a recognized CMO until the establishment of AVRS in 2015. The level of success of AVRS in reducing the incidence of copyright infringement remains unknown, but a report has it that Nollywood is the most prone industry to copyright infringements in Nigeria, thanks to the proliferation and uncontrolled use of digital platforms such as YouTube (News Agency of Nigeria, 2022).

The chapter has shown that the current copyrights regulations in the country are incapable of meeting the challenges associated with intellectual property rights in the current digital and knowledge economy. This is a major factor responsible for the poor performance of the NCC in curbing the sharp rise in online intellectual theft, especially with the pervasiveness of social media networks such as Facebook, Twitter, TikTok and Instagram. Although, policies are in the pipeline to empower the commission to fight against online intellectual theft, the process of policy formulation in Nigeria is slow due to the bureaucratic bottlenecks associated with the system of governance.

Given the aforementioned, some recommendations to optimize the capacity of the NCC in regulating and enforcing copyright laws in the fast-paced digital and knowledge economy have been highlighted in the succeeding paragraphs.

Copyright regulation in the digital and knowledge economy cannot be left to the NCC to enforce. There is a need for inter-agency collaboration and integration of other security and anti-graft agencies in the country in the fight against copyright infringement. A great deal of knowledge can be gained from collaborations with agencies, such as EFCC and the Independent Corrupt Practice Commission (ICPC), which have been at the forefront of combatting internet crime in the country. Exposure to the level of intelligence available to these agencies will be valuable to the NCC in the quest towards escalating copyright regulation to cover the online space.

The formulation of copyright regulatory policies in the country since inception had not considered including practitioners who understand the several touch points where infringements are perpetrated. Copyright policy formulation and enforcement will be strengthened with collaborations and support from industry experts. In addition, the commission could consider working with administrators of social media platforms such as Facebook, YouTube and Instagram in the use of artificial intelligence and robotics in flagging the unauthorized use of creative works in all their forms on their platforms. These outlets could be a credible source of identifying and arresting copyright violators.

Furthermore, skills deficit and corruption among officers of the NCC are major issues that must be addressed. Efforts must be directed at improving the knowledge levels of the enforcement officers on the relevant copyright laws. More so, incidences of corruption must be discouraged. As a result, adequate compensation and remuneration must be packaged to encourage loyalty and commitment from enforcement officers.

References

Adedeji, A. (2011). Combating piracy through optical disc plant regulation in Nigeria: Prospects and Challenges. *NIALS Journal of Intellectual Property*, 135–163.

Adelabu, O., and Oyeleye, M. (2022). Copyright violation and online news sourcing: Effect, challenges and panaceas. *Global Journal of Education, Humanities and Management Sciences*, 44–56.

Adelowo, C., Egbetokun, A., Abolaji, D., and Siyanbola, W. (2010). Management of copyright in the creative country industry in Nigeria: Nollywood experience. In *Globelics International Conference*. Kuala Lumpur: University of Malaysia.

Adewopo, A. (2011). *Copyright System in Nigeria*. Lagos: Principles and Perspectives,.

Adeyemi, I. (2020). Copyright issues in Nigeria: Analysis of nigerian copyright commission cases between the years 2008–2018. *International Journal of Knowledge Content Development & Technology*, 71–82.

Akoyi, Y., Raji, Z., and Olaniyan, O. (2019). *Impact of Intellectual Property Infringement on Businesses and the Nigerian Economy*. Abuja: PricewaterhouseCoppers (PWC).

Asein, J. (2012). *Nigerian Copyright Law and Practice* (2nd ed.). Abuja: Books and Gavel Publishing.

Babatunde, J. (2021, December 3). Nigeria's creative industry worth $4.5bn – Emefiele. *Vanguard*. Retrieved from: www.vanguardngr.com/, accessed August 4, 2022.

Banwo-Ighodalo. (2016). *Strengthening Intellectual Property Rights and Protection in Nigeria*. Lagos: Banwo-Ighodalo.

Nigeria: Criminal Code Act [Nigeria] (amended version of 1990) Publication Date: 1 June 1916 URL: https://www.refworld.org/docid/49997ade1a.html

Edosomwan, A. (2019). Protecting intellectual property rights in Nigeria: A review of the activities of the nigerian copyright commission. *World Patent Information*, 1–7.

Essien, E. (2016). Video film piracy in Nigeria: Interfacing to integrate the pirate. *LWATI: A Journal of Contemporary Research*, 157–166.

Federal Government of Nigeria. (1999). *Copyright Act*. Abuja: Federal Government of Nigeria.

Federal Government of Nigeria. (2021). *An Act to Repeal the Copyright Act CAP C8 LFN 2004 and To Re-Enact the Copyright Act 2021*. Abuja: Federal Government of Nigeria.

International Intellectual Property Alliance. (2009). *IIPA's 2009 Special 301 Report on Copyright Protection and Enforcement*. Washington, DC: International Intellectual Property Alliance.

Kene-Okafor, T. (2022, February 16). African fintech flutterwave triples valuation to over $3B after $250M Series D. *Techcrunch*. Retrieved from: https://techcrunch.com/2022/02/16/african-fintech-flutterwave-triples-valuation-to-over-3b-after-250m-series-d/, accessed August 5, 2022.

Moudio, R. (2013). *Nigeria's Film Industry: A Potential Goldmine*. Washington, DC: Africa Renewal.

News Agency of Nigeria. (2022, March 29). Actor drags YouTube channel to court over copyright infringement. *Peoples Gazette*. Retrieved from: https://gazettengr.com/actor-drags-youtube-channel-to-court-over-copyright-infringement/, accessed August 5, 2022.

Nigerian Copyright Commission. (2008). *International Intellectual Property Alliance (IIPA)*. Abuja: Nigerian Copyright Commission.

Nigerian Copyright Commission. (2012, November 19). Programmes, achievements. *Nigerian Copyright Commission*. Retrieved from: www.copyright.gov.ng/index.php/downloads/file/22-ncc-2012-annualreport a, accessed August 5, 2022.

Nigerian Copyright Commission. (2016, August 8). A compendium of the enforcement and antipiracy activities carried out by the Nigerian Copyright Commission within the 1st quarter (January-March) of the Year 2016. *Nigerian Copyright Commission*. Retrieved from: www.copyright.gov.ng/index.php/news-events/item/345-a-compendium-of-the-enforcement-and-antipiracy-activities-carried-out-by-the-nigerian-copyright-commission-within-the-1st-quarter-january-march-of-the-year-2016, accessed August 5, 2022.

Nwogu, M. I. O. (2014). The challenges of the Nigerian Copyright Commission (NCC) in the fight against copyright piracy in Nigeria. *Global Journal of Politics and Law Research*, 2, 22–34.

Ogwa, P. (2022, August 2). National Assembly passes copyright bill. *The Guardian*. Retrieved from: https://guardian.ng/features/national-assembly-passes-copyright-bill/

Ojoye, T. (2016, May 22). Sixty four percent of imported malaria drugs fake – Expert. *Punch Newspaper*. Retrieved from: https://punchng.com/, accessed August 4, 2022.

Okeke, F., and Ilesanmi, T. A. (2020, June 17). Nigeria: Coson V. MCSN: Let the music pay who exactly? *Mondaq*. Retrieved from: www.mondaq.com/nigeria/copyright/954920/coson-v-mcsn-let-the-music-pay-who-exactly, accessed August 5, 2022.

Okosun, V. A., and Aihie-ezomo, J. (2016). Economic diversification in a monosector economy and business management. *International Journal of Economics and*, 2(6), 67–76.

Olatunji, O. (2013). Copyright regulations under the Nigerian copyright act: a critical analysis. *NIALS Journal of Intellectual Property*, 47–83.

Oyewole, V. (2021, May 10). New report shows Nigeria's creative industry is the country's second-largest employer and has the potential to produce 2.7million jobs by 2025. *Business Insider Africa*. Retrieved from: https://africa.businessinsider.com/, accessed August 4, 2022.

Property Rights Alliance. (2022). International property right index. *Property Rights Alliance*. Retrieved from: www.internationalpropertyrightsindex.org/, accessed October 1, 2022.

Ridwan, A., Akashoro, G., and Ajaga, M. (2013). Am empirical study of the trend and pattern of video-film piracy in Nigeria. *European Scientific Journal*, 64–86.

Samuel, I. (2020). Mono economy syndrome of nigeria: reposition of manufacturing sector for sustainable diversification and development. *Research Nepal Journal of Development Studies*, 77–90.

Vanguard Newspaper. (2022, April 6). Senate passes bill to strengthen copyright law, prohibits online duplication, rebroadcasting without consent. *Vanguard*. Retrieved from: www.vanguardngr.com/2022/04/senate-passes-bill-to-strengthen-copy right-law-prohibits-online-duplication-rebroadcasting-without-consent/, accessed August 5, 2022.

9 Internet Shutdowns in Semi-Authoritarian Regimes
The Case of Cameroon

Peter Tiako Ngangum

Introduction

Internet shutdowns, which entail disconnection of the Internet within a nation's boundaries, are now a new normal in most countries across the globe (Marchant & Stremlau, 2019; Ayalew, 2019; Freyburg & Garbe, 2018; Wagner, 2018). Access Now (2019) defines Internet shutdown as "an intentional disruption of the Internet or electronic communications, rendering them inaccessible or effectively unusable, for a specific population or within a location, often to exert control over the flow of information" (Access Now, 2019, sec. 1.1, para. 1). Both the Internet Society (2019) and the Software Freedom Law Centre, India (2019), not only highlight similar features but also refer to the authorities as the principal architect of Internet shutdowns. Marchant and Stremlau (2020) argue that these definitions can help identify cases but connote a significant lack of accuracy about how information flows and Internet architecture are understood by different actors in various national contexts.

Some scholars have adopted alternative terms, evading the broad, sometimes vague, and ambivalent debate informing Internet shutdowns. For example, in their analyses, Rydzak (2019) and Purdon et al. (2015) use the term "network shutdown" to comprise suppression on social media networks but exclude more targeted restrictions, like individual website filtering. Shutdowns have occurred in many countries across the globe over the past ten years including Syria (Gohdes, 2015), Nepal, The Democratic Republic of Congo, Burundi, Ethiopia, Iraq, Kazakhstan, Pakistan, Sudan, Uzbekistan, Yemen, China, India, Zimbabwe, North Korea, Uganda, Bahrain, Bangladesh, Egypt, Turkey, Cameroon, Gambia, and Myanmar (Wagner, 2018). Internet shutdowns are unfolding against the backdrop of the initial euphoria and celebration of the Internet in Cameroon and elsewhere in Africa as an integrated democratic and dynamic network structure (Curran, 2012).

Hillary Clinton contends that "the spread of communications technology and the free flow of information would ultimately lead to greater freedom and democracy" (Polyakova & Chris, 2019: 2). However, although the Internet has given ordinary people greater access to information and provided a platform through which people can exercise their communication rights,

DOI: 10.4324/9781003388289-13

semi-authoritarian regimes often disconnect the Internet when their interests are threatened. As Freyburg and Garbe (2018) have observed, the Internet is reliant on a hierarchical architecture that provides the administrative and governing authorities and telecommunication companies with control opportunities. Based on these vulnerabilities, semi-authoritarian regimes have the power to shut down the Internet arbitrarily under the guise of *inter alia* combatting disinformation, hate speech, incitement to violence, safety, and national security concerns (Ayalew, 2019; CIPESA, 2019). Thus, *inter alia* disconnections are depicted primarily as an extreme form of online censorship (Howard, 2011).

In Africa, there were six documented cases of Internet shutdown in 2015. In 2016, that number rose to 11 out of 56 Internet shutdowns globally. By 2017, that number became 13 and 21 in 2018. Most of the Internet shutdowns in Africa were perpetuated by authoritarian regimes, with 77% of the 22 African governments that have shut down the Internet in the last five years designated as "authoritarian regimes" while 23% are "hybrid regimes" (Fisher, 2019).

While the restrictive and censorship practices of authoritarian regimes like China and Russia have been highly documented, very little focus has been devoted to overt shutdowns.

Furthermore, while all continents have now experienced Internet shutdowns, they are on the leap or upsurge in Africa, where some of the most protracted shutdowns (Cameroon and Chad) have been experienced (Marchant & Stremlau, 2019). Moreover, Africa is home to specifically broad variations in the types of Internet shutdowns including, *inter alia*, a complete Internet shutdown; a targeted Internet shutdown; an increase in state strategies, such as access restrictions (taxes) or new restrictive practices. However, the extent of current research in this area in Africa needs to be widened, including not only the socio-economic and legal contexts in which Internet shutdowns are rooted but also the various sorts of Internet disconnections that take place (Marchant & Stremlau, 2019). Unlike most existing research informing Internet shutdowns, this chapter uses the "pluralist authoritarian theory" to underpin the examination of the Internet shutdown in Cameroon and the varying modes of shutdowns that occur, their correlation to other forms of extreme censorship, and implications for the exercise of communication rights. I contend that analysing the Internet shutdown in Cameroon as a spectrum and in light of the pluralist semi-authoritarian paradigm, and not as an established democratic media sector or emerging liberal market, gives a more nuanced, clearer outlook on the range of issues at stake right now in the country. Against this backdrop, this chapter addresses the following questions: (a) What are the sociopolitical and legal contexts of the Internet shutdown in Cameroon? (b) How do the authorities restrict or compel Internet Service Providers (ISPs) to restrict connectivity by slowing or shutting down the Internet during specific events (like protests)? (c) Why does the government restrict or compel ISPs to restrict connectivity by slowing or shutting down the Internet during specific events (like protests)?

I will begin with a discussion of the relevant historical, sociopolitical, and legal contexts that inform the Internet shutdown in Cameroon. Next, I will discuss the theoretical and methodological approaches underpinning the study under investigation. Then, I will examine and/or place the Internet shutdown in Cameroon along a spectrum that helps to situate it more precisely in correlation to other extreme sorts of online censorship and information repression strategies of semi-authoritarian regimes.

Sociopolitical Context: A Synopsis

Kamerun (Cameroon) was a German Protectorate. When Germany was defeated in the First World War, Kamerun was divided between Britain and France. The League of Nations placed the Western part of Cameroon under British mandate and the Eastern part under French mandate, an arrangement which the United Nations validated in 1945, when it replaced the League of Nations. Britain administered its own part of the territory, which is British Northern and Southern Cameroon as parts of the Northern and Eastern regions of its colony of Nigeria while France governed the remaining part of Cameroon (French Cameroon) as an autonomous part of its colonial empire (Tangwa, 1999; Fonchingong, 2013).

French Cameroon became independent in 1960 and federated in 1961 with the Southern part of the British Cameroons, ushering in the Federal Republic of Cameroon. Following the political liberalization in the 1990s, the political debate in Cameroon became increasingly dominated by what came to be designated as the "Anglophone problem." The source of this problem dates back to 1961, when the political elites of two territories with distinct historical legacies (French and British) agreed on the formation of a federal state. The federation was relinquished in 1972. The country became a unitary state, first named the United Republic of Cameroon, then later the Republic of Cameroon in 1984. According to Konings & Nyamnjoh (1997: 207):

> Contrary to expectations, this did not provide for the equal partnership of both parties, let alone for the preservation of the cultural heritage and identity of each, but turned out to be merely a transition phase to the total integration of the anglophone region into a strongly centralized, unitary state. Gradually, this created an anglophone consciousness: the feeling of being "marginalized," "exploited," and even "assimilated" by the francophone-dominated state and even by the francophone population as a whole.

Drawing from this, it was, therefore, no coincidence that in October 2016, Anglophone nationalism took a dramatic lift following a series of peaceful actions instituted by common law lawyers and teachers' trade unions. The lawyers and teachers were protesting marginalization and the government's policy of assimilation.

After presenting a brief history, and sociopolitical context, this chapter moves on to examine communication rights and social media legislation in Cameroon.

Communication Rights and Social Media Legislation in Cameroon

Communication is an indispensable feature of our society, and it is central to the ways humans interconnect and participate with one another. According to Mcleod (2018: 1)

> To understand and to be understood not only enables the expression of basic needs and wants; but also enables interaction and participation at a family, community, national and global level. All humans, regardless of their age or capacity, send and receive communicative messages.

Communication is, therefore, essential to civil liberty and indispensable citizens' rights. Article 19 of the Universal Declaration of Human Rights has underlined that:

> Everyone has the right to freedom of opinion and expression; this right includes the freedom to hold opinions without interference and to seek, receive and impart information and ideas through any media and regardless of frontiers.
>
> (United Nations, 1948)

The preamble of the Cameroon constitution advocates the fundamental freedoms enshrined in the Universal Declaration of Human Rights, the Charter of the United Nations, and The African Charter on Human and Peoples' Rights, and all duly ratified international conventions relating thereto, in particular, to the following principles: the freedom of communication, of expression, and of the press. The constitution demonstrates the importance of freedom of expression, media freedom, and freedom of communication as pillars of the democratic regime. This chapter argues that fundamental democratic rights are inscribed here, that is, the freedom of communication, expression, and the press.

However, balancing media freedom, citizens' rights, and other civic liberties within an information and communication technology (ICT) context is an intricate task. In their efforts to cut down the dissemination of fake news and dissenting voices, African states have shut off the Internet (Mare, 2020) or adopted repressive measures, as evidenced in Nigeria, Uganda, and Ethiopia (Olaniyan & Akpojivi, 2021) that have undermined citizens' rights and civil liberties.

The media landscape was liberalized in Cameroon during the 1990s following the passage of law n°90/052 regulating the press. Although the constitution and the 1990 media law provide for freedom of communication, expression, and the press, these rights are subject to restrictions for the higher interests of the state. Compounding this conundrum is a persistent impasse regarding what communication rights are in a digital context and how to reconcile these rights with other competing interests.

Furthermore, while there are no specific laws regulating social media, a 2010 law relating to cybersecurity and cyber criminality contains some key provisions relating to online activity (see sections 77 and 78 of the law). I argue that some of the most relevant legislations used by the state to suppress Internet access, citizens' rights, and civil liberties are the telecommunications law n° 98/014 of July 14, 1998, (amended December 29, 2005), Cyber Security and Cybercrime law n° 2010/012 of December 21, 2010, as well as the 2014 anti-terrorism legislation.

Today, the main problem is not the law(s) itself, but how it can be highlighted or explained by a legal system (judiciary) that is void of professional autonomy. The very vague terminology used in media and terrorism laws, such as "conflict with the principles of public policy" and "attempt to undermine state security" can be applied to any media outlet, organization, group, or individual which merely criticizes the state and its institutions.

Pluralist Authoritarians and Digital Contestation

This section highlights the "pluralist authoritarian" theory developed by Frère (2015) to examine the Internet shutdown in Cameroon. From the beginning of the liberalization process in the 1990s to the start of the year 2000, most African countries were designated as nations in transition, emerging democracies, or undergoing democratic consolidation. Hence, their media has been analysed through the prism of the transition paradigm (Frère, 2015). Nonetheless, these systems were not on a course to representative government but remained in this "transitionary" state, mixing democratic features and authoritarian traits. Cameroon has a semblance of democracy in that it regularly holds elections, has opposition parties, and has a media sector that was liberalized in 1990. However, these democratic aspects are a façade. Similarly, many of the regimes in sub-Saharan Africa cannot be easily classified as either authoritarian or democratic because they display some characteristics of both (Ottaway, 2004).

Ottaway (2004: 3) argues that semi-authoritarian regimes are "ambitious systems that combine rhetorical acceptance of liberal democracy, the existence of some formal democratic institutions, and respect for a limited sphere of civil and political liberties with essentially illiberal or even authoritarian traits." It is important to note that in these systems, there is a broad-based civil society; private media do operate; multiparty elections are organized; and institutions are established, supposedly representing the interests of the various categories of the population. At the same time, the dictatorial rule is also prevalent; ongoing suppression of access and use of information, communication rights, human rights abuse, a strong governmental intolerance for free speech, electoral manipulation, and attempts to prevent any change in the regime's control over the country are commonplace. As Ottaway (2004:

163) puts it, in such an environment, a degree of self-censorship allows independent newspapers to exist but also limits their role.

Semi-authoritarian regimes exercise a certain level of political and media freedom, giving an illusion of democracy while ensuring that these freedoms will not lead to any real change, often by using restrictive strategies. Ottaway (2004) contends that semi-authoritarian regimes are not in transition. They are not emerging democracies evolving towards democratic consolidation but are semi-authoritarian by design, not by default. They are successful semi-authoritarian regimes rather than failed democracies. According to Ngangum (2019: 1), Cameroon encapsulates the same paradoxical face, mixing liberal traits with authoritarian characteristics.

Thus, in Cameroon, public authorities can claim to advocate for access to information and communication rights and media freedom by relaxing constraints on the creation of media outlets, but they may use other means (overt and disguised) to suppress the media's potential to usher dramatic changes within society. This kind of duality or ambivalence saw the authorities in Cameroon providing subsidies or special funds to stimulate private media or liberalizing the media sector through the passage of the broadcasting decree in the year 2000 and the 1990 media law while at the same time suppressing the media to curtail the flow of information into the public sphere or blocking the issuing of licences to private radio stations, which remain the principal media in sub-Saharan Africa (Ngangum, 2019). Ngangum (2019: 23) contends that:

> Administrative formalities for a broadcast license can be so burdensome and complex in Cameroon that the media can't respect the lawful authorization procedure, making the media vulnerable to punitive measures at any moment. The exorbitant cost of a license is another deterrent in Cameroon.

The concept of "pluralist authoritarian" seems to be contradictory until clarity is made between the façade and what lies beneath. In the façade, we see a diverse media sector, a market open to private media actors, political pluralism, political parties interacting with media outlets, and journalists who have gained autonomy and professionalism through the establishment of their codes of ethics, professional associations, and regulatory bodies (Frère, 2015). Nonetheless, beyond the interface, media outlets and the public have to navigate around authorities who wish to suppress the flow of information through direct political pressure, indirect economic obstacles, and manipulation of the judiciary system. Thus, despite the daily rhetoric about the diverse, plural, and representative character of the media sector, and the plurality, Cameroon does not provide an enabling environment for the exercise of communication rights and media freedom (social media).

Semi-authoritarian regimes owe their existence not only to the calculated manoeuvring of democratic institutions but also because the system is accepted by a substantial portion of the population, a support that cannot be achieved without the media's involvement (Ottaway, 2004: 17). As De Sartan (2004) argues, such regimes are distinguished by a "double speak." In this way, public norms as well as constitutional and institutional apparatus constitute a "formal language," on the one hand, and practical arrangements, unexpressed codes of daily life, and "informal language," on the other. The media are often at the centre of that double speak.

Sources

This chapter uses questionnaires and intensive interviews to inform its discussion. Furthermore, document analysis of parliamentary speech(es), media law documents, telecommunications law n° 98/014 of July 14, 1998 (amended December 29, 2005), cyber security and cybercrime law n° 2010/012 of December 21, 2010, as well as the 2014 anti-terrorism legislation were also conducted.

Fifty experts were interviewed, that is, questionnaires were sent to 50 experts on January 20, 2022 for self-completion. This was a purposive sampling motivated by the need to glean specific knowledge and experience on information and communication rights, human rights, media freedom, media and democracy, media law, information, and communication technology, and so on. The sample was composed of 15 human rights advocates and/or activists, ten journalists, ten ICT experts, ten media law experts, and five humanitarian experts. The sample was composed of 25 females and 35 males. The working experience of the respondents ranged from six years to eight years. To gain a deeper analysis of the complexities, legitimacy, and legality of Internet shutdowns, intensive interviews were used to complement self-completion questionnaires. Thus, 15 follow-up interviews, including four human rights advocates, five media law experts, four journalists, and two ICT experts, were conducted. Each of the interviews lasted 40 minutes.

Two weeks after distribution of questionnaires all the respondents had completed the questionnaire, giving a response rate of 100%. The questionnaire contained 28 questions covering, inter alia, background information, type of organization, job title, education, work experience, media freedom and freedom of expression, media censorship, access to information, communication rights, mechanisms for control, media regulation, the legality, legitimacy, and proportionality of Internet shutdowns. Both the results of the questionnaire and intensive interviews inform the research findings reported in this chapter. To protect the anonymity of the respondents, pseudonyms were used.

Internet Shutdown as an Extreme Form of Online Censorship: A Spectrum Approach

When we look at the various sorts of online censorship, we realized that Internet shutdowns are some of the most overt and incursive. Unlike other types of censorship such as closing Internet pages, websites, or certain content (De Gregorio & Stremlau, 2020), Internet shutdowns have negative effects on access to information and the exercise of communication rights. I contend that variations are often a key factor in Internet shutdowns, specifically around what or who caused the shutdown, and why it was done. This suggests a need to position Internet shutdowns in wider debates about the correlation between national security and censorship, security, and access to information and communication rights. This section introduces elements such as recurrence and time span, depth, width, and pace/tempo to highlight the spectrum approach of the Internet shutdown in Cameroon.

Recurrence and Time Span

Recurrence and time span presuppose the regularity, duration, or time span of Internet shutdown in specific contexts. In India, for example, an estimated 380 shutdowns occurred between 2014 and early 2020, even though a quarter of these Internet disconnections had a duration or time span of just 60 minutes (Software Freedom Law Centre, India, 2020). Unlike India, Cameroon and Chad have had some of the most protracted Internet shutdowns on record spanning some 230 and 480 days, respectively. While in Cameroon, the shutdown was regionalized, targeting the Anglophone regions of the country, in Chad, it was merely the blocking of access to all social media platforms rather than the Internet as a whole. According to all the experts I interviewed, the time scale or duration of the targeted Internet shutdown in Cameroon was a real tragedy for communication rights and access to information. As a senior humanitarian expert argued:

> For many Cameroonians, especially the unemployed and downtrodden, social media access and the exercise of communication rights are very important because, without Internet access, the daily existence of these people is seriously threatened. Access to social media and the exercise of communication rights can make a qualitative difference in their lives. Thus, an Internet shutdown for a long duration has serious implications for the exercise of the communication rights of the local community.
> (Tracy, Personal Communication, February 10, 2022)

Another expert underscored that:

> Communication rights presuppose that an essential context and condition are in place for a useful process of communication to take place. This process entails paying attention, accepting, communicating, and understanding as well. Therefore, recurrent Internet shutdowns for a long time or duration infringe on freedom of expression, access to information, and communication rights.
> (Ian, Personal Communication, February 19, 2022)

Depth

In looking at the depth element of Internet shutdowns, most definitions of Internet shutdowns make a difference between closing down access to the Internet completely and disabling or disconnecting access to individual and social media platforms. Thus, depth refers to the type of content that is being targeted, ranging from a complete Internet blackout to a particular platform, or even the targeting of individual bloggers, journalists, activists, or other kinds of users (Marchant & Stremlau, 2020). A complete Internet shutdown for a protracted period of time such as the case of Cameroon would mean an extreme case of the depth dimension. However, whether the shutdown is complete, partial, or just a slowdown of the network or a social media shutdown as in Chad, all of them have deleterious impacts on the exercise of citizens' rights and civil liberties.

Width

It refers to the number of people who are affected by the Internet shutdown or how widespread and diffuse a shutdown is. Even though most shutdowns are targeted and localized (Cameroon and Ethiopia), the width dimension would be equally impacted depending on the population density of the area affected. However, a nationwide Internet shutdown remains an extreme case of the width dimension.

As we have seen in the case of the Anglophone region of Cameroon, a more targeted shutdown might be just as concerning to communication rights, citizens' rights, and civil liberties as a nationwide shutdown. In Cameroon and Ethiopia, Internet shutdowns have targeted particular regions; the Oromio and the Afar regions of Ethiopia and the Southwest and Northwest regions of Cameroon. The case of the Southwest and Northwest regions of Cameroon or Ethiopia's regional Internet disconnections must be understood as strategies instituted by the national authorities to restrict access to the Internet for particular communities. As one human rights activist pointed out:

> The right to communicate and access information online means the right of every individual or community including the Southwest and Northwest communities to have their stories and worldviews heard. The exercise of communication rights, including the right to equitable access and use of information and communication resources is central to its realization.
> (Chris, Personal Communication, February 10, 2022)

I argue that targeted Internet shutdowns (Cameroon and Chad) while keeping within bounds, their effect on the general population is a worrying trend with adverse effects on access to information and communication rights not only for minorities and/or certain groups but also for the relationship between states and subgroups.

Pace (Tempo)

Pace refers to the variety of mechanisms and techniques available to achieve an Internet shutdown, which ranges from a slowdown of the network to a partial or full-scale Internet shutdown. For instance, in Cameroon, the Internet was intermittently slowed down or shut off completely between January 2017 and March 2018 (Dahir, 2018). Although a slowdown or disabling of certain networks may not be as extreme as a complete shutdown, in practice, it is important to underline that a consistent slowdown may have deleterious effects on access and use of information and the exercise of communication rights. In Cameroon and many parts of Africa, network slowdowns happen unintentionally when bandwidth demands reach the limits of a network's capacity due to poor infrastructure and unstable electricity supply. Even though a network provider can sometimes intentionally slow down a connection, there are also times when a network slowdown is a result of an intentional order from public authorities (Marchant & Stremlau, 2020). As one humanitarian expert contends:

> Man is a social being. Communication is an essential human need and therefore a human right. Without communication, no individual or community like the anglophone community in Cameroon can exist, operate, and prosper. Thus, communication rights strengthen and enhance our ability and capacity as a people, and community to use communication and information resources to attain our daily goals in the socio-economic, and political spheres.
> (Harry, Personal Communication, February 10, 2022)

After presenting a spectrum approach to the Internet shutdown in Cameroon, the following section focuses on the tradition of censorship, hostility, tension, and suspicion informing the relationship between the media and the authorities in Cameroon.

Cameroon: A History and Tradition of Media Censorship

The shutdown of the Internet in Cameroon and recent attacks on citizens' rights and civil liberties, in particular, are not new. The government has a long-standing policy of entrenched hostility towards the media. As Ngangum (2019: 1) argues:

> Although the constitution and the 1990 law, including subsequent modifications of these, guarantee media freedom, there is limited optimism for press freedom, and the role of the media in democratization for what the press supposedly gains by the new law is taken away in the same law by more severe provisions and a host of informal regulatory practices that have enhanced the arbitrary powers of the administrator.

According to a government minister:

> To ensure public order and good morals, the Cameroonian state exercises a sort of legal control on the press, thanks to some legal measures providing for censorship that is extremely light and symbolic. For poorly managed, poorly used freedom, freedom of expression can prove harmful to the consolidation of social balance and especially to national integration and peace. Some papers, the minister stressed, did not respect the law, the professional codes, and the principle of objectivity, impartiality, and search for truth dear to journalism. Censorship was thus necessary against those who would want to use freedom of expression as a pretext to install intellectual terrorism and total anarchy or a sort of return to the state of savagery.
> (Nyamnjoh, 2005: 171)

The government has labelled social media a "vicious tool" used to spread fake news and inculcate fear in the public sphere. According to the speaker of the Cameroon National Assembly, Cavaye Yeguie Djibril, social media is a new form of terrorism:

> I would like at this juncture to deplore what is developing into a new form of terrorism – the social malaise now affecting the cyberspace, that is, the insidious effects of the social media. . . . In fact, it has become as dangerous as a missile. I urge the appropriate authorities to see the pressing need to track down and neutralize the culprits of cybercrimes. Let us exercise the right to freedom of speech which, on the whole, is a noble right. However, we should know that there is a limit to freedom, for freedom without limit stifles freedom.
> (Djibril, 2016: 12)

Shutdown of the Internet by the government in the south-west and north-west regions dealt a severe blow to the burgeoning tech ecosystem "Silicon Mountain Buea." As one senior technology entrepreneur contends:

> Digital technology is a key driver of economic development and political activism, but it is also a tool for preserving and even extending political control. Within Cameroon, it is a valuable space for state censorship and control of the people. This is a travesty of the notion of the Internet as a technology of human freedom and liberation.
> (Pat, Personal Communication, February 10, 2022)

One senior broadcast journalist added:

> Although the national authorities do allow some forms of criticism and scrutiny, government critics, journalists, dissidents, and human rights advocates are nonetheless frequently arrested and detained for what

they post on popular social media sites like Facebook, and WhatsApp, both of which are aggressively monitored.

(Flore, Personal Communication, February 10, 2022)

This quote adds more impetus to the case of Mimi Mefo, a journalist for the broadcast media, *Equinoxe television*, who, on October 31, 2018, was summoned to appear before the national gendarmerie in Douala as part of a false news/information and cybercrime investigation. According to Mefo:

The regime has been using anti-terror and cybercrime laws to intimidate, threaten and silence the media. Since 2017, at least twenty journalists have been arrested and jailed in Cameroon for doing their jobs. I stopped publishing information on Facebook and my website for several months because of constant threats and intimidation.

(Mefo, 2019: 1)

One media law expert's remark was very revealing about the repressive and restrictive climate underpinning the media across the country:

This growing evolution of mechanisms for control will definitely reduce the Internet's power as a force for freedom and turn it into a tool for state repression and control of the public. By instructing operators to cause this Internet shutdown, without presenting a clear threat to public order or a pressing social need, and without presenting authorization given by a judge, the government has failed to respect the rule of law.

(Jane, Personal Communication, February 19, 2022)

However, the Minister of Posts and Telecommunications contends that:

Social media have become an important communications instrument, which unfortunately is used by people with the evil intention to propagate false information in order to threaten the public and create panic.

(Endong, 2022: 45)

Despite the reactions of the authorities and the prevailing culture of information control and censorship, most respondents believed that communication strengthens human dignity and was crucial in enhancing core human rights. A senior human rights advocate was very instructive:

Communication strengthens human dignity. Government recognition, protection, promotion, and enforcement of communication rights would mean implementing and protecting all other human rights. This is so because communication rights strengthen core human rights that collectively enhance the people's ability to communicate in their interest and for the common good of the entire society.

(Luc, Personal Communication, February 10, 2022)

Although the shutdown was lifted, the government stressed that it would be reinstated whenever necessary. Minister Libom Li Likeng was overt in his message:

> Our security forces have platforms to track and control people just as in all other countries of the world.
> (Endong, 2022: 46)

Despite the reasons that the Cameroonian authorities give publicly, critics, observers, and monitors of Internet disconnections believe these are false narratives used to conceal the principal motives to suppress opposition activity and undermine citizens' rights and civil liberties. Although this may be the case in some circumstances, I strongly argue that in certain circumstances, as illustrated by Christian, (2020), Ngange and Moki (2019), misinformation, the spread of fake news, hate speech online, and threats to national peace and security pose challenges that governments need to address. As one senior broadcast journalist in Buea argued:

> Sometimes the state does have legitimate security concerns: misinformation, the spread of fake news, hate speech, and incitement to violence on social media. Since the outbreak of the Anglophone crisis in 2016, these concerns have evolved to become a real danger to national unity, peace, and integration.
> (Emma, Personal Communication, February 19, 2022)

I contend that the essence here is not to validate the reasons that the authorities give for extreme actions like Internet shutdowns but to highlight the range of problems faced by the authorities and the lack of information that exists about how these decisions are made. Rifts between censors and communication rights advocates have intensified, and more voices continue to express concern about online censorship. According to one senior human rights lawyer:

> Internet censorship threatens access to information, it undermines communication rights and media freedom which are core requirements for the progress of our society.
> (Dan, Personal Communication, February 10, 2022)

Tom, senior counsel and human rights advocate argue that:

> Government action was lacking in good faith and all the safeguards that underpin democratic governance, such as transparency, judicial oversight, and accountability. Furthermore, Internet censorship contravenes everything that the Internet encapsulates.
> (Tom, Personal Communication, February 19, 2022)

One journalist's remark was very instructive:

> For democracy to thrive, the citizens must be able to enjoy freedom of expression, access to information, and a public space that allows rational discourse. Not all governments are fond of the notion of people being able to express themselves freely and anonymously, thus they create roundabout avenues to restrict and censor online content that does not appeal to them. Therefore, protecting the digital space from manipulation without impacting human rights will require innovation and investments from our government, tech companies, and society as well.
> (Grace, Personal Communication, February 10, 2022)

However, as the case of Cameroon has illustrated, a growing number of states are asserting hegemony over tech firms, often coercing businesses to comply with online censorship. As Mare (2020: 4244) contends regarding the case of Zimbabwe:

> Although private companies such as Econet Wireless Zimbabwe and Liquid Telecom control a huge chunk of the telecommunications infrastructure, the government often deploys political, regulatory, and lawfare strategies to force through state-ordered Internet shutdowns. Private telecommunications operators comply with the government partly to abide by their licensing obligations, for fear of political harassment and victimization, and threats of arbitrary imprisonment.

However, this often leads to censorship which undermines the exercise of communication rights. As one media law expert contends:

> Internet regulation and restrictions can present human rights risks. Communication rights build a community in which people are better equipped to receive messages, understand, and respond to them, and communicate critically, competently, and creatively. Therefore, control and restriction over Internet access and use infringe on communication rights, equitable access, and the use of digital information.
> (Phil, Personal Communication, February 10, 2022)

Thus, Internet shutdowns are often depicted essentially as an extreme form of online censorship (Howard, 2011). Today, Internet shutdowns are the most extreme form of online censorship but must be understood as an entirely distinct phenomenon from its predecessors due to its indiscriminate and disproportionate nature and the myriad of violations it serves beyond the suppression of information (Purdon & Wagner, 2015) and communication rights.

Discussion and Conclusion

The significant difference informing Internet disconnections along each of the dimensions (recurrence, time span, depth, width, pace, or tempo) is obvious. Even though a complete Internet shutdown, as well as a targeted or localized shutdown for a long time scale, may be the most deleterious to citizens' rights and civil liberties, patterns of network slowdowns and taxes also have adverse effects or where a particular region or community is targeted for exclusion. The aforementioned cases elucidate how complex the borders are between Internet shutdowns and other sorts of censorship and how context-dependent the impact of various kinds of shutdowns can be (Marchant & Stremlau, 2020). Thus, situating the case of Internet shutdown in Cameroon along a spectrum can help us to better understand their nuanced characteristics and how they are linked to other sorts of censorship and information suppression like taxation, issuing of licences for media operation, surveillance regulations, website takedowns, Facebook, or Twitter bans, closing down of media houses, and the suspension and/or banning of journalists.

Despite the existence of international human rights laws and principles, and the obligation of states to respect and enforce these laws and principles, there is often very little or no transparency and accountability when states decide to shut down the Internet, including reasons justifying shutdowns. Moreover, when authoritarian regimes rely on extemporaneous ways to decide how to mitigate Internet blackouts, their actions are rarely based on evidence, and hence they cannot justify their rationale (De Gregorio & Stremlau, 2020).

This chapter argues that the Internet (social media) plays a crucial role in spreading offensive content, like hate speech, fake news, and incitement to violence, that can infringe on national peace, unity, and integration. Serious concerns have been raised over the spread of fake news on social media, especially during the 2016 US presidential elections (Allcott & Gentzkow, 2017) and the ongoing Cameroon Anglophone conflict (Christian, 2020; Ngange & Moki, 2019). Focusing on the Cameroon Anglophone conflict, Christian (2020) contends that news stories are deficient in reliability and variability, story origin and sources, eyewitness accounts to authenticate or validate texts, and factual details such as where and when events were covered. Thus, states cannot control the dissemination of online content without regulating it (De Gregorio & Stremlau, 2020: 4229).

Even though Internet shutdowns constitute an extreme form of online censorship that infringes on access to information and communication rights, there are situations when these practices could be justified. In no way do I wish to condone such actions, but I contend that in the case of a persistent increase in the spread of hate speech, violence, and threats to national peace, security, and unity, terrorism, and the inability of social media actors to curtail such threats, there is need for a more balanced and sincere discourse about why some authorities are taking the extreme actions they take. This discourse should examine how they can be restricted, or when they might be reasonable, and how concerns about widespread online hate and fake news can be brought into debates informing the respect of communication rights. And when it comes to examining Internet shutdowns on the basis that they have negative implications on citizens' rights and civil liberties, states' grounding for Internet shutdowns must be appraised or evaluated through the prism of the principles of legality, legitimacy, and proportionality (De Gregorio & Stremlau, 2020).

Due to the significance of media freedom, access to information, and communication rights as core values for the functioning of society, the exercise of these freedoms is contingent not only on the state's duty to not interfere but also to take positive measures to formulate an effective legal framework to regulate media freedom and access to information and communication rights. In determining whether such a positive obligation exists, regard should be paid to reconciling a fair balance between the general interest of society, media freedom, communication rights, and other conflicting priorities. Thus, in the complete absence of a fair balance between protecting media freedom, access to information, the exercise of communication rights, and upholding the principles of public policy, any interference by the authorities is seen as disproportionate to the legitimate aim being pursued (Ngangum, 2020a, 2020b).

References

AccessNow., 2019. *#KeepItOn: What is an internet shutdown?* Retrieved June 12, 2019, from www.accessnow.org/keepiton/.

Access Now., 2019, July. *The state of Internet shutdowns around the world: The 2018 #KeepItOn Report.* Retrieved from www.accessnow.org/cms/assets/uploads/2019/07/KeepItOn-2018-Report.pdf.

Allcott, H., and Gentzkow, M. 2017. Social media and fake news in the 2016 election. *Journal of Economic Perspectives*, 31(2), 211–236. https://doi.org/10.1257/jep.31.2.211

Ayalew, Y. E. 2019. The Internet shutdown muzzle(s) freedom of expression in Ethiopia: Competing narratives. *Information & Communications Technology Law*, 28(2), 208–224.

Christian Tatchou Nounkeu. 2020. Facebook and fake news in the "anglophone crisis" in cameroon. *African Journalism Studies*, 41(3), 20–35, https://doi.org/10.1080/23743670.2020.1812102

CIPESA. 2019. *Despots and Disruptions: Five Dimensions of Internet Shutdowns in Africa.* Retrieved May 12, 2019, from https://Cipesa.org?Wpfb-dl=283.

Curran, J. 2012. Reinterpreting the internet. In J. Curran, N. Fenton and D. Freedman, eds, *Misunderstanding the Internet* (pp. 3–33). London: Routledge.

Dahir, A. L. 2018. This document tells the story of Africa's longest internet shutdown. *Quartz Africa*. Retrieved October 20, 2019, from https://qz.com/africa/1349108/Cameroons-internet-shutdown-blacked-out-documentary.

De Gregorio, G., and Stremlau, N. 2020. Internet shutdowns and the limits of law. *International Journal of Communication*, 2020, 1–19.

De Sartan, O. J. P. 2004. État, bureaucratie et gouvernance en Afrique de l'Ouest francophone: Un diagnostic empirique, une perspective historique. *Politique Africaine*, 96, 139–162.
Djibril, C. Y. 2016. Opening Speech by Honorable Cavaye Yeguie Djibril, Speaker of the National Assembly of Cameroon, 3rd Ordinary Session, Yaounde Cameroon.
Endong, F. P. 2022. Internet blackouts in Africa: A critical examination with reference to cameroon and nigeria. *Digital Policy Studies (DPS)*, 1(1), 39–51.
Fisher, J. 2019. New walls in cyberspace: Internet shutdowns and authoritarianism in Africa. *Mail &Guardian*. Retrieved February 5, 2020, from https://mg.co.za/article/2019-09-18-new-walls-in-cyberspace-internet-shutdowns-and-authoritarianism-in-africa/.
Fonchingong, T. 2013. The Quest for autonomy: The case of anglophone Cameroon. *African Journal of Political Science and International Relations*, 7(5), 224–236.
Frère, M. S. 2015. "Francophone Africa: The rise of pluralist authoritarian media systems?" *African Journalism Studies*, 36(1), 103–112.
Freyburg, T., and Garbe, L. 2018. Blocking the bottleneck: Internet shutdowns and ownership at election times in sub-Saharan Africa. *International Journal of Communication*, 12, 3896–3916.
Gohdes, A. R. 2015. Pulling the plug: Network disruptions and violence in civil conflict. *Journal of Peace Research*. https://journals.sagepub.com/doi/10.1177/0022343314551398.
Howard, P. 2011. When do states disconnect their digital networks? Regime responses to the political uses of social media. *The Communication Review*, 14(3), 216–232.
Internet Society. (2019, December 17). *Internet society position on Internet shutdowns*. Retrieved December 20, 2019, from www.internetsociety.org/resources/doc/2019/internet-society-position-on-internetshutdowns.
Konings, P., and Nyamnjoh F. B. 1997. The anglophone problem in Cameroon. *Journal of Modern African Studies*, 35(2), 207–229.
Marchant, E., and Stremlau, N. 2019. Africa's Internet Shutdowns: A report on the Johannesburg Workshop. In *Programme in Comparative Media Law, and Policy (PCMLP)*. Oxford: University of Oxford.
Marchant, E., and Stremlau, N. 2020. A spectrum of shutdowns: Reframing internet shutdowns from Africa. *International Journal of Communication*, 14, 4327–4342.
Mare, A. 2020. State-ordered internet shutdowns and digital authoritarianism in Zimbabwe. *International Journal of Communication*, 14, 4244–4263.
Mcleod, S. 2018. Communication rights: Fundamental human rights for all. *International Journal of Speech-Language Pathology*, 20(1), 3–11.
Mefo, M. T. 2019. Index Awards 2019. Retrieved April 4, 2019, from www.indexoncensorship.org/2019/04/awardsmimi-mefo-speech/.
Ngange, K. L., and Moki Stephen, M. 2019. Understanding Social Media's role in propagating falsehood in conflict situations: The case of the Cameroon anglophone crisis. *Studies in Media, and Communications*, 7(2), 1–13.
Ngangum, P. T. 2019. Media Regulation in Cameroon, *African Journalism Studies*, 40(3), 10–25. https://doi.org/10.1080/23743670.2020.1725777.
Ngangum, P. T. 2020a. The National Communication Council: Opportunity or constraint for press freedom and freedom of expression in Cameroon? *African Journalism Studies*, 41(1), 1–16. https://doi.org/10.1080/23743670.2019.1703776.
Ngangum, P. T. 2020b. The 'trumping effect' of anti-terrorism legislations: The case of Cameroon. In M. A. Martin Lopez, R. Rueda Lopez, C. Perez Curiel and L.

Garcia, eds, *Terre, Droits de L'Homme et Developpement: Cas et visions d'Afrique et d'Amerique* (pp. 96–123). Seville: Egregius.
Nyamnjoh, F. 2005. *Africa's Media: Democracy and the Politics of Belonging*. London: Zed Books.
Olaniyan, A., and Akpojivi, U. 2021. Transforming communication, social media, counter-hegemony and the struggle for the soul of Nigeria. *Information, Communication & Society*, 24(3), 422–437.
Ottaway, M. 2004. *Democracy Challenged. The Rise of Semi-Authoritarian State*. Washington, DC: Carnegie Endowment for International Peace.
Polyakova, A., and Chris, M. 2019. Democracy and disorder: Exporting digital authoritarianism. In *Foreign Policy Brief, Brookings*. Washington, DC: The Brookings Institution.
Purdon, L., Ashraf, A., and Wagner, B. 2015. *Security v Access: The Impact of Mobile Network Shutdowns*. London: Institute for Human Rights and Business.
Rydzak, J. 2019. *Of Blackouts and Bandhs: The Strategy and Structure of Disconnected Protest in India*. Retrieved March 30, 2019, from https://papers.ssrn.com/sol3/papers.cfm?abstract_id=3330413.
Software Freedom Law Centre, India. 2019. *About*. Retrieved March 2, 2021, from http://internetshutdowns.in/about.
Software Freedom Law Centre, India. 2020. *Internet shutdowns in India*. Retrieved February 20, 2021, from https://internetshutdowns.
Tangwa, G. 1999. Colonialism and linguistic dilemmas in Africa: Cameroon as a paradigm. *Quest*, XIII, 1–2, 1–16.
United Nations. 1948. *Universal declaration of human rights*. Retrieved July 15, 2019, from: www.un.org/en/universal-declaration-human-rights/.
Wagner, B. 2018. Understanding Internet shutdowns: A case study from Pakistan. *International Journal of Communication*, 12, 3917–3938

10 Fake News Versus Freedom of Expression

Legislating Media Trademarks Infringements on Social Media Platforms in Kenya and South Africa

Brian Hungwe

Introduction

The production of fake news and resultant infringements of media trademarks in the digital era presents challenges in balancing competing fundamental rights of freedom of expression and the accompanying constitutional limitations. Media trademarks are digitally cloned and exploited as part of a disinformation crusade. Abundant factors account for this harmful phenomenon. Apart from their reputation as a dependable information source, trademarks provide marketing visibility and reputation, where product differentiation and customer allegiance are important. Furthermore, Mirësi (2015) posits that

> When successful, trademarks become associated with perceived value to users and, consequently, are a source of higher margins for the firms that fill them. [they are] one of the main forms of intellectual property rights [IPRs] . . . [they] signal quality and good will.
>
> (Mirësi, 2015: 125)

UNESCO highlighted that exploitation of trademarks is "particularly dangerous because it is frequently organised, well resourced, and reinforced by automated technology" (UNESCO, 2018: 7). In this context, such exploitation creates "novel" and "rather vexed" interface between the guarantee of free expression and protection of Intellectual Property Rights (IPRs).

The motivating factors behind the spread of fake news range from business, extortion, political or business rivalry, elections and influencing public opinion (Conroy & Attree, 2022). The social media platforms (SMPs), ranging from Twitter, Facebook, Instagram and WhatsApp unwittingly provide podiums and stimulus for patterns of fake news disinformation. The harmful scope of fake news on SMPs is largely defined by vast global users' statistics averaging a billion users, demonstrating stiff information distribution competition patterns (Jardine, 2020). Moreover, research demonstrates that the prodigious effect of fake news could worsen, with statistics revealing that the

DOI: 10.4324/9781003388289-14

number of new smart devices collecting and sharing data should grow to 50 billion, with over 500 billion devices connected to the Internet by 2030 (Bulao, 2022). Managing IPRs becomes complex, especially where the regulatory autonomy of the state in interfering with SMPs activities is often limited by the geographical reach.

Trademark rights incorporate marketing of products and the provision of services to build a reputation, identifying and distinguishing similar goods or services of others. A trademark must be "a word, device, symbol, or other sign or any combination of these" (Rutherford, 2011: 71). The media's trusted trademarks carry enormous global goodwill deriving some measure of commercial success. Its symbols are endowed with reputable information-carrying capacity that informs decision-making processes (Barnes, 2008: 176). The established reputation provides an admissible rationale for its protection. Rutherford posits that,

> The proprietor of the trademark usually expends vast sums of money through advertising in order to build up the reputation and selling power or advertising value of his trade mark. . . . It is therefore, only fair that he should be entitled to protect this valuable asset against misappropriation.
>
> (Rutherford, 2011: 27)

Fake news trademark infringements often entail misappropriation, dilution, blurring or tarnishment. Blurring weakens the distinctive character or uniqueness of the trademark while tarnishment occurs through unfavourable associations with unlawful users such as deceptive fake news logo creations (Webster & Page, 1997: 12–44). Such harmful activities necessitate domestic regulatory measures, followed by harmonised international instruments given the corrosive global reach of the infringements.

The doctrinal research approach seeks to provide solutions to fake news based on existential workable legal principles developed over years. While literature is available exploring the motivations and psychological effects behind fake news, there is no significant work that explores the "factors that exacerbate the fake-news sharing behaviour represent[ing] a gap in the literature that needs to be bridged" (Talwara et al., 2020). This chapter in part, seeks to narrow that gap and is located in two jurisdictions, namely Kenya and South Africa. The regulatory interventions require the initial interrogation of the extent to which Intellectual Property (IP) is constitutionally protected in both jurisdictions, which are highly influential political and economic hubs driving regional trade and economic investments in East and Southern Africa (Cooper et al., 2020: 7). An economic hub creates a regional aggregation point with a "confluence of different factors such as trade lines, trade proximity, information and communication infrastructure, financial networks, social networks and logistics infrastructure" (Bernard & Moxnes, 2018). Their developed financial, logistics network and favourable regulatory environments have a domino-harmonising effect that can influence regional peers into positive legal reforms and adaptations as neighbouring spokes (Cooper et al., 2020: 4). Therefore, the jurisdictions' legislative framework effectiveness in guaranteeing trademark holders' remuneration rights will be examined. This is important because without expressly defined constitutional provisions from which to provide broad interpretations that guarantee and protect IPRs there is limited scope for trademark protection by media proprieties. Against this background, there is need to provide a fake news and journalism definitional scope. This arises because of a digitally widened network of contemporary journalists and the conceptual challenges around what constitutes fake news.

Defining Fake News and Journalism

The fake news and journalism conceptual framework are problematic given the complexities brought by the digital era. Fake news arises from the print media's relapse, supplanted by easily accessible and seamless digital media. From its original form, Vosoughi et al. have posited that fake news definition has been "irredeemably polarized", assuming different meanings to varied social constituencies with politicians referring to it as "any information put out by sources that do not support their partisan positions" (Vosoughi et al., 2018). Furthermore, scholars observe that " 'fake news' has become highly political and is often used as a buzzword not only used to describe fabricated information, but to undermine the credibility of news organizations or argue against commentary that disagrees with our own opinion" (Nielsen & Graves, 2017). Perhaps, a simple definition of fake news could be false stories published on the Internet designed to influence a particular narrative. However, determining what is "false" is problematic given different ideological and political societal persuasions. Additionally, "truth" has a "grounding of a universal truth" which is a challenge as it requires collective consensus (Molina et al., 2021). Regardless, this discussion recognises these definitional complexities and pursues the common interpretation of fake news as a deliberate digital manipulation and spread of inaccurate information.

In the digital era, journalism has also "become a collaborative and participatory practice", encompassing ordinary citizens with digital means of conveying information on SMPs without the requisite professional editorial interventions (Downie & Schudson, 2009). Nevertheless, while such platforms often gain traction, the scope of this research has been narrowed to discuss mainstream journalism and its established publications. Conventional journalism remains relevant, primarily because of its unimpeachable media trademarks, complemented by effective ethical newsgathering processes. This has to be balanced against the "exploitative manipulation of the language and conventions of news genres" by fake news, as "acts of fraud . . . [and] a particular category of phony information within increasingly diverse forms of disinformation" (UNESCO, 2018: 7). The disinformation crusade has been facilitated by the Internet and accessibility of its ancillary digital tools of information production, helping in the reconfiguration and transformation of the public sphere (Mare et al., 2019). The formerly exclusive mainstream analogue journalism has now shifted into the citizen journalism with its opaque regulatory patterns, new content production and instantaneous news consumption levels. Consumers with mobile phones can access any form of digital information through SMPs and often confuse "the popularity or virality of a shared piece of information as indication of its veracity" (Chakrabarti et al., 2018: 44). There are weak fake news digital verification tools as the information is often deceptively carried under an influential media trademark. The information is inclined to be believed primarily because of the consumers' inherent faith in the media trademark built over many years of trusted association. Trusted media trademarks provide a veneer of credibility for fake news. Against this background, fake news has become a global concern for society, governments, policymakers, international organisations and business (Talwara et al., 2020). Its false narratives, half-truths and outright disinformation are often wrapped up under the author's cover of anonymity, and enforcement of rights become complex and problematic due to seldom distant geographical reach. Given the Internet's immeasurable global reach, the impact of fake news on media trademarks' reputational implications is huge. Investigations, choice of law and enforcement mechanisms beyond jurisdictional borders are administratively costly and almost impossible. The reputational quandary of trademarks is deepened by the scale, severity and impact of fake news. Jardine (2022) postulated that

> [t]he whole edifice of democratic governance is based on the assumption of an informed citizenry with a common sense of facts, shared public narratives and a solid trust in the information provided by institutions. This entire assemblage is threatened by carefully crafted influence operations and will only grow worse as new "deep fake" technologies come into play.
>
> (Jardine, 2020)

This therefore brings to the forefront communicative rights aspects of trademarks and the corollary contestations around IPRs prompting remedial interventions to the digital conundrum. The production of fake news now threatens mainstream journalism, the pillar of effective democratic governance, often regarded as the fourth pillar of the state. The perpetrators range from malicious actions of foreign governments pursuing foreign policy agendas, (BBC, 2018), religious groups and other non-state actors with calculated political objectives (Jardine, 2022). This development can be analysed within the context of the Misappropriation Doctrine, which gave validity to legal contestations against free-riding activities on media trademarks.

Media Trademarks and Misappropriation Doctrine

The allure of influential media trademarks for disinformation purposes arises because of their historical consistency as dependable purveyors of information (Sevenzo, 2017). The difficulties in identifying the originating source of the fake news complicate legal remedies for media proprietors. The disinformation victims are both media proprietors for their unlawfully exploited trademarks and credulous news consumers inexorably exposed to an incessant erroneous diet of fake news that compromise public interest considerations. The negative psychological effect is that in general people are attracted to information which resonate with their own biases, and fake news is designed to take advantage of such human nature (Moyo, 2017). This is also known as "confirmation bias," which has been part of the digital media stratagem where they take advantage of the natural tendency by people to notice, offer any interpretation that confirms and suits their pre-existing beliefs that chime with their socio-economic political persuasions or predispositions (Bakir & McStay, 2017). The public interest dimension is crucial because fake news generates falsehoods that are potentially used in public policy formulation, because it distorts market's perception of reality and fiction. The noxious nature of fake news is captured by UNESCO's view of it as an "oxymoron which lends itself to undermining the credibility of information which does indeed meet the threshold of verifiability and public interest – i.e., real news" (UNESCO, 2018: 7). The public interest suffers because the digital tools available for the exploitation of trademarks and content are unmatched, and often mutate, providing complicated contestations for media space and audience. Solon (2017) contends:

> [T]he proliferation of powerful new technological tools. These, along with the character of social media and messaging platforms that have limited quality control standards for determining what constitutes news, make it easy to counterfeit and mimic legitimate news brands to make frauds look like the real thing.
>
> (Solon, 2017)

With poor digital verification mechanisms, and often weak legal accountability mechanisms, media trademarks are often left to wither away in the vicissitudes of such digital conflagrations. Resultantly, the commercial impact of trademark infringements is the decline in revenue as consumers shun the publications, because of an erroneous narrative developed under fake news. As such, the informal digital activities are emasculating the influence, terrain and role of journalism, with ancillary huge economic repercussions. This is because media proprietors make huge IP commercial investments into their trademarks. Such investible commercial goodwill has a pecuniary effect on potential mergers and acquisitions accompanying influential media trademarks (Macrotrends, 2022). The damaging financial implications of the infringements provide scope for the interpretation of the Misappropriation Doctrine in trademark infringements (*INS v. AP*, 1918). The doctrine provides that persons must not unlawfully appropriate investments such as trademarks without making a similar investment of their own because media proprietors make substantial investments into creating the trademarks, which are misappropriated at no cost (Barnes, 2008: 174). The doctrine which has arisen from legal precedents has three elements, namely creation, appropriation and injury.

(1) Plaintiff has made a substantial investment of time, effort and money into creating the thing misappropriated such that the court can characterize that "thing" as a kind of property right [the creation element].
(2) Defendant had appropriated the "thing" at little or no cost, such that the court can characterize defendant's action as "reaping where it has not sown" [the appropriation element].
(3) Defendant has injured plaintiff by the misappropriation [the injury element].

(Barnes, 2008: 174)

The media proprietor must prove the elements, as demonstrated in the originating United States precedent, the *International News Service (INS) v. Associated Press* (AP) (1918). The *INS v AP* case involved the plaintiff misappropriating news material from AP, an established reputable media organisation. It was argued that the INS was "endeavoring to reap where it ha[d] not sown" (*INS v AP*, 239). This reasoning is captured in probably the earliest trademark infringement case in Germany, wherein the court held that "it is opposed to the good morals to appropriate thus the fruits of another's labour in the consciousnesses that other will or may thereby be damaged" (Odol, cited in Barton, 2014: 59). The "misappropriation" of AP works entailed the abuse of the trademark, originating the doctrine.

Fake News Effect on Media Trademarks in Kenya and South Africa

In Kenya and South Africa, the proliferation of fake news exploiting media trademarks is normally associated with political electoral interest agendas (Okong'o, 2022). As such, elections in the jurisdictions have been "marred by the indiscriminate sharing of fake news and cyber-propaganda by cyber troops, citizen campaigners and digital influencers on social media platforms" (Mare et al., 2019). In Kenya, over 67 percent of the population are active Internet users (Crabtree, 2018), and in the run up to the 2022 elections, mainstream newspapers' trademarks became a magnet for fake news fabrications. A weekly influential tabloid, *The Nairobean*, published by The Standard group was deceitfully mimicked in fake newspaper headlines. (Kipng'enoh, 2015). Towards the 2022 elections, an AFP report warned it had "rounded up doctored headlines designed to stir tensions among voters, as experts warn that disinformation in Kenya is growing more sophisticated"

(Okong'o, 2022). Apart from domestic actors, there was also a foreign element behind fake news disinformation, associated with a British consulting firm, Cambridge Analytica and Harris Media LLC, a US digital advertising firm (Crabtree, 2018). Invariably, where stakes are high, a combination of domestic and international media trademarks is fabricated with "Slickly-produced news bulletins that at first glance appear to be from major international broadcasters including CNN and the BBC," and a

> fake poll video was made to look like a CNN broadcast with the familiar red and white logo carefully superimposed in the corner of the shot, but the font in the headline is very different to the one used in CNN's reports.
>
> (Sevenzo, 2017)

The BBC is a significantly recognisable media trademark in Africa (Thomas, 2020). The BBC has been an occasional victim of fake news trademark manipulation through a fake news videos and Africa Check, a not-for-profit working to promote accuracy in the media across the continent, stated:

> [V]ideos like these [fake news] can seriously influence voting behaviour [because] people who don't watch CNN or the BBC would not know that these videos were fake . . . When this fake report is putting Kenyatta ahead, [former *Kenya* President] and you're sending this video to Kenyatta's stronghold, it just reinforces the belief that he has the numbers and he's going to win.
>
> (Sevenzo, 2017)

This deceptive phenomenon is also common in South Africa. Ogilvy, a South African company that measures trends to identify how consumer behaviours are shifting with a specific lens on trademarks and publishers, revealed that most of the fake news material is connected to political or social issues, with media trademarks increasingly becoming either collateral damage or specific targets (Conroy & Attree, 2022). The eNCA, a privately owned reputable local broadcaster, expressed concern that media trademarks were being exploited to misrepresent domestic politics and shaping the national political discourse (eNCA, 2017). While politics is the dominant factor, underlying unethical profit motives designed to woo advertisement through online hits exist. Wasserman writes that some websites often hide behind parody, despite making reference to actual news events to attract audiences, often mimicking trusted news sites to deceive readers (Wasserman, 2017). Wasserman demonstrated noticeable manipulation of media trademarks to legitimate fake news:

> EyeWitness News (imitating the mainstream outlet Eyewitness News), City Sun (likely to be a combined allusion to the Sunday paper City Press and the widely read tabloid Daily Sun, or a play on the title of the newspaper The Citizen) and Times Live (easily misread as the website

for the Sunday Times and Times newspapers, Times Live). Although such imitations of names of an established brand have in certain instances been read as a form of "culture jamming," in which established news brands are subjected to parody as part of a critique on the hegemony of elite, mainstream news . . . these South African sites are in general not overly oriented towards political critique but more intent on providing "clickbait" to dupe audiences into visiting their sites and generating ad revenue.

(Wasserman, 2017)

A more brazen trademark misappropriation was aimed at the influential publications, popular talk Radio 702, the *Sunday Times* and Huffington Post SA, using Twitter handles (Evans, 2017). The harmful political messaging design sought to hoodwink the public into believing the tweets were coming from the established media houses, but a closer inspection revealed extensive, subtle and deceptive manipulations of their titles. The character of some of the fake news messages covered under the false banner of media trademarks carried deceptive psychological undertones because often they are shrewdly crafted to resonate with its readers sentiment of truth, producing what has been often termed a folkloric element (Frank, 2015). Jardine posits,

[F]ake news is appealing because it delivers a moral narrative or confirms sentiments that people already hold. [They] . . . share a common foundation: they propagate "alternative" information and present a moral narrative that people holding similar views can latch on to.

(Jardine, 2020)

Frequently, the digital exploitation of media trademarks comes deceptively in the form of parody to misinform the people (eNCA, 2017). The South African Supreme Court of Appeal held that parody is a permissible exception to infringements under fair use considerations, and specific free expression considerations (*Laugh it Off* case, para 25). While the appellants in the *Laugh it Off* case sought to hide behind freedom of expression, the South African court held that the unauthorised misappropriation of trademarks in a abusive manner was incompatible with freedom of expression (*Laugh it Off* Ibid.). With poor public digital verification tools, information disguised as parody easily pass off for facts. In both Kenya and South Africa, it's occasionally problematic extricating fake news from the arena of political and ideological contestations, where substantive arguments that seek to justify parody and or trademark infringements under the guise of freedom of expression as a communication right are used as a legal shield.

Trademarks and Communicative Rights

The U.S. First Amendment provides constitutional protection for exploitation of trademarks while expressing particular viewpoints (Rogers v. Grimaldi, 1994: 999). South African precedents have demonstrated the same

(*Laugh It Off Promotions CC v South African Breweries* para 106). The context of justifiable exploitation of a trademark under freedom of expression occurs when the public use the trademark to express a particular viewpoint, which automatically falls under the banner of defensible referential use, as opposed to proprietary uses (Barnes 178). However, the exercise of free speech has its own constitutional implications and limitations. Balancing freedom of expression and parody following a dilution of a trademark is often difficult. The court, in the *Laugh it Off* case held that "The purpose of copyright and trademark laws in an open and democratic society is not to shut out critical expression or to throttle artistic and other expressive acts in a manner that gives way to inordinate brand sway" (Laugh it Off, 2006: 13). It further noted that while the appellant did hide behind a parody defence, he had caused material detriment to the distinctive character or repute of the marks in exercising the right to free expression. The court highlighted a "predatory intent," which is arguably similar to the fake news behavioural patterns. With such predatory instincts, fake news is effectively encroaching, controlling and defining the media space, with its indeterminate communication strategies and messaging formulas. While cyber liberationists argue for self-regulation and Internet exceptionalism (Thierer, 2009), cyberpaternalists advance the need for Internet statutory interventions in regulating the exercise of the right. Given the commercial implications associated with trademark infringements, a philosophical framework that resonates with a regulatory mechanism is ideal (Goldsmith, 1998). This is so because the Internet is not a novel phenomenon "hermetically separated from the 'real' world" (Goldsmith, regulation of Internet 1119). The state in "which the harms are suffered have a legitimate interest in regulating the activity that produces the harms" (Goldsmith, 1998b). The harm on media trademarks caused by fake news ordinarily invites such regulatory interventions.

The communicative rights associated with the publication of fake news material are themselves forms of freedom of expression prompting discourse in democratic media governance, ownership and control. In the erstwhile offline domain, media owners are registered, known and operate within accountable regulatory parameters. The production and distribution of fake news was negligible, as opposed to the contemporary SMPs that often present cheap fake news reproductions with an insidious instantaneous global reach. The magnitude of media trademarks infringements with accompanying disinformation interferes with public interest considerations, compromising the quality of legitimate public discourse. This justifies regulatory mechanisms applicable to fake news communication rights. If fake news activities assume acts of criminality, this also legitimises criminal sanctions within acceptable international best practice.

The international human rights treaties obligate governments to protect the right to freedom of expression. Article 19 of the International Covenant on Civil and Political Rights (ICCPR) provides that "everyone shall have the right to freedom of expression" including "the freedom to seek, receive and impart information and ideas of all kinds." Similarly, Article 9 of the African

Charter on Human and People's Rights (ACHPR) recognises the right to "express and disseminate" opinions as well as the right to "receive information." The Kenyan and South African constitutions guarantee the right to freedom of expression, with accompanying state obligations to uphold, protect and fulfil the right. Concerns abound regulating and managing fake news online content by technology companies and governments (Iosifidis & Andrews, 2020). The existing constitutional parameters and damage to trademarks obligate the respective governments to ensure that laws and policies facilitate rather than prevent free expression while in a tough balancing act regulating to prevent anarchy. Temptations for a repressive regulatory framework are normally predictably high, especially where fears exist of foreign governments and entities encroaching into the domestic digital information sphere to subvert a sovereign government. State predispositions to draft legislation that is tailored to entrench their vested political interests become inevitable, thus providing scope for manipulating national discourse under national security considerations. This regulatory approach often breeds a regulatory framework carrying retrogressive constitutional infirmities. In a seminal judgement, a Zimbabwean court held that "freedom of expression asserts the autonomy of thinking, linguistic and communicative elements of the life of an individual and a thin slice of the universe of communication policy" (*Chimakure & Ors v Attorney General* 9). Therefore, whatever legislative framework is drafted to address fake news should not ignore the recognition of communication as an essential human need, a basic human right which facilitates meanings to be conveyed and exchanged for the production of truth, validating human dignity and equality. The Syracuse Principles on the Limitation and Derogation Provisions provide that the "Laws imposing limitations on the exercise of human rights shall not be arbitrary or unreasonable." Such scope of limitations is important and chime with Mare's admissions that the spread of fake news which subvert the rights of others calls for legitimate regulatory measures which can be implemented without undercutting the rights of citizens while balancing communication rights and other human rights (Mare et al., 2019). Confronted with such communication right contestations quandary there is need to dissect the existing trademark law regimes in the respective jurisdictions and interrogate how existing rights relate to broader communication rights in a digital context.

Legislative Interventions

The context of the proposed regulatory interventions is captured in a seminal trademark case, wherein the court held that "the mark sells the goods and therefore its positive image or consumer appeal must be saved from ruin" (*Laugh it off* 40). However, it has been argued that the protection of trademarks against dilution can create a monopoly in the trademark, limiting freedom of expression and prompting the need to create a balance of rights

(Deacon & Govender, 2007: 19). Therefore, the architecture of the trademark laws of both Kenya and South Africa should be examined.

Kenya

In Kenya, trademarks attract the most litigation of IP cases (Mbote, 2005: 23). Kenya's trademark rights statutory framework has ineffective infringement penalties despite the global agreement on Trade-Related Aspects of Intellectual Property Rights (TRIPS) encouraging deterrent penalties (TRIPS, Art. 61). Kenyan scholar, Kamau argues that "in a lenient penalty regime, the balance of risk and reward is not weighed against the offender," and yet the "objective of punishing crime is to deter future offenders" (Thuku, 2012). Furthermore, the problem is compounded by judiciary authorities with limited IP knowledge (Mbote 23). This retards the growth of jurisprudence around IP rights, because the constitution already recognises it as a fundamental right. Besides, in Kenya's statutory framework, concepts such as well-known marks are not available and therefore difficult to enforce (Thuku, 2012). However, there is a provision for trademarks registration which grants media proprieties exclusive rights against infringements (Trademarks Act s7; s5; s15). The relevant provision will be the use of a mark that is identical or similar to a registered mark without the authority of the registered owner, giving the media proprietor a right to institute proceedings (Trademarks Act, s5; s7). Unlike the pre-2010 constitution, Kenya's current constitution recognises IP rights, obliging the state to "support, promote and protect intellectual property rights of the people of Kenya" (Constitution Art. 260(c). The Trademarks Act does not expressly provide for fake news infringements, which prompted the government to enact the Computer Misuse and Cybercrimes Act (hereinafter "the Cyber Act") to address the same.

In 2020, Kenya signed the Cyber Act into law criminalising publication of false information. In particular, section 22 provides that "a person who intentionally publishes false, misleading, or fictitious data, or misinforms with the intent that the data shall be considered or acted upon as authentic, with or without financial gain, commits an offence." In this regard, it matters not if the infringer is commercially benefitting from the unlawful digital exploitation of the media trademark. The law is designed to protect, inter alia, computer systems, integrity and data, with violations under clause 12 attracting fines up to 5,000,000 shilling (nearly R620 000.00) or an imprisonment term of up to two years. While this is a complete departure from the Trademarks Act's lenient framework, the Cyber Act's retributive penalties raise fears they can "potentially inconvenience the media including online journalists, social media influencers and bloggers" (Mail & Guardian, 2018). Such reservations should however be balanced against constitutional limitations provided under Article 33, which provides for, *inter alia*, propagation of false, misleading or fictitious information that negatively affects the rights or reputation of others.

Despite the Cyber Act provisions held consistent with the constitution, (*Bloggers Association of Kenya (BAKE) v Attorney General & 3 others*, 2020), concerns remain on how to define "false" – even if the court held "false" is a plain English word, and it does not require a legal definition. It would have been prudent for the Act to criminalise prejudicial, ascertainable harm caused by the fake news, particularly on the trademarks, without overstraining itself into defining what is false. Fake news activities can cause provable commercial harm under ascertainable special damages. However, proving falsity is difficult because the right to freedom of expression applies to ideas and information of any kind, truthful or false. It was held in the *Chimakure* case that ideas and information are imparted and received for mental digestion and acceptance or rejection and that publication of false information is not necessarily unconstitutional because "freedom of thought means that the mind must be ready to receive new ideas, to critically analyse and examine them and to accept those which are found to stand the test of scrutiny and to reject the rest" (*Chimakure v Attorney General* case 11–12). The Cyber Act approach is problematic because there is no true custodian of the truth, as the "question is as old as the world" and ever evolving (Sugow et al., 2020). Furthermore, complications will emerge around establishing whether an accused person knew the information was false prior to fake news publication.

South Africa

While the Kenyan constitution provides some unequivocal provision that provides for support and protection of IP as a right, South Africa relegated the significance of IP as a human right from its Bill of Rights. Despite recognising property rights in its constitution (Constitution s16(1)(1)), South Africa apex court ruled that "IP protection is not a fundamental right" (*In re certification of the Constitution of the RSA* 799). Scholars believe the apex court should have elevated IP to a fundamental right status, given its recognition as such under article 15 of the International Covenant on Economic, Social and Cultural Rights (ICESCR) (Dean, 2015: 1–2A). In the United States, the constitution grants Congress the enumerated power "To promote the progress of science and useful arts, by securing for limited times to authors and inventors the exclusive right to their respective writings and discoveries" (U.S. Constitution Art. I, Section 8). As such, scholars have been able to debate IP protection on the basis of whether or not that protection promotes the progress of science and the arts (Pollack, 2004). The significance of such recognition lies in providing a broader constitutional interpretation and recognition of IP rights. This is deep hole in the South African constitution, given the growth of IP innovations, technology and the increasing displacement of real estate property right significance with the cumulative global capitalisation of technology and digital innovations reshaping regional and domestic legislations (*Austro-Mechana v Strato* Case C-433/20).

However, South African courts have been sensitive not to disproportionately undermine freedom of expression in trademark cases. They carefully considered "weighing-up . . . the constitutional safeguard of free expression of the unauthorised user against the right to intellectual property of the trademark owner" (*Laugh it Off* case). The free expression right is conferred under section 16 of the constitution which includes, *inter alia*, freedom to receive or impart information or ideas, with corollary limitations. While the constitution fails to guarantee IP as a human right, subsidiary legislation, however, protects trademark rights holders against infringements. The Trademark Act, section 34(1)(c) specifically prohibits dilution, blurring or tarnishment of a registered trademark. It provides that the essential elements of an infringement of a trademark would relate to "unauthorised use by the defendant of a mark identical or similar to the registered mark," and that the "the registered trademark must be well-known in the Republic" and "the use of the trade mark would be likely to take unfair advantage of, or be detrimental to the distinctive character or repute of the registered trade mark." The language of the court in the *Laugh it Off* case was that the defendant should not take "unfair advantage" of the distinctive character or repute of the trademark. Unlike the Kenyan fake news regulations, South Africa's approach is similar but confined to COVID-19 with similar interpretation challenges if juxtaposed against the limitation considerations. The Disaster Management Regulations, Issued in Terms of Section 27(2) of the Disaster Management Act, 2002 (2020), similar to the Kenya fake news statute, "are also very difficult to interpret" (Article 19 2021). Specifically, Section 11(5) criminalises publication in "any medium" of information with the "intention to deceive any other person about" about COVID-19 regulations. While the objective to "stop spreading fake and unverified news and creating further apprehension and alarm" is noble, clarity is lacking in defining "fake and unverified news" and the "intention to deceive." Such provisions are arguably "overbroad, highly subjective, and subject to abuse," because "what is to one person an 'intention to deceive' may be to another an 'intention to educate'." (Article 19 2021). As previously submitted, falsity of information is not a legitimate basis for restricting free expression.

Legislative Reforms

The difficulty in governments censoring social media information lies in that its primary infrastructure is owned by private companies, with responsibilities to manage the dissemination of unlawful content. The obligations are with both the government, providing some acceptable regulatory framework without arbitrary limitations, and the SMPs, providing effective monitoring mechanisms that control or manage the publication of disinformation content because they have the capacity to evaluate and remove flagged content using their automated detection systems. The government should provide education through its computer literacy curricula in media and digital literacy. Commendably, the South African government has been promoting a "reporting system" called Real411, whereby users can report fakes news through a sanctioned website, adjudicated by an independent Digital Complaints Committee. This independent oversight is crucial to ensure a nonpartisan balanced assessment of the flagged content.

Conclusion

Market confusion created by the advent of the digital era through fake news targeting particularly media trademarks has put consumers of news in a quandary, with challenges associated with distinguishing facts from fiction. This presents an equal challenge to the enablers of fake news, particularly SMPs, which inadvertently provide platforms for cloners who disseminate contrived fictious material as news. The regulators should keep abreast with technological developments with a view to addressing any potential legal gaps, given the unrelenting phenomenal growth of digital technology, with projections so far dictating that computing and processing capacity of computers will hit double figures almost every two years and the world producing about 500 exabytes of data by 2025 (Bulao, 2022). As such, fake news will remain a complex problem, with its malicious digital scope using new algorithmic technologies often targeting media trademarks. The attractive nature of fake news lies in its resonance with societal biases, therefore, a regulatory system consistent with international norms is desirable to protect the public susceptible to a ceaseless diet of fake news and facilitate informed and relevant national discourse. Against this background, the regulatory form should therefore seek to strike a legitimate balance between freedom of expression norms and the public's right to express itself, bearing in mind that "falsity" is not a legitimate basis for framing the scope of the regulations.

References

Bakir, V., and McStay, A. (2017) 'Fake news and the economy of emotions'. *Digital Journalism*, 1–22.
Barnes, W. D. (2008) 'Misappropriation of Trademark'. *North Carolina Journal of Law and Technology*, 9, 171.
Barton, B. (2014) *The Suppressed Misappropriation Origins of Trademark Antidilution Law: The Landgericht Elberfeld's Odol Opinion and Frank Schechter's "The Rational Basis of Trademark Protection"*. Cambridge: Cambridge University Press.
BBC. (2018) 'Russia 'meddled in all big social media' around US election'. *BBC Online*, 17 December. Available at www.bbc.com/news/technology-46590890. (Accessed: 23 August 2022).
Bernard, B. A., and Moxnes, A. (2018) Networks and Trade *Annual Review of Economics*, 10 (1): 65–85. Available at www.annualreviews.org/doi/abs/10.1146/annurev-economics-080217-053506. (Accessed: 24 November 2022).
Bulao, J. (2022) *How Fast Is Technology Advancing in 2022?* Available at https://techjury.net/blog/how-fast-is-technology-growing/#gref. (Accessed: 24 November 2022).

Chakrabarti, S., Claire R., and Minnie K. (2018) *Verification, Duty, Credibility: Fake News and Ordinary Citizens in Kenya and Nigeria*. London: BBC News. Available at http://downloads.bbc.co.uk/mediacentre/bbc-fake-news-research-paper-nigeria-kenya.pdf. (Accessed: 26 August 2022).

Conroy, P., and Attree, M. (2022) *Getting Real About Fake News Ogilvy, 2022*. Available at www.ogilvy.co.za/node/159. (Accessed: 24 August 2022).

Cooper, B., Masiiwa, R., Ferreira, M., Gatwabuyege, F., and Christine Hougaard, C. M. (2020) *Identifying Regional Economic Hubs in Africa*. Available at www.fsdafrica.org/wp-content/uploads/2020/09/Identifying-regional-economic-hubs-in-Africa_Note2.pdf. (Accessed: 26 August 2022).

Cornish, W., Llewelyn, D., and Aplin, T. (2013) *Intellectual Property; Patents, Copyright, Trade Marks and Allied Rights* (8th Edition). English, United Kingdom: Sweet & Maxwell.

Crabtree, J. (2018) 'Here's how Cambridge Analytica played a dominant role in Kenya's chaotic 2017 elections'. *CNBC*, 23 March. Available at www.cnbc.com/2018/03/23/cambridge-analytica-and-its-role-in-kenya-2017-elections.html. (Accessed: 27 August 2022).

Deacon J., and Govender, I. (2007) Trade mark parody in South Africa – The last laugh! *Journal for Juridical Science*, 32 (2): 18–46.

Dean, H O., and Karjiker, S. (2015) *Handbook of South African Copyright Law*. Cape Town: Juta & Co.

Downie, L., and Schudson, M. (2009) 'The reconstruction of American journalism'. *The Columbia Journalism Review*. Available at https://archives.cjr.org/reconstruction/the_reconstruction_of_american.php. (Accessed: 27 October 2022).

eNCA. (2017) *SA News Organisations Targeted in fake Twitter Accounts, eNCA Website*, 22 January. Available at www.enca.com/south-africa/sa-news-organisations-targeted-in-fake-twitter-accounts. (Accessed: 24 August 2022).

Evans, J. (2017) 'Oakbay denies involvement in fake news campaign'. *Mail&Guardian*, 24 January. Available at https://mg.co.za/article/2017-01-24-oakbay-denies-involvement-in-fake-news-campaign/. (Accessed: 24 August 2022).

Frank R. (2015). 'Caveat lector: Fake news as folklore'. *The Journal of American Folklore*, 128 (509): 315–332.

Goldsmith, L. J. (1998a) 'Against cyberanarchy'. *University of Chicago Law Review*, 65 (4): Article 2.

Goldsmith, L. J. (1998b) 'Regulation of the internet: Three persistent fallacies'. *Chicago-Kent Law Review*, 73: 1119.

Iosifidis, P., and Andrews, L. (2020) 'Regulating the internet intermediaries in a post-truth world: Beyond media policy?' *International Communication Gazette*, 82 (3): 211–230.

Jardine, E. (2020) 'Beware fake news'. *Center for International Governance Innovation*. Available at www.cigionline.org/articles/beware-fake-news/. (Accessed: 24 November 2022).

Kipng'enoh, W. (2015) *The Nairobian Newspaper Featured in Popular News Channel in United Kingdom, The Nairobean*. Available at www.standardmedia.co.ke/entertainment/news/article/2000162787/the-nairobian-newspaper-featured-in-popular-news-channel-in-united-kingdom. (Accessed: 27 August 2022).

Mail & Guardian. (2018, 16 June) 'Kenya signs bill criminalising fake news'. *Mail&Guardian*, 16 May. Available at https://mg.co.za/article/2018-05-16-kenya-signs-bill-criminalising-fake-news/. (Accessed: 29 August 2022).

Mare, A., Mabweazara M. H. A., and Moyo, D. (2019) ' "Fake news" and cyber-propaganda in sub-saharan Africa: Recentering the research agenda'. *African Journalism Studies*, 40 (4): 1–12. Available at www.tandfonline.com/doi/full/10.1080/2 3743670.2020.1788295. (Accessed: 24 November 2022).

Mbote, P. (2005) Intellectual property protection in Africa: An assessment of the status of laws, *Research and Policy Analysis on Intellectual Property Rights in Kenya, IELRC Working Paper*, p. 2.

Mirësi, C. (2015) 'The importance of trademarks and a review of empirical studies'. *European Journal of Sustainable Development*, 4 (3): 125–134.

Molina, D. M., Sundar, S. S., Thai, L., and Dongwon, L. (2021). ' "Fake news" is not simply false information: A concept explication and taxonomy of online content'. *American Behavioral Scientist*, 65 (2): 180–212.

Moyo, A. (2017) 'SA publications fall victim to fake news'. *ITWeb*, 23 January. Available at www.itweb.co.za/content/2JN1gP7OYy3qjL6m. (Accessed: 24 August 2022).

Nielsen, R. K., and Graves, L. (2017) ' "News you don't believe": Audience perspectives on fake news'. *Reuters Institute for the Study of Journalism with the support of Google and the Digital News Initiative*. Available at https://reutersinstitute. politics.ox.ac.uk/our-research/news-you-dont-believe-audience-perspectives-fake-news. (Accessed 25 August 2022).

Okong'o, J. (2022) 'Doctored newspaper front pages spread disinformation as Kenya elections draw near'. *AFP*, 9 June. Available at https://factcheck.afp.com/doc.afp. com.32C47U3. (Accessed: 23 August 2022).

Pollack, M. (2004) 'Originalism, J.E.M., and the food supply, or will the real decision maker please stand up? 502'. *Journal of Environmental Law and Litigation*, 19 (2): 203.

Rutherford, B. (2011) 'The law of trademarks'. In H. Klopper (Eds.), *Law of Intellectual Property in South Africa*, pp. 71–140. New York: LexisNexis.

Sevenzo, F. (2017) 'Kenya election: Fake CNN, BBC reports target voters'. *CNN*, 1 August. Available at https://edition.cnn.com/2017/07/31/africa/kenya-election-fake-news/index.html. (Accessed: 23 August 2022).

Solon, O. (2017) 'The future of fake news: Don't believe everything you read, see or hear'. *The Guardian*, 26 July. Available at www.theguardian.com/technology/2017/jul/26/fake-news-obama-video-trump-face2face-doctored-content. (Accessed: 26 August 2022).

Sugow, A., Mungai, B., and Wanyama, J. (2020) *The Regulation of Fake News in Kenya under The Coronavirus Threat*. Available at https://cipit.strathmore.edu/the-regulation-of-fake-news-in-kenya-under-the-coronavirus-threat/. (Accessed: 29 August 2022).

Talwara, S., Dhirbc, A., Singh, D., Singh, G., and Salof V. J. (2020) 'Sharing of fake news on social media: Application of the honeycomb framework and the third-person effect hypothesis'. *Journal of Retailing and Consumer Services*, 57 (2020). www.sciencedirect.com/science/article/pii/S0969698920306433.

Thierer, A. (2009) *Cyber-Libertarianism: The Case for Real Internet Freedom, The Technology Liberation Front*. Available at https://techliberation.com/2009/08/12/cyber-libertarianism-the-case-for-real-internet-freedom/. (Accessed: 24 August 2022).

Thomas, A. (2020) 'BBC News in Africa increases reach to 132 million people a week'. *Sierra Leone Telegraph*, 25 July. Available at www.thesierraleonetelegraph. com/bbc-news-in-africa-increases-reach-to-132-million-people-a-week/. (Accessed: 24 August 2022).

Thuku K. J. (2012) *Overcoming Challenges Facing Enforcement of Trademarks in Kenya*, unpublished LLM dissertation. Nairobi: University of Nairobi.
UNESCO. (2018) *Journalism, 'Fake News' & Disinformation*. Available at https://en.unesco.org/sites/default/files/journalism_fake_news_disinformation_print_friendly_0.pdf. (Accessed: 27 February 2023).
Vosoughi, S., Roy, D., and Aral, S. (2018) 'The spread of true and false news online'. *Science*, 359 (6380): 1146–1151. Available at doi: 10.1126/science.aap9559. PMID: 29590045 (Accessed 24 November 2022).
Wasserman, H. (2017) 'Fake news from Africa: Panics, politics and paradigms'. *Journalism*, 21 (1): 3–16. Available at https://journals.sagepub.com/doi/full/10.1177/1464884917746861. (Accessed: 24 November 2022).
Webster, G. C., and Page, N. S. (1997) *South African Law of Trade Marks, Unlawful Competition, Company Names and Trading Styles*, 4th ed. Durban: Butterworths.

Case Law

Bloggers Association of Kenya (BAKE) v Attorney General & 3 others; Article 19 East Africa & another (Interested Parties) [2020] eKLR
Chimakure and Anor v Attorney General SC 14–2013.
Erie Railroad Co. v. Tompkins, 304 U.S. 64 (1938).
Fin. Info., Inc. v. Moody's Investors Serv., Inc., 808 F.2d 204, 208 (2d Cir. 1986).
In re certification of the Constitution of the RSA 1996 4 SA 744 (CC) 799.
International News Service v. Associated Press, 248 U.S. 215 (1918).
Laugh It Off Promotions CC v South African Breweries International (Finance) BV t/a Sabmark International and Another 2006 (1) SA 144 (CC) para 13.
National Brands Ltd v Blue Lion Manufacturing (Pty) Ltd 2001 (3) SA 563 (SCA).
Premier Brands UK Ltd v Typhoon Europe Ltd[30] [2000] EWHC 1557; [2000] FSR 767.
Rogers v. Grimaldi, 875 F.2d 994, 999 (2d Cir. 1994).

Part IV
Politics of Digital Infrastructures

11 Politics of Digital Infrastructures in the Global South

The Case of #DataMustFall Campaign in South Africa

Tendai Chari

Introduction

The Internet has become intricately intertwined with people's everyday life, to the extent that some scholars claim that it is a fundamental right (Milderbrath, 2021; Stoycheff & Nisbet, 2016) although others argue that it is only an enabler of other human rights but not a right (Cerf, 2012). Where infrastructure for Internet access is available states are obliged "to support initiatives to ensure that online information can be accessed in a meaningful way by all sectors of the population" (Pollicino, 2019: 3). Techno optimists view Internet access as essential to achieve the 2030 Sustainable Development Goals (Hughes cited in Velocci, 2016). Even if these arguments were valid, universal Internet access in developing countries is a remote possibility, not least because the price of mobile data is beyond the reach of many.

Dominant scholarship on social movements focuses on political activism while the issue of digital rights is less explored. Consequently, there is a lacuna on hybrid social movements which combine traditional modes of collective action and digital activism, such as #DataMustFall. The concept of digital rights is problematic because it is not always clear who should protect these rights and how they should be implemented given the competing interests at stake. While governments bear the duty to protect human rights, the digital infrastructure is largely owned and controlled by private enterprises whose main motive is profit-making than protecting human rights (Human Rights Council, 2011).

Combining insights from the concept of digital rights and social movement theories, this chapter is a qualitative examination of the #DataMustFall campaign's struggle over the price of mobile data in South Africa. It illuminates on how digital rights intersect with politics of digital infrastructures from a Global South, particularly, a South African perspective. Why the #DataMustFall campaign was formed, its repertoire of tactics, and its achievements are key questions at the core of this exploration. While #DataMustFall is not a typical traditional social movement (Willems, 2010: Bond & Mottir, 2013), it has all the attributes of a social movement, albeit a hybrid one (de Wall & Ibreck, 2012). Berger and Nehring (2017: 3) rightly point out that social

DOI: 10.4324/9781003388289-16

movements are "not fixed in time and space" adding that as a concept it "is connected with utopias of community and belonging and transformation." This underscores the dynamism of social movements. The rest of this chapter proceeds as follows: after this introduction, the first section briefly surveys the literature on digital rights. This is followed by a discussion of social movement theories. The third section discusses the methodological approach adopted for the chapter. The fourth section presents the research findings and the fifth section provides the concluding remarks.

Digital Rights and Politics of Digital Infrastructures

The concept of digital rights (Mathiesen, 2014) is a useful lens to understand how the #DataMustFall campaign evolved, modalities of its activism and achievements. There is no consensus on the meaning of digital rights. However, scholars agree that digital rights entail rights in the digital era (Media Defence, 2022; Kaye & Reventlow, 2017). While digital rights are subject to varied interpretations, the dominant literature conflates digital rights with Internet rights (Karppinen & Puukko, 2020; Kaye & Reventlow, 2017). The struggle over the price of data during the #DataMustFall fits into this framework. Digital rights are thus viewed as a subset of the communication rights debate, which dates back to the New World Information and Communication Order (NWICO) debate in the late 1960s (CRIS, 2005; Thomas, 2005). The argument that digital rights should be recognized as human rights resonates with concerns raised within the #DataMustFall activism, which amplified the case for communication rights in a digital environment (Karppinen & Puukko, 2020; Mathiesen, 2014).

Debate rages as to whether the Internet should be a human right or not and if so, how can it be operationalized and by whom (Milderbrath, 2021; Pollicino, 2019; Barry, 2019; O'Rielly, 2015; Mathiesen, 2014; Cerf, 2012). Internet rights advocates assert that any disruptions or manipulation of Internet content is a violation of human rights. Mathiesen (2014) equates access to online information with a "moral standing to claim something due to one as a particular individual or particular group". Similarly, several United Nations documents recognize the natural right of individuals to dignity and to "live minimally good lives" as well as giving people "ample opportunities to exercise agency" and ensuring that they are able to "exercise important human capabilities" (Mathiesen, 2014: 3–4). As demonstrated in subsequent sections, sentiments by protagonists of #DataMustFall and comments by signers of the Amandla.Mobi petition submitted to the Competition Commission reflect this view. To protect citizens' digital rights states are obliged to put in place institutional arrangements for citizens to have access to the technology needed for Internet access (Mathiesen, 2014: 4). Yet, guaranteeing citizens' access to the Internet inserts the state into the contentious terrain of politics of digital infrastructures, thereby setting up the state against private enterprises which own and control such infrastructure. Although private enterprises have an important role to play in protecting digital rights they are driven by commercial motives (Human Rights Council, 2011: 13). As Sutherland (2021: 15) points out, the vexing question is always, "who will pay for the free service" (mobile data in the case of #DatamustFall), to ensure universal access to the Internet? Many developing countries do not have regulations that bind states or private enterprises to provide access to the Internet. Where these regulations exist institutions given the responsibility to enforce them are "ineffectual" or "timid" or simply incapacitated (Sutherland, 2021: 14). Furthermore, the dominance of the liberal market system precludes states from interfering with the production of public goods, leaving citizens to the vagaries of the market, leading to exclusion of the poor. This contradicts the state's obligations to guarantee citizens' access to the Internet because without the Internet other human rights such as the right to work, basic education, and the right to life may not be realizable (Barry, 2019).

However, some scholars reject the notion that the Internet should be a human right, because a human right is something that humans need for them to "lead healthy meaningful lives", of which the Internet is not (Cerf, 2012). Cerf argues that the Internet is a derivative right which enables other rights to be realized. Thus, "it is a mistake to place any particular technology in this exalted category (of human rights) since over time we will end up valuing the wrong thing" (Cerf, 2012). O'Rielly's (2015) stance is less nuanced, contending that the Internet is neither a necessity nor a human right. He argues that it is unreasonable to regard the Internet as a human right because people can live without it. While this could have been true before the COVID-19 pandemic, the Internet has become the fulcrum around which people's lives revolve in the post-COVID pandemic era. During the pandemic the Internet became an integral tool for realizing basic human rights such as the right to work, education, information, the right to know the truth and the right to life. Hence, digital rights have a natural affinity with epistemic rights, which are rights pertaining to "epistemic goods such as information, knowledge, understanding and truth" (Watson, 2018: 89). Epistemic rights "afford their bearer a complex set of entitlements that provide a justification for their performance and prohibition of certain actions regarding epistemic goods" (Watson, 2018: 89). A broadened conception of epistemic rights solidifies the case for Internet rights because it goes beyond the right to receive and impart information since the Internet "ensures citizens have access to multiple and diverse sources of information to ameliorate their intellectual vulnerabilities" (Habgood-Coote, 2022: 426). Contestations around the notion of digital rights discussed earlier reflect the competing interests of corporates and citizen grievances ventilated through #DataMustFall and the ambiguity of digital rights in the context of neoliberalism and the resultant commodification of digital infrastructures.

Social Movement Theories

Social movement theories illuminate on the dynamics of social movements such as #DataMustFall campaign. Defining social movements is challenging, and debate on how to classify them is ongoing (Van Stekelenburg & Klandermans, 2005). Marti and Biglia (2014: 1789) define social movements as "groups or networks of individuals, collectives, and organisations that interact with the aim of producing or resisting changes in society, cultures and/or social systems".

De Fronzo and Gill (2020: 27) define a social movement as a "persistent and organized effort involving the mobilizing of large numbers of people to work together to either bring about what they believe to be beneficial social change or resist or reverse what they believe to be harmful social change". The defining features of a social movement include "being purposeful", "highly organized", "collective cation", "interaction", and "producing or resisting change". Social movements are dynamic because they are not bound in space and time (Earle, 2011: 9). Taking after Berger and Nehring (2017), this chapter views social movements from a broader perspective which includes both formal and informal organizations and protests. Adopting this broad approach qualifies #DaataMustFall as a social movement.

Scholars try to explain why people protest, who participates in protests, and tactics employed by protest movements. Several theories have emerged to explain why social movements emerge. These are the relative deprivation theory, resource mobilization theory, political process theory, framing theory, and new social movement theory (DeFronzo & Gill, 2020; Staggenborg, 2016). The most applicable theory is the deprivation theory, which posits that people tend to rebel when their circumstances are improving because when conditions improve expectations also rise. However, when the rate of improvement does not commensurate with their expectations, they feel deprived (Staggenborg, 2016: 16). Shared grievances and "generalized beliefs" motivate people to partake in collective action (Staggenborg, 2016). Thus, the "exorbitant" price of mobile data galvanized citizens from diverse backgrounds in South Africa to participate in the #DataMustFall campaign.

While the relative deprivation theory lays a foundation for understanding the dynamics of the #DataMustFall campaign, the theory was developed in a Western context and falls short in explaining a hybrid movement such as #DataMustFall campaign, which deployed both offline and online strategies of activism (Castells, 2012). Some scholars question the relevance of Western-inspired social movement theories for the Global South (Accornero & Gravante, 2022: 15), pointing out that there is little room for dialogue between Global South and Global North epistemologies with regard to social movements. Brandes and Engels (2011: 5) argue that contemporary social movements in Africa, just like elsewhere, can be understood only against the backdrop of the historical, sociopolitical context in which they emerge. Larmer (2010: 257) argues that social movements in Africa "are unavoidably hybrid in nature, utilizing and adapting Western ideas, funding, forms of organization and methods of activism". While there is a proliferation of scholarship on social movements globally (Engels & Muller, 2019; Castells, 2012) few, if any, focus on digital rights, particularly activism for mobile data in the African context. Thomas (2006: 291) is right in his observation that "social movement theory is yet to be systematically applied to an understanding of media reform movements". In the South African context, the bulk of works focus on leftist social, political, and economic justice protest movements rooted in grassroots communities (Sebeelo, 2021; Bond & Mottir, 2013) while only a sizeable focus on social movement media (Bosch et al., 2018; Chiumbu, 2015). Although Bosch et al. (2018) have explored social movements' deployment of nanomedia in "democratising conflicts", most available studies have shied away from digital rights social movements in the mould of #DataMustFall campaign.

Methodological Discussion

The chapter sought to examine the #DataMustFall campaign's struggle over the price of mobile data in South Africa to unravel the reasons why the campaign emerged, its repertoire of tactics, as well as achievements. Accordingly, a qualitative case study design was employed. Consistent with the view that when the intention is to ask questions like "how" and "why" (Yin, 2003: 545), the case study design is the most suitable qualitative research design (Stake, 1995; Yin, 2003; Hancock & Algozzine, 2006; Baxter & Jack, 2008). Because a case study seeks to understand a contemporary real-life phenomenon within its context (Yin, 2003), data were drawn from varied sources to obtain multiple perspectives of the #DataMustFall campaign. Accordingly, data were gleaned from multiple sources, including a qualitative content analysis of purposively selected comments provided by signers of a petition submitted to the Competition Commission of South Africa in November 2017 by a social justice advocacy group, *Amandla.Mobi*.[1] While the petition was signed by 44,726 people, only 17 comments were purposively selected to illustrate motives of the campaign. The comments were anonymized by assigning codes such as P1, P2, and so on. The petition comments were complemented by a qualitative content analysis of purposively selected news articles and tweets by participants in the campaign. In addition, data were also obtained from analysis of official documents, namely the Data Services Markey Inquiry report produced by the Competition Commission, ICASA's "End User and Subscriber Charter" regulations, as well as ICASA's "Priority Markets Inquiry in the Electronic Communications Sector" report. The unit of analysis was the petition comments, news articles, tweets, and official documents. Since the main focus was to understand motives behind the #DataMustFall campaign and how the politics of digital infrastructure played itself from a citizen point of view, the main source of data was the comments from Amandla.Mobi petition document and content analysis of tweets and newspaper articles. Focus was on evolution, actors, progression, decline, and tactics of the movement between 2016 and 2023. Paying attention to the temporal and spatial setting of the campaign enabled the author to understand factors which motivated people to participate in the campaign, the repertoire of tactics used, and its achievements from the standpoints of the varied sources of information (Hancock & Algozzine, 2006: 15). Textual data was thematically coded, and themes linked to the research objectives were extrapolated. These themes are discussed in the next section.

#DataMustFall Campaign: Evolution and Issues

The #DataMust Fall campaign was started by radio Disc Jockey (DJ), TBo Touch, real name Thabo Molefe, Co-founder and Chief Executive of Touch Central FM radio station. On 15 September 2016, Molefe, through his Twitter account gave mobile networks 30 days to reduce their data prices or else "move to the network that cares about its customers" (Prior, 2020). He rallied South Africans behind the campaign using the hashtag#DataMustFall. In the weeks that followed, the campaign gained momentum, both online and offline, despite the existence of some "discordant" voices who questioned Molefe's pedigree to lead the campaign, allegedly because he was a "capitalist". The fact that actors from a wider cross section of the South African society coalesced around the issue of high data prices gave sufficient impetus to #DataMustFall campaign. While the high price of data was the original grievance, others like "collision" and "profiteering" by mobile network companies were added to the list.

The diversity of voices retweeting Molefe's original tweet reflects that the campaign was reaching a wider circle of participants. This tallies with the view that Twitter users tend to retweet information which they believe to be valuable and worth sharing with others (Lee et al., 2015). The "ever-interlinked matrix of network and the feature of retweet makes the diffusion of information on Twitter much more possible in a simpler and easier way", thereby propelling the #DataMustFall campaign (Lee et al., 2015: 190). The increased diffusion of information about the campaign is evidenced by support of the campaign by people from different backgrounds such as celebrities, politicians, government officials, civil society groups, students, and ordinary citizens. Some actors argued that through the high price of mobile data, mobile network companies were violating human rights (The South African, 2017), thereby projecting #DataMustFall campaign through a digital rights lens. This made the campaign to appeal to a wider audience, particularly the working-class people. For instance, the Communication Workers Union (CWU) declared its support for the campaign, declaring that "We also call upon all progressives to rally behind this revolutionary call to put a stop to this day light robbery that the working class in particular is subjected to" (ENCA, 2016a, 2016b). The Union implored ICASA to "investigate data costs" citing the United Nations convention concerning "human rights to

Internet and access to information". The words "progressives", "revolutionary", "working class", "human rights", and "access to information" show that the #DataMustFall campaign was framed as an anti-capitalist social movement fighting for justice (Young, 1999). This is despite the fact that some of the key actors were aligned to capital, underscoring the hybridity of the campaign. Thus, through framing, movements construct cultural meanings that resonate with the majority (Staggenborg, 2016).

As more participants from diverse social groups joined the campaign, additional grievances were brought on board. These include "unfair" rules on data and airtime expiration, rollover of data, out-of-bundle data cost, allocation of spectrum, the need for fast Internet, uncompetitive behaviour, and lack of transparency in mobile company operations. Amandla.Mobi pointed out how the market dominance by MTN and Vodacom allowed these companies to keep the price of mobile data high "while creating the illusion of competition through promotions that do not change the fact that they were making enormous profits" (Amandla.Mobi, 2017: 2). As a result, *"low-income consumers are paying disproportionately high charges and are not seeing benefits of competition* in comparison to high income consumers who are able to buy larger quantities of data" (emphasis original) (Amandla.Mobi, 2017: 2).

The ruling party, the African National Congress (ANC), argued that the high price of data negatively impacted citizens, particularly workers, youth, students, and women who could not participate in the digital economy (The Citizen, 2018). The party was also concerned that high-priced mobile data was stifling economic growth and the development of small business enterprises, adding that reduced prices of data "would be a catalyst for economic growth, unlocking economic opportunities that would lead to job creation" (The Citizen, 2018).

Civil society organizations joined the campaign, thereby amplifying citizens' voices. The Right2Know advocated for a free, safe, and fast Internet, arguing that "the Internet was at the centre of the development of societies" (Right2Know, 2022). Amandla.Mobi mobilized people to sign petitions submitted to various bodies. In a petition submitted to the Competition Commission, petition signers highlighted how mobile data had become a necessity for communication, work, and education, highlighting how excessive prices of data entrenched "a new digital apartheid" in South Africa (Huffing Post, 2016). Extracts from the petition are illustrative:

Data is very expensive, and data is being excessively even when not using Twitter etc. Older people are battling to survive. And need communication rights. (P1)
Our lives revolve around smartphones and to have an effective life, we need our phones to be connected to the Internet. So, data which is expensive deprives us of an effective life. (P2)
For once can corporates stop being greedy and think about the greater good. Internet access should be a right not a privilege. (P3)

Data costs are crippling day to day living. Everything these days is getting digital in combination with Internet-based applications. Even school children are forced to use the Internet if they have any hope of achieving good results. (P4)

Data is the currency of the ideas Economy and the Industrial Revolution; thus it must be accessible and affordable. (P5)

It is a fundamental right that data is accessible to everyone but this is currently not possible with huge data prices we are forced to pay!!! Data prices must come down!!!! (P7)

With low-cost data we will be assisting scholars without infrastructure to access medium to be able to research and communicate with the whole world. (P8)

The view that access to mobile data is inextricably linked to everyday life signifies that #DataMustFall campaigners regard data as a public good and a human right. The argument that every citizen must have access to the Internet resonates with arguments of scholars who posit that the Internet should be a human right (Mathiesen, 2014; Barry, 2019; Pollicino, 2019).

Apart from the high price of data, petition signers pointed out how loopholes in the market such as price-fixing and a duopolistic structure contributed to the high cost of data.

The collusion in price fixing between the large networks is abhorrent! It makes access to modern media to the poor virtually impossible! Data should be accessible to people of SA and not a cash cow. (P9)

The way the data providers abuse their position is exploitative and sickening. (P11)

Its not fair that cell phone companies make such an enormous profit here in South Africa when its probably half the price elsewhere. (P12)

The practice of collusion or price fixing must be brought to end. These prices must be in line with prices elsewhere . . . South Africans mustn't be subjected to exploitation . . . institutions meant to protect consumer rights must act quickly when alarms are raised. (P14)

Words such as "collision", "price fixing", "exploitation", "enormous profit", and "abuse" signify unethical business practices by mobile companies. Petition signers "unmasked" failure of the liberal market system in distributing public goods and services. This chimes with Moyo and Munoriyarwa's (2021: 365) attribution of the high cost of mobile data and voice calls in South Africa to "a combination of regulatory paralysis, collusive behaviour by oligopolistic operators, indecisive government policy and to some degree citizen in action". This links with the Competition Commission Data Services Market Inquiry's findings that the pricing strategy employed by the larger mobile networks in the country worked against the poor (Competition Commission, 2019). This shows how corporates can be stumbling blocks to the realisation of digital rights.

Apart from market failure petition signers demanded removal of "unfair" data usage rules implemented by mobile phone companies, particularly rules on expiration and rollover of data, cost of out-of-data bundles, and data usage notifications. The following quotations are insightful in this regard:

Please notify the user of his/her usage and don't steal data. Have a standard price on data and charge for extra data services if required by the user. (P15)

We are paying for the data as per contract. Why should that data expire as the service provider is not the one paying for data. There should not be any expiry of data on data we pay for. (P16)

As an IT professional, the reality is that data doesn't expire, – it's not food with a sell by date. Providers sell us data bundles which grant us access to their network. We pay upfront for this promise to use the network, so it's impossible and illogical that in this day and age, Internet access is a human right. Data sale practices that hinder access to this right should be looked at and remedied with great urgency. (P17)

Mobile network companies are viewed as irresponsible corporates, if not criminal citizens, who violate citizens' digital rights.

#DataMust Fall Campaign and Its Repertoire of Tactics

#DataMust Fall was both an online and an offline line campaign, embracing a repertoire of tactics such as demonstrations, protests, petitions, and social media boycotts, among others. Demonstrations were organized by civil society organizations such as the Right2Know and Amandla.Mobi. In September 2017, the Right2Know organized "simultaneous" protests at the headquarters of South Africa's four largest mobile network companies (News24, 2017). It accused mobile network companies of depriving citizens of the right to communicate. Amandla.Mobi also organized demonstrations, protest marches, and mobilization meetings in various communities. When ICASA issued new regulations governing mobile data expiry and out-of-bundle billing in 2018, mobile network companies struck back and took ICASA to court. Amandla. Mobi organized a demonstration at the High Court to put pressure on mobile network companies to stop "stalling" #Data Must Fall campaign (Amandla. Mobi, 2018).

That mobile network companies agreed to settle the matter out of court demonstrates the impact of the campaign. Campaigners employed a variety of tactics and alternative or small-scale media also known as "nanomedia" (Bosch et al., 2018) to drive their message to the mobile network companies as well as attract public and media attention. These include the use of posters, placards, pamphlets, circulation of photographs, community mobilization tactics, singing, *toyi-toying* (a militant march and dance), and T-shirts and caps inscribed with the messages demanding the price of data to be reduced. This chimes with Bosch et al.'s observation that with regard to how South

African social movements utilize alternative communicative strategies "to mobilise and gain visibility", particularly in a context where access to mainstream media is limited. With regard to #DataMustFall campaign, however, nanomedia were complementary rather than an alternative to mainstream media. Thus, advocacy groups conducted media interviews to saturate public spaces with their messages and to counter messages disseminated by mobile networks. To ensure that their message reached a global audience #DataMustFall campaign activities were documented through video, photography, and social media. Amandla.Mobi campaigners went door to door, "putting up posters and collecting stories about how data prices impacted on people's lives".[2] The repertoire of tactics used by #Data Must Fall campaigners were thus consistent with those used by many South African social movements which entailed a combination of traditional and online modes of protests to achieve "maximum impact" (Bosch et al., 2018: 2162). Combining traditional and digital media was strategic because it ensured that digital tools were used to reach global audiences and the middle-class participants while physical demonstrations made it possible to reach citizens who did not have access (Bosch et al., 2018: 2164).

Apart from physical demonstrations, the #DataMustFall campaign also employed boycotts; the main one being a 24-hour social media blackout championed by poet, musician, and activist, Ntsiki Mazwai on 19 June 2023. Through her Twitter account, Mazwai called upon all South Africans not to buy data or go online to force mobile network companies and the state to reduce the price of mobile data and airtime. She stated that "data costs were obscene and not affordable for people on the ground" (*The Citizen*, 2017). Mazwai tweeted, "I will not be on social media on Wednesday 21 June because #DataMustFall and it is long overdue we took action. Don't buy data. Don't log in". The following day she announced that "Next week Wednesday . . . we are putting on business". The boycott trended on social media under the hashtags "#ShutdownWednesDday", "#SocialMediaShutdown", and "#DataMustFall". In a tweet which exposed the ironies of the #DataMustFall campaign, Mazwai also tweeted "Comrades get your last fix of data. We switch off at midnight and meet back here on Thursday midday . . . It's been extended – addicts *nizwile*? (Addicts, do you hear me?).

Despite the widespread publicity on social media, the social media boycott did not hold as citizens remained active on social media. Ironically, there were more people tweeting about the social media blackout than a social media blackout. *The Citizen* newspaper observed that "The attempted one-day shutdown of Twitter in South Africa had more people tweeting about how hard it is not to go on Twitter and tweet, than people observing the shutdown" (*The Citizen*, 2017). Some of the champions of the boycott were also observed tweeting about the social media blackout meaning that they had not heeded their own calls for a boycott (Times Live, 2017).

Before the social media blackout, there were several dissenting tweets casting aspersions on its rationality, demonstrating that it would not find resonance among the generality of the population. For instance, one Twitter user questioned how it was going to be possible to stay out of Twitter given that social media had become something like "oxygen". The tweet questioned: "@***Are you trying to kill us. Its oxygen this thing hello" (Times Live, 2017, 21 June). This shows that despite the high price of data people's lives have become intricately intertwined with digitality. That Twitter users started making jokes about the boycott illuminates on the complexity of digital media boycotts and the indispensability of the Internet in everyday life. The following tweets are illustrative:

"@*** I knew it, nobody could survive without social media for a Day. #SocialMediaBlackout"
"@*** The fact that #SocialMediaBlackout is trending is too ironic for words"
"@***RT if you are online.#SocialMediaBlackout"
"@***So today is #SocialMediaBlackout?"

These tweets highlight the ironies of trying to campaign for a social media blackout in a context where the Internet has become a part of everyday life. It underscores how epistemic rights are enmeshed with broader human rights (Watson, 2018). Also, they amplify the contradictory nature of a social media blackout as a social movement tactic in the digital age. While #DataMustFall was a struggle over Internet rights, boycotting social media undermined the very right that citizens were demanding. A social media blackout violated citizens' digital rights the same way an Internet shutdown would do (Chari, 2022).

Apart from the social media boycott another tactic employed during the #DataMustFall campaign was the petition. The most notable of these was the one submitted by Amandla.Mobi to the Data Services Market Inquiry launched by the Competition Commission in November 2017. The petition was signed by 44,726 people, and signatures were collected through the organization's websites, www.mobi and www.awethu, Facebook, SMs, and well as volunteers who went door to door in various communities within the country (Amandla.Mobi, 2017). The petition specified its demands with regard to the price of data, data usage, and market failure and how poor people in South Africa were affected by these issues and the bodies expected to make decisions on them.

By specifying the issues at stake, decisions to be taken, and bodies responsible for implementing helped petition signers to understand the kind of change that their participation would bring (Maxouris, 2020). The petition on the Amandla.Mobi website required singers to put their first name, surname, email address, province, and phone number, thereby enhancing transparency since such information could be verified. In addition, signers were given an option to choose whether they wished to be contacted in future in relation to the present or future petitions.

It is difficult to gauge the impact of the petition, given that it was used in combination with other tactics. While a petition is generally perceived as a low-risk political activity which does not require much commitment, it is effective in creating awareness about campaigns (Maxouris, 2020). In addition, activities around the campaign brought large numbers from different backgrounds to support the #DataMustFall campaign, thereby emphatically setting the public agenda in a way that shook the foundation of mobile network companies.

Milestones and Setbacks

While the actual impact of #DataMustFall cannot be easily quantified, it is evident that it shook the edifice of mobile telephony companies in South Africa. As Moyo and Munoriyarwa (2021: 375) point out, for the first time South Africans found a common voice and unified approach . . . on the issue of overpriced data. After the launch of #DataMustFall campaign the state and mobile network companies started taking the issue of mobile data seriously. A few days after the launch of the campaign on social media, Molefe was invited by the Parliamentary Portfolio Committee on Telecommunications and Postal Services to address the issue of high prices of mobile data (Times Live, 2016). Molefe tweeted thus: "History in the making, parliament ICT Committee has invited me to speak next Thursday! Our government is listening" (ENCA, 2016b, 16 September). Molefe also disclosed that he had received a call from the chairperson of ICASA who requested a meeting to discuss issues around #DataMustafall. Molefe tweeted: "We are making progress. I just got off the phone with Chair of ICASA Mr Mohlaloga, he promised a meeting this week. #DataMustFall".

The ICASA chairperson stated that his organization welcomed "consumer activism in our sector" adding that consumers had rights which needed to be protected. "We take bringing down the cost to communicate very seriously . . . I hope that the operators are listening to the consumers" (News24, 2016). While sceptics could view these statements as political rhetoric, given allegations that ICASA was "a lame duck" regulator (News24, 2016; Moyo & Munoriyarwa, 2021), the fact that the head of a critical public institution made this statement illustrates that the #DataMustFall campaign was making waves within the corridors of power.

The most significant acknowledgement of the campaign from a political office came from President Jacob Zuma during his State of the Nation Address (SONA) when he committed to reduce the cost of mobile data. Zuma stated: "We assure the youth that the lowering of the cost of data is uppermost in our policies and plans" (Republic of South Africa, 2017). Although Zuma did not divulge concrete plans to reduce the price of data, the fact that the highest office on the land acknowledged concerns registered by the campaign speaks volumes about its success. A similar promise was made by President Cyril Ramaphosa during his SONA address in June 2019, when he pledged to reduce the price of mobile data adding that the Minister of

Communications would issue a policy direction to ICASA to start the process of licensing spectrum. Ramaphosa pointed out that bringing down the cost of data was essential for "economic development and unleashing opportunities for young people" (Prior, 2020). Unlike his predecessor, Zuma, Ramaphosa spelt out concrete measures to bring down the price of mobile data.

Apart from merely raising awareness about the issue of high price of data, there were several developments triggered by the #DataMustFall campaign. Notable examples are enquiries into the price of mobile data conducted by two significant regulatory institutions, namely the Competition Commission and ICASA. In July 2017, ICASA launched an enquiry to determine priority markets in the electronic communications sector. The enquiries identified "relevant wholesale and retail markets or market segments" in the telecommunication industry which were susceptible to *ex ante* regulation (based on forecasts rather than actual results). Markets that should be prioritized for market reviews and potential regulation were also identified. ICASA also announced plans to conduct a market review to identify priority markets which would be followed by possible regulatory interventions in terms of the existing law (ICASA, 2018).

ICASA amended the End-User and Subscriber Charter Regulations of 2016 (as amended) to protect consumers. A significant milestone was that the review brought four changes beneficial to mobile data users; thus:

- Mobile network service providers were mandated to notify users when their data fell below 50%, 80%, and 100%. This was meant to help consumers monitor their data usage so that they could control their spending on data.
- Network service providers were obligated to give consumers the option to roll over unused data to the following month to ensure that they did not lose their data as was the practice at the time.
- All network service providers were obligated to allow consumers to transfer data to other users who were on the same network.
- Network service providers were no longer allowed to charge consumers out-of-bundle rates when their data ran out without the permission of the consumers.

(Review Online, 2018)

According to Amandla.Mobi, the amendment of regulations was a significant victory in the sense that new regulations helped "to stop networks from profiting from the poor".

> Our campaign eventually secured victories such as pro-poor regulations that benefited over 30 million users. The campaign also resulted in an agreement with the mobile networks to reduce the cost of some of their data bundles by 30% and 50%. This reduced the cost of mobile Internet for over 13 million people in South Africa.
> (Amandla.Mobi https://amandla.mobi/data-must-fall-campaign/)

Although amendments to these regulations brought much relief to mobile data users, some mobile network companies resisted their implementation by mounting a legal challenge against ICASA and other stakeholders. This exposes how in a neoliberal free market environment corporate interests can easily collide with citizens' digital rights.

The Competition Commission's 2017 Data Services Market Inquiry revealed that the pricing of data services by the leading mobile network operators was "exploitative", "discriminatory", and "antipoor" (Competition Commission, 2018:20). The Commission ordered mobile networks to introduce immediate relief on data pricing regardless of the fact that mobile companies had reduced their data prices before. Big mobile operators in the industry, MTN and Vodacom, were ordered to reduce the price of their data by up to 50% thereby providing immediate relief to mobile data users (Competition Commission, 2018; MyBroadband, 2019). The Commission also ordered mobile companies to give all citizens on prepaid packages a "life-line" package of daily data to "ensure that all citizens have data, regardless of income levels" (Mail & Guardian, 2019). Other notable benefits emanating from the Competition Commission's Data Services Market Inquiry include cessation of "exploitative" practices such as partitioning and price discrimination, zero-rating of content from public benefit organizations and educational institutions, and operators to inform every subscriber the effective price of data used by the subscriber every month (Competition Commission, 2018). In the immediate and long run, the Commission's directive to ICASA to release more spectrum would lower the price of mobile data (Competition Commission, 2018). This would lead to social inclusion and full citizen participation in the Fourth Industrial Revolution in the long term.

Notwithstanding these milestones, the price of mobile data in South Africa remains beyond the reach of the majority who spend a significant portion of their salaries on mobile data. Mobile operators were still resisting the price of data. Vodacom and MTN agreed to reduce their prices only after threats of prosecution by the Competition Commission (Research ICT Africa, 2020). Due to lack of regulation and imperfect competition, prices of mobile data remain anti-poor, and South Africa is still ranked eighth out of nine countries in terms of the cheapest data (Research ICT Africa, 2020).

The #DataMustfall campaign also suffered numerous setbacks, which include resistance or delays by mobile networks to comply to with some of ICASA regulations and the Competition Commission's recommendations. This resulted in court battles and the subsequent delays in the implementation of End-User Subscriber Charter Regulations. Campaign tactics such as the social media blackout did not gain traction because they contradicted demands for Internet rights. From the beginning, the campaign had exhibited internal contradictions. It was ironic that the man who is credited for starting the campaign was not a poor person but a "media mogul" who betrayed the movement by allegedly striking a deal with one of the mobile networks (Times Live, 2019). The campaign also exposed the contentious relationship between digital rights and the moral tenets of business. It would seem that attempts to include goods and services produced by private enterprises as human rights is a complicated affair. De Villiers (2017) succinctly illustrates how making connectivity a human right renders the notion of private enterprise meaningless:

> If the connectivity at hand is being provided by a company, then unfortunately, it is not a basic human right. The connectivity is being provided through someone else's work. If you are denied the absolute right to the product of your mind and your own effort, and someone else or the state decides how to dispose of it, you are a slave. Somehow the notion of rights has been expanded to include a right to what others produce. It is easy to call government to provide basic rights, but it can only provide them if they collect enough taxes. So, at the end of the day, someone is paying for the data service which some are demanding should be free.
> (De Villiers, 2017)

This quotation underscores how the moral tenets of corporate capitalism are at variance with the dictates of digital rights. Given the competing interests and a "weak regulator in a tough game" (News 24, 15 November) the notion of Internet rights becomes complicated.

Concluding Remarks

This chapter explored citizen struggles for digital rights, using #DataMustFall campaign in South Africa as a case study to shed insights on the intersection between digital rights and the politics of digital infrastructures from a South African perspective. It has revealed that the campaign was triggered by circumstances of deprivation where citizens could not access the Internet due to the exorbitant cost of mobile data. Although #DataMustFall was a hybrid social movement, some of its tactics were similar to those deployed by traditional South African social movements, which encompass both traditional and online modes of activism to achieve "maximise impact" (Bosch et al., 2018: 2162). The campaign achieved several milestones, which include reduced prices of data, amendments to mobile data-use regulations, and exposure of the "exploitative" practices employed by mobile network companies. However, these were counterbalanced by resistance by mobile networks to implement regulations and recommendations made by public bodies such as ICASA and the Competition Commission. Such resistance signals gloomy prospects for the realization of digital rights, particularly universal access to the Internet in South Africa.

The #DataMustFall campaign exposed the contentious relationship between digital rights and the moral tenets of commercial enterprise, signalling the complexity of attempts to include goods and services produced by private enterprises as human rights (De Villiers, 2017).

While #DataMustFall campaign originated online, offline activities such as physical demonstrations and protests highlight the extent to which social movements are evolving. This hybridity makes it difficult to "pigeonhole" social movements such as #DataMustFall, whose modes of operation were hybrid while its membership was eclectic, defying prototypical and ideological straitjacket classifications. Thus, #DataMustFall was as much a working-class movement as it was a middle-class cause. Whether this attribute weakened or strengthened the movement is a matter of conjecture. What is clear is that the movement was characterized by some ambiguities and contradictions from the beginning. However, it would be erroneous to attribute the decline of the movement to these internal contradictions.

To expand the line of enquiry taken in this study, future studies could employ in-depth interviews with key stakeholders in the mobile telephony sector to glean deeper insights on structural weaknesses of the movement and causal factors of its ultimate decline. This is crucial in a context where issues that triggered the #DataMustFall campaign remain germane while "ineffectual", "timid", and "amnesiac" (Sutherland, 2021) state bodies demonstrate policy ambivalence, giving mobile cellular companies "carte blanche to act as they please, thereby exposing citizens to unbridled extortion" (Moyo & Munoriyarwa, 2021: 376).

Notes

1 At the time of writing, the petition had been signed by over 75,000 people on the organization's website.
2 Amandla.Mobi. Retrieved from https://amandla.mobi/data-must-fall-campaign/

References

Accornero, G., and Gravante, T. (2022). Bridging Social Movement Studies between Global South and Global North. *The Open Journal of Socio-Political Studies*, 15(1): 193–202.

Amandla.Mobi. (2017). *Registration Form for Witten Submission*. Retrieved from www.ellipsis.co.za/wp-content/uploads/2018/09/Amandla-Mobi-DSMI-Submission_Non-confidential-1-Nov-17.pdf. Accessed 17 January 2023.

Amandla.Mobi. (2018). *Data Must Fall*. Retrieved from https://amandla.mobi/data-must-fall-campaign/. Accessed 17 January 2023.

Barry, J. J. (2019). *Information Communication Technology and Poverty Alleviation: Promoting Good Governance in the Developing World*. London: Routledge.

Baxter, P., and Jack, S. (2008). Qualitative Case Study Methodology: Study Design and Implementation for Novice Researchers. *Qualitative Report*, 13(4): 544–559.

Berger, S., and Nehring, H. (2017). Introduction: Towards a Global History of Social Movements. In S. Berger and H. Nehring (eds.), *The History of Social Movements in Global Perspective: A Survey* (pp. 1–35). London: Palgrave Macmillan.

Bond, P., and Mottir, S. (2013). Social Movements and Massacre in Africa. *Journal of Contemporary African Studies*, 31(2): 283–302.

Bosch, T., Wasserman, H., and Chuma, W. (2018). South African Activists' Use of Nanomedia and Digital Media in Democratisation Conflicts. *International Journal of Communication*, 12: 2153–2170.

Brandes, N., and Engels, B. (2011). Social Movements in Africa. *Stichprobem Winer Zeitschrift fur Kristiche Afrikastien*, 20: 1–15.

Castells, M. (2012). *Networks of Outrage and Hope*. Cambridge. Polity Press.

Cerf, G. V. (2012, 4 January). Internet Access is not a Human Right. *New York Times*. Retrieved from (Opinion | Internet Access Is Not a Human Right – The New York Times) nytimes.com. Accessed 30 January 2021.

Chari, T. (2022). Between State Interests and Citizen Digital Rights: Making Sense of Internet Shutdowns in Zimbabwe. In A. F. Kperogi (ed.), *Digital Dissidence and Social Media Censorship in Africa* (p. 76). London: Routledge.

Chiumbu, S. (2015). Social Movements, Media Practices and Radical Democracy in South Africa. *French Journal for Media Research*, 4: 1–20.

Competition Commission. (2019). *Data Services Market Inquiry*. Retrieved from www.compcom.co.za/wp-content/uploads/2019/12/DSMI-Non-Confidential-Report-002.pdf. Accessed 17 January 2023.

CRIS. (2005). Assessing Communication Rights: A Handbook. *CRIS Campaign*. Retrieved from https://archive.ccrvoices.org/cdn.agilitycms.com/centre-for-communication-rights/Images/Articles/pdf/cris-manual-en.pdf. Accessed 6 January 2023.

de Wall, A., & Ibreck, R. (2012). Hybrid Social Movements. *Journal of Contemporary African Studies*, 31(2): 303–324.

De Villiers, J. (2017). OP-ED:#DataMustFall Providers to decide for themselves. *CNBC Africa*, 23 June. Retrieved from www.cnbcafrica.com/2017/data-providers/. Accessed 24 June 2023.

DeFronzo, J., and Gill, J. (2020). *Social Problems and Social Movements*. London: Rowan & Littlefield.

Earle, L. (2011). Literature Review on the Dynamics of Social Movements in Fragile Societies and Conflict Affected States. Issue Paper. *GSDRC Emerging Issues Research*. Retrieved from https://gsdrc.org/wp-content/uploads/2015/07/EIRS13.pdf. Accessed on 30 April 2023.

ENCA. (2016a, 15 September). *Data Must Fall, Warns Tbo Touch*. Retrieved from www.enca.com/south-africa/datamustfall-demands-cellular-providers-to-lower-their-prices. Accessed 14 January 2023.

ENCA. (2016b, 16 September). *Tbo Touch Takes DataMustFall Campaign to Parliament*. Retrieved from www.enca.com/south-africa/tbo-touch-takes-datamustfall-campaign-to-parliament. Accessed 20 January 2023.

Engels, B., and Muller, M. (2019). Northern Theories, Southern Movements? Contentious Politics in Africa through the Lens of Social Movement Theory. *Contemporary Journal of African Studies*, 37(1): 72–92.

Hancock, D. R., and Algozzine, B. (2006). *Doing Case Study Research: A Practical Guide for Beginning Researchers*. New York: Teachers College Columbia University.

Huffing Post. (2016, 8 December). *#DataMustFall – The High Cost of Data Has Created a New Digital Apartheid*. Retrieved from www.huffingtonpost.co.uk/entry/datamustfall-the-high-cost-of-data-has-created-a-new-digital_uk_5c7e8e58e4b078abc6c09824. Accessed 28 January 2023.

Human Rights Council. (2011). Report of the Special Rapporteur on the Promotion and Protection of the Right Freedom of Opinion and Expression, *Frank La Rue*. A/HRC/17/27. Retrieved from https://digitallibrary.un.org/record/706200. Accessed 23 December 2022.

ICASA. (2018). *Findings Document on Priority Markets Inquiry in the Electronic Communications Sector.* Retrieved from www.ellipsis.co.za/wp-content/uploads/2018/08/findings-document-priority-markets-inquiry.pdf. Accessed 21 January 2023.

Karppinen, K., and Puukko, O. (2020). Four Discourses of Digital Rights: Promises and Problems of Rights-Based Politics. *Journal of Information Policy,* 10: 304–328.

Kaye, D., and Reventlow, N. (2017). *Digital Rights are Human Rights.* Retrieved from https://slate.com/technology/2017/12/digital-rights-are-human-rights.html. Accessed 6 July 2023.

Larmer, M. (2010). Social Movements in Africa. *Review of African Political Economy,* 37(125): 251–262.

Lee, M., Kim, H., and Kim, O. (2015). Why do People Re-Tweet? Altruistic, Egoistic and Reciprocity Motivations For Retweeting. *Pyschologia,* 58: 189–201.

Mail & Guardian. (2019, 6 December). *From Data Must Fall to Data for All.* Retrieved from https://mg.co.za/article/2019-12-06-00-from-data-must-fall-to-data-for-all/. Accessed 24 January 2023.

Marti, J. B., and Biglia, B. (2014). Social Movements. In T. Teo (ed.), *Encyclopedia of Critical Pedagogy.* Springer: New York.

Mathiesen, K. (2014). Human Rights for the Digital Age. *Journal of Mass Media Ethics,* 29(1): 2–18.

Maxouris, C. (2020). *Online Petitions Work Best When You Do More Than Just Sign.* Retrieved from https://edition.cnn.com/2020/06/23/us/do-online-petitions-work-trnd/index.html. Accessed 19 January 2023.

Media Defence. (2022). *Introduction to Digital Rights.* Retrieved from https://www.mediadefence.org/resource-hub/introduction-to-digital-rights/. Accessed 30 April 2023.

Milderbrath, H. (2021). Internet access as a Fundamental Right: Exploring Aspects of Connectivity. *Brussels: European Parliamentary Research.* Retrieved from www.europarl.europa.eu/RegData/etudes/STUD/2021/696170/EPRS_STU(2021)696170_EN.pdf. Accessed 7 July 2023.

Moyo, D., and Munoriyarwa, A. (2021). 'Data Must Fall': Mobile Data Pricing, Regulatory Paralysis and Citizen Action in South Africa. *Information, Communication and Society,* 24(3): 365–380.

MyBroadband. (2019, 2 December). *Vodacom and MTN Must Cut Prices by 50% and Give Free Data.* Retrieved from https://mybroadband.co.za/news/cellular/331043-vodacom-and-mtn-must-cut-prices-by-50-and-give-users-free-data.html. Accessed 23 January 2023.

News24. (2016, 15 November). *Icasa a Weak Ref in a tough Game.* Retrieved from www.news24.com/fin24/icasa-a-weak-ref-in-tough-fight-20161115. Accessed 15 January 2023.

News24. (2019, 19 September). *Right to Know to Lead Protest for Cheaper Data Prices.* Retrieved from www.news24.com/news24/right2know-to-lead-protest-for-cheaper-data-prices-20170919. Accessed 17 January 2023.

O'Rielly, M. (2015). What is the Appropriate Role for Regulators in an Expanding Broadband Economy? Remarks of Commissioner Michael O'Rielly before the Internet Alliance, June 25, 2015. Retrieved from https://transition.fcc.gov/Daily_Releases/Daily_Business/2015/db0625/DOC-334113A1.pdf. Accessed 30 April 2023.

Pollicino, O. (2019). The Right to Internet Access: Quid Iuris. In A. Von-Arnaild, K. Von Der Decker and M. Susi (eds.), *The Cambridge Handbook of New Human Rights* (pp. 1–14). Cambridge: Cambridge University Press.

Prior, B. (2020). #DataMustFall: The Complete Story. *MyBroadband*, 2 August. Retrieved from https://mybroadband.co.za/news/telecoms/341887-datamustfall-the-complete-story.html. Accessed 4 January 2023.

Republic of South Africa. (2017, 9 February). *President Jacob Zuma: 2017 State of the Nation Address*. Retrieved from www.gov.za/speeches/president-jacob-zuma-2017-state-nation-address-9-feb-2017-0000. Accessed 23 January 2023.

Research ICT Africa. (2020). Despite Reduction in Mobile Data Tariffs Data Still Expensive in South Africa. *Policy Brief Number 2*. Retrieved from https://researchictafrica.net/wp/wp-content/uploads/2020/06/Tapiwa-Chinembiri-Mobile-Data-Pricing-Policy-Brief2–2020-FINAL.pdf. Accessed 23 January 2023.

Review Online. (2018). *#DataMustFall – 4 Icasa Regulations that Will Affect Your Data*. Retrieved from https://reviewonline.co.za/261030/datamustfall-4-icasa-regulations-will-affect-data/. Accessed 21 January 2023.

Right2Know. (2022). *The Right to Know Campaign Will Continue to Fight for a Free, Fast and Safe Internet*. Retrieved from www.r2k.org.za/2022/02/19/the-right-2know-campaign-will-continue-to-fight-for-a-free-fast-and-safe-internet. Accessed 17 January 2023.

Sebeelo, T. B. (2021). Hashtag Activism, Politics and Resistance in Africa: Examining #ThisFlag and #RhodesMustFall Online Movements. *Insight on Africa*, 13(1): 95–109.

Staggenborg, S. (2016). *Social Movements*. Oxford: Oxford University Press.

Stake, R. E. (1995). *The Art of Case Study Research*. Thousand Oaks, CA: Sage.

Stoycheff, E., and Nisbet, E. K. C. (2021, 20 July). *Is Internet Freedom a Tool for Democracy or Authoritarianism? The Conversation*. Retrieved from https://theconversation.com/is-internet-freedom-a-tool-for-democracy-or-authoritarianism-61956. Accessed 20 November 2022.

Sutherland, E. (2021). Data Must Fall – The Politics of Mobile Telecommunications Tariffs in South Africa. Paper Presented at the South African Association of Political Studies (SAAAPS) 15th Biennial Conference, Rhodes University, 26–28 August. Retrieved from https://papers.ssrn.com/sol3/papers.cfm?abstract_id=2154165. Accessed 30 April 2023.

The Citizen. (2017, 1 June). Ntsiki Mazwai Tell People Complaining about Data to 'Shut Up'. Retrieved from https://www.citizen.co.za/news/south-africa/ntsiki-mazwai-tells-people-complaining-data-to-shut-up/. Accessed 30 April 2023.

The Citizen. (2018, 18 October). *ANC to Make Submissions Inquiry Into Data Prices*. Retrieved from www.citizen.co.za/news/south-africa/anc-to-make-submissions-at-inquiry-into-data-prices/. Accessed 17 January 2023.

The South African. (2017, 20 June). #Data Must Fall Campaign to Slash the High Cost of Data Tariffs Starts with Social Movement Boycott Tomorrow. Retrieved from https://www.thesouthafrican.com/news/datamustfall-campaign-to-slash-the-high-cost-of-data-starts-with-social-media-boycott-tomorrow/. Accessed 30 April 2023.

Thomas, P. (2005, 28 October). CRIS and Global Media Governance: Communication Rights and Social Change. *Paper Presented at the 21st Century Conference*. Center for Social Change Research, Queensland University of Technology, Queensland. Retrieved from https://espace.library.uq.edu.au/view/UQ:102463. Accessed 31 December 2022.

Thomas, P. (2006). The Communication Rights in the Information Society (CRIS) Campaign: Applying Social Movement Theories to an Analysis of Global Media Reform. *The International Communication Gazette*, 68(4): 291–312.

Times Live. (2016, 20 September). *Tbo Touch to present #DataMustFall Campaign in Parliament.* Retrieved from www.timeslive.co.za/tshisa-live/tshisa-live/2016-09-20-tbo-touch-to-present-datamustfall-campaign-in-parliament/. Accessed 20 January 2023.

Times Live. (2017, 21 June). *Despite #SocialMediaBlackout Boycott the Social Media Streets Were Lit Up!* Retrieved from www.timeslive.co.za/news/south-africa/2017-06-21-despite-socialmediablackout-boycott-the-social-media-streets-were-lit-up/. Accessed 17 January 2023.

Times Live. (2019, 4 April). *Tbo Touch Labelled a 'Sell Out' in #DataMustFall Fight.* Retrieved from www.timeslive.co.za/tshisa-live/tshisa-live/2019-12-04-tbo-touch-labelled-a-sell-out-in-datamustfall-fight/. Accessed 23 January 2023.

Van Stekelenburg, J., and Klandermans, B. (2005). Social Movement Theory: Past Present and Protest. In E. Stephen and I. van Kessel (ed.), *Movers and Shakers: Social Movements in Africa* (pp. 17–43). Leiden: Brill.

Velocci, C. (2016). Internet Access is Now a Basic Human Right. *The Verge*, 4 July. Retrieved from https://gizmodo.com/internet-access-is-now-a-basic-human-right-1783081865. Accessed 15 December 2022.

Watson, L. (2018). Systematic Epistemic Rights Violations in the Media: A Brexit Case Study. *Social Epistemology*, 32(2): 88–102.

Willems, W. (2010). Social Movement Media in Post-Apartheid South Africa. In J. Downing (ed.), *Encyclopedia of Social Movement* (pp. 492–495). London: Sage.

Yin, R. K. (2003). *Case Study Research: Design and Methods.* London: Sage.

Young, T. R. (1999). Marxism and Social Movements. *Contemporary Sociology*, 28(3): 268–270.

12 Silence and Silent the SóróSoké Generation

The Politicisation of Social Media in Nigeria

Ufuoma Akpojivi

Introduction

The right to communicate, conceived by Jean d' Arcy in 1969 (O'Siochru, 2005), has been a fundamental discourse within Africa and continues to be a dominant issue in contemporary African states for two reasons. First, the right to communication is considered a fundamental human right (Oyedemi, 2014), where every citizen should be able to access and impart information. This right is covered in international and regional treaties, such as Article 19 of the Universal Declaration of Human Rights and Article 9 of the African Charter on Human Rights, which allow citizens to receive and impart information. The importance of the right to communication in any democratic society cannot be emphasised. As Habermas (2006) argues, communication is central in deliberative liberal democracy, as it affords citizens the opportunity to be part of the democratic process, express themselves, and shape public polity. However, there has been an increasing attempt by postcolonial[1] African states to control and mediate these citizens' rights to communication, whereby states across the continent are either policing citizens' rights to communication by formulating and implementing policies to curtail this communicative right (see Olaniyan & Akpojivi, 2021) or abruptly restricting access to infrastructure that facilitates communication (see Mare, 2020). This trend is worrisome for a postcolonial state such as Nigeria with an extensive history of censorship and government control of the communication sphere and its impact on democratic culture and stability.

Ogbondah (2018) argues that following the third wave of democratisation in Nigeria that commenced in 1999 after many years of military rule, expectations were high that the communicative rights of citizens would be upheld. However, there has been a systematic decline and suppression of this right due to poor state–media and citizen relationships. For example, Ogbondah (2018) argues that journalists and media practitioners have been harassed and arrested, media houses closed, and restrictive regulatory measures have been implemented. Similarly, Freedom House (2021) stated that infrastructure deficits, including unreliable access to electricity, uneven infrastructural spread, and digital divide, are among other factors that have hindered the communication rights of Nigerians. Furthermore, for the first time in the history of Nigeria, the government of President Buhari issued a directive to the regulatory body requiring the banning of Twitter on June 5, 2021. While the ban was generally attributed to the contestation between the government and Twitter for the deletion of President Buhari's tweets, which made reference to Nigeria's civil war of 1967–1970, threatening to deal with agitators from the South Eastern region, that is, 'those misbehaving today' in 'the language they will understand' (BBC, 2021), the call to further regulate Over The Top (OTT) services reiterated the broader desire of the government to regulate citizens' communicative rights. The desire of the state to control or restrict the communication space is not a new phenomenon, as the government of President Buhari, since its assumption of power in 2015, has sought to regulate social media through mechanisms such as the proposed "Protection From Internet Falsehood and Manipulative Bill 2019" and the "National Commission for the Prohibition of Hate Speech Bill 2019", which has generated uproar and contestation between the state and other stakeholders (Olaniyan & Akpojivi, 2021). Hence, the contestation and struggle between the state and citizens over the state's attempts to silence its citizens.

Therefore, this chapter seeks to examine the politicisation of the internet and its affordances by the Nigerian government and the contestation between the state and citizens over this politicisation. Additionally, the chapter aims to interrogate why postcolonial African states such as Nigeria have abrogated this right to themselves as they determine this right for their citizens, that is, who gets it, when, and how. To this end, this chapter seeks to address the following research questions: why has social media become a dominant tool of contestation between the Nigerian state and citizens? What conversations occurred following the Twitter ban of June 5, 2021? Do these conversations reinforce postcolonial issues of regulation and politicisation of free speech and media freedom?

This chapter is structured as follows: the next section will provide a brief conceptualisation of communication rights and provides clarity on the context of its usage within the chapter. This is followed by a brief historical background to the Twitter ban, followed by a detailed discussion of communication as fundamental human rights, the contestation between government and citizens and the mechanism used by the state to limit these rights in the fourth Republic of Nigeria. This discussion is followed by the theoretical framework underpinning the chapter and the methodological approaches adopted in the chapter. This is followed by a detailed discussion of the politicisation of social media and the internet in Nigeria. The last section provides the conclusion and recommendations.

What Is Communication Rights?

Communication rights as a concept is a common parlance in media and communication studies. Despite being prevalent, it does not have a universally acceptable definition and application in nation states. Communication rights or the right to communicate was propounded by Jean d'Arcy in 1969 (Moyo, 2010). D' Arcy's conceptualisation of communication rights seeks to extend the universal declaration of human rights from mere right to information of individuals to holistic rights to be informed, the right to communicate, and rights to participate in public and societal discourses (Howard, 1984). This means that the right to communication or communication rights goes beyond just seeking, receiving, and imparting information but for individuals to participate in the societal discourse using the information they have collected. This means that communication rights involve expressing and participating (communication) and seeking and receiving information, thereby updating and extending the universality and practicality of the universal declaration of human rights (Corredoira, 2021).

Within the context of this chapter, communication rights means the ability of citizens to seek, receive, impart information and participate in public and societal discourse, and these should be universal across countries because information and participation are central to the sustenance of any democracy. Consequently, this study seeks to interrogate the politicisation of the internet and its affordances by the Nigerian government, its impact on the communication rights of Nigerians, and the contestation between the state and citizens over this politicisation.

Contextual Background to Study

Prior to the Twitter ban on June 5, 2021, the issue of communication rights, which entails the right to receive and participate in media and societal discourse was a topical issue in Nigeria. As Jean D' Arcy (1969) argues, true communication and attainment lie in our hands, and this should be recognised and organised for both individuals and communities in which they exist. This means that communication rights become a fundamental human rights that should be protected and respected by the state. Consequently, democratic nation states are expected to provide and protect this right (Montiel, 2013), and Nigeria is no exception, as section 39 of the 1999 constitution provides for this right. Despite the constitutional provision for freedom of speech, there have been regulatory frameworks that seek to limit this freedom of expression, as there is an increasing attempt by the state to censor and dictate what to communicate and how to communicate. For instance, Wodu (2021) stated that the Nigerian government tends to issue directives to media houses to toe certain lines when reporting on the security challenges confronting the country. This assertion buttresses the argument of numerous scholars that freedom of expression and freedom of the media are in decline in the fourth republic as media houses are either banned or fined, and journalists are arrested or disappear (see Olukotun, 2018).

However, one fundamental issue confronting the Nigerian state is whether section 39, subsection 1, which states: 'Every person shall be entitled to freedom of expression, including freedom to hold opinions and to receive and impart ideas and information without interference', applies to the communicative rights of Nigerians online. This is important because scholars have criticised the Nigerian constitution for its failure to provide for media freedom, as the available rights are vaguely restrictive to the right of speech, which is easily withdrawn under section 39 subsection 3 under national interests. Therefore, there is need to conceptualise and theorise this online communicative right within the context of Nigeria's legislative provisions because according to the Freedom House[2] report of 2022, there is an increasing decline of this right in Nigeria due to digital restrictions and legislation of the government to criminalise online speech and content. Following the inauguration of President Buhari under the fourth republic, the government has on numerous occasions expressed concerns over the impact of these new media technologies and their affordances on the country. The government blamed the internet and social media in particular for the 'surge in the propagation of hate speech, fake news, seditious and treasonable messages' (Oluwole, 2021). This is despite some social critics and scholars attributing the rise of fake news and mis/disinformation within the media space to the government (Olaniyan & Akpojivi, 2021).

The positionality of the state towards the digital rights of citizens and the internet is largely attributed to Nigerians using these new media platforms to hold their leaders and state institutions accountable by fostering good governance. According to the NOI social media report of 2019, over 61% of Nigerians have access to the internet, and the majority of users use the internet and social media platforms for social advocacy. This advocacy could be seen in the #EndSars protest of 2020, where Nigerians used Twitter not only to highlight, campaign, and amplify the issue of police brutality that had become endemic but also occupied strategic spaces to demand the necessary social change. Hakeem (2020) argues that through the #EndSars[3] of 2020, Nigerians were not only protesting against the colonial legacy of policing which is rooted in brutality that has continued in the postcolonial Nigerian state, but also they were responding to issues of good governance and accountability that have been a bane. This reinforces the desire of the state to curtail the online communicative rights of Nigerians. This is evident in President Buhari's statement in which he blamed social media and the internet for what he called the 'unrest' of citizens. According to President Buhari,

> In October 2020, we all witnessed an escalation in the use of the social media for dissemination of subversive messages and incitement of violence which played a part in heightening tensions, causing unrest and spurring widespread acts of looting and destruction across the country.
> (Cited in Oluwole, 2021)

This resulted in the 'indefinite suspension'[4] of Twitter by the government and the call to have other OTT platforms regulated. While the government blamed the ban on Twitter for taking down the tweet of President Buhari on June 2, 2020, which went against their content policy, Nigerians saw the ban as an attempt by the government to censor and restrict their communicative rights.

According to Obia (2021), the government tried to avoid censoring social media, as it did not ban Facebook despite the platform taking down a post similar to that of President Buhari. The suspension of Twitter reflects the fact that Twitter has become a dominant tool for 'dissident' 'being vocal', and presenting a platform for speaking truth to power. According to the NOI Poll (2019), 84% of Nigerians use Twitter for advocacy, therefore, the perception that the resultant ban was a way of silencing the SóróSoké[5] generation that wants to speak out against injustices and maladministration by the Nigerian state. Thus, the assertion that due to the inherent role Twitter played in providing a public sphere for debates and advocacy, and the former CEO, Jack Dorsey's public support of #EndSars (Obia, 2021), contributed to the 'indefinite suspension'. However, this chapter seeks to examine the increasing trend of the politicisation of the internet and social media, which I argue goes beyond just the Twitter ban but a persistent attempt by the government to regulate social media and OTT platforms either via state authoritarianism or by asking service providers to shut down certain services or through draconian legal frameworks. For example, on June 13, 2022, the National Information Technology Development Agency (NITDA) issued a directive on the code of practice governing computer service platforms and internet intermediaries in Nigeria. According to the NITDA, internet intermediaries and computer service platforms must

> establish a legal entity with the Corporate Affairs Commission, appoint a representative to interface with the Nigerian authorities, comply with all applicable tax obligations under Nigerian law, provide a comprehensive compliance mechanism to avoid publication of prohibited contents and unethical behaviour on their platform and provide information to authorities on harmful accounts, suspected botnets, troll groups, and other coordinated disinformation networks and delete any information that violates Nigerian law within an agreed time.
> (NITDA, 2022)

These provisions further reveal the desire of the Nigerian state to access social media platforms and control and dictate the conversations occurring online, as the said code of practice is vague on what constitutes harmful content, thereby empowering the state to decide what is harmful content and account, thus leading to censorship. This goes against the fundamental principles of communicative rights as a 'social right' that is rooted in freedom (Mallen, 2021).

Communicative Rights of Digital Citizens

Scholars have approached digital citizenship differently due to conceptual issues. The notion of digital citizenship arises from the proliferation of the internet and its associated affordances, such as social media. The idea of digital citizenship suggests a community (online) to which citizens belong where they are able to share information, interact, and engage with each other and mobilise to bring about social change in society. This community is bounded and sustained by technology (Mossberger et al., 2008). While this 'community' to a certain extent is 'imagined' or 'abstract' in nature due to the lack of physicality, its existence in shaping societal discourse cannot be overlooked as technology and the digital inclusion of citizens are pivotal tool for development.

In a lucid review of the African Union's (AU) policies, such as the 'digital transformation strategy for Africa (2020–2030)' and the policy and regulation initiative for digital Africa (PRIDA), the inclusion of African citizens within this imagined community is for economic rights and perspective. Both policies see technology as central to the economic transformation and development of the African continent, and the appropriation of these technologies by the youths on the continent is considered by the AU as a strategic tool for empowering citizens, especially the teeming youths that use this technology the most and are mostly unemployed. According to the digital transformation strategy for Africa (2020–2030), digital inclusion is germane to improve the overall well-being of African citizens and strengthen economic growth and diversification within the continent. Therefore, there is a call for accessibility and affordability of broadband across the continent and the formulation and implementation of legislative frameworks that will enable this digital inclusion for social and economic development (see AU, 2019, The Policy and Regulation Initiative for Digital Africa). Furthermore, the call is that by 2030, Africans should be digitally empowered and be able to access the Internet freely and securely at least 6 mb/s at all times in any location within the continent (AU, 2020).

Such an approach to digital citizenship by the AU is rooted in economic rights (social rights), a salient aspect of citizenship (see Marshall, 1950). The attainment of this social right is dependent on the citizen's communicative right and the use of technology to facilitate the social rights of improved economic well-being and welfare. Mallen (2021) substantiated this by stating that the actualisation of freedom, whether economic, political or social, is facilitated by communicative rights facets of seeking, receiving, and imparting information. That is, the ability of citizens to be empowered economically as encapsulated in the various policy initiatives of the AU, as mentioned previously, is based on the ability of citizens to seek, receive, and impart information, which are vital components of communicative rights. Therefore, making communication and the right to communication *sine qua non* to citizenship and digital citizenship. Meaning, within the African continent, the communicative rights of citizens cannot be ignored, as the actualisation of the AU policy goals of digital inclusiveness is vested in the ability of citizens to seek, receive, and impart information.

This means that while the Nigerian government does not have a clear policy on digital communicative rights, the desire to achieve economic inclusiveness and the digital economy at the supranational level (AU) has influenced

Nigeria's approach to digital inclusiveness and citizenship. According to Nigeria's National Digital Economy Policy and Strategy (2020–2030), citizens are the 'greatest asset to the realisation of a digital economy' (Federal Ministry of Communications & Digital Economy 2020). The notion of a digital economy and citizens within the policy suggests that digital citizenship within the Nigerian state drives the digital economy. A digital economy is rooted in digital citizens who are knowledgeable and possess the appropriate skills to drive this digital economy. As the internet and other ICTs have permeated every aspect of our lives, they have also created a web of interconnections between people and things (Isin & Ruppert, 2020). Such an interconnection has shaped how politics is played, economies are structured, and culture is defined. Digital citizens are actively reinventing themselves online and the social structures of society using technology. Such reinvention could be seen in the mobilisation of citizens online demanding social justice, good governance, and accountability.

Oyedemi (2020) argues that the space for digital citizens to participate in rudimentary societal discourses is changing due to easy-to-access information from the internet and ICT, as citizens are able to effectively participate in political, economic, and cultural debates occurring within society. Such participation has enabled once disenfranchised and neglected citizens to speak out and hold governments accountable. The last two decades have witnessed citizens across the African continent utilising the internet and its affordances to hold governments accountable and pushing for social change. From #OccuppyNigeria, #EndSars, #BringBackOurGirls, and #OurMumuDonDo, among others, Nigerians have taken to the openness of the internet and its infrastructure to participate in societal discourses and push for reforms. Therefore, juxtaposing Nyamnjoh's (2016) argument that we currently live in an era where everything must fall due to the active participation of citizens in this imagined community as they use these technologies to disrupt normative politics and polity and push for a better society (see Isin & Ruppert, 2020). According to Oyedemi (2020), the act of citizens actively using technology to source information, perform their civic duties, and actualise their economic and financial goals makes them digital citizens.

The argument about technology being central to the attainment of digital citizenship or achieving a transformed society and digital economy as stipulated by both the AU and Nigerian policies means there is need to rethink the relationship between states and citizens' communicative rights in a postcolonial state such as Nigeria in relation to technological access and legislative frameworks that governments have historically suppressed. Olaniyan (2022), while buttressing this further, argues that at the dawn of independence, there were only 18,724 telephone lines in 1960 and less than 500,000 in 2000. Nevertheless, 2019 figures from Nigeria's Communication Commission (NCC) indicate an internet penetration rate of 55.7% out of a population of over 200 million. Despite this slight improvement, Obijiofor (2015) argues that the communicative right of Nigerians is perpetually in decline due to factors such as the digital divide, technological and legislative frameworks. Communication (both technological infrastructure and framework) has become a tool of control and itself an item of contestation (see Castells, 2009). According to Mare (2020), this control manifests itself at the infrastructure level of granting licensing to telecommunication operators, ownership, and surveillance of infrastructure.

Within the Nigerian context, during the fourth republic, this control is reflected in the government's active control of determining telecommunication players, determining infrastructural expansion and services offered (Owoeye, 2018), recently surveilling the infrastructure (monitoring calls/text) (see Idris, 2018), and shutting down telecommunication services – calls or internet services – in some states as part of the strategy to fight Boko Haram and terrorists, and banning OTT services such as Twitter. These technological interventions have shown that the communicative rights of citizens have been 'hijacked and melded' and that this technology is not 'intrinsically an instrument of freedom', as government intervention and control have betrayed the original purpose of enabling digital citizenship (Price, 2021). This, according to Price (2021), is rooted in the market of loyalties due to the contestation between the state, telecommunication operators, citizens, and other stakeholders. To maintain and curry favours from the state and recoup profit from their continued existence, these telecommunication operators willingly carry out government interventions/control.

Theoretical and Methodological Underpinnings

This chapter uses Stuart Mill's philosophical argument of the tyranny of the state and contestation between freedom and regulation in 'On liberty' and Jurgen Habermas's 'Public Sphere' as theoretical lenses. Mill (1859) argued that nation states have the desire to control and limit the liberty of their citizens and that such control goes against the tenet of democracy and the attainment of truth. To him, the opinion and views of any individual should not be suppressed, as suppressing such could mean silencing a view or opinion that could be true. According to Mill, even when an opinion is wrong, there is an element of truth, as to him 'though the silenced opinion be an error, it may, and very commonly does contain a portion of truth' (1859: 72). Therefore, the only time the state should intervene is when such freedom impacts the freedom of others and overall state interests. This brings about contestation, as in postcolonial African states such as Nigeria, governments have used national interests, which in most cases refer to the interests of the government and not citizens as the basis to suppress the communicative rights of its citizens (Akpojivi, 2018). For instance, a lucid review of government (military and democratic) attempts to control communicative infrastructure from 1960 to date all have a common feature of the need to protect national interests; thus, the distrust among citizens who believe that due to lack of effective conceptualisation of what constitutes 'national interests', the national interest argument has become a tool for control (Akpojivi, 2018).

Such control hinders the formation of public opinion and debate that should occur within the communicative space (McNair, 2000). Habermas (1989) argues that the structural transformation of the communicative sphere should enable citizens to meet and deliberate on issues of the public sphere due to the autonomy, equality, and access that it provides. While some scholars might limit Habermas's conceptualisation to coffee shops and traditional media, Dahlgren (2005) extended Habermas's conceptualisation of the public sphere to internet-mediated communication. Technology and the internet have expounded on the communicative sphere and rights of the public. Therefore, any control from the government, whether at the infrastructural and framework levels, means that citizens' universal communicative rights have been hindered (Corredoira, 2021). As de Pool (1983: 5) stated, 'freedom is fostered when the means of communication are dispersed, decentralised and easily available as are printing presses or microcomputers'.

Data for this study were collected using a qualitative approach. Data were collected from Twitter using the Twitter Archiving Google Sheet (TAGS) and the Twitter Application Programming Interface (API). Tweets that were collected and analysed in this study were archived on a daily basis from June 4 to June 13,[6] 2021, using the following hashtags: #TwitterBan, #TwitterSuspendBuharisAccount, #Nigeria, #RefuteTwitterBan, #EndTwitterBanInNigeria, #KeepItOn, #OpenInternet, #FixNigeria, and #WeMove. This period was selected because Twitter was officially 'indefinitely suspended' on June 5. However, Nigerians became aware of this on the night of June 4. Therefore, I started collecting tweets on June 4. In addition, the aforementioned hashtags were trending, and thus, tweets under these hashtags were collected. Over 500,000 tweets were collected during the said period and were purposively sampled and selected[7] to understand the contestation between the state and the citizens over the politicisation of the internet, the kind of conversations during the period, and if these conversations reinforce postcolonial issues of regulation and politicisation of free speech and media freedom. These tweets were analysed using thematic analysis, as they were read and grouped into different emerging themes. It should be noted that tweets that were purposively used in the analysis did not fully account for all discourses on other social media platforms such as Facebook. To address the ethical concerns of collecting and using social media data during this period of heightened contestation, I anonymised the data by removing the Twitter handles and names of tweets used in the analysis. Likewise, in some instances, I have paraphrased some of the tweets used to avoid easy identification by Google or Twitter search.

Findings and Discussion

Contestation Between the SóróSoké Generation and the Nigerian State

From the collected data, six themes emerged: freedom of speech versus digital authoritarianism, politicising technology, internet shutdown, regulating social media, content moderation policy, and deliberative liberal democracy.

However, because of space limitations, this discussion will focus on freedom of speech versus digital authoritarianism, politicising the technology, and internet shutdown.

Freedom of Speech Versus Digital Authoritarianism

Following the news of the 'indefinite suspension' of Twitter, there was contestation between the citizens and the state over the broader implications of this 'indefinite suspension' on the communicative rights of Nigerians and economic development. There was contestation over why the Twitter platform was banned in a democratic era (Obadare, 2022). Most of the tweets linked the ban to Twitter, removing President Buhari's tweets, which were deemed to go against Twitter policy and Twitter acting as a platform for citizens to express themselves and hold their leaders to account.

> @*** tweeted 'You're right. Buhari, which banned Twitter because his Tweet was deleted, is truly just a woman in disguise. Obas'.
> @*** tweeted 'because twitter deleted his tweet we all have to suffer. Demons in their white agbada looking meek and angelic'.
> @*** tweeted 'APC govt and Buhari used social media to get to power but now twitter ban because of their ego being bruised'.
> @*** 'PMB once led protests against the previous administration freely. However, today, he sends security forces to attack peaceful protesters'.

From these tweets, citizens blamed the ban on the government's displeasure over the deletion of President Buhari's tweet and thus the need to restrict the deliberative space for all Nigerians. Furthermore, some attributed the ban to Twitter becoming a critical space for citizens to deliberate and hold the government accountable, which was exacerbated by the #Endsar protests in which people were killed in Lekki, Lagos. See the following selected tweets:

> @*** 'till this day, I still can't believe the poverty capital of the world is Nigeria!!!Imagine over 50% of Nigerians living in poverty'.
> @***They promised us $1 will become I Naira, but they haven't fulfilled this promise and they decided to gag us.
> @***We need more people to speak the truth to the powers
> @***it's time to end bad governance in Nigeria
> @***Our Mumu don do. Enough is enough. We don't tire to suffer. Enjoyment no be bad thing. We want a better Nigeria.

Mwaura (2022) argues that microblogging platforms such as Twitter have shaped national discourses as people take to these microblogging platforms to highlight the ills in society at the expense of the government, thus resulting in contestation. This contestation is over the democratic rights of citizens to express themselves, as this is a fundamental component of a democratic society. For instance,

> @*** tweeted #Democracy guarantees right to free speech and peaceful protest.
> @*** democracy is threatened wherever and whenever free speech is threatened. For the sake of Nigeria's democracy and our heroes' past, we shall keep it.
> @*** I stand with Nigerians for free speech and true democracy, free speech, free choice and free assembly.
> @***Thank you to everyone using their voice/platform/on the streets/online protesting.
> @***God I love my generation . . . they speak up.
> @***Stop deceiving the world with this democracy day, Nigeria is currently in a dictatorship.
> @***This is not the country we pray and hoped for. Anyone who supports this dictatorship administration is sure part of the problem. Fix Nigeria and not break it.

From these tweets, freedom of speech (both online and offline) is considered a central tenet of democracy. As democracy is grounded in plurality and diversity of views, it will enrich the democratic space and discourse, as argued by Mill (1859). In addition, Chari (2022) argues that technology and its affordances enable the realisation of the communicative rights of citizens. The inability of Nigerians to express themselves online results in digital authoritarianism, as expressed in the following tweets.

> @***Stop deceiving the world with this democracy day, Nigeria is currently in a dictatorship.
> @***this is not the democracy we fought for, that people died for, that we want. We cannot claim to be in a democracy where people cannot express themselves online.

The basis of digital authoritarianism is that in the history of Nigeria's fourth republic, this is the first time that Nigerians were unable to express themselves online, where their digital rights were being infringed upon, and as Ikome (2007) argued, this is a feature of postcolonial states. Postcolonial states use violence or what Mbembe (1992) called the banality of power to suppress the rights of citizens. Olaniyan and Akpojivi (2021) argue that the government's growing attempt to censor or limit communicative rights online through regulatory mechanisms, and the 2021 Twitter ban were the heights of such digital authoritarianism. It goes against available national and international conventions such as Article 19 of the Universal Declaration of Human Rights and the African Charter of Human Rights, which guarantee the digital rights of citizens to seek, receive, and impart information. According to Corredoira (2021: 37), these international conventions expound on the 'existing principles to the realities of the internet, based on the idea that access is a right that facilitates other rights'. Therefore, the question of to what extent such digital authoritarianism has impacted the economic/social rights of Nigerians remains.

Obadare (2022) argued that the Twitter ban within six months of the Fourth Republic's existence had broader economic implications for citizens and the country at large. Citing the NetBlocks, Obadare notes that 'the total loss to the country from the ban ran in excess of $250,000, every hour'. Therefore, the salient question is why the deletion of President Buhari's tweet should result in a ban with such a grave impact on the communicative and economic/social rights of Nigerians. While the Nigerian state has justified its actions by citing national interests, as the Minister of Information Lai Mohammed claimed, 'the ban came after citing the persistent use of the platform for activities that are capable of undermining Nigeria's corporate existence' (Infomant247, 2021). Akpojivi (2018) argues that within postcolonial African states such as Nigeria, there is a tiny dichotomy between personal interests and national interests, as most personal interests are hidden within the national interest clauses to censor or limit media and human rights/freedom. This has actively been the case right from colonial to independence era and post-independence era where media and its regulatory mechanism have always reflected personal interests.

Politicising Technology

Chari (2022) posited that the internet and its affordances are enablers of freedom of expression and communication, as people can seek, receive, and impart information with minimal restrictions, unlike the mainstream media. To Svensson (2020), the proliferation of mobile technology and the internet has provided platforms and opportunities for citizens once disenfranchised to participate and contribute to national discourse. For example, opportunity has become a sore point of contestation. Olaniyan (2022) argues that following the deregulation of the telecommunication industry and the proliferation of the mobile telephone and the internet, a significant number of Nigerians have access to the digital space and are able to contribute to national discourse and hold government to account. Such a process of holding them accountable has led to the desire of the state to censor the internet and its affordance, thus the politicisation of the technology. This was evident in the tweets collected, as seen in the following selected tweets:

> @*** tweeted 'Jack has done more for Nigerians in this short period than Buhari did for Nigeria in his entire existence'.
> @*** tweeted 'I cannot even tweet anytime I like, been trying to gain access to Twitter since morning 😔 🖤'.
> @*** tweeted 'I'd rather be a rebel than a slave'.
> @*** tweeted 'My generation will forever be remembered for our doggedness in the face of adversity, we refused to back down'.

These tweets highlight the contestation between the technology provider, the state, and citizens. For instance, the first tweet acknowledged the germane role of Twitter and its founder Jack Dorsey in providing a platform for strengthening Nigeria's democracy, which is believed to be more than what the Nigerian government has done. This juxtaposes Akpojivi's (2013) argument that democracy and democratic culture go beyond the regular conduct of elections and are rooted in the ability of citizens to communicate and use this communicative right to hold their leaders accountable. Thus, the third tweet expounds that they will rebel against the state politicisation of the internet by censoring and shutting down Twitter rather than being a slave.

This notion of rebellion highlights the contestation between the citizens and the state over the politicisation of the internet and technology, as the Nigerian state following the ban criminalised the use of Virtual Private Network (VPN) to access Twitter. Likewise, the state approached the Cyberspace Administration of China (CAC) to discuss 'plans to build an internet firewall' that would enable the government to censor and surveil the online activities of Nigerians by filtering and blocking access to certain websites (Mbamalu, 2021). This goes against the argument of the 'oneness' principle within the internet, thus leading to internet fragmentation (Tropina, 2022). Therefore, there is a need to speak against such politicisation of the internet and technology, as reflected in the following tweets.

> @***tweeted 'VPN to the rescue'.
> @***tweeted 'We want our voices to be heard, do not try to shut us up. We have a right to peaceful protest NG is our home!!! Nigeria'.
> @*** tweeted 'If you're still using VPN to access Twitter this morning, it is the duty of You and I to massively support this movement'.
> @*** tweeted 'Either you're physically out there or at home, everyone has a voice. Use it wisely, speak up'.
> @*** tweeted 'I do not have 100k followers or a blue tick, but I will still lend my small voice with my 5 followers in agreement 👍❤️□'.

Additionally, this rebellion resulted in offline protests during Nigeria's democracy day,[8] as protesters used both offline and online opportunities to speak to power. The protest actions were across the major cities in Nigeria and witnessed the state further resisting such rebellion by use of security (police/military), as evident in the following tweets.

> @*** tweeted 'Today, is simple. Join the protest or be their voice online. It's Either you match (march) or Tweet. Don't be useless!!!'.
> @*** tweeted 'Buhari protested against the previous government, but since he became president protest has become a crime'.
> @***tweeted 'Never knew we had so much Military Personnel in Nigeria? Where have they been hiding? Why are our streets suddenly filled'.

@***tweeted 'I may not be out there to join the protest but I'll do my best here online. Enough is enough we can't continue like this!!'

@*** tweeted 'So much respect for everyone out there fighting for their rights. Please, please, stay safe 💚♡'.

@*** tweeted 'Major protests across #Nigeria's major cities including #Lagos #Ibadan #Kano and #Abuja planned. European embassies'.

@***tweeted 'The boy getting arrested in this video is my Neighbour's son please retweet aggressively to raise awareness for God's sake'.

@***tweeted 'Don't ever let anyone tell you that #EndSARS wasn't a success. The government has completely lost the plot since then'.

@*** tweeted 'Let it be known that the Buhari led administration deployed more security on peaceful protesters than it did against Boko haram'.

@*** tweeted 'Do not go and face Gun o, buhari does not CARE o, be safe, this people see us as animals shooting is not far from them'.

Despite the brutality of the state, citizens were able to speak back to power and demand their rights to freedom of communication. The politicisation of the internet raises issues of how effective tech giants such as Google, Facebook, and Twitter should be regulated and who regulates them and their content, as the Nigerian government claimed these platforms have become tools for the dissemination of hate speech, misinformation, and disinformation. Chari (2022), while buttressing further held that states use the ideas of the internet as a public good and national interest to censor or politicise infrastructure technology. However, the boundaries and expertise on how to decide this should not be on the state based on selfish interests (Akpojivi, 2018). Olaniyan and Akpojivi (2021) argue that there are regulatory provisions within the Nigerian state to address these concerns, but the desire to politicise the internet and control its infrastructure has led to ignoring existing frameworks and formulating more policies. Such politicisation and contestation of technology were further expounded with the establishment of Crowwe App by Adamu Garba, a microblogging and social networking service as an alternative for Nigerians and backed by the Nigerian state. This was resisted as the App was reported on available platforms by Nigerians, which subsequently resulted in the removal of the App from all platforms (BBC, 2021b).

Internet Shutdown

As argued in this chapter, the internet and social media affordance act as enablers of communicative rights, and the Twitter ban was perceived as a strategy of the state to suppress the communicative rights of citizens to continually speak out against the ills in the country (see Chari, 2022). This was evident in the following tweets, as not only did the citizens complain about the Twitter ban and its broader impact, but it was also seen as a way to silence them due to the high costs of VPN to access the platform and likewise to stop them from highlighting societal ills and holding the state accountable.

@***tweeted 'We're proud to be speaking out against Internet shutdowns at @accessnow's @rightscon. Internet shutdowns restrict exercise'.

@***tweeted 'Apparently, all the VPNs seems expensive especially if one wants to be here on twitter. At these trying times we truly need medias that government cannot shutdown anytime they like'.

@*** tweeted 'Dictatorship, Corruption, Daily Killings, Banditry, Herdsmen, Police Brutality, Unemployment, Internet Shutdown, Twitter Ban, + a million more. Nigerians have had enough'.

@***tweeted 'my Airtel Internet Has Completely Shutdown and my MTN Internet Is Super Slow'.

@***tweeted 'Twitter did not create #KeepitOn, it was a created by an amalgam of progressive organisations protesting rampant network/internet shutdowns'.

@***tweeted 'They want to shutdown the internet #KeepitOn https://t.co/tGAUP7a0p0'.

@*** tweeted '#June12Protest #KeepitOn we also have big organisations too collecting bribe. Banks froze the accounts of protesters without due process, telecoms shutdown Twitter without due process, and media houses change stories to favour the government. All this they do for reward. Aluta Continua https://t.co/2Ava5RDkQm';.

Conclusion

Communication rights have always been contested between the state and citizens in Nigeria. Such a contestation is not new and is due to failure by the state to recognise the universality of communication rights of seeking, receiving, imparting, and participating in societal and national discourse (Howard, 1984). The inability of the Nigerian government to extend and operationalise the universality of communicative rights is reflected in its desire to regulate social media and all OTT services and to monitor citizens' communication through control of the infrastructure and promulgation of regulatory mechanisms to curtail further citizens' communication under the banner of national/public interests. This was evident during the over six months' Twitter ban that affected Nigerians' communicative and social/economic rights. Such a ban was seen as an attempt by the government to shut down the communicative space (Twitter) that enables citizens to hold the government accountable, thus an attempt to silence them.

Such attempts by the government have resulted in what Tropina (2022) called 'fragmentation' of the internet, where universally accepted standards are not upheld. That is, within the context of this chapter, this fragmentation is due to the failure of the state to grant and guarantee communication rights, which resulted in digital authoritarianism via the Twitter ban and other proposed restrictive regulatory mechanisms. This fragmentation restricted the ability of Nigerians to access, send, and receive global information and was resisted through the use of VPN to advocate for freedom of communication, which is a salient tenet of democracy. Mare (2022) sees this fragmentation as beneficial, as it allows for online pluralism, that is, it increases the possibility of marginalised voices being heard, thereby promoting diversity of views.

While this chapter has shown that such fragmentation has enabled silent voices to be heard, it has further called for a rethink of how communication rights can be achieved within a country such as Nigeria that seeks to promote the digital economy and digital citizenship but wants to maintain their authoritarian enclave by splinternet and curtailing communication rights. The broader implication of this cannot be overemphasised, as universal principles underpinning communication rights are discarded and giving room to the state to selectively abrogate what should be said and when. Such acts threaten democratic sustenance, as democracy is rooted in freedom and the ability of citizens to express themselves and make informed decisions. Only when people exercise their communicative rights can the desired digital economy formulated in policies at the national and supernatural levels of the AU be achieved.

Acknowledgement

I wish to thank Samuel Olaniran, who assisted with the data collection in 2021.

Notes

1 Postcolonial states are states that experienced colonialism and recovering from colonialism and experiencing neocolonialism in the forms of economic and cultural imperialism, globalisation and aids to directly or indirectly control the development of a country. According to Ikome (2007), postcolonial states exhibit structures and behaviours of violence, exploitation, alienation, and deconstruction of their colonial masters. Therefore, my usage of postcolonial states falls within Ikome's (2007) argument.
2 Freedom House, like other international organisations such as Article 19, produces an annual report detailing the state of freedom across the world. While these reports are invaluable in providing insights, however, scholars have critiqued and questioned their yardsticks or methods used at arriving at their assertions.
3 The #EndSars protest of 2020 wasn't the first protest concerning police brutality. There was a similar protest under the #EndSars in 2017 and that was when the hashtag was first used.
4 According to the government, Twitter wasn't banned but suspended indefinitely. There isn't any clear-cut difference as Twitter wasn't accessible to Nigerians, and individuals and media houses were warned not to use VPN to access the platform as doing so could lead to persecution.

5 SóróSoké is a Yoruba phrase that means speak up. In addition, it was used using the #EndSars protest of 2020 as a way to communicate the message that Nigerians are tired of police brutality, poor governance, and maladministration.
6 Following the indefinite suspension, Nigerians used VPNs to access their Twitter accounts, thus the study focused on the first ten days of the suspension to examine the conversations occurring.
7 For privacy issues and in line with the POPIA of South Africa, I have removed the Twitter handles of the tweets used in the analysis to protect their identities. Additionally, in some instances, I have paraphrased some tweets.
8 June 12 is regarded as democracy day in Nigeria to commemorate the annulled MKO Abiola election in 1993 which was considered free and fair election.

References

African Union. (2019). *The Policy and Regulation Initiative for Digital Africa*. Online: https://au.int/fr/node/38115, accessed August 3, 2022.
African Union. (2020). *The Digital Transformation Strategy for Africa (2020–2030)*. Online: https://au.int/sites/default/files/documents/38507-doc-dts-english.pdf, accessed August 3, 2022.
Akpojivi, U. (2013). Looking Beyond Elections: An Examination of Media Freedom in the Re-Democratisation of Nigeria. In A. Olorunnisola and A. Douai (Eds), *New Media Influence on Social and Political Change in Africa* (pp. 84–100). Hershey: IGI Global.
Akpojivi, U. (2018). *Media Reforms and Democratisation in Emerging Democracies of Sub-Saharan Africa*. New York: Palgrave.
BBC. (2021a). *Muhammadu Buhari: Twitter Deletes Nigerian Leader's 'Civil War' Post*. Online: www.bbc.co.uk/news/world-africa-57336571, accessed April 25, 2022.
BBC. (2021b). *Crowwe App: Adamu Garba Tok Why Google Remove Crowwe App from Playstore*. Online: www.bbc.com/pidgin/tori-57479605, accessed August 1, 2022.
Castells, M. (2009). *Communication Power*. Oxford: Oxford University Press
Chari, T. (2022). Between State Interests and Citizen Digital Rights: Making Sense of Internet Shutdowns in Zimbabwe. In F. Kperogi (Ed), *Digital Dissidence and Social Media Censorship in Africa* (pp. 76–97). Abingdon: Routledge
Corredoira, L. (2021). Communication Rights in an Internet-Based Society: Why is the Principle of Universality So Important? In L. Corredoira, I. Mallen, and R. Presuel (Eds), *The Handbook of Communication Rights, Law, and Ethics: Seeking Universality, Equality, Freedom and Dignity* (pp. 30–46). New Jersey: Wiley Blackwell.
Dahlgren, P. (2005). The Internet, Public Spheres, and Political Communication: Dispersion and Deliberation. *Political Communication*, 22(2): 147–426.
D'Arcy, J. (1969). Direct broadcast satellites and the right to communicate. *EBU Review*, 118: 14–18.
Federal Ministry of Communications and Digital Economy. (2020). National Digital Economy Policy and Strategy (2020–2030). *Lagos, Federal Government Press*. Online: www.ncc.gov.ng/docman-main/industry-statistics/policies-reports/883-national-digital-economy-policy-and-strategy/file, accessed April 25, 2022
Freedom House (2021). *Freedom on the Net 2021*. Online: https://freedomhouse.org/country/nigeria/freedom-net/2021, accessed April 25, 2022.

Habermas, J. (1989). *The Structural Transformation of the Public Sphere* (Translated by T. Burger and F. Lawrence). Cambridge: Polity.

Habermas, J. (2006). Political Communication in Media Society: Does Democracy Still Enjoy an Epistemic Dimension? The Impact of Normative Theory on Empirical Research. *Communication Theory*, 14(4): 411–426.

Hakeem, Y. (2020). *#EndSars Protest in Nigeria: Police Brutality and Beyond*. Online: www.derby.ac.uk/blog/endsars-nigeria-protest-police-brutality/, accessed May 12, 2022.

Howard, A. (1984). The Right to Communicate. *Santa Clara Law Digital Commons*, 13(2–3): 219–236.

Idris, A. (2018). *Nigerian Government is Spying on Your Phone Calls-NCC*. Online: https://technext.ng/2018/03/07/nigerian-government-spying-phone-records-ncc/, accessed August 4, 2022.

Ikome, F. (2007). The Nature and Character of the PostColonial African State, in Good Coups and Bad Coups. *Institute for Global Dialogue*. Online: www.jstor.com/stable/resrep07759.7, accessed November 15, 2022.

Informant247. (2021). Breaking: FG Suspends Twitter's Operations in Nigeria. Online: https://theinformant247.com/breaking-fg-suspends-twitters-operations-in-nigeria/, accessed June 5, 2021.

Isin, E., and Ruppert, E. (2020). *Being Digital Citizens*. London: Rowman & Littlefield International.

Mallen, I. (2021). Freedom as the Essential Basis for Communication Rights. In L. Corredoria, I. Mallen and R. Presuel (Eds), *The Handbook of Communication Rights, Law and Ethics: Seeking Universality Equality, Freedom and Dignity* (pp. 9–19). Hoboken: Blackwell.

Mare, A. (2020). Internet Shutdowns in Africa State-Ordered Internet Shutdowns and Digital Authoritarianism in Zimbabwe. *International Journal of Communication*, 14: 4244–4263.

Mare, A. (2022). Beyond Unity in Global Internet Governance: Embracing Fragmentation in a Multipolar and Multicultural World. *Centre for Global Cooperation Research, Quarterly Magazine*. Online: www.gcr21.org/publications/gcr/gcr-quarterly-magazine/qm-2-3/2022-articles/qm-2/3-2022-mare-beyond-unity-in-global-internet-governance-embracing-fragmentation-in-a-multipolar-and-multicultural-world?type=%27%27nvopzp%3B%20and%201%3D1%20or%20%28%3C%27%27%22%3Eiko%29%29%2C, accessed November 18, 2022.

Marshall, T. H. (1950). *Citizenship and the Social Class: And Other Essays*. Cambridge: Cambridge University Press.

Mbamalu, S. (2021). *Presidency Meets With China's Cyber Regulator to Build Nigerian Internet Firewall*. Online: https://fij.ng/article/exclusive-presidency-meets-with-chinas-cyber-regulator-to-build-nigerian-internet-firewall/, accessed October 12, 2022.

Mbembe, A. (1992). The Banality of Power and the Aesthetics of Vulgarity in the Postcolony. *Public Culture*, 4(2): 1–30.

McNair, B. (2000). *Journalism and Democracy: An Evaluation of the Political Public Sphere*. London: Routledge.

Mill, S. (1859). *On Liberty* (4th ed.). London: Longman.

Montiel, A. (2013). Prologue. In A. Montiel (Ed), *Communication and Human Rights*. Coyoacán: Universidad Nacional Autónoma de México.

Mossberger, K., Tolbert, C., and McNeal, R. (2008). *Digital Citizenship: The Internet, Society and Participation*. Cambridge: MIT Press.

Moyo, L. (2010). Language, Cultural and Communication Rights of Ethnic Minorities in South Africa A Human Rights Approach. *The International Communication Gazette*, 72(4–5): 425–440.
Mwaura, J. (2022). Digital Dissidents or Whistle-Blowers? A Critical Analysis of Microbloggers in Kenya. In F. Kperogi (Ed), *Digital Dissidence and Social Media Censorship in Africa* (pp. 175–195). Abingdon: Routledge.
NITDA. (2022). *Code of Practice for Interactive Computer Service Platforms/Internet Intermediaries*. Online: https://nitda.gov.ng/wp-content/uploads/2022/06/Code-of-Practice.pdf, accessed October 24, 2022.
NOI Poll. (2019). *Social Media Poll Result*. Online: https://noi-polls.com/wp-content/uploads/2019/11/Social-Media-Poll-Report.pdf, accessed May 12, 2022.
Nyamnjoh, F. (2016). *#Rhodesmustfall: Nibbling at Resilient Colonialism in South Africa*. Bamenda and Buea: Langaa Research & Publishing CIG.
O'siochru, S. (2005). *Assessing Communication Rights: A Handbook*. New York: CRIS.
Obadare, E. (2022). *Twitter Ban Shows Limits of State Power in Nigeria*. Online: Council on Foreign Relations. Online: www.cfr.org/blog/twitter-ban-shows-limits-state-power-nigeria, accessed August 1, 2022.
Obia, V. (2021). *Twitter versus Government of Nigeria: Power, Securitisation and the Politics of a Social Media Ban*. Online: https://inforrm.org/2021/06/22/twitter-versus-government-of-nigeria-power-securitisation-and-the-politics-of-a-social-media-ban-vincent-a-obia/, accessed January 2, 2022.
Obijiofor, L. (2015). *New Technologies in Developing Countries: From Theories to Practice*. Hampshire: Palgrave.
Ogbondah, C. (2018). State-Media Relations: Constraints on Freedom of the Media. In A. Olukotun (Ed), *Watchdogs or Captured Media? A Study of the Role of the Media In Nigeria's Emergent Democracy 1999–2016*. Lagos: Diamond Publications Ltd.
Olaniyan, A. (2022). *From Iwe Irohin to Saharareporters.com: Hardcoding Citizen Journalism in Nigeria*. PhD Thesis. Witwatersrand: University of the Witwatersrand.
Olaniyan, A., and Akpojivi, U. (2021). Transforming Communication, Social Media, Counter-Hegemony and the Struggle for the Soul of Nigeria. *Information, Communication & Society*, 24(3): 422–437.
Olukotun, A. (2018). Introduction and Overview. In A. Olukotun (Ed), *Watchdogs or Captured Media? A Study of the Role of the Media in Nigeria's Emergent Democracy 1999–2016* (pp. 1–18). Lagos: Diamond Publications LTD.
Oluwole, V. (2021). *President Buhari Blames the Internet for the Rising Spate of Insecurity in Nigeria*. Online: https://africa.businessinsider.com/local/leaders/president-buhari-blames-the-internet-for-the-rising-spate-of-insecurity-in-nigeria/8k2nmq2, accessed May 12, 2022.
Owoeye, F. (2018). *These Factors are Threatening the Survival of Nigeria's Telecom Sector*. Online: https://nairametrics.com/2018/10/22/these-factors-are-threatening-the-survival-of-nigerias-telecom-sector/, accessed August 4, 2022.
Oyedemi, T. (2014). Internet access as Citizen's Right? Citizenship in the Digital Age. *Citizenship Studies*, 19(3–4): 450–464.
Oyedemi, T. (2020). The Theory of Digital Citizenship. In J. Servaes (Ed), *Handbook of Communication for Development and Social Change* (pp. 237–255). Singapore: Springer.
Pool, I. (1983). *Technologies of Freedom*. Cambridge: Harvard University Press
Price, M. (2021). Preface. In L. Corredoira, I. Mallen, and R. Prequel (Eds), *The Handbook of Communication Rights, Law, and Ethics: Seeking Universality, Equality, Freedom and Dignity*. New Jersey: Wiley Blackwell.

Svensson, J. (2020). Empowerment as Development: An Outline of an Analytical Concept for the Study of ICTs in the Global South. In J. Servaes (Ed), *Handbook of Communication for Development and Social Change* (pp. 217–235). Singapore: Springer.

Tropina, T. (2022). Internet Fragmentation: What's at Stake? *Centre for Global Cooperation Research, Quarterly Magazine*. Online: www.gcr21.org/publications/gcr/gcr-quarterly-magazine/qm-2-3/2022-articles/qm-2/3-2022-tropina-internet-fragmentation-whats-at-stake, accessed December 1, 2022.

Wodu, N. (2021). *Nigerian Press Freedom in Grave Danger. Council on Foreign Relations*. Online: https://www.cfr.org/blog/nigerian-press-freedom-grave-danger, accessed January 2, 2022.

Index

Note: Numbers in *italics* indicate figures on the corresponding page. Numbers in **bold** indicate tables on the corresponding page.

Abubakar, Sule 134, 137
Accountability Lab (Zimbabwe) 122
activism, virtual space (usage) (Mozambique) 102
Adejumo, Moses Olaiya 130
advanced metalinguistic knowledge 31–32
advanced persistent threat (APT), usage 100
Africa, communication rights 1
Africa Check, accuracy (promotion) 189
African Charter on Human and Peoples' Rights, The (ACHPR) 12, 168, 191–192
African Charter on Human Rights, Article 9 223
African National Congress (ANC), data argument 209
African Union (AU): Data Policy Framework 12; digitization policy guidelines 12
Ajira centres, number **51**
Ajira Digital Program, establishment 50
Akingbade, Olutobi 14, 70
Akpojivi, Ufuoma 1, 13, 15, 223
alternative information, propagation 190
alternative media, impact 6
Amandla.Mobi: demonstrations, organization 211; door-to-door campaigning 212; market dominance highlight 209; petition submission 207, 213
Amazon platform, exploitation (limitation) 135
Anglophone problem (Cameroon) 167
anti-piracy device, usage (Copyright Act of 1970, Section 21 (1)) 152–153

anti-terror laws, state usage (Cameroon) 176
Application Programming Interface (API), Twitter usage 231
appropriation (Misappropriation Doctrine element) 188
Arab Spring 9, 103
Arasere: language, learning 29; separate sounds, examples **26**; speaking 32
Arid and Semi-Arid Lands (ASALs), ICT usage 41
Association of Movie Content Owners and Producers/Distributors of Nigeria (AMCOP) 134
Audio-Visual Rights Society of Nigeria (AVRS), CMO responsibility 155
authoritarian regimes, designation 166
autonomy (South Africa) 62–63

Baba Jukwa engagement 120
Babangida, Ibrahim 149
Bakassi Boys 131
Balogun, Ola 130
BBC, fake news misinformation 189
bilingualism, power 30
biliguality, psychological state 25
"Bill for an Act to Repeal the Copyright Act CAP LFN2004 and to Re-enact the Copyright Right Act 2021" (Nigeria) 156–157
Bloggers Association of Kenya (BAKED) v Attorney General & 3 Others 194
"Bridging the Digital Divide for People with Disabilities" 62–63
#BringBackOurGirls 229
broadband, affordability (desire) 228

Index

broadcast licenses, administration formalities 170
broadcast media, urban area confinement 112
business, rights (relationship) 6

Cable News Network (CNN): fake news misinformation 189; impact 121
Cabo Delgado (Mozambique): attacks, initiation 101; political conflict 14
Cabo Delgado Também é Moçambique (Cabo Delgado is also Mozambique) 91; case study 100–101; civil society organisations, involvement 104; slogan, misunderstanding 105; students/non-governmental organisations, inclusion 104; Twitter awareness 103; virtual action, campaign support/strategies steps (explanation) *104*; "We don't want support; we just want the war to end" (illustration) *103*; WhatsApp meeting, advantages 103–104
Cabo Delgado Também é Moçambique (Cabo Delgado is also Mozambique) campaign: blocking, attempt 105; illustration *101*; success, limitations 103, 105
Cambridge Analytica, fake news disinformation 189
Cameroon (Kamerun): administrator, arbitrary powers (enhancement) 174; Anglophone problem 167; anti-terror/cybercrime laws, state usage 176; broadcast license, administration formalities 170; censorship, necessity (state decision) 175; control mechanisms, evolution 176; culture heritage/identity, preservation 167; democratic governance safeguards, government (impact) 177; democratization, media (role) 174; digital information, infringement 178; digital space, protection (requirements) 178; Facebook information, publication cessation 176; Facebook, usage/arrests 175; family/community, interaction 168; Federal Republic of Cameroon 167; government action, good faith (absence) 177; human rights risks, Internet regulation/restrictions (impact) 178; individuals, operations (impossibility) 174; information access, importance 178; information access (threat), Internet censorship (impact) 177; Internet access, control/restriction (problems) 178; Internet disconnections, monitoring 177; media arrests 175–176; media censorship, history/tradition 174–178; media landscape, liberalization 168–169; Mefo, national gendarmerie appearance 176; National Assembly, social media perspective 175; platforms/people, security forces tracking 177; pluralist authoritarians, digital contestation (relationship) 169–171; press, state legal control 175; Republic of Cameroon 167; research sources 171; Silicon Mountain Buea, Internet shutdown (impact) 175; sociopolitical context 167–168; WhatsApp, usage/arrest 175
Cameroon (Kamerun), communication rights 168–169; exercise, importance 172; infringement 178
Cameroon (Kamerun), Internet shutdowns 165; citizen rights/civil liberties, government attacks 174; depth 173; discussion 179–180; online censorship, spectrum approach 171–172; pace (tempo) 174; recurrence/time spans 172; width 173
Cameroon (Kamerun), social media: access, importance 172; communication instrument, state perspective 176; legislation 168–169
censorship: NFVCB requirements/decisions 137; violations 141
Centre for Innovation and Technology (CITE) 122
Chari, Tendai 1, 13, 15, 203

Charter of the United Nations 168
Chibuzor, Chukwudi 134–135, 139
Children's Act 38 of 2005 58
China, authoritarianism 166
cinematograph films: availability (Copyright Act of 1970, Section 37(5)) 152; copyright provisions, infringement (avoidance) 151
CIPESA 96
citizen journalism (Zimbabwe) 110; civil society-supported citizen journalism 121–123; definition 110–111; individual practice 119–121; practice, attention 117–118; subaltern public sphere function 115–116; subaltern, social transformation 116–117
citizen journalists, impact (Zimbabwe) 117–118
citizen rights/civil liberties, government attacks (Cameroon) 174
citizenship, exclusion/inclusion 8
Citizen, The 212; imitation 189–190
citizen unrest (Nigeria) 226
City Sun, fake news misinformation 189–190
civic space, threats (Mozambique) 102
civil rights, impact 4
civil society organisations, involvement (Mozambique) 104
civil society-supported citizen journalism (Zimbabwe) 121–123
clickbait, impact 72, 190
climate justice 113
codes, cultural concept 26
cognitive advantage (Ubang community) 28–31
Collective Management Organization (CMO) 150; Copyright Regulations of 2007 161–162; impact (Nigeria) 154–155
coloniality, Global South context 111
communication: civil rights 4; cultural rights 4; impact 176; instrument, Cameroon state perspective 176; needs 3; resources, usage (importance) 173
communication rights (Cameroon) 168–169; exercise, importance 172; infringement 178
communication rights (CR) 4–5; assessment 21; concept in progress 1–2; concept,

recognition/endorsement 3; context/condition, presupposition 172; defining 224–225; digital citizenship, relationship 7–11; discourse 1; entrenchment (Zimbabwe) 110; government recognition/protection/promotion/enforcement, benefit 176; information communication technology (ICT), relationship (Nigeria) 71–73; international perspectives 11–16; pillars 4; political/socio-economic rights, interdependence (Lagos State) 70; strengthening, importance 174; trademarks, relationship 190–192; undermining 177
Communication Rights in the Information Society (CRIS) 4
Communication Workers Union (CWU), #DataMustFall campaign support 208–209
communicative activity 115
communicative power, reconfiguration 80–81
communicative rights 191
community, cultural concept 26
Competition Commission, Data Services Market Inquiry 216
Computer Misuse and Cybercrimes Act (Cyber Act 2020) 193–194
confidence (Ubang community) 28–31
confirmation bias 187; fake news, relationship 190
connectivity, human right 217
consciousness levels, increase 118
Constitution of the Federal Republic of Nigeria, Section 39 (impact) 141
Constitution of the Republic of Mozambique, private life protections 99–100
consumerist content, proliferation 6
content moderation policy 232
conversation, cultural concept 26
copyright: infringement-related activities, arrests (Nigeria) 150; international copyright treaties, Nigeria compliance 156; laws (Nigeria), appraisal 148–150, 156; laws (Nigeria), NCC enforcement 157, 160–161; milestones (Nigeria) 158–159;

order (2012), materials levy 155–157
Copyright Act 2021 (Nigeria): Section 29(1), impact 157; Section 30(1–2), service provider (infringement notification) 157
Copyright Act of 1970 (Nigeria): anti-piracy device, usage (Section 21 (1)) 152–153; enactment 148; hologram stamp, usage 153; Section 37(5), cinematograph film availability 152; Section 37(3), copyright inspector authority 151; Section 38, copyright investor powers 150
copyright inspectors (Nigeria): appointment 150–151; authority, Copyright Act of 1970, section 37 (3) (impact) 151
copyright regulations (Nigeria) 150–161; Collective Management Organization (CMO), impact 154–155; Optical Disc Plan regulation 153–154; security devices 152–153; video rental regulations (1999) 151–152
Copyright Society of Nigeria (COSON) registration 154
Copyright Unit (Department of Culture), impact 149
Corporate Affairs Commission (Nigeria), legal entity (establishment requirement) 227
COVID-19: challenges, overcoming 12; digitally marginalized netizens, focus 14; impact 98; Internet, importance 205; outbreak 81; pre-COVID-19 online communication/engagements, social media (impact) 76–79; SMP information 76; South Africa approach 195
COVID-19 lockdown 72; digitally marginalised netizens, lived experiences (examination) 70; online communication/ engagements, social media usage 79–82; regulations, querying 82
creation (Misappropriation Doctrine element) 188
creative audiovisual, usage 156
creative works access (limitations/ exceptions), Nigerian bill (passage) 156

Criminal Code Act (Section 491) purpose (Nigeria) 148–149
cross-generational sensitivity 113
cultural bilingualism 31
cultural identities 39–40; homogenization, increase 6
cultural rights, impact 4
culture: communication 27; jamming 190
cybercrime laws, state usage (Cameroon) 176
Cyber Security and Cybercrime law n° 2010/012 169
cybersecurity training, usage 100
Cyberspace Administration of China (CAC), internet firewall construction 235

Daily Sun, imitation 189–190
Dalvit, Lorenzo 13, 55
d'Arcy, Jean 223, 225; communication right 3; Universal Declaration of Human Rights, future 2
#DataMustFall campaign (South Africa) 15, 203; awareness, raising 215; collusion, practice (cessation) 210; Communication Workers Union (CWU) support 208–209; Competition Commission, Data Services Market Inquiry 216; connectivity, human right 217; data bundles, sale 211; data, expense 209, 210; data providers, position (abuse) 210; data theft, cessation (need) 211; demonstrations 211–212; evolution/issues 208–211; ideas Economy, data (currency) 210; Internet access, right 209; issues, specification 213–214; low-cost data, importance 210; methodological discussion 207–208; milestones/setbacks 214–217; mobile network service provider mandates 215; network service provider obligations 215; petition 209–211; price fixing, cessation (need) 210; smartphones, usage/importance 209; social groups, alignment 209; social media blackout 212–213; social media publicity 212; social movement theories 206–207; tactics 211–214
data rollover, unfairness 211

Data Services Market Inquiry report 207, 216
data usage notifications, unfairness 211
decolonial critique (South Africa) 59–60
deep fake technologies, growth 186
deliberative liberal democracy 231
democratic citizenship, journalism form 112
democratic governance: basis 186; safeguards, Cameroon government (impact) 177
democratic society, communication needs 3
democratisation (Nigeria) 223–224
democratization, media role (Cameroon) 174
Development, Democratization, Decolonization, and Demonopolitization (4Ds) 2
digital affordance, definition 6
digital authoritarianism, freedom of speech (contrast) 232–234
digital blackout 10
digital centres, uncertainties 50–51
digital citizens, communicative rights 227–230
digital citizenship: communication rights, relationship 7–11; impeding 10
digital contestation, pluralist authoritarians (relationship) 169–171
digital economy, backbone 49
Digital Economy Blueprint 49
"Digital Economy Strategy" document release 48
digital identity systems, exclusionary nature 45–48
digital inclusion (South Africa): policy/practice 60–62; southern epistemological perspective 55
digital inclusion, importance 228
digital inequalities 56–57; complexities 42–43
digital inequality, systemic problem (Global South) 95
digital information, infringement (Cameroon) 178
digital infrastructures (Global South): commodification 205; digital rights 204–205; politics 203, 204–205
digital infrastructures, access 44–45

digitally marginalised netizens, lived experiences (examination) 70
digital rights 5–7; debates, limitation 93; definition/controversies (Mozambique) 93–94; emergence 93; Global South 94–96; issue, exploration 203; status (Mozambique) 99–101
Digital Satellite Television (DSTV), provision 119
digital space: escape route 102; protection, requirements 178
digital technology, impact 95
digital trade, non-digital trade (blurring) 49
"digital transformation strategy for Africa" 12
disability: social construction 58–59; South African Human Rights Commission (SHRC) recognition 58; terms, usage 59
Disabled People of South Africa (DPS), anti-apartheid role 55
Disabled Women of South Africa (DWSA), disability focus 58
Disaster Management Regulations 195
disinformation, spread 7
Djibril, Cavaye Yeguie 175
Dorsey, Jack 227, 235
Dosunmu, Sanya 130
dual-language phenomenon (Ubang community) 22–26
DVDs, pirate usage 146–147

e-commerce uptake, drivers 49
Econet Wireless Zimbabwe, telecommunications infrastructure control 178
Economic and Financial Crime Commission (EFCC), relationships 160
editorial interventions 185–186
Edosomwan, Aifuwa 14, 146
Electronic Transactions Law 99
email phishing security, usage 100
Employment Equity Act 55 of 1998 57
#EndSars protest 226–227, 229
#EndTwitterBanInNigeria 231
End-User and Subscriber Charter Regulations of 2016: ICASA amendment 215; implementation, delays 216–217
environmental protection 113
equality, goal 71–72

248 Index

ethnographic cultural communication theory, adoption 26
European Union (EU) Commission, digital transformation proposal 94
expression, freedom 3, 168; fake news, contrast 183; Internet shutdowns, impact 172
EyeWitness News, fake news 189–190
Eyewitness News, imitation 189–190

Facebook (FB): access, maintenance 0; advertising audience, overview (Mozambique) 99; arrests (Cameroon) 176; information, publication cessation (Cameroon) 176; self-expression 78; usage 156, 162; usage, absence (impact) 82; usefulness 76; video calls 75
fake news: appeal 190; defining 185–186; disinformation 189; freedom of expression, contrast 183; impact 188–190; noxious nature 187; spread, concern 7
Federal Commissioner for Trade, empowerment 149
Federal Republic of Cameroon 167
filmmakers, Kano State Censors Board arrests 136
#FixNigeria 231
Foucault, Michel 114
freedom, actualisation 228
freedom of expression 3, 168, 172, 183; impeding 44–45
freedom of speech, digital authoritarianism (contrast) 231–234
Freedom of the Press and Expression Ranking 100
free speech, laws/restrictions (imposition) 5
Fuelling Poverty (documentary ban) 132

Gadzikwa, Wellington 14, 110
Gbadamosi, Kemi 134–135, 139, 142
gender justice 113
gender parity, absence 113
General Data Protection Regulation (GDPR), privacy protection 57
girl-child, communication rights (assessment) 21
girls, Ofre language (learning complaints) 29
global goodwill 184

global mass media, corporate/consumerist/northern bias (impact) 6
Global South: digital inequality, systemic problem 95; digital infrastructures, digital rights 204–205; digital infrastructures, politics 203, 204–205; digital rights 94–96; digital rights abuse, reduction 95; digital technology, impact 95; North domination 95; social movement theories 206–207
Global System for Mobile communication (GSM) 9
governance structures, encoding/institutionalizing 93
government (Kenya) policies/projects, inequality 48–50
Gramsci, Antonio 14
gross domestic product (GDP), pastoralism (contribution) 41
Gukurahundi 120

Habermas, Jürgen 14, 16, 113–114, 230–231
Halilu, Adamu 130
Hall, Edward 27
Harris Media LLC, fake news misinformation 189
hate speech, spread 7
hologram stamp, usage 153
Huduma Namba Bill 2021 (Kenya) 43
Huduma Namba Card, digital identity card 45
Huffington Post SA 190
Human Development Index 55
human dignity (strengthening), communication (impact) 176
human rights: advocates, deficit (South Africa) 60; communication, importance 174; digital space manipulation, relationship (Cameroon) 178; naming, avoidance 55; realization 6; risks, Internet regulation/restrictions (impact) 178; struggle 1; universal declaration, framework 12
Hungwe, Brian 183
Hwedza News (newsletter) 122

Ibang, Oliver 23
ideas Economy, data (currency) 210
identity documents, acquisition (difficulty) 46–47

Index

illiteracy, problem 43–44
Imasuen, Lancelot 131
independent communication, facilitation 8–9
Independent Communications Authority of South Africa (ICASA): data costs, investigation 208–209; #DataMustFall meeting 214; End-User and Subscriber Charter Regulations, Data Services Markey Inquiry report 207; End-User and Subscriber Charter Regulations of 2016, amendment 215; End-User and Subscriber Charter Regulations of 2016, amendment (victory) 215–216; lawsuit 211
Independent Corrupt Practice Commission (ICPC), internet crime battle 162
Industrial Revolution, data currency 210
inequality, spread 42
informal language 171
information: absence, problem 43–44; diffusion, increase 208; freedom 3; negative psychological effect 187; receiving/imparting, human right 3; shared piece, popularity/virality 186; sharing, conservatism (Mozambique) 105; usage, importance 173
information access: importance (Cameroon) 178; infringement 172; threat, Internet censorship (impact) (Cameroon) 177
Informational Justice, rights vehicle 6
information communication technology (ICT): communication rights, relationship (Nigeria) 71–73; context, difficulty 168; "Digital Economy Strategy" document release 48; emergence 7–8; permeation 229; studies 40; study (Kenya) 43; usage 9; usage, initiatives 41
informed citizenry, assumption 186
inhibitory control (Ubang community) 28–31
injury (Misappropriation Doctrine element) 188
Instagram, usage 156, 162
intellectual property (IP): constitutional protection 184–185; enforcement 160; infringement 7; NCC protection 147

Intellectual Property Rights (IPRs): management 160, 184; protection 183–185
intellectual property rights (Nigeria), review 146
intellectual theft 146
international attention/solidarity, promotion (Mozambique) 103
international copyright treaties, Nigeria compliance 156
International Covenant on Civil and Political Rights (ICCPR), Article 19 191–192
International Covenant on Economic, Social and Cultural Rights (CESCR) 194
International News Service (INS) v. Associated Press 188
International Telecommunication Union (ITU) 64, 96
internet: connectivity, cost implications 77; contact, need 81; cost 102; derivative right 205; exceptionalism 191; human right, rejection 205; policy formulation/implementation 94; politicisation, interrogation 225; poor people access, impossibility 80; price fixing, cessation (need) 210; proliferation 10; subscribing/connecting, affordability (absence) 79–80, 82
internet access: control/restriction problems (Cameroon) 178; Mozambique 98; right 209
Internet disconnections, monitoring (Cameroon) 177
Internet-Protocol-based services 5
Internet Service Providers (ISPs), authorities (restriction) 166
Internet shutdowns (Cameroon) 15, 165; depth 173; impact 175; online censorship, spectrum approach 171–172; page (tempo) 174; recurrence/time span 172; state-ordered Internet shutdowns, force 178; width 173
Internet shutdowns (Nigeria) 236–237
intrusion prevention system (IPS), usage 100
Ishaw, Ishaq Sidi 134
Issabaka (Imasuen) 131

250 *Index*

journalism: citizen-centred form 110–111; defining 185–186; innovation 116
Judeo-Christian creation mythology 24

Kamerun (Cameroon) 167
Kano State Censorship Board (KSCB) 129; bypassing 140; establishment 132–133; filmmaker arrests 136; filmmaker awareness 136
KeepItOn (campaign) 94
#KeepItOn 231
Kenya: Arid and Semi-Arid Lands (ASALs), ICT usage 41; digital centres, uncertainties 50–51; digital identity systems, exclusionary nature 45–48; digital inequalities, complexities 42–43; digitisation policies/strategies/projects 38; e-commerce uptake, drivers 49; election, fake news misinformation 189; government policies/projects, inequality 48–50; Huduma Namba Bill 2021 43; media trademarks, fake news (impact) 188–190; National Education Management Information System (NEMIS) 47–48; pastoralist communities 39–42; pastoralist communities, digital marginalisation 43–45; pastoralist counties, Ajira centres (number) **51**; Public Procurement Information Portal (PPIP), establishment 49; research methodology 43; social media platforms, media trademarks infringements (legislation) 183; trademarks, legislative interventions 192–194; Trade-Related Aspects of Intellectual Property Rights (TRIPS) 193
Kenya Universities and Colleges Central Placement Service (KUCCPS), student placement 48
knowledge, communication 4
Kwangwari, Kudzai 122
Kwara State, pirating evidence 152

Ladebo, Ladi 130
Lagos State Film and Densor Board (LSFCB) 136; establishment 132

Lagos State, Nigeria: communication/political/socio-economic rights, interdependence 70; COVID-19 lockdown, digitally marginalised netizens (lived experiences, examination) 70; COVID-19 lockdown, online communication/engagements (social media usage) 79–82; hunger, impact 81–82; internet connectivity, cost implications 77, 82; internet, contact (need) 81; physical chats, closed door process 78; political views, harassment/physical attacks 78; pre-COVID-19 online communication/engagements, social media (impact) 76–79; public meetings, speaking up (danger) 78; research methodology 74–76; self-expression, social media (usage) 77–78; social media, usage 76–79; social media, usefulness 76; theoretical framework 73–74
language: barriers, impact 11; bidirectional movements 25; dynamics, acceptance 33–34; exploitative manipulation 185–186
language-cultural barrier 21
language-cultural phenomenon (Ubang) 31–32
Laugh it Off case 190, 195
levy disbursements, sharing formula (Nigeria) 155
Levy on Materials (Copyright Order 2012) 155–157
LGBTQ vulnerability 58
liberalization process 169
liberation, consideration 62–63
liberties, support 8
Likeng, Libom Li 177
linguistic code, access 25
Liquid Telecom, telecommunications infrastructure control 178
Living in Bondage (Nnebue) 130

MacBride report, recommendations 3
Magamba 122
marginalisation: digitising 38; pastoralist communities, digital marginalisation 43–45; perpetuation 116

mass media, non-print forms (popularity) 73–74
materials levy (copyright order 2012) 155–157
media. *see* social media: censorship, history/tradition (Cameroon) 174–178; characterisation 113–114; commercialization, impact 6; development indicators (UNESCO) 113; freedom, undermining 177; press, Cameroon legal control 175; reform movements, understanding 207; social media platforms, media trademarks infringements (legislation) 13; suppression 170; trademarks, fake news (impact) 188–190; trademarks, Misappropriation Doctrine (relationship) 187–192; vulnerability 170
Media Centre (Zimbabwe) 122
Media Development Indicators (UNESCO) 113
media diversity, increase (absence) 6
Media Institute of Southern Africa-Zimbabwe Chapter (MISA-Zimbabwe) 122
Mefo, Mimi (Cameroon national gendarmerie appearance) 176
Mekwuenye, Ekene 134, 140
Mental Health Care Act 17 of 2002 58
messaging platforms, quality control standards (absence) 187
meta journalism 111
Mgbeadichie, Chike 13, 21
microblogging platforms, impact 232–233
Milkmaid, The (film cut requests) 132
Misappropriation Doctrine 15; elements 188; interpretation 188; media trademarks, relationship 187–192
mobile data, price (impact) 26
mobile phone networks, reach (inadequacy) 40
Mobile Telephone Network (MTN): data price reduction, order 216; market dominance 209
Mohammed, Lai 234
Molefe, Thabo (TBo Touch) 208, 214
monolingual counterparts 29–30
moral narrative, presentation 190
Motion Picture Practitioners Association of Nigeria (MOPPAN) 134

Mozambique: activism, virtual space (usage) 102; background/context 96–97; Cabo Delgado attacks, initiation 101; *Cabo Delgado Também é Moçambique* (Cabo Delgado is also Mozambique) 91; civic space, threats 102; civil society organisations, involvement 104; digital divide 94–96; digital landscape 98–99; Facebook advertising audience, overview 99; governance structures, encoding/institutionalizing 93; information sharing, conservatism 105; international attention/solidarity, promotion 103; internet access 98; normative ideals, encoding/institutionalizing 93; power relations, encoding/institutionalizing 93; research methodology 97–98; results/discussion 101–106; speaking out (courage), virtual space (usage) 102; students/non-governmental organisations, inclusion 104; terrorism, discussion (difficulty) 103; virtual action, campaign support/strategies steps (explanation) *104*; WhatsApp meetings, advantages 103–104; youth digital activism, paths 91
Mozambique, digital rights: debates, limitations 93; definition/controversies 93–94; status 99–101
M-Pesa, money transfer 39
Mudzengi, Earnest 10, 14
Mukapiko, Nyasha 122
Multichoice Zimbabwe, impact 119
multi-pronged citizen journalism, calls 115
Musa, Khalid 134–135
Musical Copyright Society of Nigeria (MCSN), emergence 154
#MustFall 9
Mwaura, Job 13, 14, 38

Nairobean, The (publication) 188
nanomedia, deployment 207
"National Commission for the Prohibition of Hate Speech" 72, 219
National Council for People with Disabilities (NCPD), disability focus 58

National Cyber Security Policy and Strategy 99
National Development Plan (NDP) 61
National Digital Economy Policy and Strategy (Nigeria) 229
National Education Management Information System (NEMIS) 47–48
National Film and Video Censors Board (NFVCB): censorship requirements/decisions 137; filmmakers, regulation 129
National Information Technology Development Agency (NITDA), internet intermediaries/computer service platforms (interface requirement) 227
National Institute of Information and Communication Technologies (INTIC), cybersecurity proposal 100
National Paralympic Committee (NPC), disability focus 58
negative liberties, protection (digital rights) 5
Netflix platform, exploitation (limitation) 135
New International Economic Order (NIEO) 2
news brands, counterfeiting/mimicking 187
news genres, exploitative manipulation 185–186
New World Information and Communication Order (NWICO) 2; debates 111, 204
Ngangum, Peter Tiako 15, 165
Ngozi Okonjo Iweala (NOI): social media report 226; Twitter usage poll 227
Nigeria: anti-piracy device, usage 152–153; Audio-Visual Rights Society of Nigeria (AVRS), CMO responsibility 155; "Bill for an Act to Repeal the Copyright Act CAP LFN2004 and to Re-enact the Copyright Right Act 2021" 156–157; citizen unrest 226; communicative rights, indefinite suspension 232; Copyright Act 2021 157; Copyright Act of 1970, enactment 148; Copyright Society of Nigeria (COSON) registration 154; creativity, promotion (levy disbursements) 155; Criminal Code Act, Section 491 (purpose) 148–149; democratisation, wave 223–224; digital economy, impact 228–229; digital restrictions 226; freedom of speech, digital authoritarianism (contrast) 232–234; hologram stamp, usage 153; intellectual property rights, review 146; Internet shutdown 236–237; levy disbursements, sharing formula 155; Levy on Materials (Copyright Order 2012) 155–157; materials levy (copyright order 2012) 155–157; media, distrust 71; Motion Picture Practitioners Association of Nigeria (MOPPAN) 134; Musical Copyright Society of Nigeria (MCSN), emergence 154; National Digital Economy Policy and Strategy 229; National Film and Video Censors Board (NFVCB) 129, 137; online audiovisual work, author nonconsent (broadcast/reproduction ban) 156; prohibited contents/unethical behavior, publication (avoidance) 227; social media, politicisation 223; SóróSoké, contextual background (study) 225–227; SóróSoké, silence 223; Special Anti-Robbery Squad (SARS), disbanding 73; state, SóróSoké generation (contestation) 231–232; technology, politicisation 234–236; Twitter ban/suspension 225, 227
#Nigeria 231
Nigeria, copyright: inspectors, appointment 150–151; laws, appraisal 148–150; laws, NCC enforcement 157, 160–161; milestones **158–159**; order (2012), materials levy 155–157; owner, infringement notice (issuance) 157; regime, strengthening 156; regulations 150–161
Nigeria film industry: audience, filmmaker concerns 140–141; background 130; blood, display (problems) 137–139; Censors

Board decisions, impact 138; censorship, NFVCB requirements/decisions 137; discussion 141–143; film classification, submission reason 136; filmmaker suppression/arrests 136; issues 137; Kano State Censorship Board (KSCB), impact 132–140; Netflix/Amazon, exploitation (limitation) 135; orientation, need 138; private self-censorship 133–134; public self-censorship 133–134; regulation/self-censorship 129; research findings 135–141; research methodology 134–135; restricted classification, example 137; restrictions 139; self-censorship 133–134; smoking, film display (prohibition) 138, 140; state agency, politician control 136; stories/popular culture, censors (impact) 130–133; storytelling, destruction 137; violence, filming (restrictions)(139; YouTube, patronised platform 135

Nigeria (Lagos State): communication/political/socio-economic rights, interdependence 70; COVID-19 lockdown, digitally marginalised netizens (lived experiences, examination) 70; COVID-19 lockdown, online communication/engagements (social media usage) 79–82; hunger, impact 81–82; information communication technology, communication rights (relationship) 71–73; internet connectivity, cost implications 77, 82; internet, contact (need) 81; physical chats, closed door process 78; political views, harassment/physical attacks 78; pre-COVID-19 online communication/engagements, social media (impact) 76–79; public meetings, speaking up (danger) 78; self-expression, social media (usage) 77–78; social media, usage 76–79; social media, usefulness 76–77

Nigerian Copyright Commission (NCC) 15; anti-piracy programme, levy disbursements 155; capacity, enhancement 156; copyright laws enforcement 157, 160–161; intellectual copyright protection 47; responsibilities 149–150; video rental business, registration 152

Nigerian Copyright Council, renaming 149
Nigerian Criminal Code 148
Nigeria Police Force, relationships 160
Nnebue, Ken 130
Nollywood, moniker 130, 142
nomadism 40
non-digital trade, digital trade (blurring) 49
normative ideals, encoding/institutionalizing 93
Northflix platform, usage 135

Obiaya, Ikechukwu 14, 129
objective politics, subjective/partisan politics (contrast) 116
Occupy movements 9
#OccupyNigeria 229
Ofre: learning, questions 29; separate sounds, examples 26
Ogunde, Hubert 130
Ojetola, Elder Adetunji 134–135
Oladele, Francis 130
Olaiya, Seun 134
oligopoly capitalism 113
One Lagos Night (Mekwuenye) 136
On Liberty theory (Mill) 16
online audiovisual work, author nonconsent (broadcast/reproduction ban) 156
online censorship, spectrum approach (Cameroon) 171–172
online communication/engagements, social media usage (Nigeria) 79–82
online information, access (moral standing) 204
open data, questions 93
#OpenInternet 231
Open Parly 122
opinion, freedom 3, 168
Optical Disc Plant regulation (Nigeria) 153–154
#OurMumuDonDo 229
out-of-data bundles, cost (unfairness) 211
Over The Top (OTT): platforms, regulation 226–227; services, regulation 224

Paradigm Initiative (PIN), digital rights 96
Parliamentary Portfolio Committee on Telecommunications and Postal Services, mobile data issue 214
pastoralism, conceptualism 39–40
pastoralist communities 39–42; digital marginalisation 43–45; ICT adoption 40
pastoralist counties, Ajira centres (number) 51
Penal Code 99; Article 252 100
people, Cameroon security forces tracking 177
people with disabilities: digital inclusion, southern epistemological perspective 55; empowerment, fight 62
physical chats, closed door process (Nigeria) 78
plaintiff, injury 188
platforms: exploitative nature 56–57; messaging platforms, quality control standards (absence) 187; security forces, tracking (Cameroon) 187
pluralist authoritarians, digital contestation (relationship) 169–171
pluralist authoritarian theory (Frère) 169
Policy and Regulation Initiative for Digital Africa (PRIDA), digital economy support 12, 228
political activism, focus 203
political office holders, mistrust 78
political rights, communication/socio-economic rights (interdependence) 70
political views, harassment/physical attacks (Nigeria) 78
poverty eradication 112
power: banality 233–234; concentration 6; relations, encoding/institutionalizing 93
pre-COVID-19 online communication/engagements, social media (impact) 76–79
predatory intent, court examination 191
press: Cameroon legal control 175; freedom 3
Press Law, revision 97
PricewaterhouseCoopers (PwC) intellectual theft survey 146

"Priority Markets Inquiry in the Electronic Communication Sector" (ICASA report) 207
privacy: GDPR protection 57; laws/restrictions, imposition 5; right 3
privacy (South Africa) 62–63
private censorship 133
private radio station licences, issuance (blocking) 170
private rights, state obligations (relationship) 5–6
private self-censorship (Nigeria film industry) 133–134
Promotion of Equality and Prevention of Unfair Discrimination Act 4 of 2000 (PEPUDA) 57–58, 61
property right: characterization 188; segregation 113
pro-poor economic growth 112
"Protection From Internet Falsehood and Manipulative Bill 2019" 224
Protestantism, impact 120
publication, participation right 3
public censorship 134
publicity, usage 723
public meetings, speaking up (danger) 78
public policy, principles (conflict) 169
Public Procurement Information Portal (PPIP), establishment 49
public rights, state obligations (relationship) 133–134
public self-censorship 142
"Public Sphere" (Habermas) 230
public sphere, communication 4

Radio 702 190
Ramaphosa, Cyril (SONA address) 214–215
#RefuteTwitterBan 231
Reporters Without Borders International report 100
Republic of Cameroon 167
Right2Know, Internet advocacy 209, 211
rights, business (relationship) 6
Russia, authoritariansim 166

Said, Edward 24
Sarai, Ahmad 134
saviour mentality, persistence 60–61
security forces, tracking (Cameroon) 177
self-censorship (Nigeria film industry) 129; private self-censorship 133–134; public self-censorship 133–134

self-expression, social media (usage) 77–78
self-regulation, cyber liberationist argument 191
semi-authoritarian regimes: Internet shutdowns 165; political/media freedom 170
Short Message Service (SMS), usage 119–120
Silicon Mountain Buea, Internet shutdown (impact) 175
Smart Africa Alliance initiative 48
smartphones, usage/importance (#DataMustFall campaign) 209
smoking, film display (Nigeria prohibition) 138, 140
Social Assistance Act 13 of 2004 58
social communication 25
social history, chronicles 131
social justice, goal 71–72
social media (SM): access, importance (Cameroon) 172; access, maintenance 80; account, usage 77; charter, quality control standards (absence) 187; communication instrument, Cameroon state perspective 176; Facebook (FB), usefulness 76; legislation (Cameroon) 168–169; politicisation (Nigeria) 223; pre-COVID-19 online communication/engagements, social media (impact) 76–79; terrorism, Cameroon state perspective 175; Twitter chats, importance 77; Twitter pages, following 76; usefulness 76–77; WhatsApp, usage 76
Social Media Platforms (SMPs) (social media platforms) 183; access, blocking 172–173; administrators, interaction 162; agitations, channeling 83; capacity 74; COVID-19 news 76; creative audiovisual, usage 156; fake news, sharing 188; media trademarks infringements, legislation 183; usage 70–72, 226
social media (SM), usage: importance 81; increase, state perspective 226; narratives 82
social movements: dynamism 204; features 206
social rights, development 3

society (democratization), communication (impact) 3
socio-economic rights, communication/political rights (interdependence) 70
SóróSoké (Nigeria): contextual background, study 225–227; digital citizens, communicative rights 227–230; findings/discussion 231–234; freedom of speech, digital authoritarianism (contrast) 232–234; generation, Nigerian state (contestation) 231–232; Internet shutdown 236–237; silence 223; technology, politicitisation 234–236; theoretical/methodological underpinnings 230–231
South Africa. see #DataMustFall campaign: autonomy 62–63; Bill of Rights 194; Competition Commission, Data Services Market Inquiry 216; decolonial critique 59–60; digital inclusion, policy/practice 60–62; digital inequalities 56–57; disability service organisations, presence 60; disabled people, human rights advocates deficit 60; Disabled People of South Africa (DPS), anti-apartheid role 55; Disabled Women of South Africa (DWSA), disability focus 58; End-User and Subscriber Charter Regulations of 2016, ICASA amendments 215; media trademarks, fake news (impact) 188–190; National Council for People with Disabilities (NCPD), disability focus 58; National Paralympic Committee (NPC), disability focus 58; people with disabilities, digital inclusion (southern epistemological perspective) 55; people with disabilities, empowerment (fight) 62; privacy 62–63; Promotion of Equality and Prevention of Unfair Discrimination Act 4 of 2000 (PEPUDA) 57–58, 61; rights, disability (relationship) 57–59; social media blackout 212–213; social media platforms, media trademarks infringements

(legislation) 183; trademarks, legislative interventions 192, 194–195; trademarks, legislative reforms 195–196
South African Human Rights Commission (SHRC), disability recognition 58
South African Schools Act 84 of 1996 57
southern epistemological perspective 55
speaking out (courage), virtual space (usage) 102
Special Anti-Robbery Squad (SARS), disbanding 73
state obligations, private rights (relationship) 5–6
State of the Nation Address (SONA), Zuma mobile data commitment 214–215
state-ordered Internet shutdowns, force 178
state-owned fixed communication company (TDM), state management 99
students/non-governmental organisations, inclusion (Mozambique) 104
subaltern (Zimbabwe): public sphere function 115–116; social transformation 116–117
subaltern communities, problems 117
sub-Saharan Africa (SSA): digital/economic/sociocultural elements 57; digital inequalities 95–96; internet usage, survey 38–39; mobile Internet, cost 10; pastoralists/agro-pastoralists, population estimate 40; private radio station licence, issuance (blocking) 170; regimes, classification (difficulty) 169
success stories 63
Sunday Times 190
Sunday Times, misinformation 190
surveillance, impact 10
Syracuse Principles on the Limitation and Derogation Provisions 192

#Tajamuka 121
TBo Touch (Thabo Molefe) 208, 214
TDM, statement management 99
technology: leveraging 49; politicisation (Nigeria) 232, 234–236; tools, proliferation 187

telecommunications: industry, *ex ante* regulation susceptibility 215; infrastructure, control 178; players, government determination (Nigeria) 230
Tell Zimbabwe Trust and Community Podium 122
terrorism: Cameroon state perspective 175
terrorism, discussion difficulty (Mozambique) 103
#ThisFlag 121
TikTok, usage 156
Times Live, misinformation 189–190
Touch Central FM (radio station) 208
toyi-toying (militant march/dance) 212
trademarks: communication rights, relationship 190–192; fake news, impact 188–190; legislative intervention (Kenya) 192–194; legislative intervention (South Africa) 192, 194–195; legislative reforms 195–196; media trademarks, Misappropriation Doctrine (relationship) 187–192; proprietor expenditures 184; quality/good will signal 183; reputation, relationship 184
Trademarks Act 193–195
Trade-Related Aspects of Intellectual Property Rights (TRIPS) 193
traveling theory 24
truth, single source 45
Tsandzana, Dércio 14, 91
Twitter: access, maintenance 80; Application Programming Interface (API), usage 231; ban (Nigeria) 225; Cabo Delgado awareness 103; chats, importance 77; handles, usage 190; pages, following 76; self-expression 78; suspension (Nigeria) 227; usage 156; usage, absence (impact) 82
Twitter Archiving Google Sheet (TAGS), usage 231
#TwitterBan 231
#TwitterSuspendBuharisAccount 231

Ubang community: advanced metalinguistic knowledge 31–32; boy-child, communication switch (expectation) 23; boys/girls,

intelligence bias 29; characteristics 22; cognitive advantage 28–31; confidence 28–31; dual-language phenomenon 22–26; dual-language practice 22; females, responsibilities 31; husbands, control 31; inhibitory control 28–31; language-cultural barrier 21; research methodology 27–28; thematic analysis 28–32; theoretical framework 26–27; women, second-class personas 32; YouTube videos, textual/visual analysis 32–34
Uchendu, Victor 25–26
Ugbomah, Eddie 130
Undie CC 32–33
United Nations Convention on the Rights of People with Disabilities (UNCRDP) 61
United Nations (UN) declaration of freedom of expression 21
United Nations Declaration of Human Rights (UNDHR) 94
United Nations Scientific and Cultural Organization (UNESCO), Media Development Indicators 113
United Republic of Cameroon, initial name 167
Universal Declaration of Human Rights (UNDHR): Article 19 8, 11, 38, 168, 223; future 2; inalienable rights 94
Ushahidi (crisis mapping application) 39

video rental (Nigeria): business, NCC registration 152; regulations 151–152
Virtual Private Network (VPN): criminalisation 235; usage 16, 238
Vodacom: market dominance 209; price reduction agreement 216
VOD platforms 135
voices (diversity), alternative media (impact) 6

#WeMove 231
WhatsApp: arrests (Cameroon) 175; meetings, advantages 103–104; video calls 75
WhatsApp, usage 76

White Paper on the Rights of Persons with Disabilities 58
women: communication rights, assessment 21; second-class personas (Ubang community) 32
workiing-class conditions, degradation 113
World Health Organization (WHO), anti-malaria drug falsification report 147
World Intellectual Property Organization (WIPO), treaties (absence) 147
World Trade Organisation (WTO) 64; Agreement on Basic Telecommunication services 56

youth activism, tools 101
youth digital activism, paths (Mozambique) 91
YouTube: platform, patronisation (Nigeria film industry) 135; usage 23, 162; videos, textual/visual analysis 32–34

Zhowezha, Morris 122
Zimbabwe: citizen journalists, impact 117–118; civil society-supported citizen journalism 121–123; communication rights, enrichment 110; Short Message Service (SMS), usage 119–120
Zimbabwe African National Union-Patriotic Front (ZANU PF), ZBC (relationship) 118–119
Zimbabwe Association of Community Radio Stations (ZACRAS), community radio initiatives 119, 122
Zimbabwe Broadcasting Corporation (ZBC), ZANU PF (relationship) 114–119
Zimbabwe, citizen journalism 110; context 118–119; individual practice 119–121; subaltern public sphere function 115–116
Zimbabwe Electoral Commission, presidential election results withholding 119
Zuma, Jacob 214–215

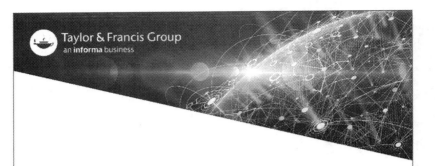